The Age of
Mackenzie King

The Age of
Mackenzie King

Henry Ferns and Bernard Ostry

Introduction by John Meisel

James Lorimer & Company, Publishers
Toronto 1976

ISBN 0-88862-115-9 cloth
ISBN 0-88862-114-0 paper

Photo credits:

All photographs are from Public Archives Canada. The following are the Public Archive negative numbers. The order of the numbers corresponds with the order of the photographs in the book.

C-7332	C-7318	PA-25971	C-46324
C-55534	C-3184	C-46311	C-25281
C-7314	C-55526	C-29350	C-84803
C-2853	C-71510	C-46317	C-24305
C-79190	C-28574	C-46298	C-46319

Cover design by Don Fernley

5 4 3 2 1 76 77 78 79 80

James Lorimer & Company, Publishers
35 Britain Street
Toronto, Ontario

Printed and bound in Canada

Canadian Cataloguing in Publication Data

Ferns, Henry S., 1913-
    The age of Mackenzie King

First published 1955 under title: The age of Mackenzie King: the rise of the leader.

Includes bibliographical references and index.
ISBN 0-88862-115-9 bd.   ISBN 0-88862-114-0 pa.

1. King, William Lyon Mackenzie, 1874-1950.
2. Canada—History—1867-1914. 3. Canada—History—1914-1918. 4. Industry and state—Canada—History.
I. Ostry, Bernard, 1927-   II. Title.

FC581.K5F47 1976   971.06'22'0924   C76-017137-8
F1033.K53F47 1976

To the memory

of

Flying Officer William Paterson

and

Pilot Officer Leon A. Titof

of the

Royal Canadian Air Force,

two young Canadians who enlisted in the armed forces of their country for the conscious purpose of helping to banish from the earth the inhuman principles of Fascism. They hoped for the creation of a nation and a world in which all men may live in peace as brothers. In their idealism and in their sacrifice they were not alone. This comradeship was their happiness and their consolation, for they knew that the battle they fought, like other struggles for liberty and human brotherhood, was necessary for the well-being and decency of mankind.

CONTENTS

William Lyon Mackenzie—Isabel Grace Mac-
kenzie—John King—The Birth of Industrial
Canada—Mackenzie King at the University of
Toronto—The Student Strike of 1895.

The United States in the Mauve Decade—The
Education of Mackenzie King at the Universities
of Chicago and Harvard—Jane Addams and Hull
House—Scholarship and Journalism—Experiment
in Political Negotiation—Travel in Europe during
the *Fin de Siècle*—Academic or "Real" Life—The
Choice—Deputy Minister of Labour.

The Government and the Civil Servant in
Ottawa, 1900—Henry Albert Harper, a Friend—
The Labour Gazette—Conciliation—The Strike at
Valleyfield, P.Q.—The Royal Commission on
Industrial Disputes in British Columbia—A
Lesson Learned—The Policy of the Deputy
Minister and the Fundamental Political Problem
of an Industrial Community.

The Industrial Disputes Investigation Act—A
Problem of the Labour Market—The Race Riots
in British Columbia—The Law of Competing
Standards—Negotiations on Indian Immigration
—Opium and Chinese Immigration—*The Secret
of Heroism*—Laurier's Minister of Labour.

The Combines Investigation Act—The Grand
Trunk Railway Strike of 1910 and the Failure of

the Industrial Disputes Investigation Act—An
Attempted Settlement at Public Expense—Mac-
kenzie King Takes over the Negotiations—The
End of the Strike—The Defeat of the Workers
Revealed—Criticism in Parliament and the
Country—The Strike and the Electoral Defeat of
the Liberal Party.

Introduction to the 1976 Edition

It is difficult to recollect, now that virtually all of Mackenzie King's seemingly endless memorabilia are available to students, and after he has received more attention from biographers than any other Canadian politician, what things were like, in 1955, when *The Age of Mackenzie King* burst on the scene. Most interested Canadians remembered the tenth person to become their Prime Minister as something of an enigmatic figure who, though he could never be said to have enjoyed the affection of the people, had been unprecedentedly successful in garnering their votes. A highly readable, unpretentious biography by Bruce Hutchison, which appeared two years after King's death, provided a generally sympathetic, although by no means uncritical, portrait. The scholarly community was awaiting the more thorough and searching official biography of Professor MacGregor Dawson, who had been given access to all the former Prime Minister's papers, including the immense diary, running in its later years to some 1200 pages of typescript annually. While no one doubted Dawson's mastery of Canadian politics, his lively style or his integrity as a scholar, it was generally assumed that the official biographer and his numerous helpers and colleagues would take a friendly position towards King and that in any event, they shared King's commitment to the bland politics of non-doctrinaire, compromising, pluralist democracy.

In this, of course, the official biographical team was broadly representative of Canada's academic establishment. The latter's ethos was essentially liberal, democratic, bourgeois and genteel. Harmony at all cost, rather than conflict, was indisputably deemed by virtually everyone to be the most desirable form of interaction, whether in the social or academic spheres. Even the break of CCF-affiliated scholars eschewed confrontation and placed supreme confidence in the intrinsic worth of moderation, amelioration and the likelihood that sweet reason —and the public good—would triumph if men of goodwill only confronted in a spirit of tolerant and civilized give-and-take. The quintessence of this atmosphere is illustrated in the career of F.H. Underhill — probably the greatest guru of the social democratic left—who, after years of stimulating sharpshooting directed at the Liberals and particularly their seemingly indestructable leader, found it possible to retire from the University of Toronto to become the curator of Laurier House, Lady Laurier's gift to King which he in turn bequeathed to the nation as a Liberal museum and research centre.

Ferns and Ostry's book splashed onto this benign scene and mightily disturbed the smooth academic calm enveloping the official King biographers and the not inconsiderable number of King watchers. In somewhat strident, acerbic tones it presented an unsympathetic picture of the former Liberal leader, questioning his motives, his effectiveness as a mediator, and in some measure even his integrity. The reception of the book was mixed: reviewers generally liked the focusing of the investigation on the pre-leadership days and particularly on King's activities in the labour field, either on behalf of the government or on that of the Rockefellers and their friends. The meticulous exploration of available documentary sources, the careful footnoting which distinguished this biography from Hutchison's, the relating of political events to economic phenomena — all were noted with approval. The tone adopted by the young, virtually unknown scholars, on the other hand, was universally deplored. The somewhat bad tempered, merciless and in the view of many reviewers, tendentious flaying of King, denying him any spontaneous human reaction and showing him as something of a priggish careerist was usually condemned as being unfair and as weakening the otherwise impressive research of the authors. Some even argued that the fruits of the exhaustive inquiry were used all too selectively so as to achieve the desired effect. And then there were those who questioned whether anyone should have attempted to write a study of Mr. King without having access to his papers. To this, as to many of the other charges, persuasive replies were available, underlining the very special place of this book.

Historiography, like other arts and sciences, is inevitably subject to many biases and fashions. No one scholar, one school, nor even one age can produce a 'complate', satisfactory reconstruction of bygone events. The most realistic and useful account of the past (or present for that matter) is achieved when several attempts at understanding are made, embracing many schools, many ages, many perspectives and, of course, many sources. Circumstances forced Ferns and Ostry to confine their searches to only some existing sets of documents and informants. This restriction was not an unmixed blessing: while it obviously diminished their scope and effectiveness, it compelled the authors to make do with limited documents and so to subject the sources to the most painstaking winnowing. It also encouraged them to remain within fairly narrow bounds with respect to both the scope of their inquiry and the factors which modified their assumptions about King's life and behaviour. The result was perhaps a limited image of their protagonist but it enabled them to etch a sharp portrait which not oi focused on some critically important characteristics of the original but also invited refutation, modification and correction, thereby challenging the official biographers to address themselves to issues and aspects of their problem they would almost certainly otherwise have overlooked or underplayed.

I am not suggesting that the book's chief virtue was to act as a foil to later writers, although it undoubtedly did perform this role. It achieved considerably more than that. It tackled a controversial subject forthrightly, even aggressively, from a point of view not currently in fashion, one which examined King's early life from a perspective mindful of the importance of class tensions in society and of the relation between them, the economy and politics. This biography is thus conceived in the political economy tradition, a mode of integrating political and economic realities into a meaningful whole. This tradition is happily at present experiencing a revival in most western countries, including Canada, and the publishers are to be commended for making an earlier study undertaken in this context available to a wide audience.

Readers will no doubt wish to compare the portrait and interpretation of Ferns and Ostry with those of Professor Dawson's *W.L. Mackenzie King: 1874-1923* and Professor Stacey's recent *A Very Double Life: The Private World of Mackenzie King.* This comparison is certain to modify some of the features stressed by Ferns and Ostry's work but *The Age of Mackenzie King*, in turn, will complement the other biographical studies and will correct some of their biases and idiosyncracies.

I have just noted that the publishers are to be commended for reprinting this book, thus adding to the several other historically important reprints and translations (including, among the latter, Pierre-Elliott Trudeau's *Asbestos Strike*). They are also to be congratulated on their timing. One of the fundamental questions opened up by the present volume is the relation between King and labour on the one hand and the corporate interests on the other, and ultimately, of course, the relation between these two interests and the Liberal party. At a time when the Liberal government is endeavouring to apply its anti-inflation policy — one vitally affecting both labour and industry—it is particularly appropriate to be reminded of one of the Liberal party's chief architect's and leader's earlier connections with these two powerful actors on the national scene. The topicality of the current reprint does not, of course detract from the more enduring interest of the book.

John Meisel
Hardy Professor of Political Science
Queen's University

Preface to the First Edition

This book is presented to the reader not as a definitive study, but as an essay contributed to a public discussion of the thoughts and policies of a man who reflected and in some measure shaped the character of Canadian society. We have undertaken this work, not as professional biographers or historians, but as citizens of Canada, as members of the Commonwealth and the United Nations, interested in the political behaviour of one of our outstanding countrymen. Our object has been to discover something of the process by which a successful parliamentary leader emerges in an industrial society; of the nation which he led; and of the age in which he lived.

The studies of Mackenzie King, upon which the public have so far been obliged to rely, have passed lightly over the first forty-five years of his life. The information about the period prior to his selection as leader of the Liberal Party is exceedingly thin and repetitious. Much of it is inaccurate, and all of it has been interpreted with the knowledge of his subsequent success as a politician constantly in mind. We have found that a factual examination of his early political life throws a vivid and revealing light upon his years of power, and that in order to understand the man and the party he led so long, students of Canadian politics must devote more attention than hitherto to Mackenzie King's career before 1919.

Evidence concerning this period is abundant and some of it is public property, but this evidence has been little studied nor has any substantial and important part of it been placed before the public for consideration and discussion. An examination so focused will serve to correct the deficiencies of past and current accounts of that period of Mackenzie King's life when he played a considerable role both in Canada and the United States in the shaping of some of the most fundamental of all social relationships. For these reasons we believe that this book will be of interest to that growing body of people concerned with the development of Canadian democracy and its role in world affairs.

September, 1955   *H. S. Ferns*
BIRMINGHAM   *B. Ostry*
ENGLAND

Acknowledgments

We owe a great debt to all those who have helped us, in one way or another, in writing this book. We, alone, are responsible for what appears in these pages, and we do not expect that those who have our gratitude will necessarily support the conclusions we have come to in this study.

For their kind cooperation we wish to thank, particularly, the Rt. Hon. Arthur Meighen, the Hon. Charles A. Dunning, LL.D., Mr. M. J. Coldwell, M.P., H.E. Sri V. K. Krishna Menon, the Hon. L. B. Pearson, the Hon. Paul Martin, Senator Norman P. Lambert, Mr. Henry Borden, Mr. Fred MacGregor and Dr. L. W. Brockington, C.M.G., Q.C.

For information and advice on special subjects, we are indebted to Mrs. Grace MacInnis, Mrs. F. M. Pratt, Mrs. N. W. Rowell, Rev. Canon A. Harding Priest, Mr. H. W. Herridge, M.P., Mr. R. Finlayson, M.P., Mr. Mark Shinbane, Q.C., Mr. R. B. Russell, Mr. R. Slocombe, Mr. Lewis St. G. Stubbs, and Mr. Joseph Mills. In Great Britain, Miss Ann Ashley, Miss Ann Cunningham and Mr. Frank Owen have kindly helped us clarify several points.

We are indebted, too, to Mr. Alistair Stewart, M.P., who has given us not only valuable help but also has interested himself in the accessibility of information. In this last connection we wish to remember, also, the late Rodney Adamson, M.P.

Many persons of great professional experience who had dealings with Mr. Mackenzie King before World War I have offered us information and suggestions. We are especially grateful to Dr. R. H. Coats, formerly Dominion Statistician and one of Canada's most distinguished social scientists, for documentary material and instructive comment. From one of the few men living who enjoyed the confidence of Sir Wilfrid Laurier, Mr. A. K. Cameron of Montreal, we have learned much and we thank him cordially both for his reminiscences of times past and for the opportunity to examine the many documents in his possession.

In spite of great physical distress the late Edward L. Doyle, sometime Secretary of District 15, United Mine Workers of America, spent much of the last energy of his life in supplying us with information from his private archives. We wish to remember him with gratitude for his invaluable help. Mr. Adolph Germer, one of the leaders of the Congress of Industrial Organisations has also guided us to many useful facts.

Among our colleagues in British universities we wish to thank particularly Professor W. H. B. Court and Professor Gilbert Walker of the University of Birmingham, and Mr. H. L. Beales and Mr. Ralph Miliband of the London School of Economics and Political Science. Among those in North America, Dean J. A. Gibson of Carleton College, Ottawa, Professor R. MacGregor Dawson of the University of Toronto, Mr. Fred Gibson of Queen's University, Kingston, Professor V. H. Jensen of Cornell University and Mr. Clifford K. Shipton of the Archives of Harvard University have given us much assistance.

We have received permission from Mr. Mackenzie King's literary executors to use certain copyright material in their charge and we wish to acknowledge this courtesy.

To a number of institutions and their officers we are grateful for the information they have made available and for the help and understanding they have accorded us: the Public Archives of Canada, the British Museum, the President and Fellows of Harvard University, the Parliamentary Library, Ottawa, the Lawson Library of the University of Western Ontario, the Royal Empire Society, The British Library of Economic and Political Science, the Toronto Reference Library, the Manitoba Provincial Archives, the Harding Library, University of Birmingham, and the Library of Canada House, London, England.

The families and dearest friends of authors are notorious for their helpfulness and tolerance. Ours are no exception. They have had a hard assignment for which our poor thanks are little reward.

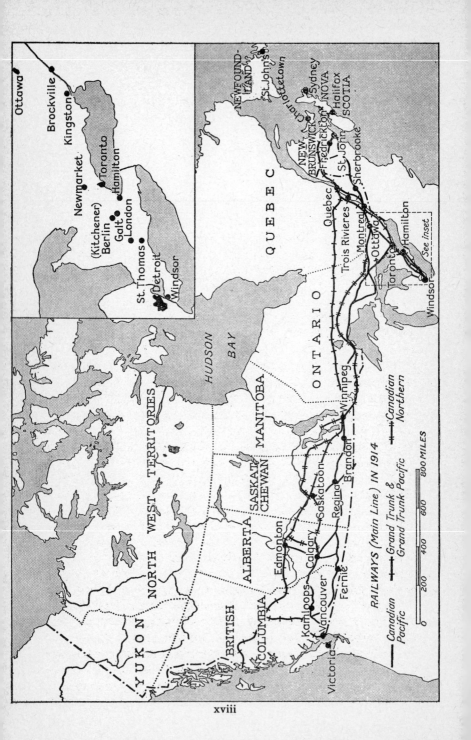

RAILWAYS (Main Line) IN 1914

Canadian Pacific
Grand Trunk & Grand Trunk Pacific
Canadian Northern

0   200   400   600   800 MILES

xviii

Introduction

The Right Honourable William Lyon Mackenzie King was the most successful parliamentary politician in history. What do we mean by successful? We mean that he was the Sovereign's first minister longer than Walpole, longer than the younger Pitt, longer than Gladstone, longer than his Canadian predecessors Sir Wilfrid Laurier and Sir John A. Macdonald, longer than any Prime Minister who had ever previously advised the Crown in Australia or the Union of South Africa or any other nation of the Commonwealth.[1] In the parliamentary tournament, Mackenzie King was peerless.

This longevity in office is the more remarkable when one considers the Age of Mackenzie King—a time for the world at large of political troubles of vast dimensions, of wars, revolutions, economic catastrophes, fanaticism and violence. At a time when his neighbour, the President of the United States, never moved in public except behind a cover of secret service protectors, Mackenzie King walked the streets of the Canadian capital unattended and unharmed. Politicians of other nations who used more drastic means than he failed to last as long. So successful was Mackenzie King that without resort to violence he managed to create the closest approximation to a one party state among those nations which admit the possibility of two or more political parties. A champion of any kind attracts the interest of his fellow men, and Mackenzie King commands the attention of every student of politics searching to discover the secrets of social peace or to analyse the elements of power.

In considering the record of Mackenzie King how much may we accord to the man and how much to the community he

[1] In 1955, Mackenzie King's record was surpassed by Sir Godfrey Huggins, Prime Minister of Southern Rhodesia since 1933.

governed? Was Canada in his day a uniquely peaceful and contented community, or was he a uniquely talented politician?

When Mackenzie King first appeared upon the political stage during a dispute at his university in 1895, Canada was a country hardly known to the world at large and lacking a clear identity in the community of nations. During Mackenzie King's political life, Canada experienced a most astonishing transformation. This was primarily economic. In the last sixty years the Canadians have done phenomenal things in the way of producing wealth. Like the Iranians they have oil; like the Americans iron; unlike anyone else they have nickel. They produce more electrical energy *per capita* than any nation on earth. In spite of an enormous expansion of industrial output they have continued to produce a food surplus. Richly endowed by nature, the Canadians have established for themselves a remarkable character as workers and producers.

In the essentials of its economic organization and the super-structure built upon this foundation, Canada differs in no important particulars from other industrial free-enterprise nations. Its long run political problems are those commonly found in communities which produce industrially in a market economy. But there is a complication. Canadians are not mere economic men. In its spiritual and mental life, which in the short run is a matter of some political importance, Canada possesses a character of its own. Compared with the nations of Europe and Asia, and even with those of Latin America, Canada is a young community. Because it is a community built in a largely empty wilderness—in this respect like the United States, Australia and Argentina—by immigrants of from three weeks' to barely three hundred years' standing, its people have frequently very old ideas brought from the lands of their forebears where the ideas they cherish may have died long since or are in the process of passing away. Thus, Canada is a new nation of old and often conflicting ideas and traditions. In Canada there flourishes an ecclesiastical organization whose authority in the community, whose ideas about the physical and moral world and whose conceptions of human society would have been largely agreeable to Innocent III. Another fundamental group in Canada are the spiritual as well as physical descendants of the United Empire Loyalists. For other Canadians the Battle of the Boyne is a lively and significant memory. Mennonite and Hutterite communities, possessing the most modern machines for doing their work, still cherish forms of social organization and ideas of the world and of God which their ancestors devised before the days of Martin Luther. The Orthodox Church, traditionally regarding the Roman Catholics as a schismatic body, flourishes in Canada. Orthodox Jewry of even more ancient lineage is no less nourished on Canadian soil. Now men and women from eastern Europe are flooding in hot with their wrongs and their mistakes. The spiritual heirs of every social conception since the collapse of the Roman Empire have found a means of renewing their lives in the open, rich environment of Canada.

If Canada depended for its unity upon the community of its myths, its dreams and its memories, it would not exist. Canada is united by its physical and economic apparatus: its railways, airlines, pipelines and telegraph lines, its gigantic industrial and commercial organizations and the interdependence of Canadians upon one another in the production and marketing of commodities. When a Canadian is at work in a factory, a mine, on a farm or in an office he or she is a part of an organization of continental dimensions, of international connections and of recent growth. When he goes to a bowling alley or a golf club or a hockey game, he is doing something hundreds of thousands of other Canadians do. But when he turns within himself and listens to the imponderable notes which sound through eternity and give us character, who can say what he then may hear? Canadians have not lived long and intimately together in the manner of the peoples of Europe, nor have they experienced great political revolutions such as the English and American Civil Wars or the American, French and Russian Revolutions which have indelibly imprinted themselves upon and given a character to the peoples of whose social experience they are a part.

The heroic experiences of the Canadian people have been of a rather different character. Their deeds of valour have invariably had a conservative purpose: the preservation of their political personality from exterior forces seeking to mould Canada for their own ends. They resisted the blandishments of the American revolutionaries, and in the war of 1812 drove out the American invaders. When the Canadians divided against each other and came briefly to blows in 1837 both the rebels and the Government had the common objective of seeking to repel what each esteemed to be exterior influences. During the two wars against Germany, Canadians differed and for the same reasons: one party feared the consequences for Canada of an alteration in the balance of power in Europe and the other the consequences of seeking to preserve it. Both by their own lights were devoted to the preservation of things as they are, as they have been and as it is hoped they will always be.

In the presence of so many traditions and in the absence of any tradition common to all Canadians, the politician who aspires to govern Canada has no easy task. If he immerses himself in the tradition of a particular group and learns to command its support, he may well cut himself off from other groups. If he steps forth as a mere economic man, he may discover himself similarly isolated. The Canadian politician must operate, therefore, at two levels, concerning himself, on the one hand, with the variety of sentiments which are rooted in the past of the people and, on the other, with the tensions and conflicts of an industrial society as it exists in the present. The tensions of the second description may, and often do, express themselves in terms of the differences of the first, but an independent zeal for race and religion may also interfere with the functioning of the complex industrial mechanism. What is the order of the importance of the problems of Canadian politics and from where are they derived? These are the questions which any serious Canadian politician must answer, for the battlefield of Canadian political life is strewn with the corpses of leaders who did not know the answers to them.

It is the argument of this book that Mackenzie King did know the answers to these questions, and that this knowledge explains why he succeeded where men superior to him in many respects and capable of commanding more affection and regard failed. Readers are bound to differ in their estimate of Mackenzie King's methods and of his objectives (and the authors do not count themselves among his admirers on this account), but they are bound to agree, we believe, that in his conception of what politics is about he had an understanding which worked. Not all politicians are so endowed.

During recent years the political philosopher, Michael Oakeshott, has given his attention to the development of a general theory of politics applicable to the modern world.[1] His theoretical inquiries have led to the conclusion that a style or character has emerged during the past four hundred years which distinguishes the political behaviour of modern man from that of his medieval and ancient ancestors and from that of the few examples of non-industrial society which survive today. The style or character of politics which Oakeshott has discerned is, he argues, universal. Whether men call themselves parliamentarians, republicans or communists, men living in industrial societies, or aspiring to do so, entertain common expectations of the State and common views of its role in the community. Without arguing the truth or falsity of this proposition we would go further and say that the subject matter of politics is common to all.

Our study of Mackenzie King appears to be a small piece of evidence in support of this theoretical conclusion. At a first inspection no two politicians would seem farther apart than Mackenzie King and Lenin. They differed in their objectives and their techniques to be sure, and they lived in markedly different circumstances. But they had something in common besides the fact of success. They had a common view of what politics is about in an industrial society. Both recognized the forces at work beneath the surface of social life shaping its course without regard for the sentiments and memories of men. Both knew how to use these forces: one for one purpose, one for another.

Mackenzie King played an important role in the politics of Canadian industrial society almost from its birth. He entered the newly formed Ministry of Labour as its expert head in 1900 only a few years after the commencement of the vast expansion of Canadian enterprise which accompanied the revival of world business in 1896. He brought to this task a fund of social theory acquired from European and American sociologists and political scientists who had been privileged to observe the coming into being of industrial society in Europe and the

---

[1] M. Oakeshott, *The Idea of Character in the Interpretation of Modern Politics.* This paper was read to the Political Studies Association of the United Kingdom meeting at Cambridge 27 March, 1954.

United States. Some of his teachers were men who knew that certain features of free-enterprise society are not "natural" and cannot be taken for granted but are artifacts. For this reason Mackenzie King was more of a realist and more of a genuine scientist in his basic ideas about politics than many of his sophisticated contemporaries and most of his successors, whose theoretical assumptions are based upon the world around them with little regard for historical forces.

Thus, Mackenzie King commands attention both as the leader of an interesting, wealthy and powerful member of the community of nations and as an example of a politician handling problems typical of industrial capitalist society.

CHAPTER I

". . . Home and Native Land . . ."

The subject of this work was born in Berlin, Ontario, on December 17th, 1874. He was the eldest son and second child of John and Isabel King. They gave him the honourable and famous name of his maternal grandfather, William Lyon Mackenzie. Thus, at his christening, the infant was enrolled, in an important sense, in the profession of politics, for the grandparent whose name he bore was one of the most interesting and challenging figures in the history of Canadian public life.

William Lyon Mackenzie came from the Highlands of Scotland, "a pedlar's lad", in the contemptuous phrase of Sir Francis Bond Head, the Lieutenant-Governor of Upper Canada. Self-education and migration to Canada shortly after the Napoleonic Wars transformed this "Scotia's son of rustic toil" first into a shopkeeper then into a newspaper proprietor and finally into a political leader. In the age which produced Chartism in Britain and Jacksonian democracy in the United States, William Lyon Mackenzie proclaimed himself the leader of the "mechanics and freeholders of Upper Canada". Had his political enterprise succeeded he might well have joined the great company of American liberators, his name inscribed with those of Washington, Adams, Bolívar and San Martín in the gallery of heroes who brought to an end the colonial epoch in the Americas. But history had ordained otherwise for William Lyon Mackenzie. Instead of a hero he became a traitor. There did not exist in his case that agreement between the inward and

7

spiritual vision of society and external social circumstances, which is the first condition of political success.

William Lyon Mackenzie was a man of strong and often inconsistent views about the practical concerns of the colony of Upper Canada. Like Cobbett, he began as a reverent admirer of the monarchy, the aristocracy and the constitution of Great Britain. He even rejoiced in the memory that his forebears had sacrificed themselves in the service of their Lord and their Clan, fighting to preserve the legitimate claims of the House of Stuart. Like Cobbett, too, he came to execrate the objects of his youthful reverence. Half Jacobite and half Chartist he spoke contemptuously of "Victoria Guelph, the bloody Queen of England", and of her government as "Victoria Melbourne's bloody divan". He ended his life embittered by the conviction that "responsible government" was not a democratic triumph but a conspiracy of "talkative attorneys and land speculators . . . all want[ing] to get rich at once".[1] This progress from one political pole to another had been the result of two emotions within himself: a deep conviction that the guinea stamp upon society was evil, and an unshakable and romantic courage which never counted costs. He was a most unusual type of politician for he was genuinely disinterested in a way which the poor and ambitious can seldom afford to be. He lived as if he could see glaring within the despicable love of money and respectability the hydrogen fires of hell.

A man so endowed with the prophetic qualities was bound to have an awkward time in a society such as that which existed in Upper Canada in the 1820's and 1830's. At that time old loyalists and new immigrants were scrambling to possess the wealth of one of North America's treasure houses and to determine the principles upon which men would work, wealth would be shared, and the government of the community be conducted. William Lyon Mackenzie's views on these questions are not susceptible to any brief or comprehensive statement, for he was a man who proliferated words and ideas with neither discipline nor let. He entertained four abiding ideas, however, which grew stronger in their expression as his experience of society ripened: firstly, that government should be created by

[1] Quoted in R. A. MacKay, "The Political Ideas of William Lyon Mackenzie," *Canadian Journal of Economics and Political Science*, Vol. 3, 1937, p. 21.

and answerable to the whole people; that Church organization should be separated entirely from the State; that the public authorities should maintain a comprehensive secular system of education available to all; and that the whole produce of labour should be distributed to all the labourers. If these things were done, society would know peace, for then there would be no rich and no poor, no rulers and no ruled.

This was not a vision widely entertained by an important and powerful part of the community in Upper Canada. A gang of respectable toughs in Toronto threw his presses into Lake Ontario. He was elected to the Legislature five times and expelled five times. He was elected first Mayor of Toronto. He frightened the governing clique; he frightened the Colonial Office and its governors in Upper Canada. He frightened the preachers and the Churches. He frightened the bankers and merchants; for if he was not a prophet armed, he was, at least, a prophet supported. In 1836-37, depression descended upon the business world of North America. The love of money Mackenzie hated as a moral disease. This moral disease now became an economic disease which everyone could understand. Mackenzie believed the time had come for an armed settlement of social ills. He proclaimed a constitution for Upper Canada in which the people would have power and in which there would be none of those engines by which the rich robbed the poor, such as banks and joint-stock companies. Then he began to arm.

If William Lyon Mackenzie possessed vision in abundance, he lacked judgment in like measure. The old Canadians had experienced the aggressions of an army bearing at the end of its bayonets liberty and democracy. Many of the new Canadians had come not to find Utopia in the forests of Upper Canada but the very things William Lyon Mackenzie abominated: money, office, power and respectability. Many were willing to complain, but few were willing to fight, and so Mackenzie was isolated by his courage and rendered impotent by his prophecy. His rebellion failed, and he fled to the United States, in that age a haven of refuge for the enemies of kings and tyrants.

From a distance he had admired the United States as a land of democracy and progress. Actual experience there opened his eyes. Some Americans he admired, such as Martin Van Buren, whose life he wrote, but he hated "the monstrous slave power" which controlled the United States and gave character to its institutions. His exile was, therefore, a wretched misery. The successful Canadian newspaper proprietor became an unhappy hack journalist and petty political conspirator, living in a foreign land beset by depression.

For breaches of American neutrality legislation he was sentenced to serve eighteen months in the gaol at Rochester, New York. Gaols were rather more liberal institutions in the 1840's than nowadays, and Mackenzie edited the *Carolina Almanac* from the privacy of his cell. A gaol sentence was no solution for his personal problems, however. The gaol authorities could only provide for the prisoner himself, and Mackenzie had a wife and thirteen children. Some of these died and all were pinched with want. Added to this was the knowledge (which never in any way moved Mackenzie himself) that powerful people in the city which his family called their home despised and hated the head of their house. During the course of this exile, in such circumstances of distress, the mother of Mackenzie King was born, the thirteenth and last child.

In 1846, the British Government, yielding to the popular movement which Mackenzie had helped to stimulate, and finally persuaded by the philosophers of *laissez faire*, decided that the government for the British North American colonies was best which governed least. From 1846 onward, the Colonial governors in North America were instructed to govern in accordance with the advice given them by those ministers who had the support of the elected legislatures. Thus, government, for all practical purposes, was amenable to the influence and theoretically under the control of those residents of the colonies who had the vote. Something resembling one of Mackenzie's ideas had been realized. As a consequence of this, the elected Legislature of Canada enacted legislation forgiving all treasons in the cause of change. A respectable mob burned down the Parliament Buildings in Montreal to register their rage, but they no longer had the power to prevent the return of the exiles. William Lyon Mackenzie re-established himself and his family in Toronto in 1850, and in a contest with the rich and respectable Liberal, George Brown,* was elected to the Legislature in 1851.

But William Lyon Mackenzie was no happier under the new regime of "responsible government" than he had been under the old regime of the "Family Compact". The object of the government was still, he believed, not the just ordering of society but the distribution of patronage and public favours and the erection of a new governing class as selfish as, and probably more corrupt than, the old. He talked furiously against banks and joint-stock companies and in favour of free, secular education and the prohibition of alcoholic beverages. In his lively youth he had refused to be silenced by the offer of a high position and an income of £1,500 a year, made to him by the Secretary of State for the Colonies, Lord Goderich; now in his poverty-stricken old age he again refused to be silenced with an office in the government. In an age of buying and selling his incapacity to sell himself attracted the greatest attention, and he became known as "the Unpurchasable Patriot". To such a level did his persistent opposition reduce him that his friends were obliged to take up a collection for the "much maligned and persecuted Champion of Popular Rights and Honest Government".[1] But even this gesture of affection and respect brought William Lyon Mackenzie no peace. Two years later, in 1858, he resigned from the Legislature in disgust. He was esteemed mad. In 1861 he died, but he was not forgotten.

The family life of prophets is reputedly uncomfortable. This was certainly the case with William Lyon Mackenzie's. Only persons of great intellectual powers, extreme stupidity or unusual saintliness can adjust themselves undamaged to the circumstances of poverty, pride, constant agitation, bitterness and hope which the character of William Lyon Mackenzie imposed upon his family like an edict of fate. Isabel Grace Mackenzie possessed no unusual intellectual powers, nor was she stupid nor a saint. She was an average girl who hankered after the security the daughter of the Unpurchasable Patriot had never known. She loved her father and never proposed to

* On pp. 338 *et seq.* of the book readers will find brief biographical notes, arranged alphabetically, about various personalities whose names are marked throughout the text with an asterisk.

[1] *The Mackenzie Homestead*, Minutes of Proceedings (Toronto, 1856).

repudiate him, but she was not equipped either in disposition or in talent to take up his quarrels with the foe. Her father had been called an atheist; she was content to go to the Presbyterian Church and happy to do its work. He scorned to use his proven capacity to make money; she was quite willing to take a practical view of that useful talent. She had endured poverty and despite, and she sought to come to terms with the community in which she lived; to discover in its virtues the means of living agreeably both with her father's memory and society as she found it.

Isabel Mackenzie was a young woman and there were few opportunities, save marriage, for a girl of her associations to solve the problem of building up her life. It was, therefore, in her marriage that Isabel Mackenzie found her solution. John King presented himself to her as a man of respectable accomplishments, a university graduate in the days before vast numbers attended university, a professional man who had once won a prize for an essay entitled "Our English Shakespeare". He was a patriot who served against the Fenians and a newspaper editor at the age of twenty-two who wrote against the Tories in Berlin, Ontario. His Liberalism was an advantage, but he had an additional attraction in the eyes of Isabel Mackenzie, for John King was one of those rare Liberals who still admired her father. That was one asset. He had another. His father had fought her father in 1837. Her father was a Highland pedlar boy of radical hue; his was a Scots officer of the Royal Horse Artillery of a distinctly bluish tinge.

When John King married Isabel Mackenzie he had already established himself, in accordance with the Canadian practice, as a barrister and solicitor in Berlin (now Kitchener), Ontario, at that time a small market town of less than 3,000 people. It was, however, an important stopping place on the railway from Toronto through the rich farm lands of western Ontario to Windsor, on the Canadian frontier, opposite Detroit. John King was a familiar Canadian type, a young man from the metropolis moving to an area of expected economic growth where he hoped to make his fortune, or at least, to establish a respectable place in a new community. And he succeeded. John King prospered moderately and soon came to occupy a position in the top strata of provincial society. He was the attorney for the municipal and county authorities. He was counsel for the local bank. He acted as Crown Prosecutor on many occasions. The volume of his private legal business was so great that he was obliged to open a branch office in the nearby town of Galt. He lived in a house which bore a name. He kept a carriage. Domestic servants and not "just a hired girl" attended to the duties of his household. He was an elder of the Presbyterian Church, a representative of the Arts Graduates in the Senate of the University of Toronto and a Queen's Counsel.

John King was also a politician. He was for some time the president of the North Waterloo Liberal Association, and several endeavours were made, which for some reason he always resisted, to have him stand for the constituency in the Liberal interest. He wrote much in the newspapers and weekly journals on political topics, and he was a wide-ranging speaker on behalf of his Party. It was reported to Sir Wilfrid Laurier* in his favour that he took "an active part for many years on the stump and [had] written for Liberal papers in the counties of Waterloo, Wellington, Perth, Kent, Lennox and Addington and York".[1] If he was active politically on the county level, John King also had his connections in the Provincial metropolis. In the Law School he had met many of the future political and business personalities of Ontario. One of the most important men in the Liberal Party in Ontario, and one of the shrewdest and richest men in the community, W. (later Sir William) Mulock,* was his friend.

Mackenzie King was born and grew to young manhood in the secure and peaceful circumstances of a simple provincial community in which his family occupied a position of some consequence. He attended the local primary and secondary schools publicly supported and administered in accordance with one of the essential principles for which his grandfather had fought. In them there was very little for the mind, for these schools were dedicated to the service of the average children to the neglect of those with the divine talents. In these schools Mackenzie King showed no aptitude as a scholar. He never acquired that facility with languages and the arts of mathematical reasoning which it is the business of any rational system of secondary education to impart to children able enough

[1] *Laurier Papers*, Ritchie to Laurier, 31 January, 1901, enclosure.

to acquire them. Only when Mackenzie King found his mind stimulated and more heavily tried in the University did he begin to reveal his outstanding mental qualities.

The real educative influence of Mackenzie King's youth was his home, and the emphasis he placed in later life upon the influence of his parents upon his career was justly conceived. From his mother he derived a blood connection with one of the outstanding personalities of his country. Her pride in her father's memory was one of the great experiences of her son's life which partly explains the enormous importance Mackenzie King came to attach to his mother as the presiding deity of his household and his life itself.[1] From his father he gained as much as from his mother, for his father's position in the community taught him both the responsibilities of public life and the modes of its pursuit. His father was not only interested in political questions and made them the staple of his daily conversation, but he understood in practical terms what it meant to be a Canadian politician. At a time when the respectable classes in Canada were learning to consider the making of money as preferable to the pursuit of public honours, Mackenzie King was encouraged by his father in the old-fashioned notion that a political career was the noblest and best a man could follow. But if he was taught to admire such service, he was also afforded an opportunity to see how such service is carried on and by what practical devices reputations are made and offices are won.

His father, indeed, was qualified more to teach his son these arts than to inculcate political principles. John King esteemed himself "a friend to liberty and to liberty's friends",[2] but he was a conventional and partisan Liberal only unusual on account of his family connection with radicalism. When his father-in-law was attacked John King sprang to William Lyon Mackenzie's defence, but it cannot be said that in his defence

[1] Isabel Mackenzie King was not all sweetness and light. She had some of her father's talent for bitter enmity, which she exercised within the bosom of her family. She quarrelled with two of her sisters, Mrs. Charles Lindsay of Toronto, and Miss Elizabeth Mackenzie who lived in the United States, and she pursued this feud with such acerbity that when Miss Elizabeth lay dying in poverty in the Y.W.C.A. in Chicago she refused to hear any appeal for help. *Laurier Papers*, J. King to Superintendent of the Y.W.C.A. Chicago, 6 June, 1901; cf. Mrs. Lindsay to Miss T. Raske, undated.
[2] J. King, *The Other Side of the Story* (Toronto, 1886), p. 3.

he displayed, conspicuously, any understanding of his father-in-law's ideas or the nature of the Canadian society which in-spired his prophetic insight. John King was content to adopt the familiar notion that William Lyon Mackenzie had fought for "responsible government" and that he had won and was, therefore, deserving of the eternal gratitude of all Canadians. With scant respect for his father-in-law's example, John King liked the middle ground, without much knowing why he liked it except for the practical reason that it might be the winning ground. He liked the Liberalism which is "popular with the middle party, which is the party that must be convinced in order to win when the fight is on".[1] The fact is that John King understood very well the art of practical politics and very little about the theoretical foundations of political life.

The Kings attached the greatest importance to their chil-dren's education. Having completed his secondary schooling in Berlin in 1891, the youthful "Willie" was sent to the University of Toronto in the autumn of that year. Two years later his father was appointed by the Law Society to a lectureship in Osgoode Hall, the Society's professional school in Toronto, and the King family removed from Berlin to the metropolis, to a nameless shared house on the corner of Beverley and Baldwin Streets in a fashionable part of the city. There, within the space of two years, the life not only of Mackenzie King but of his whole family was transformed in a manner the significance of which was beyond their powers of estimation.

The transformation of the King family ran parallel with and was, indeed, part of a transformation taking place in Canada as a whole. When John King had first established himself in Berlin it was a slow-moving market town of commercial establishments and small manufactories serving the needs of a simple farming community. This agrarian society of Ontario in the 1870's possessed an almost Utopian excellence in the eyes of the farmers themselves, for there were no landlords in the European manner, no tithes and no burdens imposed upon them from above. They worked hard, but they possessed the means with which to work. The land was rich and abundant. Fuel and building material were close at hand in the forests and

[1] *Willison Papers*, J. King to Willison, 29 November, 1902

wood lots. In their hay fields they raised the fuel for the motive power of their ploughs and farm machinery. They sold their surplus produce in order to buy the few necessities with which they could not supply themselves. Life for them was abundant and sometimes good. For others, the merchants and professional people, however, Canada was hardly the "go-ahead" country of their dreams. Canada did not progress like the United States. Fortunes were not as easily made; population did not grow as rapidly; land values did not rise so swiftly. Immigrants came to Canada by one door, but more Canadians left by another for the United States. In Canada it was harder for the ambitious promoter to find workers willing to leave the land and turn their labour into industrial capital, in spite of the many remedies for the situation tried by the Government.

By the time John King decided to depart from Berlin a remedy had begun to emerge. Canada had commenced moving away from the age of farming, lumbering and commerce into the age of industrialism and high finance. By the device of imposing tariffs the Canadian Government had encouraged industrialization. In spite of many disappointments, towns like Berlin had doubled in size within a decade. A class of factory owners had come into being, and so had an industrial wage-earning class. A new and perplexing age was dawning when first Mackenzie King, and then his father, mother, sisters and brothers abandoned the provincial town, where they had enjoyed success and social esteem, for the metropolis of Toronto, where all the conflicting forces of the new age were focused.

For John King and his family the move to Toronto was laden with dramatic possibilities. How would they meet the importunities of the larger society they had chosen to embrace once more? They were not a family whose ears were sealed to the sounds around them or whose eyes were attracted only by the gleam of gold beginning to glitter along Bay Street in Toronto. Not all talk in Toronto, only the loudest, was of money and the opportunities of the times. Questions were being asked symptomatic of moral perplexity such as William Lyon Mackenzie had known. ". . . The present evils of society are due to the prevalence of individualism," declared one speaker before the Ontario Teachers' Association in 1892.

"... In a social system such as that which obtains at present, the tendency is for capital to aggregate and labour to segregate: and that therefore the position of the capitalist is getting more and more omnipotent, and that of the labourer more and more precarious and dependent; and that the result of this competitive individualism will be, that the condition of the labourer will become intolerable (as indeed it has already become in some measure) and that, as a consequence, social disruption and horrible anarchy will inevitably ensue."[1]

When Mackenzie King entered the University of Toronto in 1891, it was involved intimately in the social crisis of the times; and there could be seen, on the intellectual plane, repercussions of the forces in conflict in Canadian society at large. The authority of the classical and theological studies in the University had lately undergone a diminution in favour of the natural and social sciences. In 1888, the Provincial Government of Ontario had intervened in the affairs of the University to the extent of providing a new Chair of Political Economy and Constitutional History. The Provincial Premier, Sir Oliver Mowat*, and Edward Blake,* one of the most intellectually distinguished Liberals of his generation, both interviewed the applicants for the new post because they were, as the Minister of Education said,

"organizing a department of political science in the earnest hope that it would be able to afford to the undergraduates . . . a comprehensive course of training in economics and political philosophy, which could fit them for dealing with the many social and constitutional problems which require particular attention in a rapidly expanding country like Canada."[2]

The man appointed to do this work was W. J. (later Sir William) Ashley,* an Oxford don of formidable intellect and industry. He brought with him to Toronto a wide acquaintanceship with the historical method in the social sciences and a scepticism about the *a priori* theorizing of the classical economists. "A Political Economy", he said in his inaugural address, three years before Mackenzie King came up to the University,

"is possible which shall be of real value to society; in it the old doctrines will be shown not to be untrue, but to have only a relative

[1] J. E. Bryant, *Education in the Twentieth Century* (Toronto, 1892), p. 11.
[2] A. Ashley, *William James Ashley, A Life* (London, 1932), p. 54.

truth. . . . The direction for fruitful work is no longer in the pursuit of the abstract deductive method which has done as much service as it is capable, but in following new methods of investigation—historical, statistical, inductive. . . . The method of investigation, in my opinion, most fruitful, I would call the historical . . . the method of direct observation and generalisation from facts, whether past or present. . . . It seems to me that the economist could examine, for instance, the position of the agricultural interest in Ontario by just the same sort of method. . . ."

Ashley was not only dissatisfied with the methods of the traditional political economy but with its purposes.

"The very term Political Economy stank in the nostrils of intelligent working men. . . . (They) had been fed upon it for half a century to show artisans how everything in the industrial world was for the best; or, at any rate, that it could not be improved by combinations or by interference by the State. . . ."[1]

To remedy the situation Ashley helped to found and became the first editor of the *Toronto University Studies in Political Science*, in which were published treatises upon such subjects as "The Condition of Female Labour in Canada" and "Municipal Monopolies, and Their Management". He soon won the admiration of the trade unionists of Toronto who heard him "lecture on economic questions from time to time and always with advantage and satisfaction".[2]

Ashley left Toronto for Harvard at the end of Mackenzie King's first year in the University. His successor, James Mavor, presented a remarkable contrast. Ashley was an aloof and rather forbidding scientist who believed that academic men should study the community around them but should not involve themselves in such a way as to prejudice their capacity to ask and answer questions in a disinterested fashion. Mavor was a mercurial Scots adventurer who in the course of his life believed many things and nothing long. While he was a young teacher in Glasgow he became a socialist, and he was a close friend of William Morris. He ended his career denouncing the socialist tyranny and corruption of The Hydro-Electric Power Commission of Ontario. In the course of this political progress he became the intimate of railway promoters, an adviser of Sir Clifford Sifton,* a patron of the Doukhobors, a friend of

---

[1] Ashley, *William James Ashley* etc., pp. 49–50.
[2] *The Mail*, Toronto, 19 January, 1895, p. 4.

Kropotkin, a visitor at Tolstoy's home Yasnaya Polyana, and the author of a book on Russian economic history. When Mavor arrived in Toronto he specialized in the denunciation of socialism, criticism of the trade union movement and academic politics. Students are usually more perceptive than professorial appointment boards of the quality of their teachers. So it is not surprising that many students were unsympathetic towards Mavor's opinions. Mavor, however, filled his office to the general satisfaction of the authorities in Toronto for he possessed social charm, an eccentricity which concealed his lack of originality and a goodly supply of the favourite prejudices of his employers, stated with a novelty which persuaded them that both he and they possessed brilliant social and political insight.

Mackenzie King enrolled in the newly formed department of political science of which Mavor was a leading figure. He encountered an intellectual atmosphere little calculated to form his mind or to provide him with a knowledge of scientific method. The list of courses he took is, indeed, formidable. They included practically everything the University had to offer in the field of political economy, political science, history and law. He added to these some courses in languages, psychology and philosophy. But these courses were still organized and presented in a manner calculated to tax the memory rather than the understanding and the imagination. So little do they appear to have stimulated a true excitement in the young student's mind that Mackenzie King never continued the study of one of these subjects, save political economy, when he had broader opportunities afforded him at the Universities of Chicago and Harvard. A study of his thought suggests, indeed, that the formative intellectual experiences of his life took place after he left the University of Toronto and were the product of Chicago and Harvard and of his residence in the United States.

As a student in Toronto " Rex " King was outstanding in his scholarship. He headed his class in the examinations twice and was at other times close to the top. Otherwise, he did not command attention. A rather solemn, moon-faced young man displaying a studied sense of social responsibility, he was not so much unpopular as ignored, in spite of his persistent interest in student affairs and a habit of seizing every available opportunity

c

to state his views. His fellow students say they thought of him as "practising" for something. The very selfconsciousness of his effort seems to have been a barrier to wide and spontaneous popularity and even to membership in a small circle based upon the welling up of some youthful intellectual or cultural interest. Canadian students are characteristically preoccupied with "getting on in the world" and Mackenzie King was in no way unusual in his serious attention to what he thought could be useful in later life.

But he was unusual in one particular, apart from his scholastic abilities. He moved around and about the community beyond the limits of the University rather more than most students. Like other students he followed the North American custom of working at some paid employment during the vacations. He was a newspaper reporter. The exceptional element in this social experience, however, was the attention he paid to welfare work. He helped to entertain youngsters in the Toronto Hospital for Sick Children on Sunday afternoons. He helped young newsboys clubs. He helped with church work. He was gaining experience of people, and particularly of those people beyond the limits of the middle class.

Mackenzie King's life as a student at the University of Toronto would hardly be worth recording were it not for a dramatic event which filled a part of his last year of undergraduate study. This was the great student strike of 1895. It was no adolescent rag, which can safely and humorously be remembered in the pages of an alumni magazine, but a manifestation of the intellectual crisis through which the University was passing. If Ashley had tried to encourage and Mavor to discourage the contemplation and critical appreciation of social questions, the community in Ontario itself was feeling the desire to inquire and think.

Questioning of the kind then developing can be ignored or stifled, but sometimes the human propensity to question and discuss exceeds the powers of administrative repression. This happened in the University of Toronto in 1895. The strike generated the greatest anxieties in the breasts of the respectable classes in Toronto. It caused a sharp reaction in working-class circles in Ontario. It raised the question of intellectual freedom and the right principles of university government, still unsettled in the Canadian community. In the end the turbulence of the strike could only be smothered by the report of a Royal Commission which enquired into the conduct of the University's affairs.

Mackenzie King's part in the events of 1895 has been variously interpreted. Some have seen in it an evidence of rebel zeal and a manifestation of the fiery militant Mackenzie inheritance.[1] Others recall a rumour that Mackenzie King "ratted" on his fellow students.[2] Discussing the matter some half century later, Mackenzie King asserted in a private conversation that at a certain stage of the disturbance, when matters had become thoroughly confused, the students asked him to assume the leadership in order to deal with the authorities. As nearly as we can discover, the facts are these.

The tenure of the office of President of the University of Toronto by James Loudon seems to have been a troubled one. Whether there was one root cause of the trouble we cannot say. Several factors seem to have affected the situation. The decline of metaphysical and theological studies appears to have excited considerable anxiety in the hearts of the various clergymen and professors of theology who still swarmed within the precincts of the University. They hardened as their power shrank, and their influence in the community seems to have rendered the University administration apprehensive. This was one element of friction.

Another was the alleged incapacity and bad manners of some of the staff. Ashley had commanded the admiration and the affection of the students, but Mavor's bohemian manners and "arty" bearing, joined with his indifferent lecturing and teaching and a hostility to criticism of the old-fashioned doctrines of the orthodox economists, were sufficient to provoke the remark that "he neither knew his subject nor how to impart what he did know". The Professor of German, Herr Vandersmissen, absented himself from lectures so frequently that wide comment was made on his casual attitude. One wag

---

[1] E.g. *The Globe and Mail* (Toronto), 15 February, 1940.

[2] Writing to the daughter of the leading figure in the strike, the late Mr. B. K. Sandwell, former editor of the Toronto *Saturday Night*, stated: "The sad thing is that the truth about King is so bad it can't be printed even yet, for all the evidence goes to show that after making a most stinging speech at the *first* Strike meeting he ratted on the whole business and attended lectures as usual!" Sandwell to Mrs. F. M. Pratt, February, 1949.

appended to his frequently posted notice of absence "Vander's missin' again." Of another two members of the staff, the student newspaper *Varsity* remarked: "There are members of the staff of Toronto University whose manners are indelicate and whose speech is barbarous." This referred to the unsettling habit of the Professor of French, who insisted on vigorously clearing his throat during classes, and to the Professor of Philosophy's frequent inability to join singular subjects to singular verbs.

A further factor appears to have been the direct interference of the political officers of the Provincial Government in the affairs of the University. This interference may have been well meant, for it was rooted in a determination, in the case of Ashley's appointment, to bring the curriculum more into line with the intellectual requirements of society. But the Provincial Government was liable to regard any public institution as a pork barrel. A clergyman, G. M. Wrong,* who was related to the prominent Liberal politician, Edward Blake, was appointed Professor of History at a high salary; and although he later became a distinguished historian, he turned out to be a poor lecturer. When a clergyman related to a politician was appointed a professor of history, naturally some barbed and cynical comments were made. But even this roused neither the students nor the public, immediately.

The focal point of the troubles of 1895 was the question of the right of students to think, organize and discuss without the supervision and censorship of the University Administration. In 1892 there had been a series of student expulsions which remained without satisfactory explanation. Then, the Administration had taken over the control of the gymnasium which appears to have been a place of assembly for the students. In 1895 this authoritarian tendency in dealing with the students culminated in an endeavour to dictate to the Political Science Club the character of their programme and to determine who should be invited to address the members of the Club. There were, of course, complex and hidden forces at work in the situation created. One of these was James Mavor, the Professor of Political Economy, busily and unskilfully playing off both ends against the middle. The student president of the Political Science Club was a young man of spirit, Hamar

Greenwood* (later Rt. Hon. Lord Greenwood) who once challenged Professor Mavor, in the presence of the President of the University, to a bare-knuckle fight on a point of honour. Greenwood submitted a programme of lectures for the winter term, 1894–95, to the Professor of Political Economy, a requirement in itself humiliating enough and contrary to civilized principles of student self-government. Mavor accepted the programme and agreed to recommend it to a higher level of the academic bureaucracy, the Council. The programme finally obtained official approval. Then Greenwood and his associates did something which challenged the whole system of authoritarianism employed by the University.

They invited two trade unionists to speak to the Club, and added their names without permission to the approved programme. One of the trade unionists was Mr. A. P. Jury,* a free thinking Canadian follower of Charles Bradlaugh and an advocate of the Single Tax. The other was Mr. Phillips Thompson,* a socialist. The topics on which Jury and Thompson were invited to speak were "The Labour Question" and "Practical Socialism". The action of the Club enraged Mavor, who was already hostile to the trade union and socialist movement. Behind him stood the ranks of the clerical party whose influence had been exerted some eight years previously to keep from the students the contaminating influence of Messrs. Jury and Thompson. When the Club submitted the amended programme Mavor and the University Council rejected it and vindictively withdrew permission for the entire programme. The students decided to hold their meetings in spite of the authorities.

Mackenzie King was a member of the Political Science Club, but there is no evidence that he had any part in these events. From his subsequent conduct we may suppose that he approved of what the leaders of the Club were doing.

In response to the action of the University authorities, *Varsity*, the student newspaper edited by J. Montgomery, published an editorial on student rights and the principles of student self-government which recommended the University Council to "act on some manifestly honest principle, [and to] ... take a stand without fear or favour that would be intelligible to the outside world". While the students were thus attacking the University authorities, the Trades and Labour Municipal Committee also joined in the attack, accusing the authorities of snobbery and clerically inspired obscurantism.[1]

The reply to the attack upon the University authorities by the labour organisations took the form of a press campaign to maintain "University discipline". To the trade unionists the University Council made the lame reply that they were not really attacking Messrs. Jury and Thompson, because they had banned one of their own professors when they cancelled the Club's entire programme. If they were lame in their replies to outside criticism they became a very Goliath towards the students. Montgomery was summoned before the Council, and ordered to apologize for his editorial and to print his apology. This he agreed to do, but the students would not permit such a course. The editor resigned. Mackenzie King was an assistant editor, but the students passed over him and re-called to the editorship James A. Tucker, a poet, a man of brains and courage who had once served as editor of the paper. Tucker refused to apologize, and made it plain that the University authorities could expel him if they so desired, for he intended not to compromise on the question of the right of students to comment freely on affairs of interest to themselves. To back up his statement he wrote a letter to the press over the signature, "Student," calling attention to the state of affairs in the University and asking the public to look at the situation objectively and not to be stampeded by unsubstantiated press campaigns about University discipline.

Tucker was called before the Council. He asked to be represented by counsel. This was refused. He was asked to answer three questions concerning his conduct. He answered them. Then he was ordered to apologize. This was on January 29th, 1895. On January 31st a special meeting of the Literary and Scientific Society was called to discuss the course the students should take. A petition was already being circulated asking for a public inquiry into the affairs of the University. Mackenzie King was one of a number of speakers at the meeting of January 31st, but we do not know what he said or what stand he took. He neither moved nor seconded the resolution calling upon the public to reserve judgment. The star of the meeting

[1] *The Mail*, Toronto, 19 January, 1895.

was, of course, Tucker, who plainly stated his determination not to apologize and to insist on the right of students to free comment. The students' case was prepared for publication. It was signed by five students of whom Mackenzie King was not one.

In spite of the commotion of late January, 1895, the critical temperature for an explosion had not yet been reached. On February 6th, G. M. Wrong, who probably did not realize that he was one of the focal points of tension, wrote a letter to *The Mail*, Toronto, suggesting a means of compromise and reform. On February 11th Tucker was suspended. A few days later the Professor of Latin, William Dale, wrote a letter to *The Globe*, Toronto, attacking the method of appointing professors, alleging that Professor Wrong's was an unsuitable appointment, that he was paid more than previous holders of the post, and implying that he owed his appointment to his relationship with Edward Blake. Dale was immediately asked to resign, which he did. His subordinate, F. B. R. Hellems, a Fellow in Classics, resigned in support.

When news of Dale's dismissal reached the students, there was an uproar. Dale has been described by some of his students as an excellent teacher. He was very popular and much respected. On the day they learned of his resignation, students began to absent themselves from classes. Mavor was already being boycotted, but the strike began to spread to all classes. President Loudon became ill. A mass meeting was called. Tucker and Greenwood were the most impressive speakers, but Mackenzie King was well received. In fact, he moved the resolution, seconded by Greenwood, calling upon the students to strike. Such a blow to the prestige of the University authorities and their friends in the Provincial Government could not go unanswered. It was now a question of who could stand up for their principles most firmly and for the longest time.

On February 20th, the students received a letter from President Loudon consenting to an inquiry. A mass meeting was called and a committee of fourteen, of whom Mackenzie King was one, was appointed to handle the interests of the students. At this critical moment Greenwood, the future British Cabinet Minister, and King, the future Prime Minister of Canada, respectively moved and seconded a resolution calling on the students to end the strike.[1] The strike had been called as a last resort to bring the grievances of the students to the attention of the public. They had put their faith in a public inquiry; now it was to be tested.

The Royal Commission for which the students had been calling was appointed. The Chief Justice of the Province of Manitoba was the Chairman. Judges, lawyers and professors were his fellow commissioners. W. R. (later Mr. Justice) Riddell* was named counsel for the students, and S. H. Blake, Q.C., for the University. One by one the students, professors and University officials were examined.

Tucker and Greenwood were impressive witnesses on behalf of the students, but otherwise the students were unable or unwilling, examinations being only a few weeks away, to testify against their teachers and examiners. Such were the circumstances when Mackenzie King was called to the witness stand to undergo examination in the presence of the Royal Commission at the hands of Mr. Blake, one of the most skilful members of his profession.

Mackenzie King was in many respects a key witness. He was not a hothead. Caution, indifference or conscientious scruples had prevented him from playing a leading role in the early development of the dispute, but he had come forward at a critical moment to take an important place in the strike. His family connection lent him much authority, for his father was a Queen's Counsel, a lecturer in the Law School, one of the founders of *Varsity* and a member of the University Senate. His father, too, had been honoured only a few months previously by the Press Association for his work on the law of libel. If the students were eager to hear what Rex King had to say, they had good reason.

H. J. Scott, the junior counsel for the University administration, commenced the cross examination. He addressed a few simple and apparently not very relevant or important questions to Mackenzie King. Had the witness heard it said that the University would be the better without Professor Mavor? Yes, Mackenzie King had heard such comments. "What," Mr. Scott asked, "did the witness *think*?" The witness said that he was one

---

[1] It is perhaps worth noting in this regard that this was the only resolution which the students did *not* pass unanimously.

of the few students who thought Professor Mavor's lectures were "any good". What about Professor Wrong? The witness thought Professor Wrong's lectures were rather weak. Mr. Scott then delivered the witness to his senior colleague Mr. Blake. It was difficult at this stage to see just where the witness stood on the issues before the Commission.

Mr. Blake started with a few casual questions. The witness answered perfunctorily. Then the famous courtroom actor drew himself up tensely, and, in the terrifying manner he was accustomed to employ in these circumstances, went up to the young student and said, very slowly, his voice inflected with threats of proceedings for perjury: "Now, Mr. King just tell me briefly, in two words: have you *personally* anything to complain of in President Loudon?" This trick question was based upon the popular fallacy that if an individual is personally unaffected by a situation, he has, therefore, no grounds for complaint about that situation. The witness fell into the trap. He admitted that he had discovered no fault himself in President Loudon. "I must say he has always treated *me* with respect," he concluded. The Commissioners and the public in the galleries dissolved in laughter. Mr. Blake dismissed the witness. The young Mackenzie King was for many years embarrassed to recall the humiliation he had suffered; for it was said of him that he, who had moved the resolution to strike, had publicly stated he knew nothing of which to complain.[1]

The outcome of the whole episode provides an interesting commentary on life in Canada under the domination of the seekers after money and respectability. The Royal Commission found the University authorities "Not Guilty" but mildly censured them for want of tact. President Loudon and Professors Wrong, Mavor, Vandersmissen, etc. kept their posts. Professor Dale and Mr. Hellems were not reinstated. Hamar Greenwood found it wise to make his career in Great Britain. Tucker remained expelled, and with the aid of a fund subscribed by his

[1] The most valuable information concerning the strike is to be found in the correspondence of Mrs. F. M. Pratt, Tucker's daughter, the Rev. Canon A. Harding Priest, Tucker's nephew, and Mr. A. M. Chisholm, Tucker's friend, who with Greenwood, formed the actual triumvirate of the strike. Unfortunately, this material is not at present available to the public, and until it is, the attitude of Tucker and King in this episode will not be fully appreciated. Cf. Hector Charlesworth, *More Candid Chronicles* (Toronto, 1928), pp. 72–92.

friends at the University he went into exile in the United States where he completed his education.[1]

For Mackenzie King, the consequences were hard to define. As far as he himself was concerned they were mild and in keeping with his conduct on the witness stand. He was not seemingly punished at all. He was placed first in the examinations which were held shortly after his appearance before the Royal Commission, but for some reason or other he failed to obtain the fellowship for which he applied, in 1896, and which by any ordinary calculation based upon his academic record he could legitimately have expected to receive.[2]

But if the youth appeared to escape the wrath of authority his father does not seem to have been so fortunate. In his father's case the story is rather more complicated. It would be hard to prove that the sight of someone bearing the name of William Lyon Mackenzie moving a strike resolution had so frightened ruling circles in Toronto that they thereupon decided to chasten John King and drive out his son, but the curious coincidence remains that, until 1895, the experiment of moving to Toronto seems to have gone well for John King. After 1895, John King gradually ceased to flourish. He failed to obtain the Chair of Constitutional and International Law, "because the appointment . . . [was] virtually left to President Loudon against whom Mr. King had taken an independent stand in University matters."[3] Twice he sought elevation to the judicial bench and twice he was denied. Why should these things be, he cried out to his friend Willison.*

> "I care less personally and professionally for the position, than for what it will enable me to do in many ways for my family. My regard and duty for them is the paramount consideration. . . . It seems hard that I should be barred . . . but I think it is only . . . [because] I am not an active politician, a conservative and an R.C. I could have no doubt worked up a good practice in Toronto if I had been ready to do things which no honourable professional man should do . . . we can't afford to retire. We must keep the wolf from the door. . . ."[4]

[1] Since writing this we have discovered in the Parliamentary Library, Ottawa, a manuscript entitled *Famous Canadian Trials,* vol. xviii *Student Rebellion* by Edwin C. Guillet, M.A. This account of the student strike confirms many of the details and conclusions which the authors have come to in the course of their own study.

[2] *Willison Papers,* King to Willison, 6 April, 1923.

[3] *Laurier Papers,* Ritchie to Laurier, 31 June, 1901.

[4] *Willison Papers,* J. King to Willison, 14 March, 1904.

When Mackenzie King emerged upon the scene as a young man fresh from the simplicity of Waterloo County in Ontario, both his home and his native land were entering upon a course of transformation. In that earlier transformation of his grandfather's day, the Highland pedlar's lad, his forebear, had been kicked hard by the vested interests of society and he had resisted and endured. Now in this new transformation of Canada into an industrial community old social habits were decaying and new were being born, and the Mackenzies and the Kings were being tried again. The father, for much less reason—for no discernible reason of principle—and in a more genteel manner, was being kicked as William Lyon Mackenzie before him had been kicked. In this school of cynicism Mackenzie King was learning his lessons, but as yet what he learned and what conclusions he drew were not clear.

CHAPTER II

Germinal

In the making of his career as a politician the years 1896–1900 were, for Mackenzie King, the most important of his life. During these years he made the map of the social world which guided him through the political mazes where he was destined to travel for more than half a century. It was then he discovered the forces at work in society and decided upon his course in relation to them.

Of equal importance to these intellectual and spiritual processes was the establishment before his twenty-sixth birthday of a position within the edifice of government itself which enabled him to lay the foundations of his parliamentary career. Subsequent to 1900 he encountered many perils to this career; at times his political life seemed nearly in ruins and he made many serious mistakes of detail. But so apt to reality were the discoveries he made, during the dying years of the nineteenth century, that he seemed for the rest of his life endowed with a mysterious power, which men called luck, but which was in fact little more than relevant knowledge.

In the year when Mackenzie King departed from the University of Toronto, the transformation of Canada manifested itself in sharp political change. In June, 1896, the Liberal Party under the leadership of Sir Wilfrid Laurier had triumphed at the polls. A kind providence appeared to preside. With the triumph there dawned an unexampled prosperity and growth for Canada. The disappointing frontier beyond the Great Lakes, acquired and traversed at so much expense after the formation of the Dominion in 1867, was transformed, in the epoch of Sir Wilfrid Laurier, into a vast wheat farm and cattle ranch capable of feeding millions at home and overseas. If the development of the Canadian West was the dramatic event of the times, the rapid growth of industrial and mining enterprises was of even greater importance, and of more social significance. The seedlings planted by Sir John A. Macdonald began to bear fruit for Sir Wilfrid Laurier.

But at this time, there was still little opportunity for a Canadian to see the shape of things to come. Canadians were still described as colonials, and they were beginning to resent the term. In fact Canada, in 1896, was not a colony and had not been one for half a century, if by a colony we mean a community lacking the powers of self-government. Being a colonial is, however, something vastly more than a matter of self-government. It is the condition of being isolated, undeveloped, unsure and inexperienced. In this sense Canada was still a colony, and it was necessary for Canadians wishing to grasp the world and to understand it to go abroad for experiences they could not have, yet, in their native provinces. When Mackenzie King went to the United States in 1896 he was going to live amidst the realities of a developed industrial capitalist community well set upon its turbulent course through its "mauve decade".

In Canada the society William Lyon Mackenzie had known was passing away. In the United States the traditional America of Jefferson and Adams had long since disappeared. A new America had come into being of great cities, great industrial corporations, great corruption, great wealth, great poverty, great prosperity and great depression. Arcadia was in ruins and, amid the smoke, Jefferson's dream of a rural society of peasant proprietors as rational and as conservative as the Chinese had vanished. The Yankee admiration for ingenuity and labour-saving gadgets had become a worship of technology. Prudent thrift had become a passion for profit and the accumulation of vast piles of wealth. Dislike of shiftlessness and laziness had become a contempt for everyone content to work for a weekly wage. Pity for misfortune had become fear of the ill-paid. The factions, which Madison had believed inevitable in any society based on private property, had become great conglomerations arming and organizing against each other.

When Mackenzie King first went to the United States, the American Republic was already the greatest industrial power in the world. In terms of energy produced, manpower employed in industry, total productivity *per capita*, steel output, coal output, indeed, by almost any measuring rod, the United States was economically the most highly developed nation on earth by 1895. Its growth was greater than that of any other industrial state. Although the great powers of Europe did not yet realize the fact, the material centre of gravity had passed to the North American continent, where there was united under the authority of a single constitution a community possessed of more useable natural resources and animated by more determination to exploit them than any other. By 1895, there were only three nations in the world comparable with the United States in size, resources, and population: Russia, India and China; but in none of these countries was the structure of society and the political institutions such as to evoke from the people the will and the energy to create a vast industrial community like that growing so rapidly in the rich environment of North America. Mackenzie King was witnessing the birth of a giant exemplar of a thorough-going capitalist power, which, in the simplicity of its social dynamics and the structure of its social relations, might have served as an illustration in a lecture by one of the early socialist theorists.

In a new society, whose economy was afflicted with rapid cyclical movements, prophecy flourished and social criticism abounded. The incarnation of heaven or hell was freely predicted. W. D. Howells, the novelist and literary critic, noted the rising of a "blood-mist". In a widely read book, *Caesar's Column*, a social cataclysm was confidently predicted, and the learned and sophisticated Henry Adams took comfort in the second law of thermo-dynamics upon which he relied hopefully for the end of the world. Bellamy invited his readers to believe in the coming of a collectivist Utopia which took the form of an enlightened and all-embracing trust. People were advised to believe in technology and not to believe in God, while the Roman Catholics grew strong on the medicine of Papal infallibility. Panaceas and nostrums, faith-healing and elastic currency, all found their advocates and their market in a society inflamed with greed and fear, hope and despair. The most enlightened survivors of the old America viewed the whole scene with contempt, unmitigated in any way by respect for the ascendant class of millionaires. Charles Francis Adams declared that, although he knew a multitude of "successful" men of the period, there was not one "I would care to meet again either in this world or the next". His brother, Henry, improved upon this by remarking that "America contained scores of men worth five millions or upwards, whose lives were no more worth living than those of their cooks".

The evident chaos of the American moral world in the 1890's must not be allowed to deceive, however. In spite of an absence of any consistent intellectual or religious patterns, the millionaires and their cooks, for whom Henry Adams expressed his contempt, had a firm grip upon social reality. Neither party was much bemused by economics, political theorizing or religious sophistries. Theirs was the realism of the balance sheet. Employers knew, frankly stated, and revealed by their actions, that their capacity to make fortunes depended principally upon economizing their expenditures upon the largest item of their costs: wages. They could do this in two ways: either by keeping wages absolutely low or, if allowing them to rise, to increase productivity per man at a greater rate or at least at the same rate as the rise in wages. Employees, for their part, saw very clearly what seemed to be a solution of their problems: increased wages. No one, from Eugene V. Debs* to John D. Rockefeller,* seriously questioned the nature of the social cleavage or its causes or its ramifications in politics.

Mackenzie King experienced the American community through the agency of universities, and he approached it with some detachment as a student and a foreign observer. He studied first at the new University of Chicago and then at the old institution of Harvard. His subjects were political economy, economic history and sociology. He studied under some of the most famous and creative social scientists of the day, and he was a fellow student of several others who have altered the course of thinking about economic and social questions. Thorstein Veblen was a teacher and Wesley C. Mitchell was a student at Chicago when Mackenzie King was there. Sir William Ashley, and Archdeacon Cunningham* of Cambridge University, taught him economic history at Harvard. J. Laurence Laughlin, the *laissez faire* dogmatist, lectured to him on economics at Chicago. At Harvard he attended Ec. II where F. W. Taussig* expounded the classical economists and taught his students both to believe in the immutability of classical economic categories and to criticize all they learned.

The men who taught Mackenzie King were among the foremost minds in North America meditating upon the character and destiny of the complex industrial communities in which they lived. The dark star, Thorstein Veblen, pronounced a curse on the conspicuous waste he saw around him, but he also taught the lords of the jungle the comforting doctrine that the war between the predatory elements and the industrious elements in society is inevitable and eternal, and that by an exercise of ingenuity the financial magnates, like the feudal lords before them, can clothe their interest in ethics and thus identify their interest with the general interest. Wesley C. Mitchell was attracted to study the cyclical fluctuations of the American economy for the purpose of laying bare the laws governing its wild excitements. Ashley and Cunningham taught that the mode of men's work determines the character of society and that the state must positively consider the work and well-being of the community. Taussig rather contradicted this historical viewpoint and this willingness to turn towards the state as an agency in economic development. He opposed governmental intervention in economic life and considered the social welfare programmes of Germany as excessively humanitarian and unduly costly. The idea that capital and the productive apparatus of society could "belong to" or be administered by or in the interest of any group except "business men" was not even considered by him to merit discussion. But Taussig, more than any of Mackenzie King's other teachers, was expressive of the most advanced thought of American big business. He questioned the advantage of protectionist policies at a time when American business was succeeding to the international position of Great Britain as a supplier of manufactured goods and a consumer of raw materials. He was critical, too, of the labour relations policies of some big American business men. Discussing the Homestead Steel Strike and the conduct of Henry C. Frick, Taussig once declared:

"No doubt a man of action must fret at the incongruity of a conference with an unwieldy committee of twenty-five slow-witted workmen. But with tact, patience, friendliness of bearing, the cultivation of a spirit of confidence and goodwill it is possible—whether probable, who can say?—that the struggle might have been avoided; and these qualities were conspicuously absent in the Manager."[1]

Taussig's assumption that labour disputes arise because workers are stupid and employers are high spirited and that a drop of kindness will solve everything, corresponded with some of the ideas of the young Canadian student who sat at his lectures and visited his tea parties.

At Chicago Mackenzie King devoted part of his attention to the study of money. At this time William Jennings Bryan* was preparing a descent from the cross of gold on which the people of the United States were reported to be crucified. Mackenzie King presented seminar papers on "The Function of Money," "The Quantity Theory of Money", "A History of Prices in the United States since 1850", "Currency Elasticity" and "State Banking Systems, 1837–63". His companion interest was the history and organization of the labour movement and the development of social welfare services. When he transferred to Harvard in 1897 he continued these interests, but broadened the scope of his studies to embrace economic history, the foundations of the study of which were then being laid by the two Englishmen, Ashley, who was on the staff of Harvard, and Cunningham, who was a visiting lecturer.

While attending the University of Chicago Mackenzie King was reported to have satisfactorily carried a full course of instruction in the field of political economy and sociology, but he left without taking a degree. In later life, Wesley C. Mitchell could not remember him making any impact among the graduate students of his day, and he seems to have remained very much in the background there. At Harvard he attracted much more attention. In the examinations in the course work there he won an A rating in all his courses save one. At the end of his first year he was elected to the Henry Lee Memorial Fellowship, worth considerably more than the Townsend scholarship "for the benefit of indigent scholars" which had enabled him to

[1] J. Dorfman, *The Economic Mind in American Civilization* (New York, 1949), iii, p. 267.

D

enter Harvard. In 1899, when he completed all his course work for a Ph.D. degree, his fellowship was renewed and he was given leave of absence to study in Europe. In the American universities he had repeated the pattern of Toronto, a pattern which became characteristic of his life: he started obscurely, attracted little initial attention and ended triumphantly.

And he repeated another pattern. Just as he had gone to school in Berlin and learned his essential lessons at home, so in Chicago he attended classes at the University and learned other lessons among people who knew neither the campus nor the classroom. His academic work was untheoretical, severely descriptive and lacking in moral overtones, but it is plainly revealed that at this time he was discovering what he explicitly stated twenty years later in the pages of *Industry and Humanity*, i.e. that the central subject matter of politics in an industrial community is the tension between the great groupings: those who buy labour power in the market and those who sell it there.[1] Other questions—constitutional questions, racial questions, economic questions are but particular manifestations of what Michael Oakeshott has so aptly called the style or secular character of modern politics. In relation to the contending groups Mackenzie King discovered also his position. In this discovery his experiences at Hull House in Chicago and his connection with Jane Addams,* its founder, were of the highest importance.

Chicago, in the 1890's, surveyed the continent, east, west, north and south, and seemed the centre of all things. Along the lake front, on the Gold Coast, dwelt the hog butchers, the traction magnates, the mail-order tycoons and the farm machinery princes. Inland lay the "jungle" where, in the shadow of the slaughter-houses, dwelt the old Americans, the Poles, the Germans, the Hungarians, the Jews, the Negroes, the Russians, the Italians, the Greeks, the Slovaks, the Irish, working, breeding, fighting, praying and dying. On a hot afternoon, when the breeze was blowing off the torrid plains of Illinois and Iowa, Kansas and Nebraska, the sweet, nauseating odour of death from the slaughter-houses used to penetrate into the Gold Coast, and the rich men and their servants and their women knew whereof their substance came. The air would clear only

[1] See Chapter IX below.

when the hot winds hit the cold air rising off the blue water of Lake Michigan. Then, the lightning and thunder were loosed and the cold torrential rains fell, flooding the streets and purifying the air for a few days.

Away from the Gold Coast and some distance from the slaughter-houses, the University, which the young Canadian had chosen to attend, had been founded in 1892 by a contribution from the oil fortune of John D. Rockefeller. Three years earlier, Jane Addams, the daughter of a well-to-do family, founded Hull House in Halstead Street in the "Jungle" and much nearer the stockyards of Chicago. Hers was an "impulse to share the lives of the poor", that twinge of conscience which from time to time produces a St. Francis or a Shaftesbury. She could not have chosen a better spot to exercise her talents, for Chicago in the 1890's was the focal point of every social tension afflicting the United States at that time. In 1886 Chicago had witnessed the Haymarket Riots and the judicial assassination of the anarchist leaders. In 1892, Governor Altgeld of Illinois had reinflamed the old passions by attempting to undo some of the injustice perpetrated by the courts, the newspapers and the pulpits of the millionaires. When Mackenzie King went to live in Hull House, in order, as he said: "to conduct in a more effective and satisfactory manner some of my sociological researches,"[1] the terrible Pullman strike was only lately over, and Eugene V. Debs was still in gaol. The socialists had been killed, beaten and gaoled, but American labour was organizing, in spite of this assault, more rapidly than at any time in its history.

If industrial unrest was the central problem of the time, there was the subsidiary problem of poverty, and its attendant vices, crime, superstition and political corruption. Miss Addams and her associates, "young persons who had sought relief from the consciousness of social maladjustment in the anodyne of work offered by philanthropic and civic activities ... ",[2] devoted their attention both to the major problem and its subsidiary. According to Miss Addams, the leading citizens of Chicago had decided, following the bloody proceedings in Haymarket Square and in the courts of the State of Illinois, that "the only cure

[1] W. L. M. King to Harvard University, 26 April, 1897.
[2] J. Addams, *Twenty Years at Hull House* (New York, 1910), p. 177.

for acts of anarchy was free speech and an open discussion of the ills of which the opponents of government complained". Hull House became a forum for ventilating grievances and for the virulent and ceaseless discussion of the large ideas of the European immigrants about the need to constitute the world in accordance with new principles.

Miss Addams for her part could see no rational objection to socialism or communism, but she refused to be drawn into participation in any movement. She found the European immigrants soaked in Christian traditions. This meant that they, whose ancestors had for 1500 years taken seriously the symbols of crucifixion, death and resurrection to a more abundant life, had come easily to believe that through the crucifixion of revolution the old society could be buried and a new one resurrected on earth, more just, more perfect and more divine than the one around them which they abominated. To Miss Addams the European immigrants were fanatics because "finding no contradictions to their theories ... (they) believe that the very universe lends itself as an exemplification of their point of view". Her object was to draw the teeth of their fanaticism by teaching them to think not about the ventilation of grievances but the ventilation of factories, not about the reconstruction of society but about the reconstruction of city streets, not about the crimes of classes but about the crimes of individuals. She invited them to abandon the European disposition to think at once about the past, present and future and to become Americans with only one time dimension in their lives—the here and now. What does it matter who owns a factory as long as the factory is clean and well lit? Who cares what a factory produces as long as the pay envelope is large enough?

The coincidence between the ideas of Hull House and its practical activity on the one hand, and the ideas behind Mackenzie King's activities on the other, is so close that we must conclude, in the absence of other evidence, that here was the seminal experience of his mental life. And this should not surprise us. He was born of a respectable and reasonably well-to-do middle class family. He had an introvert sensitivity and a political imagination. His mind comprehended more than his home, his neighbourhood and his city. The Hull House solution had, therefore, its attractions; for he, like Miss Addams, remained uncommitted in the conflict around him, moved by a belief in a tranquil Arcadia which they thought existed somewhere in up-state New York or in rural Ontario, but which has never existed outside the hopes of Thomas Jefferson.

During his first year as a graduate student he began to write. The literary remains of these years enable us to see something of the mind which was following a path back and forth from the academic life of contemplation and study to the practical life of the settlement houses and the jungle. At Chicago he published two learned papers in the newly founded *Journal of Political Economy*, "An Outline History of Trade Union Organisation in the United States" and "The International Typographical Union: a Study in Trade Unionism". These were the product of the classroom and the seminar.

During his vacation from the University in 1897, he began to work in the Hull House style and to concern himself in the manner of Jane Addams with practical questions loaded with political implications and possibilities. Although he was a Liberal he took the surprising step of arranging, with the Conservative *Mail and Empire* of Toronto, for a series of articles on slums, the foreign-born, and sweating systems as they existed in Toronto. Less than a year later we find him engaged in similar work for the Consumers' League of Massachusetts, preparing a brief for presentation to the State Legislature on the working conditions of Boston shop girls. Almost simultaneously he was at work preparing a report for the Canadian Government on sweating systems in relation to government contracts.

His writings during the period reveal his capacity for descriptive work. He could gather facts and put them down with clarity, and this capacity seems to have been the foundation of his academic success. He showed little interest in or capacity for theoretical or critical analysis. He exhibited no originality as a scholar, but, having regard for the intellectual and political environment of his native province, he was obviously well in advance of his own community in his interests and in his recognition of what were coming to be the central problems of industrial society. For the most part his writings bore upon them the stamp of Germano-American scholarship. They were dry, flat, neutral and factual. In his articles in the

Toronto *Mail and Empire*[1] he permitted himself one tiny flash of indignation when he described the treatment of Negroes in Toronto and the evil consequences of the sweating system. He ventured also to state that membership in a trade union on the part of a foreign born Canadian was a mark of good citizenship. This was a bold statement for a Toronto Liberal to make in the 1890's. The subject of race, which so interested his countrymen, hardly interested him at all, and in discussing the foreign born in Toronto, he classified the French-speaking Canadians and English Jews together as foreigners, while he regarded Anglo-Saxon Yankees and persons born in the United Kingdom as Canadians.

Although still primarily a scholar, he was already experimenting as a politician. His articles in the *Journal of Political Economy* were proof that he was that new social type, "the expert"; but he already realised that mere achievement as a scholar is not enough for the man who seeks power. The articles he published in the *Mail and Empire* were used as the means to launch his career, for they became a counter in a bargaining process which placed him inside the apparatus of Government. Published in a Conservative newspaper the articles were in fact an exposure of the official denials that such abuses existed in Canada. The articles did not represent, however, all the shot Mackenzie King could have fired. He has told us the reason why he omitted some facts from his study of sweat shops which appeared in the Toronto *Mail and Empire*, on Saturday, October 9th, 1897. He had discovered that uniforms for the employees of the Canadian Post Office were being manufactured by sweated labour. Although he had related an instance of government discrimination against Negroes by refusing them the right to join the militia and play in the regimental bands, this instance of governmental participation in abuses he suppressed. "I decided at all events", he wrote, "not to publish the article on 'sweating' till the government had had its chance."[2]

In the company of his father, he waited on the Postmaster-General and Liberal Party boss, William Mulock. The old

---

[1] The articles were anonymous. They appeared as follows: "Crowded Housing, its Evil Effects," *The Mail and Empire*, Toronto, 18 September, 1897; "Foreigners who live in Toronto," 25 September, 1897; "Toronto and the Sweating System," 2 and 9 October, 1897.

[2] W. L. Mackenzie King, *Industry and Humanity* (Toronto and Boston, 1918), p. 70, henceforth cited as *I.H.*

friends of the Law School, who knew the game of politics as it is played in Canada, talked for a space of time. "It was even better than I had anticipated."[1] Mulock professed indignation at what Mackenzie King had to reveal. He asked for suggestions. A "day or two later", the government invited Mackenzie King to report officially on government clothing contracts. He had a job in the government, and his career had begun: not as a muckraker exposing abuses, not as a popular leader demanding change, but as a servant of government with a very acute idea of how a political reputation may be made.

In the original edition of his chief work, *Industry and Humanity*, published in 1918, Mackenzie King related frankly this story of suppressing facts about the Federal Government's connection with the sweating system through its contractors. In the edition published in 1935, much matter was excised from the original edition of 1918, but only two paragraphs were rewritten: those relating to this incident. In the edition of 1935, Mackenzie King's father has disappeared from the scene entirely, and the young Galahad appears alone fighting labour's battle. All mention of "giving the Government a chance" was deleted. William Mulock appears, not as a politician threatened with exposure, but as an ardent reformer eager to learn the way to righteousness and Mackenzie King as the author of enlightenment. If the version of 1935 presents some difficulties of interpretation in the light of the original version of the incident, the original itself is ambiguous. In the 1918 edition King emphasized his father's connection with Mulock. Although he did not say so, his account suggests that more than one meeting between his father and Mulock took place; for, after describing the common membership of his father and Mulock of the Senate of the University of Toronto, Mackenzie King wrote: "On the *ensuing* Sunday afternoon, my father and I called on Mr. Mulock. It was even better than I had anticipated."[2] Ensuing from what? What had he anticipated? The "ensuing" may refer to a previous meeting between the elder King and Mulock, or it may refer to the Saturday, October 9th, when the article on sweating was published from which unfavourable reference to the Post Office Department had been deleted. Or it may refer to both. In any event Mackenzie King's

[1] *I.H.*, p. 70.   [2] *I.H.*, p. 70. Our italics.

account seems to suggest that a bargain was struck on his behalf between the wily lawyer and real estate operator, who ran the Canadian Post Office, and his father.

The connection with the Government which he thus established was never broken. When Harvard gave him the means of studying in Europe he improved upon the means by persuading the authorities in Ottawa to assign him the task of reporting on the methods employed by European governments to prevent government contractors from sweating their employees. Thus, he was able to kill two birds with one stone, for the thesis he proposed to submit for a Ph.D. was entitled "Sweating Systems and the Clothing Trade in the United States, England and Germany". When he departed for England in the autumn of 1899 (J. S. Woodsworth* was making the same journey at the same time) he had two roads open to a career.

Originally he had intended "to study at a German University [and] spend a short time in England . . . with a good part of the time on the thesis. . . ."[1] For some reason he never carried out this plan. Most of his time abroad was spent in England, although he visited Germany, Switzerland and Italy and boarded in Paris for some weeks with Archdeacon Cunningham's aunt. The Harvard Alumni Bulletin reported that he attended the London School of Economics and Political Science, but the School itself has no record of Mackenzie King ever having entered, attended or left. He met the Webbs, however, and moved among the Fabians. He left some traces of his activities in the Passmore Edwards Settlement House in Bloomsbury, where he addressed some meetings on "What is the Main Feature of the Labour Problem?" and others on "Some Current Industrial Troubles".[2] Altogether, however, his year in Europe remains an indistinct period in terms both of his work and of his experiences and impressions.

This is somewhat surprising because he landed in England shortly before the outbreak of the Boer War at a moment of growing crisis in the moral, political and economic life of the British community. As the nineteenth century drew to a close so did the assurance and moral certainty of the Victorian age

---

[1] Archives of Harvard University.
[2] The Star Weekly, Toronto, 14 August, 1943.

begin to wane. The age of political turbulence and growing state power, of moral perplexity and of external challenge was dawning. In Africa, a small colonial nation was challenging, with amazing vigour, the power of Great Britain. In Europe and overseas, Germany, the United States and Japan were challenging Britain in the markets of the world. The armaments race of our time had begun. After the long course of popular improvements during the last half century, real wages had begun to move uncertainly, and the British labour movement was turning towards independent political action. The free competitive market, which the Victorian had regarded as the dispenser of natural justice, had been largely undermined by combinations to control and rationalize the flow of goods to consumers and to stabilize producers' incomes. Humane and sensitive people, troubled by the violence the state employed in international intercourse, initiated pacifist movements while at the same time they advocated more use of the state authority to wipe out social evils and injustices. Others, complacent about the growing military power of the state, were alarmed by prospects of growing taxation and state interference in private economic activities. The ends and means of social action were coming increasingly under review. If the United States had presented the young Mackenzie King with an example of industrial youth and vigour, Great Britain provided him with an example of maturity.

In the absence of public knowledge of his many letters to his parents during the period of his first stay in Europe, we cannot say finally how his experiences in Europe influenced his mind and formed the course of his life. His fellow Canadian, J. S. Woodsworth, was shocked by the poverty he discovered in the East End of London, and he could see as yet no way out for the victims save the minor comfort which charity could bring.[1] Mackenzie King had long passed this stage of development. He saw the problem of poverty and its political consequences in the clear light of reason and not as an emotional experience. But if he saw more than Woodsworth he reacted less. The reasons for this were various. Intellectually, he was more mature and

[1] See Grace MacInnis, *J. S. Woodsworth* (Toronto, 1953), pp. 28–44; cf. Woodsworth Diaries and Correspondence for this period in the Public Archives of Canada, Ottawa.

the range of his scientific knowledge was greater. He had the advantage of learning from vastly more capable teachers than Woodsworth. He was also colder and less willing to commit himself. Already he had the professional politician's capacity for shrewd silence, and Britain, because of Canadians' emotional involvement whether for or against, is ever a subject upon which a Canadian politician will talk with circumspection.

But there were other reasons why he did not leave any recorded public impression of what he saw and learned in Great Britain and in Europe. By the time he departed from Harvard in 1899 he was already deeply involved in making a choice of a career, and the brief moment of intellectual freshness of youth had passed. Before his departure from Harvard he had discussed his future with several of his teachers and his father. In the summer of 1899, Archdeacon Cunningham and his family visited Toronto where they dined with John King and "the boy" for the purpose of discussing the alternative of a political or academic career. In his old age Cunningham had the distinct and gratifying impression that he had influenced Mackenzie King to undertake the work of politics because, as he told him at the time, "it was real life".[1]

When he travelled across the Atlantic Mackenzie King had a commission from the Canadian Government to report on questions of labour policy in Europe. Simultaneously Harvard offered him an instructorship in economics. Thus he had his feet in the camps of both government and university. In fact he had already chosen his course. It only remained to wait and see what might come of the two connections. In the spring of 1900 this situation ripened in accordance with his expectations. The Canadian Government had reached the point where it required a department of labour to handle the growing volume of business arising from the several pieces of labour legislation passed by the Laurier Administration. William Mulock, who had just been appointed Canada's first Minister of Labour, offered Mackenzie King the editorship of the *Labour Gazette* about to be established. His father exchanged several letters with Taussig on the subject. Mackenzie King hesitated. The editorship of the *Labour Gazette* would involve more money than the instructorship at Harvard, but did it offer an opportunity

[1] Miss Ann Cunningham has supplied us with this information.

for social service? Mr. Mulock was able to convince him "of the exceptional opportunities of social service which [the position] afforded".[1] And he was able to add another inducement: the Deputy Ministership of Labour. The opportunity for service being thus assured him, Mackenzie King turned down the offer from Harvard and returned from Europe to a desk at Ottawa.

Mackenzie King had chosen well. He was entering a field where, by comparison even with the best men, he was exceptionally well equipped intellectually. Those who work should win the prizes, and Mackenzie King had demonstrated that he could work. In the University of Toronto, in Europe, but above all, in the United States, he had acquired a knowledge of the social problems of industrial communities about which few Canadians, no matter how intelligent and perceptive, could, necessarily, know much. Before his twenty-sixth year he had discovered those things essential to the success of a politician in the North American industrial community of that time. To this knowledge he added a shrewd capacity to bargain in his own interest.

Mackenzie King was catching the tide at the flood. Canada had at last begun to grow rapidly. As the industrial production of a vast range of raw and finished products developed, the political problems familiar to the older industrialized communities proliferated. Wages, hours of work, unemployment, methods of collective bargaining were becoming more and more questions of immediate concern to an ever-increasing body of Canadians. Questions of a more remote but more fundamental sort were being raised continually concerning the purpose and nature of society.

Mackenzie King was twenty-five years old and he was in business.

[1] J. Lewis, *Mackenzie King, the Man: His Achievements* (Toronto, 1925), p. 29.

CHAPTER III

The Sorcerer's Apprenticeship

At the beginning of this century, when Mackenzie King established himself in Ottawa, the political organization of Canada was relatively simple. Although the Canadian Government was of the parliamentary type, the main structure and principles of which had been borrowed from Great Britain, it had evolved in the North American social environment and consequently had undergone certain modifications and developed certain features unknown to the parent institution. In French-speaking Canada a hierarchical Church had managed to survive and, indeed, to strengthen its hold on the peasant population. This Church was strong, partly because it ruled alone without the competition of a self-confident landed aristocracy and without the interference of the lay government established by the British Crown in the eighteenth century. Under the guidance of the Church, which set the tenets of policy but generally refrained, except in moments of mistaken clerical pride, from interfering in the immediate political life of the community, the French-speaking population of Canada had fashioned out of the parliamentary and democratic instruments of government a weapon which they employed for the protection of their race, their religion and their culture. In English-speaking Canada, on the other hand, the forces of the free market, the abundance of land and the existence of numerous Protestant sects, had worked together to dissolve the hierarchical social patterns which, in spite of many revolutionary upsets, still survived in Europe. In Canada, the parliamentary form of government had been adapted to the task of effecting bargains among the multifarious interest groups which flourished in the agrarian-commercial community of the nineteenth century. For both the French- and the English-speaking Canadians, Parliament, and particularly the House of Commons, was the focal point of their political life.

Neither the Crown nor the bureaucracy, which in contemporary European communities enjoyed so much influence and exercised so much power, could then claim in Canada much authority. The office of Governor-General was filled by a member of the British landed and official aristocracy, but the power he wielded was almost negligible. Lacking the mysterious powers of hereditary monarchs, Governors-General were compelled to forego part of the influence and prestige which derives from the sacred symbols of patriarchal social values. Their capital, Ottawa, was a country town wanting in everything, save natural grandeur, which lends enchantment to the royal name; while in the centres of wealth they were but elegant birds of passage who might adorn for the moment the soirée of a rich hardware merchant or railway contractor, but were incapable of leading the nascent plutocracy of the young Dominion to new levels of dignity and conceptions of public service. Formally, by the terms of the British North America Act, the Governor-General had a considerable authority, indeed, near omnipotence; but the conventions of politics, the wisdom of the Colonial Office, and the realization in Britain that Canadians, like beavers, thrive best when left alone, had combined to transform the representative of the Crown in Canada. From being a man of great formal authority, he had become a man whose influence—deriving from his prestige and social connections— depended on his capacity to give advice and on the willingness of his first minister to accept it.[1] Only as a guardian of the conventions of parliamentary and cabinet practice was he still truly independent.

The Civil Service of Canada, in 1900, was a body of clerks

[1] The argument of this paragraph applies more to the domestic than to the foreign policies of Canada. In the latter case Lord Minto, for example, displayed a considerable independent initiative in securing Canadian participation in the South African War and he was very active in the development of the system of imperial preference. His successor, Lord Grey, conducted a lively correspondence with President Roosevelt and his Secretary of State on matters affecting Canadian-American relations.

charged with the duty of inscribing in the books of law the decisions of Parliament, of collecting the meagre revenues of the
State and dispersing to the bondholders and the contractors of
the Government the moneys they had collected, largely in the
Customs Houses. These clerks may have known how to phrase a
law or to discover a point of procedure by which one politician
might baffle another, but they neither thought about policy nor
made it. Ottawa, their home, was uncharacteristic of Canada,
generally. Modest security based on paper shuffling was alien
to Canadian conceptions of the whole duty of man. Poets, like
Archibald Lampman and Duncan Campbell Scott, sat at desks
in Ottawa, but their deskmates were not unusually party hacks
nourishing themselves in retirement upon the bounty of the
Government. Life was slow and leisurely. The clerks in the
Privy Council Office commenced their labours at 10.30 in the
morning; they adjourned for lunch and billiards at 12.15. At
2.30 they returned to their chambers to perform their duties,
but, except in anxious moments when Parliament was in session,
they generally played whist, not in their offices, but in a tower
room in the East Block. At 4.30 they strolled home through the
quiet leafy streets of Ottawa to cultivate their gardens, to chat,
to pray and to quarrel. Theirs was a life of peace, of intrigue
and of routine, *mais ce n'était pas le Canada.*

Ottawa was not a typical Canadian city in another important
respect. It was small—no bigger in 1900 than a small English or
French provincial city and no bigger than Regina, Saskatchewan today—but it possessed a social hierarchy gilded and
plumed in the official manner of the secular state such as no
other community in North America could display. The sun had
not yet set on Government House, and from its aristocratic
drawing rooms the fifty significant families of Ottawa took their
tone and learned the order of their precedence. The invitation
to Government House determined whether one was on the
inside or the outside, and the frequency of one's visits was the
visible sign of one's standing—not be it said in Canada, but in
the capital city itself.

Mackenzie King, of course, was on the inside from the very
start. His position of deputy minister insured him an instant
entrée. The puritanical and democratic suspicions which
prompted one of his friends to express the fear that "with many

people here in Ottawa . . . the social round is becoming an end in itself and therefore a danger . . ."[1] do not seem long to have damped the ardour with which Mackenzie King pursued the phantom of pleasure. On New Year's mornings, customarily, he would call on the three dozen houses on Metcalfe Street and in Sandy Hill where lived the distinguished beings who enjoyed the Vice-Regal acquaintanceship. He attended the tea parties of Miss Elliott who taught the daughters of the Earl of Minto* the art of music. One of the numerous and lovely daughters of a highly placed official, loved the young bachelor. But she was a Roman Catholic and he was a Presbyterian. The echoes of ancient gossip whisper the name of another beautiful girl to whom the young expert on labour relations used to show his collection of autographs of the famous in his rooms in Somerset Street. But tender and spontaneous romance did not dominate Mackenzie King's life, although he endured the round of skating parties, drives in the country, weekends and evenings at Kingsmere, the picnics and garden parties which animated the Ottawa scene. He was a man of sensibility but he was also a man of reason and design. A noble lady became the object of his marital ambitions. This noble lady however, was a different proposition from her predecessors. She and her two noble sisters were known as "the destroying angels", such havoc did they wreak among the hearts of Ottawa's young manhood. Mackenzie King acknowledged that, if the noble lady had less beauty, she had more brains than her sisters. With these she eluded pursuit.

In Ottawa, Mackenzie King soon organized his own show. He founded the Canadian Club there and tactfully became its first vice-president. With equal tact he was not a member of the floundering Fabian Society of Ottawa. He knew everybody. One of those who was much in his company in those forgotten days in Ottawa has observed: "King had something for everybody. He was always promoting something or selling something." He was in fact a young man of high spirits and energy who liked to be noticed and liked to leave no hour unimproved and no scene untouched by his attention. He was a type frequently found in English-speaking Canadian communities,

[1] W. L. M. King, *The Secret of Heroism* (Toronto, 1906), pp. 89–90, henceforth cited as King, *The Secret*, etc.

but he differed from the type in the reserved and conscious skill with which he organized his life. In his youth he appeared an extrovert to all those who failed to detect in his exuberance the conscious plan which some, at least, noticed there.

Once at his desk in Ottawa Mackenzie King sent for the only intimate friend of his student days in the University of Toronto, Henry Albert Harper. A strained emotional relationship existed between these two young men

> "full of . . . the evenings they spent together in company with books, from which each in turn read aloud to the other, and which were laid aside only that a deeper searching of the heart might follow, accompanied by pledges of mutual loyalty and resolve, long after the embers had burned out upon the hearth and all things were in the sacred keeping of the night."[1]

They were nature worshippers together, and, just as Mackenzie King later developed an aptitude for reading tea leaves and interpreting the significance of objects falling on the floor,[2] Harper revealed a capacity for discovering the messages hidden in the geological features of the Cambrian Shield. After looking at Montmorency Falls Harper once wrote to Mackenzie King: "To me the message it conveyed was of chastity and purity, like a beautiful, faithful woman, who had gone through the world to a white age, unspotted and unstained."[3]

The "deeper searchings" of the Mackenzie King-Harper relationship can be safely left to the study of those interested in psychology. To the political scientist, Harper's scepticism about Parliament, his faith in social science and social scientists, his philosophic idealism (ever the congenial mental equipment of bureaucrats) are of extraordinary interest. "I am becoming more and more convinced", he wrote,

> "that the true rulers of the nation are outside of our parliaments and our law courts, and that the safety of society lies in informing those who form public opinion. . . . The poor downtrodden have more to hope for from men who, having a specialized training in the operation of social forces, apply themselves to the proper remedy, than from all the windy, ultra-radical demagogues."[4]

This is representative of the thought of the young bureaucrats.

[1] King, *The Secret*, etc., p. 68.
[2] *Psychic News*, London, 12 January, 1952.
[3] King, *The Secret*, etc., p. 63.
[4] King, *The Secret*, etc., p. 114.

How far a cry from the Liberal doctrine of Bentham and the elder Mill that only individuals can know their own good and express it!

Mackenzie King installed Harper in his office as his immediate assistant, authorized to substitute for himself both as Deputy Minister of Labour and Editor of the *Labour Gazette*. This was an advantageous arrangement, for Mackenzie King was thus free from onerous and time-consuming administrative tasks and had more opportunity for getting about the country, thinking and planning for the future. To Harper it was an acceptable arrangement for he believed that he saw in his friend Rex the man capable of realizing his nebulous but strongly felt ideals.

The first duty of the two friends was the establishment of the *Labour Gazette*, "to gather from all parts of the Dominion facts, figures and information bearing on industrial conditions and the state of the labour market." Mackenzie King's instructions suggest that Parliament intended that there should be established an impersonal official organ of information carrying statistical and legal information. But just as he made the new department into a friendly society of his own, so he organized the *Labour Gazette* as a personal organ. His name was prominently displayed as Editor and Deputy Minister. Lest there be any doubts about who founded the Department of Labour, the first number of the *Gazette* contained Mackenzie King's letter to the Hon. William Mulock, of September 2nd, 1897, on sweating and his report on the same subject of January, 1898. In the pages of the *Labour Gazette* we can follow the thinking, the coming and the going of the young Deputy Minister of Labour with great ease. He was from the first the star of the show, and the impression was created that he was the author of all thought and action relating to labour.

His thought itself centred around the word *conciliation*. He recognized the social tensions developing in industrial Canada. To vanquish the dread spectre of social conflict, feared alike by both employees and employers, he proclaimed this blessed word to the Dominion. Those who believed in the word were reported at length in the *Labour Gazette*; those who spoke darkly were seldom heard. Mackenzie King emerges from the pages of the *Labour Gazette* as a messenger from the gods come to still the

E

troubled waters in Valleyfield, P.Q., in Rossland, B.C., and all the other spots from the Atlantic to the Pacific, where men disputed about wages, hours of work, human rights and human dignity.

But what did the word mean and to what real problems was it an answer? In whose interest did he propose to conciliate? In the public interest? What did that mean? Such questions cannot be discussed without first appreciating the problems which faced Canadian labour at that time. These centred round two questions: the recognition of unions as bargaining agencies, and the open shop. Both of these questions were but aspects of the general problem of income distribution.

Like their American brothers across the border the Canadian wage earners in the first decade of the twentieth century were not well organized except in a few industries such as the railroads and the old craft trades. The labour market was extremely fluid and competitive, rendered so by the heavy flow of immigrants from Europe, the Mediterranean and Latin America. Endeavours were being made to make this market even more competitive by opening the gates to immigrants from the Middle East and the Orient. Wage increases seriously lagged behind increases in productivity, and capital accumulation was very rapid, as it was everywhere in North America. If the wild cyclical swings of the economy were to be checked, it was necessary for the pattern of income distribution to be substantially altered.

The flow of immigrants into North America created for the labour organizations a complex and difficult problem— no less difficult and complex in Canada than in the United States. Immigrants were difficult to organize, and native-born men and women, newly come into industry from the countryside, hardly less so. For this reason union recognition and the closed shop were matters of fundamental concern. To the employers, the refusal to do business with unions was the first position to occupy in endeavouring to keep low the wages bill. By insisting on negotiation only with individuals or through leaders employed in the plants concerned, employers were able to hold the whip hand so long as there were alternative workers available in a fluid labour market. To bargain with a union meant to bargain with experienced negotiators who could not be fired or victimized.

The unions regarded the closed shop as essential in the circumstances because the fluid labour market, in which alternative workers newly come from Europe or native-born workers driven to the wall by immigrant competition, made it extremely difficult to raise both money and real wages so long as employers were free to hire and fire at will, regardless of the unions. Under the open shop system a strong union dealing with an employer willing to negotiate could very easily negotiate him into bankruptcy and their members into the street, so long as the employer's competitors were able to employ cheap labour in open shops. Under that system and in the presence of a fluid labour market no employer could afford for long either to recognize or to deal with unions.

In order to understand his methods it may be useful to watch Mackenzie King at work settling an actual labour dispute or devising a policy to meet a set of circumstances. Let us examine the disturbance at Valleyfield, P.Q., in October, 1900, one of the first disputes in which Mackenzie King tried his hand, and the commotions in British Columbia in 1901–03. These disturbances were similar in their beginning and in their course to thousands of other conflicts which had taken place in Lancashire in the 1820's and 1830's, in the Rhineland in the 1870's and in Illinois and Pennsylvania in the 1880's. They were signs of Canada's industrial adolescence.

A joint stock company, Montreal Cottons Ltd., owned and operated a spinning mill at Valleyfield in the Province of Quebec, a small industrial town thirty-five miles from Montreal. About 3,000 operatives, of whom two-thirds were women and girls, were employed. There was a union, L'Union Ouvrière, in the mill, but we know nothing about its strength, policy, membership or outside affiliations. Evidently it was ineffective, for it does not appear to have succeeded either in starting, stopping or directing the events of October, 1900. These were not initiated in the mill itself. The strike started among a group of 200 labourers employed upon some excavations connected with an extension of the mill premises. These labourers were being paid $1.00 a day, and they downed tools to secure $1.25 a day, which, they asserted, was the wage paid for similar work in the district and in particular by the municipal authorities. The company refused the labourers' demand. The workers quit on a Monday. On Tuesday, some of the strikers interfered with the unloading of cement for the company. On Wednesday, a sufficient number of strikers assembled to prevent the delivery of coal to the mill. The local constabulary was called to the scene, but it either could not, or would not, break up the picket. The company applied to the Mayor for the assistance of the militia. The Mayor thereupon signed the requisition necessary to obtain the services of the militia from Montreal. Two companies of infantry arrived on Thursday evening, and on Friday two companies of cavalry and two more companies of infantry.

The arrival of the troops on Thursday evening transformed the situation. On Friday morning, none of the spinning operatives turned up for work, and the same thing happened on Saturday. There were no disturbances, but the operations in the mills of Montreal Cottons had come to a dead stop. A "hard" solution seemed in the making when Mackenzie King appeared upon the scene.

Along with the Hussars from Montreal there arrived in Valleyfield two telegrams from Aurora, Ontario, one addressed to Louis Bertrand, the Secretary of L'Union Ouvrière and the other to J. N. Greenshields, Q.C., the solicitor of Montreal Cottons Ltd. They were from the Hon. W. Mulock, the Minister of Labour, and they arrived on the Saturday, while the mills were shut down completely. In these telegrams, the Minister of Labour proposed to the employers and the Union that they join forces with the Federal Government to appoint a Board of Conciliation to inquire into the dispute. In the meantime it was proposed that the workers return to their machines. The telegrams from the Federal Minister of Labour immediately became known to the workers. They belonged to that mass whom Sir Winston Churchill has so well described as "the common man or woman who had nothing but a precarious week's wages between them and poverty, and owned little more than the slender equipment of a cottage, and the garments in which they stood upright".[1] They had already lost two days' work in protest against the use of soldiers. The promise of conciliation under

[1] W. S. Churchill, *The World Crisis* (London, 1923), p. 13.

the auspices of the Federal Government was sufficient for them. On Monday morning, they began to return to work, and Mackenzie King appeared in person in Valleyfield, visiting "the parties concerned".

In the meantime, Mr. Greenshields had politely rejected the offer of the Federal Government. He knew of no strike, he said. The company had discontinued their excavations and no work was available for the labourers who had left their employment. As for the mill operatives, "they are not working but for what reason we do not know."[1] While Mackenzie King negotiated, the Company was firing those individuals whom it considered responsible for the absenteeism which Mr. Greenshields found inexplicable. To Mackenzie King the operatives made it plain that they would come out again unless the troops were withdrawn and unless the company stopped its reprisals against individuals.

By this time, the case of the labourers who wanted an additional 25 cents a day had been lost sight of; and, since the company's main interest was in paying $200.00 a day instead of $250.00 for excavating labour, they agreed to a withdrawal of troops, to stop dismissing any more employees and to review the cases of already dismissed persons. On Tuesday, eight days after the labourers had left their employment, the troops began to withdraw leaving only a token force behind for police purposes. Simultaneously the mill operatives began to return to their work. Who had won?

The person who asks this kind of question will find little with which to satisfy himself in the affair at Valleyfield. Nothing in the affair can appeal to the lover of consistency, justice or heroism. On the other hand, the person who loves social quiescence and the *status quo*, cannot help but admire the way in which a dramatic situation loaded with many possibilities, suddenly dissolved into anti-climax. In the traditional sense of the word as it was employed by a medieval guildsman, the Valleyfield strike was Mackenzie King's "masterpiece". Subsequently he worked on a larger canvas, but he never did anything new again. Just as Thomas Wolfe spent his life re-writing *Look Homeward Angel*, so Mackenzie King spent his years re-writing Valleyfield, elaborating, refining, embellishing and

[1] *Labour Gazette*, Vol. 1, 1900, p. 102.

adapting to new media, but always adhering to the basic pattern.

The question still remains: who won? From Mackenzie King's account in the *Labour Gazette* we are asked to infer that everyone won. The operatives resumed work. The troops were withdrawn.

"Many of the labourers obtained work from the municipality almost immediately after the commencement of the strike, others received employment elsewhere, and at the time the settlement was arrived at between mill operatives and the company, but few of the labourers were still out of employment."[1]

The plain fact is that the effort of 200 labourers to compel their employers to pay them $1.25 a day failed. If you consider this failure desirable, then you may say justice was done and order maintained. You may think, however, that the employers won their point and that superior power in society was employed to baffle and defeat a group of workmen who were striving to improve their incomes. How the pattern of income.distribution was maintained may variously be described as deceit and bamboozlement or persuasion and consultation. Mackenzie King described it as *conciliation*, and recorded it as the first of his victories.

If the Valleyfield strike affords us an early instance of Mackenzie King's techniques in handling specific labour troubles in individual plants, his activities in British Columbia tell us something about his response to the wider possibilities of the social tensions of the period.

Almost from the first moment of his entry into the new Department of Labour, Mackenzie King found the problem of British Columbia on his doorstep. In that Province, more boldly outlined than in the older communities of Ontario and Quebec, could be found the complex social conflicts of a newly-established and rapidly developing industrial society. The industrial pattern of social organization predominated in British Columbia almost from the first moment of its history. Lumber camps, sawmills, shingle camps, fish canneries, mines, collieries, railroads, harbour works and steamship lines were all industrial organizations owned by private interests on the one hand, and, on the other, worked by landless and nearly homeless wage workers congregated from all over the world: from the ebullient American frontier, from the British Isles, from the older parts of Canada, from Australia and from the Orient. This simple social and economic division was complicated by racial hatred directed at the Oriental workers from China, Japan and India, whose numbers, experience of extreme poverty and cultural differences from white men, introduced a new element into the labour market very favourable to the employers.

The intensity of the social tensions in British Columbia, not unexpectedly, generated an interest on the part of the people in the broad questions of social reorganization raised by the advocates of socialism, syndicalism, anarchism and the single tax. Movements with which Mackenzie King could have had only a casual acquaintance in the older parts of Canada were living realities in British Columbia.[1] They were not easily susceptible to solution by the use of well-meaning phrases picked up in Ec. II at Harvard. Instead, they meant involvement and decision. Where did Mackenzie King stand and what did he propose to do? What kind of advice did he propose to give his Minister? The finding of an answer precipitated a conflict, perhaps within himself, but certainly between himself and his friend Harper.[2]

The establishment of the Department of Labour was watched with considerable interest not only by the labour organizations but also by organized Canadian business. The Canadian Manufacturers' Association wanted to know in whose interest the new Department proposed to be neutral. In order to encourage the Government and the Department to make up its mind, the Association began firing broadsides during the summer of 1901. The Manufacturers demanded that the department be reorganized scarcely before it had time to organize. This kind of pressure was kept up at a time when the most serious trouble was brewing on the Pacific Coast. In its presence Mackenzie King apparently wanted to swing to the right; his friend Harper wanted him to pursue a middle course.

[1] See J. T. Saywell, "Labour and Socialism in British Columbia: a Survey of Historical Development before 1903". *British Columbia Historical Quarterly*, Vol. XV, Nos. 3 and 4.

[2] One who shared a table with Mackenzie King at Mrs. Turner's celebrated boarding house has informed us that there was much gossip at this time about the growing rift between the young Deputy Minister and his principal assistant.

In November, 1901, we find Mackenzie King travelling to British Columbia equipped "with the strong arm of a commission", for the purpose of dealing with a widespread outbreak of industrial unrest centred at Rossland, B.C., where the Western Federation of Miners, District 6, was fighting the coal operators on the question of union recognition and better pay. Mackenzie King and Harper were still on terms of personal cordiality, but Harper was deeply worried by the course his friend and superior officer was taking. Shortly after Mackenzie King had departed from Ottawa, Harper wrote to him. "Perhaps," he said, "it is this very mission of yours which has set my mind so strongly of late upon the question of man's duty." Both Mackenzie King and Harper possessed a great facility for words on this particular theme and Harper penned several pages of high moralizing. In the end, however, he got down to cases. "Out there (i.e. in British Columbia) where the country is just finding itself, where standards are few and hastily put together," he continued,

> "men are apt to emphasize the importance of the *immediate* thing. Here, in the East, men try to get away from the truth by demanding 'of all the thousand nothings of the hour, their stupefying power'. Both sides of the continent have perplexities and heartaches for the well-wisher of mankind. But, however distressing may be the rash radicalism of British Columbia, I doubt if its position is not relatively better than that of the indifferent East. For where there is manly force and rude contact with nature—in Carlyle's sense—there is apt to be more of a result where an appeal is made, as it must be in both cases, to the manliness of men, the trueheartedness of true hearts. The main difference, it seems to me, lies in this, that British Columbia requires the curb, and the East the spur. Both need light. And the men who would give it to them must have their confidence, so much have men come to associate the truth and its exponent. Confidence requires trust and faith; and these, to be lasting, must be based upon strength and honesty in the individual who would be the guide. Hence it behoves every man who would be of lasting service to his country to see that he, too, is clean."[1]

Whether Mackenzie King succeeded at this time in keeping himself clean, we cannot say. In any event he had no success in bringing peace to the embattled forces of industrial politics in British Columbia. During most of 1902, the lines were being

---

[1] King, *The Secret*, etc., pp. 158-59.

drawn for a more comprehensive struggle than that which had taken place in 1901. In February, 1903, the battle exploded into the open, when the Canadian Pacific Railway Company dismissed several employees whose union activities on behalf of the United Brotherhood of Railway Employees were discovered by the company's labour security service. The clerks and baggagemen struck. In support of the United Brotherhood, locals of the Western Federation of Miners closed down the collieries supplying the railway. Stevedores and seamen came out, and even across the Pacific in Australia an effort was made by organized labour to tie up Canadian Pacific ships. Nor was this all. In 1902, the Provincial Progressive Party was formed in British Columbia with the object of uniting labour, the small farmers and farm labourers in a single political party under leaders over whom the working people might have some control.[1] This, viewed in the light of the minor successes won by the Socialists in the provincial elections of 1900, was alarming to the Liberals. And Mackenzie King was a Liberal.

Thus, in British Columbia, economic and political issues had become so intermingled that fundamental questions of social organization were raised. The men who raised these issues were the organizers and leaders of the American Labour Union and the Western Federation of Miners. While these men differed widely on particulars they were in general agreement not only about the necessity for trade union organization among wage workers but also about the necessity for eliminating private ownership in industry. Organization was, these leaders considered, the indispensable element in achieving the objective of victory upon "the political battlefield where capitalism will be assassinated once and forever".

Contrary to the popular belief—expressed by Mark Hanna* and Jane Addams—that socialism was an idea alien to the American labour movement, that it was an importation from Europe, the militant socialist and anarcho-syndicalist leaders of the American Labour Union and the Western Federation of Miners were nearly all native-born Americans of Anglo-Saxon stock, men of the American frontier fed on and fed-up with American democracy from Daniel Shays to William Jennings Bryan. These home-grown militants of the American

[1] Saywell, *B.C. Hist. Quart.*, Vol. XV.

working-class movement were tough, uncompromising men, committed to the proposition that the wage worker has only the alternative: power or slavery. Their language and imagery were drawn from the evangelical religion of the frontier. Their grandiose dreams, their hatred of government and their militant egalitarianism were social passions very old in North America. They belonged to the United States which marched gladly to the Battle Hymn of the Republic, which had been moved by the death of John Brown and which, at an earlier date, had received unto itself the exile William Lyon Mackenzie.

The workers of British Columbia responded with some enthusiasm to leadership provided by the Western Federation of Miners and the American Labour Union. The Western Federation was very strong among the miners, and it had scored some successes in the field of organization. The strike on the Canadian Pacific Railway represented an attempt not only to penetrate a new and important part of the industrial apparatus of the Canadian west but also to begin a movement to push aside the conservative railway brotherhoods who controlled the engineers, conductors, firemen and trainmen of the Canadian and American railways.

The Company called upon the members of the conservative brotherhoods to operate the trains which brought in blacklegs. The principal ally of the Union, the Western Federation of Miners, attempted to answer this manoeuvre by cutting off the railway's supplies of fuel, but this was unsuccessful. Equally ineffective was the effort to reduce the supply of alternative labour by beating up blacklegs. The Canadian Pacific Railway was able to break the strike.[1]

The entire character of the dispute and the conduct of both parties revealed that the foundations of society in British Columbia were being challenged as a result of the struggle for money and economic power. The railway may have won a pitched battle with the American Labour Union and its ally the Western Federation of Miners, but it was by no means clear which side was going to win the contest so evidently developing. To consider this question the Government appointed a Royal Commission consisting of the Hon. Gordon Hunter, Chief

[1] *The Report of the Royal Commission on Industrial Disputes in the Province of British Columbia* (Ottawa, 1903), pp. 10 and 75, describes the methods employed by the Company.

Justice of British Columbia, a sometime Conservative politician, and the Reverend Elliot S. Rowe, a Christian Socialist clergyman. Sitting in the middle as Secretary to the Commission, was W. L. Mackenzie King. The formal responsibility for the Report of the Commission, of course, rested with the Commissioners, but they made it plain that the Secretary, too, was involved. To Mackenzie King's "unceasing efforts and interest in the work of the Commission (was) due much of any value that may be found in this Report".[1]

The Commission found that the American Labour Union and the Western Federation of Miners were in favour of a policy which would tear open capitalist society and rescue the workers from "famine ... whoredom ... and slavery."[2] Neither the Commission nor the Secretary sympathized with this enterprise. Reading over the propaganda, educational material and policy directives of the American Labour Union, it is clear that a worker in British Columbia might have been puzzled to know in particular instances whether he was being advised to strike for five cents an hour on his pay or to usher in the millenium. The Commission chose to interpret this confusion favourably to the latter objective. They reported a breakdown of morality revealed by their study of the unrest in British Columbian society.

In the presence of the amoral circumstances which they had found, the Royal Commission engaged in a ritual wringing of hands on the subject of man's want of moral integrity. They then turned to the task of devising the means by which the state could rid the Canadian Labour movement of the influence of the American Labour Union and the Western Federation of Miners, and make it impossible for any union to use its power for social change or even to bargain at any level above that of the single factory or plant.

The Commission was concerned with "how far there should be legislation directed against foreign interference with Canadian workmen". Too far, it seemed to all the union leaders of any consequence in Canada. It was proposed by the Commission to make it a crime punishable by a fine in minor cases and imprisonment in major cases for any person not a British subject and resident for less than one year in Canada

---

[1] *Report, Royal Commission*, etc., p. 1.   [2] *Report, Royal Commission*, etc., p. 69.

"to procure or incite any employee in Canada to quit the employment without the consent of the employer; or for *any* person within Canada to exhibit or publish, or in any way communicate to any employee or employees the contents of any order, request, suggestion or recommendation ... by any person or persons ordinarily resident without Canada, that he or they quit the(ir) employment. . . ."[1]

The proposal was aimed particularly at the officers and organizers of the affiliates of the American Labour Union and the Western Federation of Miners, "who are not trade unionists, but socialistic agitators of the most bigoted and ignorant type."[2] Its effect, however, would have been to make every activity of an international union connected with bargaining an illegal activity and open to attack by the lawyers of the employers.

Two years before the Royal Commission began its labours the Taff Vale decision had been delivered by the judicial authorities in Great Britain. This judgment made unions legally responsible for the losses suffered by employers in the course of an industrial dispute. The full meaning of the Taff Vale decision was appreciated by the Commission. It proposed that Canadian trade unions be incorporated and made liable for breaches of contract and actionable for damages. Then, with a fine gesture of sympathy towards the unions, it proposed to exempt union benefit and insurance funds from claims for damages and to limit the rights of appeal in order to prevent prolonged lawsuits.

In order further to limit the freedom of action of unions, the Commission recommended the prohibition of "unfair" and "scab" lists. Boycotts and intimidation should be made crimes. Picketing was condemned, but its outlawry was not specifically recommended. The Commission referred to the practice of "blacklisting" by employers. "Time did not admit of full investigation. . . ."[3] but the Commission believed it to be a "natural" response to the "unnatural" practices of the unions. The Commission limited itself to suggesting that employers be obliged to state in writing the reason for dismissing an employee. Nothing was said about co-operation among employers to bar individuals from employment.

The Report revealed a remarkable sensitivity to the im-

[1] *Report, Royal Commission* etc., p. 76.
[2] *Report, Royal Commission*, etc., p. 75.
[3] *Report, Royal Commission*, etc., p. 76.

ponderables of propaganda. It, too, talked about the "millennium". But men must not rush the millennium and take it by storm in the style of the Western Federation of Miners. A regime of shorter hours will mean, said the Commissioners, an "advance . . . a long way towards the millennium". If we do well to keep the millennium in view, let us keep our feet on the ground, let us be sensible. ". . . We feel," concluded the Report, "quite free to admit that while much good can be accomplished by wise legislation, the labour problem, so-called, is incapable of final solution, and that it will be with us as long as human nature remains what it is, and present civilization endures."

The Commissioners were right. The solution they proposed created more problems than it settled, particularly for the Secretary. When the Canadian Trades and Labour Congress met at Brockville in September, 1903, a strong attack was made upon the Report of the Commission, and the committee of the Congress appointed to inquire into their activities made a charge which hit directly at the Secretary and his endeavours to establish himself as "a friend of labour". The committee reported "that labour interests and experience were neither directly nor indirectly represented on the Commission". The underlying theories of the Commissioners were rejected outright. "The ground that appears to be taken is that the organization of a trade union is the natural cause of a strike, overlooking the causes that make the trade unions an absolute necessity."[1] Had the recommendations of the Commission been translated into legislation the Canadian trade union movement would have been nearly destroyed. It would have been cut off from co-operation with the American trade union movement. It would have been so saddled with legal difficulties that very few new unions could have been started and many of the old ones would have been forced to liquidate. Thus, even the most conservative of Canadian unions were forced to unite with the most radical unions to fight a system of union control which would have substituted for the "hard" policies of employers a "hard" policy of courts and gaols by the Government.

Mackenzie King's first effort to translate his aspirations for social peace into terms of institutions and laws had, thus, brought him into association with an exceedingly unpopular

[1] *Labour Gazette*, Vol. 4, p. 325.

endeavour to cripple the power of labour to bargain and to assert itself in the community. We have remarked already that Mackenzie King had the capacity to look at situations from the outside; that he possessed the power of judgment. Now he called upon this capacity. It has often been charged that he was an inconsistent man. This charge hurt him and he performed some fantastic feats of verbal ingenuity to prove that he was ever consistent in all he did. But he was consistent: consistent in his ambition to achieve power and consistent in his cold intellectual capacity to detach himself from every situation, and from his own most ardent ideas in order to judge them in relation to the requirements of his search for power. In this instance, he quickly disengaged himself from the findings of the Commission.

In January, 1904, there was renewed strife in British Columbia centred in the mines of the Crow's Nest Pass Coal Company at Fernie, B.C. In February, King visited the troubled area, and reported most sympathetically to the Minister of Labour in spite of the fact that the Western Federation of Miners was involved. So generally sympathetic to labour did his interventions in 1904 seem, that the distinct impression is left by the *Labour Gazette* that conciliation by the Deputy Minister of Labour was beginning to be regarded in labour circles as "a good thing". But not always; the strike of steel workers in Sydney, Nova Scotia in June and July, 1904, was settled by the Deputy Minister to the advantage of the employers. Mackenzie King's swing to the right was thus checked, and so was his swing to the left. He had recovered the middle ground.

One of Mackenzie King's recent biographers has painted a picture of his hero at this stage of his career as a radical sympathizer with the labour movement working among politicians who were either indifferent or hostile to the claims of the wage-earners.[1] Such a picture involves a double exaggeration. In the first place it underrates the importance of men like Sir William Mulock and Sir Wilfrid Laurier, who concerned themselves with labour problems well before Mackenzie King appeared upon the scene. Secondly, there is no evidence presently available which suggests that in terms of policy, as distinct from technical advice, Mackenzie King contributed anything to the

[1] B. Hutchison, *The Incredible Canadian* (Toronto, 1952), pp. 22–24.

activities of the Government beneficial to labour. On the contrary, there is much evidence that he and the Government, which first he served and of which later he was a part, placed obstacles in the way of labour and limited the powers of labour to bargain. There is no evidence that Mackenzie King ever worked to strengthen the legal and political foundations of union recognition or to limit the effects of the open shop system on the power to bargain. He consistently advocated legislation directed to strengthening the state's power to investigate labour disputes, to compel arbitration and conciliation, and by this device to blunt the ultimate weapon possessed by the wage-earners, i.e. their power to withhold their labour. The effect of his policies, as he himself subsequently admitted, had the effect of preventing workers from co-operating together to employ their social power.

In studying the activities of Mackenzie King it is always necessary to distinguish what he persuaded himself he was doing; what he persuaded others he was doing; and what he actually did. When we look at what he actually did we can more readily appreciate his contribution to the evolution of politics. He had some knowledge of economic history and critical sociology: enough to frighten him and to open his eyes to the several possibilities of the situation in which Canada now found itself. He could see what economic history plainly teaches: that the early stages of industrialization have been characterized by acute social tension.

Mackenzie King established himself as a serious adviser of the Canadian Government and an architect of its policies at a time of transition. When we look back upon the history of Canada from the 1880's to the Treaty of Versailles, we can see many similarities to the condition of political tension which prevailed in Britain during its industrial revolution and in Germany, the United States and Russia during their transitional phases. In every country there appeared the virile, "no nonsense" school of politicians who advocated "hard" policies for the resolution of the social tensions of the nascent industrial community. Even in the United States, which lacked a military or aristocratic caste from which a Wellington or a Bismarck might come, the virile, "no nonsense" school flourished. But in all the great industrial states other schools of thought have

existed. They have offered "softer" solutions of social antagonisms. Like Sir Robert Peel, they have realized that it may be
more dangerous to stand behind the Duke of Wellington than
on his left.

Canadian experience, examined comparatively in the light
of the history of other nations, was not unusual. It is clear
that the Royal Commission on Industrial Disputes in British
Columbia marks a critical point in Canadian political history;
for in it we can clearly see the possibility of "hard" tactics developing. The enthusiasm for such policies was abundantly
present among the high-spirited employing class of Canada.
Mackenzie King himself might have gone in the direction the
Royal Commission indicated. But he drew back, and changed
his direction towards the "soft" policies which both tradition
and training fitted him to pursue. This does not mean that
Mackenzie King's "soft tactics" were to inaugurate a new epoch
of industrial peace. Quite the contrary. Principally, he had
benefited himself politically, for now he not only had something
for everybody in Ottawa, but seemingly something for every
major faction in the Dominion. He was now in big business.

CHAPTER IV

What Colour is "Liberty, Equality, Fraternity"?

The years 1905–08 constitute a phase in the life of Mackenzie King which has its own unity, coherence and emphasis. These were the years when he found a policy, gained a following in the community and, in possession of these, forced himself upon the attention of the parliamentary politicians. By the end of 1908 he was, judged by his own standards, the most successful young politician in Canada. Not yet thirty-five years of age, he had achieved ministerial rank in one of the two large parties. Although neither he nor his policies were uniformly acceptable to the trade union hierarchy and to the broad mass of wage workers, he was, perhaps, better known to a wider group of voters than any but the oldest and most influential of his Liberal colleagues. Too often the prestige and connection of Canadian cabinet ministers is purely local or provincial. Through his association with the labour movement Mackenzie King was known to, if not always approved by, a group of national dimensions and considerable voting strength.

His policy, evolved in these years, had two positive foundations. The first was a programme of conciliation based upon an acceptance of the existing degree of organization prevailing among workers and employers. The second was a programme of limiting the supply of labour available in the market. He developed both these programmes simultaneously during the years when he was Deputy and later Minister of Labour, but for the purposes of discussion we propose to deal with them separately.

We have already noticed the attention which he gave to the magic word *conciliation* during the years of his apprenticeship as a deputy minister from 1900 to 1904. During that period Mackenzie King does not appear to have had any definite conception of the meaning of the word which could be translated into legislation and given the form of a social institution. Arbitration and conciliation were part of the programme of labour legislation recommended by the Royal Commission on Industrial Disputes in British Columbia, but the forms of organization, which it was proposed to impose on labour by law, were wholly unacceptable to the labour movement. The labour movement itself advocated conciliation at certain times, for certain purposes and under certain conditions. Originally the demand for conciliation had found much favour in the Canadian labour movement. Many trade union leaders were led to believe that it would involve recognition of the right to bargain. By the time Mackenzie King appeared upon the scene, however, labour leaders were of two minds on the subject, while employers were beginning to see other possibilities in legislation along these lines. Indeed, there was a meeting of minds on the subject between those employers who saw in conciliation a means of sapping the militant energies of the labour movement and of making difficult the unity of labour, and those conservative trade unionists who saw in legislation compelling conciliation a means of defence against rival bodies advocating industrial unionism or socialism. Before Mackenzie King entered the government's service, one of the Vice-Presidents of the Canadian Trades and Labour Congress was advocating machinery for conciliation as a device for combating the "irresponsible" unionism of the American Labour Union and the Western Federation of Miners.[1] Conciliation was likewise advocated by the Canadian Manufacturers' Association on the basis of their conception of what should be the proper form of organization for wage workers and employees. Mackenzie King, himself, never troubled to state on what terms he proposed to inaugurate a system of conciliation.

[1] *Laurier Papers.* James Wilks to Laurier, 27 February, 1900.

There can be no doubt about the popularity of the word. It contained within it the promise of an easy way out of social difficulties and of a possible end to industrial tension, without any alteration in the structure of society. The earliest and most carefully worked out effort to establish such a system of conciliation in Canada and one which, perhaps, best reveals its appeal as an easy and conservative "solution" of the tensions of society, was that undertaken by Archbishop Bégin* of Quebec in the year 1900.[1]

At that time the boot and shoe industry of the city of Quebec, employing nearly 4,000 workers, was threatened with disruption by the resistance of the operatives to certain small changes in the industry which involved the discharge of employees. In order to maintain managerial control and flexibility, the employers attempted to smash the unions. A lock-out brought the industry to a standstill. Both parties were so hard hit that they agreed to refer their differences to the Archbishop of Quebec. As a result of his deliberations a system of arbitration and conciliation was established in the industry, the terms of which provided that the employers set up a Board of Conciliation representing themselves; the employees establish a Board of Complaint, the equivalent of a union committee; and a representative of each of these bodies meet to choose a chairman and third member of a Board of Arbitration, which would settle differences. Archbishop Bégin worked out the details of the system upon the basis of the principles of the Papal Encyclical, *Rerum Novarum*. This presupposed a permanent gradation of human beings according to function and the automatic operation of the economic system in accordance with a Divine Plan for human well-being which curiously resembled the simpler systems postulated in equilibrium economics.

Both the theory of conciliation and the methods finally adopted by Mackenzie King and translated into legislation in the form of the Industrial Disputes Investigation Act closely resemble those of Archbishop Bégin. The Archbishop considered that the Laws of God transcend the interests of groups of men. Mackenzie King translated this idea into a conception of a transcendent Public Interest. The device of bringing the opposites together to select a third party and thus to form collectively

[1] *Labour Gazette*, Vol. I, 1900, pp. 134–35.

a means of discovering the Divine Will or Public Interest is present in both plans. The Archbishop, however, conceived of the workers' difficulties as complaints, as if they were servants of superior creatures, their employers, whereas Mackenzie King realized that conciliation involved a bargaining process between parties willing and able, in the final phase, to fight each other on nearly equal terms.

Mackenzie King has left us an account, often repeated and embroidered by others, of the drama which led to the conception and birth of the Industrial Disputes Investigation Act which he regarded as one of the corner-stones of his career.[1] There was a coal strike in southern Alberta in the autumn of 1906. The operators refused to meet the officers of the union or to recognize them. Coal stocks dwindled as the bitter Canadian winter approached. Settlers on the plains watched with dismay their dwindling coal piles. Calamity hung over the prairies. Mackenzie King was far away in Europe on a government mission.

Then Mackenzie King landed in New York. A telegram from Sir Wilfrid Laurier, the Prime Minister, informed him of the dangerous situation. He sped out to the foothills of the Rockies. On the plains of Saskatchewan the settlers huddled round their closely banked fires as the blizzards howled out of the Arctic void. In southern Alberta the sun shone, however; and the employers and workers pursued their anti-social vendetta. Mackenzie King met the parties concerned. No luck—too stubborn. Meanwhile in Ottawa, Sir Wilfrid Laurier was assaulted by letters from anxious and freezing citizens. Then came a break in the tension. For what reason we are not told. Mackenzie King returned to Ottawa. Sir Wilfrid Laurier summoned him to his office. "The situation has been very critical. Such may occur again. Can you do anything?"

"Yes." Mackenzie King had the answer. It was the season of Christmas, but Mackenzie King got out his glue pot and scissors, and sent for copies of the legislation establishing systems of conciliation in New Zealand and several states of the American Union. He was pasting together a draft of the Industrial Disputes Investigation Act.

[1] *I.H.*, pp. 505 ff.

He did not always describe its birth in these terms. More often it was depicted as an instance of parthenogenesis. On one occasion, however, Mackenzie King told the story of the Industrial Disputes Investigation Act in these words: "The act is not original, it is based on legislation in other countries. The phraseology of it, a good part of it, is from legislation in other countries and some of it is copied from State Laws in this country (the United States)."[1] So much for the widely publicized statement of President Eliot* of Harvard that "the Hon. W. L. Mackenzie King invented this legislation and got it put into effect".[2] So much, too, for the story Mackenzie King told the Editor of the *Manchester Guardian* at the time of the British General Strike that he had devised the means of making industrial disputes on a grand scale impossible.[3]

In *Industry and Humanity*, written in 1918, Mackenzie King asserted that he consulted with the officers of the Trades and Labour Congress of Canada in preparing the draft of the Industrial Disputes Investigation Act. They were, he said, astounded at the good fortune of the labour movement in being offered such legislation, which "surpassed the liveliest expectations of Labour at the time".[4] But they were doubtful whether Parliament would pass so radical a measure.

Testifying before the United States Commission on Industrial Relations in 1915, Mackenzie King gave a somewhat different account of the part played by the labour movement in the preparation of the draft Bill. Before the Commission he stated that he "took the matter up with some of the officers of the Canadian Federation of Labour (sic)".[5] According to the version given in 1915, the Industrial Disputes Investigation Act was the result of a bargain made with the miners in the Alberta coal fields during the strike of 1906. "The men", he said,

"were very much incensed at the company being unwilling to meet them, and they were equally provoked at the inability to get the facts when we were working on them, and I said to them, when we were discussing the matter, that if we could not get this information that we were after or get this meeting we were trying

---

[1] *Final Report and Testimony of U.S. Commission on Industrial Relations to the United States Congress*, (Washington, 1916), p. 714; hereafter cited as *R.C.I.R.*
[2] Norman McLeod Rogers, *Mackenzie King* (Toronto, 1935), p. 45.
[3] *Murphy Papers*, A. S. Wallace (of the Staff of the *Manchester Guardian*) to Murphy, 11 November, 1926.
[4] *I.H.*, p. 513.   [5] *R.C.I.R.*, p. 716.

to bring about in a voluntary way, I would get legislation through Parliament to compel it if they would back me up on it, and they were highly agreeable to that point of view at that time."[1]

This version of labour's agreement to the Industrial Disputes Investigation Act thus differs from the usual version,[2] in that the support appears to have come from a local group of labour leaders who were induced to believe that compulsory conciliation was a means of securing recognition and information from their employers.

Whatever may have been Mackenzie King's ideas about the purposes of the Industrial Disputes Investigation Act and the real circumstances of its birth, Sir Wilfrid Laurier never had any doubts about his intentions in this connection. In 1908, when Laurier was reproached by a Manitoba politician, the Hon. J. D. Cameron, with criticisms of the Liberal Administration's labour policies, Laurier replied concerning the Act:

"The Lemieux Act was not passed with the object of conciliating the labour vote. It was passed with the sole object of preventing the untold misery and mischief wrought by strikes. When the Bill was under discussion some sections of the railway organization fought it most strenuously, and they may perhaps attack it again next session, certainly during the present Parliament; notwithstanding this view of a most important class, I persist in believing that the Act is a most meritorious piece of legislation."[3]

In the first draft of this letter Laurier expressed his unrevised and uncalculated sentiments with regard to the labour movement, for he spoke of the opposition to the Industrial Disputes Investigation Act not as strenuous but vicious, and he wanted to tell Cameron that "even at the risk of losing the whole labour class, I do not think the measure should be repealed". But this candour he struck out and had the letter re-typed as we have quoted it.

The labour leaders whom Mackenzie King consulted may have been sceptical about the willingness of Parliament to accept so radical a measure as the Industrial Disputes Investigation Act, but their fears were completely unfounded. The measure passed almost without debate. The Canadian House of Commons is esteemed a dull place. This probably explains why the drama which followed Mackenzie King's landing in New York during

---

[1] *R.C.I.R.*, p. 716.   [2] e.g. in *I.H.* and elsewhere.
[3] *Laurier Papers*, Laurier to Cameron, 12 November, 1908.

the critical months of 1906–07 has failed to leave a trace in the brief parliamentary debates on the Industrial Disputes Investigation Act.

But there may be another explanation. The events in southern Alberta in 1906 were in no way remarkable. They were but a small wave upon the growing tide of unrest and violence which accompanied the development of mining and industrial enterprise in Canada. Mackenzie King himself was not unaware of the significance of what was occurring. He placed the State above the strikers and employers, above classes, above society— above the people. There were always two equal sides to every question—the State would appear to travel directly down the centre road and the people would follow.

Politically, in the short run, he was correct. In his report on Lethbridge he appealed to the sentimentality of his readers and presented a superficially logical case with a superficially beneficial solution.

> "When it is remembered that organized society alone makes possible the operation of mines to the mutual benefit of those engaged in the work of production, a recognition of the obligations due society by the parties is something which the State is justified in compelling if the parties themselves are unwilling to concede it"

were his words. But he did not end here. He wanted to recommend machinery to prevent the recurrence of the Alberta strife. If Parliament really were interested in promoting industrial peace, then, with the existing conciliation legislation in mind, they would enact

> "something like the Railway Labour Disputes Act for strikes and lockouts. Such an act, it would appear, might be achieved, at least in part, were provision made whereby, as in the case of the Railway Disputes Act, all questions in dispute might be referred to a board empowered to conduct an investigation under oath, with the additional feature, perhaps, that such reference should be not optional, but obligatory, and pending the investigation and until the board had issued its findings, the parties be restrained, on pain of penalty, from declaring a lock-out or strike."[1]

And it was precisely this idea, the only original feature in an otherwise unoriginal piece of legislation, which became the Liberal law of the land.

[1] F. A. Acland, "The Canadian Industrial Disputes Investigation Act." *The Annals of the American Academy of Political Science*, Vol. XXXVI, 1910, pp. 419–37.

In the debate on the Bill, R. L. Borden* (later Sir Robert), the leader of the Conservative opposition, welcomed the willingness of the government to face the problem. Strikes and lockouts were all too frequent in his opinion; 577 in the five years 1901–05 inclusive. More and more frequently the militia were being called out to keep order. This cost money, and too often the Federal Government was unable to recover the cost of restoring order from the municipal authorities and the business enterprises in whose interest the soldiers had been used. Perhaps the Industrial Disputes Investigation Act would be cheaper. When moving the second reading of the Bill, the Liberal Minister of Labour, the Hon. Rodolphe P. Lemieux,* took essentially the same view of the situation.

The debate, brief as it was, reveals why a measure as simple as the Industrial Disputes Investigation Act could be con- sidered by its author a major contribution to the solution of the social tensions of an industrial, private enterprise society. Apart from knowing that there had been 577 industrial disputes in five years in Canada, the farmers, lawyers and shopkeepers who sat in the Canadian Parliament knew nothing about the subject on which they were being invited to legislate. Strikes were the work of an unkind providence. Mr. Borden, to his credit, wanted the House to appoint a committee of inquiry so that the members might learn something, but the Government, without any challenge, dismissed the idea of an inquiry on the grounds that the Department of Labour knew all there was to know about labour relations. The Canadian House of Commons was willing to be worried by industrial unrest but it wanted a quick, sure, easy solution. "This is not a party issue," the Minister of Labour declared.

> "The principle involved in the Bill is too vital and too important a one to be made a party issue. It is, indeed, essentially a national issue, which in these days of organized capital and organized labour, should command the hearty co-operation and sympathy of everyone who takes an interest in industrial questions. I contend, Mr. Speaker, that this is both a Liberal and a Conservative measure."[1]

The Hon. Rodolphe Lemieux never spoke truer words than these; for the Industrial Disputes Investigation Act was not a

[1] *Debates of the House of Commons*, 1907, Vol. XLXXIX, p. 3002.

labour measure. The labour leaders, who were dumbfounded by its radicalism when they first heard it from the lips of the Deputy Minister of Labour during the winter of 1906–07, soon discovered that it meant very little in terms of the development of the labour movement. Samuel Gompers,* the president of the American Federation of Labour, told the Canadian leaders that they had been fools ever to have given any support to a measure which tended to take from labour a tactical weapon and to put a premium in negotiation upon the services of highly paid lawyers. What experienced labour leaders knew empirically, social scientists later discovered. In the state of Colorado, Mackenzie King's system of conciliation was worked out to its logical conclusion as a comprehensive and all-embracing scheme of labour relations, and there a careful study of the system over a period of years has led to the conclusion that compulsory conciliation has been an obstacle to the organization of labour and its power to bargain.[1]

The Act was not, of course, intended to assist in the development of the power of the wage-workers. Quite the contrary; and it must be judged as a measure devised to prevent strikes and lockouts.[2] Whether it did this is hard to say. The Industrial Disputes Investigation Act operated for 18 years until it was found unconstitutional by the Imperial Privy Council in 1925. Mackenzie King was the Prime Minister at the time, but neither he nor Parliament, nor the labour movement, nor the employers, nor any of the political parties, made any successful move to re-establish the system. Clearly, the community, after a lengthy experience, had ceased to consider the Act indispensable. When the parties to collective bargaining are experienced, a conciliation board only affords them an opportunity to air their difficulties in public, and to that extent gain outside support. But the factors which make the parties agree or disagree are more often than not outside the scope of a conciliation board's attention. A board can do nothing to alter the character of the labour market at a particular time, nor the

---

[1] C. E. Warne and M. E. Gaddis, "Eleven Years of Compulsory Investigation of Industrial Disputes in Colorado," *Journal of Political Economy*, XXXV, 1927, p. 681.

[2] During the Grand Trunk Railway strike Laurier still wished to see the introduction of compulsory legislation and he thought the moment of the strike particularly auspicious for the development of such a system. *Laurier Papers*, Laurier to King, 2 August, 1910.

power of the parties in the market. The most that a conciliation board can do is to estimate the balance of power in a situation, to translate this balance into a finding and to persuade the parties that, the facts being what they are, such is the settlement which each will have to accept, whether or not they strike or lock out their employees. The parties to disputes regard the procedure as a matter of course, and of little consequence.[1]

The operation of the Act was left by Mackenzie King to his department. The legislation almost failed during its first year because of the practice adopted of emphasizing the compulsory aspects of the Act and permitting lawyers to act on boards. Their attitude was narrowly legal and their tendency was to turn facts into evidence and to apply legal tests to the evidence. It was not until Adam Shortt of Queen's University introduced the technique of conciliation by bargaining that the boards were employed as devices for making compromises. Once this was done the Act began to work and to produce the very modest results which can be claimed for it.[2]

Scientifically considered, the Industrial Disputes Investigation Act is hardly worthy of attention as a significant element in the structure of industrial relations. Politically, however, it was of great consequence for Mackenzie King's career. American big business, more hardly pressed by the tensions of its own maturing system, became interested in it almost at once. President Eliot of Harvard declared that he would "like to bring the Act to the attention of some of my friends, who are at the head of large corporations and much exposed to strikes. . . ." By the year's end Mackenzie King was able to report to Eliot that this course had "already begun to bear good fruit" and that he had received "a very large number of letters from interested parties in the United States. . . ."[3] Thus was a connection with powerful elements in the United States established. On the other hand, the Act was useful politically in Canada, for it embraced the blessed idea of social peace and appeared a harmless device for achieving that goal so greatly desired by Canadians as well as all mankind.

---

[1] The argument of this paragraph is based upon personal experience in conciliation work under the authority of provincial legislation.

[2] See H. D. Woods, *Canadian Collective Bargaining and Dispute Settlement Policy—An Appraisal*, Address to the Canadian Political Science Association, 1 June, 1955.

[3] *Eliot Papers*, Eliot to King, 2 May, 1907; King to Eliot, 31 December, 1907.

Although much has been written about Canadian immigration policies and the character of immigration movements, very little study has been devoted to the various and many reactions of the Canadian wage-working class to the effect upon the labour market of the influx of immigrants from Europe, the United States, Latin America and Asia, during the years 1896–1914. That this was a source of constant concern to the labour movement is evident enough from a glance at the reports of the annual meetings of the Trades and Labour Congress of Canada. Writing to Sir Wilfrid Laurier in 1900, James Wilks, one of the Vice-Presidents of the Trades and Labour Congress, described the effects of the migration of Finns and Scandinavians from Minnesota upon the labour market. In one tremendous sentence he told the Prime Minister that,

> "The situation is of such a serious character that if the Government does not deal with it in a firm manner by enforcing the present law [the Alien Contract Labour Act] if it possesses sufficient efficiency, or by amending it in such a way as to give it sufficient force to prevent these importations, the consequences will simply be this, that hundreds in fact probably thousands will be driven from their homes and Country because there is an unlimited supply of foreigners in the Middle Northwestern States, and I regret to say that there are men in British Columbia who by reason of the liberality and justice of our provincial and national laws, have reached prominence, power and publicity and amassed wealth, but who nevertheless have such little regard for the public interest that they would not hesitate and nothing but government interference can stay the calamity, to fill this country with an ignorant, unfortunate horde of non-English speaking aliens thereby working irreparable and permanent injury to the whole community."[1]

Mackenzie King was first called upon to deal with the effect of immigration upon the labour market in a highly particular way in 1905. Immigrants were being imported for strike breaking purposes, and several unions, notably the International Typographical Union, had complained. Mackenzie King conducted an investigation, and, in 1906, he went to England to discuss the matter with the British Government with a view to having the British Parliament legislate to prevent fraudulent practices connected with inducing residents of the British Isles to migrate to Canada. He was successful in his negotiations.

[1] *Laurier Papers*, Wilks to Laurier, 27 February, 1900.

Simultaneously, he investigated the influx of Italians into Montreal and recommended a strengthening of the laws governing the importation of contract labour.

These were relatively minor matters, but they provided an opportunity for Mackenzie King to take a stand clearly in sympathy with a demand of the organized section of labour. In 1907 an explosive crisis developed which brought Mackenzie King into the centre of a situation of national magnitude and international ramifications. This crisis was created by the anti-Oriental riots in British Columbia in September, 1907.

Since 1891, the labour movement in British Columbia, with the assistance of miscellaneous interests in the community, had been endeavouring to prevent Asians from entering the province and, if possible, Canada itself. Chinese were subject to a heavy head-tax which kept the number of Chinese immigrants very small. Numerous acts of the provincial legislature were passed designed to make it difficult or impossible for Chinese, Japanese and East Indians to procure employment, but these acts were invariably disallowed by the Federal Government for reasons of national or imperial policy. Imperial relations were not alone the reason for preventing absolute exclusion of Asians. Powerful interests in British Columbia and elsewhere saw numerous advantages to be derived from cheap labour. If European immigrants were prepared to crowd ten in a room in order to live on small wages and save, Chinese immigrants were prepared to cut the room in two horizontally in order to double the floor space of their flop houses.[1] Chinese immigrants were "steady in their habits, reliable in their work and reliable to make contracts with. They won't strike when you have a big pile of fish in your dock. They are less trouble and less expensive than whites".[2]

Until 1906, the immigration of Oriental labour was not considered by the exponents of exclusion as sufficiently serious to warrant sharp action. The Chinese Government was too weak to insist upon equal treatment for Chinese. The Japanese Government was extremely cautious because, during the period between the Sino-Japanese War and the Russo-Japanese War,

---

[1] *Report of the Royal Commission on Chinese and Japanese Immigration* (Ottawa, 1902), p. 15.
[2] *Report*, etc., as above, p. 145.

it was laying the foundation of a new international position, and was unwilling to deal with all questions of international prestige at the same time. Before the *Report of the Royal Commission on Chinese and Japanese Immigration* in 1902, the Japanese Government, on its own initiative, limited the emigration of Japanese to British Columbia. The Anglo-Japanese Commercial Treaty of 1902 made provision for the equality of treatment of the subjects of the contracting powers, but Canada was not specifically bound by this provision. After the Russo-Japanese War, however, the British Government urged Canada to become a conscious party to the treaty by legislation in the Canadian Parliament. Sir Wilfrid Laurier was willing to do this provided it in no way committed Canada to treating Japanese on a par with Europeans in the matter of immigration. The Japanese Imperial Consul-General in Canada, Nossé, gave the Canadian Government a positive assurance that the Japanese Government would continue to limit emigration to Canada.

Some time in 1906 the Japanese Government changed its policy, and began to issue passports to emigrants bound for Canada. This change was connected, to some extent, with economic difficulties following the cessation of hostilities with Russia. Companies were formed in Canada and in Japan to handle the flow of emigrants. Although there were only 7,500 Japanese in British Columbia in 1906, the number of Japanese who landed at Canadian ports in the first ten months of 1907 was 8,125 of whom 4,429 remained in Canada.[1] Only 1,614 came from Japan directly and the rest from the Hawaiian Islands. But they were all Japanese. In August, 1907, organized labour in British Columbia formed the Anti-Asiatic League. On September 7th riots broke out. The Lieutenant-Governor of the Province, a wealthy mine owner who employed Asian labour, was burned in effigy, and an assault was delivered on the Chinese quarter in Vancouver. Considerable damage was done to property. Then an assault was made on the Japanese quarter, but the Japanese fought back with guns and fists, and the rioters retreated. The Canadian Government acted with decision: they appointed a Royal Commission to investigate. There was one Commissioner: W. L. Mackenzie King.

[1] *Lemieux Papers*, W. L. Mackenzie King, *Report* . . . [on] *Methods by which Oriental Labourers have been induced to come to Canada*, pp. 7–8.

The situation which confronted him was loaded with some of the most fundamental ethical as well as political questions of the twentieth century: those connected with race relations. He came to the task in a state of comparative innocence. Although he shared a few of the automatic responses of middle-class Toronto on the subject of race (he and Harper read, with approval, Kipling on the White Man's burden[1] and he thought of French Canadians as foreigners), there is no evidence of racial bigotry in the literary remains of his student days. One of the two sparks of indignation which lighted his study of the Toronto slums was struck by the injustice which Negroes in Toronto encountered at the hands of their white fellow citizens. All his life he possessed a talent for social intercourse with foreigners and non-Caucasians, free of patronage and condescension and distinguished by good manners and personal sympathy. This was particularly true where the Japanese were concerned. During the inquiry into the anti-Oriental riots he was one of the few whites concerned in the matter who kept his temper and preserved his self-respect. Indeed, he seemed able to leave the impression with the Japanese under investigation that, although he had seized their archives and was exposing them to hatred and enmity, he was their personal friend whose sympathy for them was boundless.

Unless we admit the difficulties of the racial question, we can never adequately assess what Mackenzie King attempted and what he achieved. It is easy enough to preach the doctrine that in Christ all men are brothers, and that the ethics of brotherhood require us to love one another and cherish men of all races. Does loving one another involve admitting men of an alien culture and yellow skin to the same labour market as white men in order that mine operators, fish canners and railway contractors can strike a more advantageous wage bargain? Does not exclusion of yellow men, or brown or black from the labour market mean that those who exclude them are depriving their coloured brethren of an opportunity to labour on the world's resources and its accumulated capital to the end that they too may live and prosper? On the other hand, is not the responsibility of Chinese, Japanese or Indians the same as that of white men: to make their own communities into rationally organized,

[1] King, *The Secret*, etc., p. 70.

just and productive societies where men can live well without departing far from the graves of their ancestors and the soil which they love? Or, is it not the duty of white men to bring to an end the severe discipline of the labour market by insisting that workers with black or yellow skins be paid an equal wage for equal work, and that these wages correspond to the productive capacity of industry?

We have deliberately framed the questions before Mackenzie King as ethical dilemmas; for he constructed for his own guidance in handling these problems and in presenting them to the parties involved (and at least one party involved, the Japanese Government, was a formidable one) a general ethical proposition related to what he believed to be the facts of political economy. This general proposition he defined as "The Law of Competing Standards."

The Law of Competing Standards, stated in Mackenzie King's own words, is this:

> "Assuming there is indifference in the matter of choice between competing commodities or services, but that in the case of such commodities or services the labour standards involved vary, the inferior standards, if brought in this manner into competition with a higher standard, will drive it out, or drag the higher down to its level."[1]

There is nothing startling in this law. It is only a special case of the general propositions about competition framed by the classical political economists. It has, however, a special interest for the use to be made of it; for he decided that the state must protect higher standards and prevent lower standards from coming into competition with them.

In the light of this law and the moral decision he made in favour of higher standards, at least in this case, his policy was clear: to work for the exclusion of Asians from the Canadian labour market. This policy had the advantage of providing a scientific and ethical justification for what the mobs of British Columbia had already decided to do, and which was already expressed in the legislation against Chinese immigrants. The usefulness of the Law of Competing Standards, quite apart from its alleged scientific validity, was not the discovery of a policy for Canada, but a means of persuading first the Japanese

[1] *I.H.*, pp. 66–80.

and then the Indian Governments to accept the decision of the Canadian Government to exclude their countrymen.

Mackenzie King asserts that the Japanese Government became co-operative once they understood the Canadian motives explained in this scientific and ethical fashion.[1] This is an exaggeration. The negotiations with the Japanese Government were conducted by the Hon. Rodolphe Lemieux and Sir Claude Macdonald,* the British Ambassador to the Imperial Court, assisted by Mr. (later Sir) Joseph Pope.* In his own account of the negotiations, Lemieux did not mention the Law of Competing Standards, and, indeed, seems to have been unaware of its existence. Count Hayashi, the Japanese Foreign Minister, simply stated that, if the Imperial Japanese Consul in Canada had given an assurance about the restriction of Japanese emigration to an extent which amounted to their exclusion from Canada, he had exceeded his instructions, and that the Imperial Japanese Government would never accept the indignity of admitting that Japanese should be treated by a friendly power any differently from the citizens of other powers friendly to Canada. Lemieux was obliged, on instructions from Sir Wilfrid Laurier, to inform the Japanese Government that the Canadian Parliament would never consent to a treaty which implied free admission of Japanese immigrants. In the end Count Hayashi consented to a face-saving agreement which preserved the appearance of equality but bound the Japanese Government voluntarily to limit the issue of passports for Canada to a small number of Japanese of the professional classes, to Japanese already resident in Canada and to a very small number of labourers.

In his report to the Cabinet of January 12th, 1908, Lemieux rationalized the anti-Oriental sentiment of the mob in British Columbia. The economic causes of the riots he recognized, but he did not think that the problem was simply economic. "Be that as it may," he wrote,

"the fact remains that British Columbians object to a vast alien Colony, exclusive, inscrutable, unassimilative, with fewer wants and a lower standard of living than themselves, maintaining intact their peculiar customs and characteristics, ideals of home and family life, with neither the wish nor the capacity to amalgamate,

[1] *I.H.*, p. 76.

which gradually by the mere pressure of numbers may undermine the very foundations of their province."[1]

This is an example of an approach to race relations which neglects what may be done by humane leadership, education and the operation of practical democracy to make it possible for peoples of different races, cultures and history to come together, intermingle and develop a new community. Lemieux simply accepted what the prejudice of the anti-Asian racialists suggested, and Mackenzie King supported him in this. A letter which he wrote to Lemieux from Toronto on December 30th, 1907, reveals this and much else. "We are all expectantly waiting", the would-be Cabinet Minister wrote to his superior,

"for the opening of the sealed packet which you are bringing with you from the Orient. Your mission to Japan has been followed with intense interest throughout the whole Dominion, an interest which has deepened as the Canadian people have come to realize how important and far reaching is the outcome of the issues with which you have to deal. 'Momentous' is not too strong a word to apply to the situation even at this which may be but the initial stage.

"It is fortunate, I think, for Canada that you should have had your difficulties with the advisers of the Mikado. The people of Canada have not been unmindful that you were their representative and each delay and obstacle which you encountered has only served to stiffen their backs. You will come back, I am sure, realizing that Japan is a power greater than the people of this continent have ever dreamed and that as Canadians in dealing with the Orient, if true to our country, we will realize there is no strategy too subtle or diplomacy too fine for us to be prepared to meet. You have guarded your secret well, and to no word of your reported utterances have I heard exception taken. A dispatch to the effect that the American Embassy was not altogether satisfied in that you preferred to act independently of its co-operation and assistance, have served to evoke from our press an appreciation of the care and wisdom with which you have conducted your negotiations.

"When interviewed by the press it seems to me that you could not do better than tell the people of British Columbia that on a great question of this kind there can be no diversity of interest as between any one part of the Dominion and the whole, and that their problem is Canada's problem and that in all your negotiations you have been mindful of this.

"In case you should think of calling at Government House or be invited to do so on landing at Victoria, I would suggest that in view of the somewhat compromising position in which the

[1] *Lemieux Papers,* report to Cabinet, 12 January, 1908, p. 9.

G

Lieutenant Governor has been placed in the disclosures which came out during my last inquiry it would on the whole be expedient for you to avoid meeting him if you are able to do so. Any conference with him would probably be misunderstood or misinterpreted by the Opposition press."[1]

Here is not the voice of science explaining to suspicious and resentful Orientals the great truths of political economy which cast out fear and hatred. Instead, we have an example of expediency based on the proposition that the average current prejudices on the subject of race are the only foundation of policy and the right policy.

Almost at once, Mackenzie King took over the role of negotiator-in-chief for the Canadian Government. To make a system of excluding Asians from Canada effective, the Canadians and Americans, obviously, would have to work together, and in order to achieve the necessary harmony, Laurier sent Mackenzie King, late in January, 1908, to speak directly with President T. Roosevelt and Secretary of State Root, on the subject.

Canadian relations with the United States were not good at this time. The memory of the Alaskan boundary dispute and Roosevelt's high-handed pressure on that occasion still rankled. Partly due to indifference and partly to the absence of machinery for direct negotiation between Ottawa and Washington, the efforts of Roosevelt and Root to restore good feeling and, if possible, to exclude what they conceived to be European influences from Canadian-American relations, met with small success. The arrival of Mackenzie King in Washington delighted Roosevelt. In the company of Lord Bryce, the British Ambassador, Mackenzie King was soon in close conference with the President and Secretary of State. Roosevelt quickly converted a Canadian desire to co-operate against Japanese immigration into "a happy omen of the future". Roosevelt described to "dear Sir Wilfrid" his "particular pleasure" in meeting Mr. King and "at the steps that have been taken to bring our several peoples into a closer and more friendly connection".[2]

After thus demonstrating his amiability to the President of

[1] *Lemieux Papers*, King to Lemieux, 30 December, 1907.
[2] Described in J. M. Callaghan, *American Foreign Policy in Canadian Relations* (New York, 1937), Chapter XX.

the United States, Mackenzie King was shortly off to London. In March, he visited Whitehall with the object of effecting an arrangement with the Government of India for preventing the emigration of Indians to Canada. In this instance the negotiation involved some delicate points unknown to the negotiators in Tokio. Canadians and Indians were alike subjects of the British Crown. If the British Empire meant anything besides big ships, big guns and monarchical ceremonial it surely meant equality of all His Majesty's subjects in the market. Equality of opportunity in the market was the earliest, the most abiding and the most fundamental of all the principles of the liberalism for which Locke contended, Bentham wrote and James Mill tortured his children. As a result of the impact of the free market the ancient civilization of India had been undermined and its crafts destroyed. A consistent application of liberal principles would seem to require that the possessions of His Majesty would be free to all His Majesty's subjects on terms of equality under the law to the end that, if the old had been destroyed, at least something new might be built. So the Indians thought. The principle *Civis Romanus Sum* had enabled inhabitants of Asia Minor to live in the province of Britain if they so desired. But the proud claim to be a British subject did not, it was to be discovered, involve the right of a Punjabi or a Bengali to cut down trees in British Columbia or dig for diamonds on the Rand. Liberalism in politics was not, it seemed, consistent with liberalism in economics, and so one of the pillars of the Empire built by exponents of the free market received another shaking.

Mackenzie King met Lord Elgin* at the Colonial Office, Sir Edward Grey* at the Foreign Office and Mr. John Morley* at the India Office. After they had agreed upon a clever device for keeping Indians out of Canada, while saving the face of the India Office, in the same way that the Japanese Government had been allowed to save its face, Mr. Morley said:[1]

"I do not mind mentioning to you confidentially, though I would not like this said outside, the situation is none too good in India to-day. There is a great deal of unrest; there is consequently a

[1] *Lemieux Papers*, "Memorandum Accompanying Report of W. L. Mackenzie King, C.M.G.... On his Mission to England to Confer with the British Authorities on the Subject of Immigration to Canada from the Orient, and Immigration from India in Particular," 2 May, 1908, p 13.

great political situation at stake in the enactment of any legislation [regarding the prohibition of emigration] in India."

Mr. Mackenzie King replied that he

"thought Sir Wilfrid Laurier fully recognised this; that the extent
to which a great political situation would be affected by legislation
in India was also a consideration, in a remoter way, to be kept in
mind in regard to any legislation which Canada might be obliged
to enact. It was for this reason amongst others, that Sir Wilfrid
Laurier was anxious if possible to avoid the necessity of legislation
and to meet the difficulty by some other means. Both Mr. Morley
and Lord Elgin expressed words of strong approval of this
attitude."

Mackenzie King commenced the negotiation by denying
that he had anything to suggest to the British Government and
the India Office; that he wished to inform the British Government about the situation in Canada. The Canadians feared the
Japanese, he said, but they pitied the Indians who came to
Canada. Once again he called science into the service of political
argument. India was hot; Canada was cold. Therefore, Indians
were unsuitable immigrants in Canada. Lord Elgin ventured
the observation that India also possessed cold and moun-
tainous regions, but Mackenzie King countered by remarking
that the Indians who came to Canada came not from these
happy climes. Where he thought the Sikhs in British Columbia
came from he never revealed. In order to paint an adequate
picture of the horrors of life in Canada, Mackenzie King stated
that "their foreign customs and manners had subjected them to
ridicule, and where they had come in numbers many of them
had been unable to secure employment". Finally to clinch his
argument Mackenzie King dragged in the threat of Socialism.
"I also ventured the opinion", he reported to the Prime
Minister,

"which I said was distinctly personal and might not be concurred
in by others, that it was a better thing for the province of British
Columbia that it should develop slowly, under conditions which
permitted the mass of the white population becoming holders of
small properties, rather than that, with the aid of Asiatic labour,
a more rapid progress should be made by a few enterprises such as
mining and railroading, with the result that individuals connected with these corporations might become wealthy, and the
mass of men remain wage earners with no stake in the community;

that as a matter of fact British Columbia was the only province in which Socialism had made any headway, and that one of the main reasons Socialism made such headway was because people did not hold property, and this in part was explained by immigration from the Orient. ... Mr. Morley said that such an inference might be fairly drawn."[1]

Mr. Morley wanted Mr. Mackenzie King to make some suggestions, and Mr. Mackenzie King wanted Mr. Morley to do something. Finally Mr. Mackenzie King put it to Mr. Morley that the people of India needed protection from the evil shipping companies who dispatched people for a profit to a land of cold, misery and tragedy. To this suggestion Mr. Morley assented. "That is quite right," he said, "she must protect herself." Mr. Mackenzie King told him about the way in which the traffic in Japanese was regulated. "Well," said Mr. Morley, "let me see how it would apply to my Indians."[2]

Mr. Morley was prepared to control contract labour more strictly. Then he felt a twinge of liberalism.

"But the men who have come in have not come in under contract. I can see where it is desirable to prevent contract labour in certain instances, but to endeavour to restrict men from selling their farms and going where they please is an interference with individual liberty, and prohibition of this kind would be obnoxious."[3]

Mr. Mackenzie King helped Mr. Morley over this difficulty by asking his co-operation in enforcing a Canadian regulation that an immigrant must travel by a direct route on a single ticket from the place of his origin to a Canadian port. In as much as no steamship company ran directly from Indian ports to Vancouver, Indians were barred. Mr. Morley promised to help.

As a result an informal agreement was arrived at by which the Indian Government undertook to publish "the conditions imposed by Canada widely in India".[4] In 1909, Mackenzie King stopped off in India on his way to a meeting of the International Opium Commission in Shanghai. His object was to discuss the matter of Indian immigration further and to tighten up, perhaps, the system of exclusion. In Calcutta he saw the

[1] *Lemieux Papers*, "Memorandum," etc., as above, p. 6.
[2] *Lemieux Papers*, "Memorandum," etc., p. 9.
[3] *Lemieux Papers*, "Memorandum," etc., p. 12.
[4] O. D. Skelton, *Life and Letters of Sir Wilfrid Laurier* (Toronto, 1921), Vol. II, p. 353. Lord Minto to Sir Wilfrid Laurier, 1 March, 1909.

Viceroy, Lord Minto, and "two members of the Viceroy's Council, and the heads of several Departments, and other gentlemen whom it was thought advisable . . . (to) see". He found that

> "the Indian Government ha[d] only the highest opinion to express of the conciliatory attitude adopted by Canada, which ha[d] been of a nature to save embarrassment such as had been experienced as a consequence of the action of other self-governing colonies, in particular South Africa . . . and also Australia."[1]

Canada had not been "brought into the discussion at all" which accompanied the outcry against anti-Indian measures. In the circumstances Mackenzie King advised the Cabinet in Ottawa to let sleeping dogs lie. An attempt to formalize the system of exclusion would only start them barking at Canada.

Mackenzie King also asked "a direct question" about the "deportation of destitute Indians" from Canada. The Anglo-Indian officials did not mind the Canadian Government deporting people for the crime of destitution (a very likely possibility in view of the legislation in British Columbia limiting their opportunities of employment), but they were worried by the thought of mass deportation which would excite popular indignation in India. "A clear statement to the effect that destitution and suffering is the sole cause for the step would be received without causing a stir," Mackenzie King reported to Laurier, "but the authorities are of the opinion that it would be advisable in such a case to avoid the appearance of anything like wholesale deportation as tending to raise a doubt as to the object with which it was made." The Viceroy's Government "approved" of the deportation of Indians from Canada to British Honduras. On the Mosquito Coast, it was believed, the destitute would find their salvation.

Mackenzie King's visit to India convinced him that the Indians were "entirely unsuited to the Dominion" and that, "it is in every way desirable that Canada should be kept for the white races and India for the black, as Nature appears to have decreed." Steamships were overcoming the decrees of nature, and Mackenzie King inquired about what the Indian Government was doing to stop shipping companies from selling passages from India to Canada.

[1] *Laurier Papers*, King to Laurier, 31 January, 1909.

"Mr. Harvey, of the Viceroy's Council, assure[d him] that the companies concerned have been given to understand that any further action of this kind will be strongly disapproved of by the Government, and he believe[d] that this of itself [would] prove an effective deterrent against a repetition of such practices."[1]

Mackenzie King studied the political situation during his journeys in India. "As to the unrest in India," he wrote to Laurier, "from what I have learned in conversation from those in authority, as well as from impressions I gathered by careful observation, I should say that the extent and amount of unrest appears much exaggerated." But he was not unduly bemused by the comfort officials had to offer. He thought the problems of government in India were much like the problems of governing Canada in the days before responsible government. The only difference was that Indian problems were a thousand times more complex and difficult than those in Canada. With the penetrating eye of a man trained by Ashley and Cunningham he went beyond politics. "Nothing should give us greater concern," he told Laurier,

"than the introduction of western methods of production by this country as well as by China and Japan. Already there are a few factories scattered about India, but for the most part industry is carried on entirely in the home and by hand. This was the position of England a century ago. What is to become of England and the rest of us when the same development takes place in the Orient seems to me a problem of a like, if not greater magnitude than that arising out of the possible migration of the Oriental peoples to our shores."

The Chinese Government was the last to experience the refinements of a negotiation with Mackenzie King. This was in the spring of 1908. His Chinese opposite number at the Tsungli Yamen was a Yale man, Liang Tun-Yen, and, as Mackenzie King explained, he was Harvard.[2] If Yale cannot talk to Harvard then, of course, human intercourse is well nigh impossible. The Harvard man produced the Law of Competing Standards and asked the Yale man what he had to say about this latest discovery of western economic science. The Yale man asked,

"if there was this difference in the standard of living between the peoples of the two countries (Canada and China) would not the

---

[1] *Laurier Papers*, King to Laurier, 31 January, 1909.
[2] *Laurier Papers*, King to Laurier, 22 March, 1909.

best way to remove the difference be to allow the Chinese to enter without restriction and permit free movement everywhere. Wages and prices were rising in China and labour by emigrating could gradually bring about one level in all countries."[1]

The Yale man had obviously read Adam Smith. The Harvard man, who had improved upon the classical economists, "replied that this might be quite true, and it illustrated the difficulty which the Canadian people foresaw." Chinese standards might go up, but Canadian standards would go down. The Yale man was prepared to limit contract labour because coolies were shamefully exploited, but "free labour should, on the other hand, . . . be at liberty to emigrate as it pleased." The Harvard man was then obliged to tell the Yale man that Canada would keep the Chinese out in any case, and could not Canada and China agree to keep their labourers at home. With a naïve logic the Yale man "remarked that as Canadian labour would not desire to come to China, such an agreement was very one sided and not truly reciprocal".

Intercourse between Harvard and Yale was obviously breaking down. Liang Tun-Yen became a simple, patriotic Chinese. He spoke feelingly on the attitude of foreigners toward China. The nations had come hammering upon her door; told her that she must mix with other people; must share their trade and enlightenment, and were now seeking to exclude her peoples from their shores. China did not want the foreigners; she would rather be left alone. He recognized, however, "that intercourse with other nations was necessary, and that there were advantages to be gained by the admission of men from other countries."

The Yale man had become a Chinese, but Mackenzie King was still playing the Harvard gambit.

"I replied that Chinese of the classes foreign nations were asking China to admit, were not excluded by them, restriction had to do with labourers only; and was because of the difference in standard and numbers. . . . Greeks and Italians and the like were being excluded for much the same reason as Chinese labourers. . . ."[2]

Finally Liang Tun-Yen capitulated to Mackenzie King's

[1] *Laurier Papers*, Memorandum of an Interview with the Acting President of the Waiwupu (Chinese Foreign Office), 9 March, 1909.

[2] *Laurier Papers*, Memorandum of Interview with Acting President of the Waiwupu, 17 March, 1909.

arguments. "He was prepared to admit there was a difference in standards which . . . should receive consideration." Harvard had won 1-0. A draft agreement was prepared. Mackenzie King sailed for home with an understanding that something concrete might be agreed to once the Chinese Consul General had been able to discuss the matter in Ottawa.

During June, 1910, Mackenzie King, holidaying in Berlin, Ontario, sat in the sun drawing a uniform system of exclusion which would keep out Indians, Japanese and Chinese by a single, simple device of passport control.[1] The agreement with China, which could have fitted into this system, was never concluded. The Imperial Chinese Government collapsed, and the Chinese embarked upon the business of reorganizing society without reference to the Law of Competing Standards.

Mackenzie King accepted the policy of limiting the labour market through racial discrimination, more whole-heartedly than any of the other and more wholesome policies of Canadian labour which he might have supported.

By the time Mackenzie King had completed his essay in manipulating the Mandarins, he was already a Parliamentary politician in his own right. Having successfully completed his mission, he was made a Minister of the Crown. In September, 1908, he had resigned his office of Deputy Minister of Labour and stood as the Liberal candidate in his native constituency of North Waterloo. He had been returned to Parliament, and was recommended by Sir Wilfrid Laurier for appointment[2] as Minister of Labour following the passage through Parliament, in May 1909, of legislation creating a separate Department of Labour under the charge of a single Minister. In the Commons there was considerable hostile criticism by the Opposition, who asserted that the Minister's salary was too big for so soft a job, but on June 1st, 1909, Mackenzie King took the Privy Councillor's oath.

Mackenzie King had always cherished political ambitions. In his university days those who listened to him lecturing to newsboys, reading to sick children and orating to students had the impression that he was practising, "always practising". When

---

[1] *Laurier Papers*, King to Laurier, 6 June, 1910.
[2] He was formally appointed Minister of Labour on 22 June, 1909.

exactly Mackenzie King decided to make the transition from the bureaucracy to Parliament we cannot say. All we can do, on the basis of the evidence at present available, is to indicate several of the convolutions in the transformation of the civil servant into the Parliamentary politician.

The first overt sign of ambition for a public career exhibited itself in January, 1906, when he published *The Secret of Heroism*. *The Secret of Heroism* is ostensibly a memoir of his friend and colleague, Henry Albert Harper. Harper was drowned in the Ottawa River in December, 1901, while endeavouring to save the life of Miss Bessie Blair, "a girl of rare and beautiful character," who in the company of a gentleman skated into an open patch of water and drowned. By the time *The Secret of Heroism* went to press, five years after the event, Harper had already been commemorated in bronze in the form of a statue of Sir Galahad which still stands on Wellington Street, in Ottawa, with its back to the Parliament of Canada and its eye on the Rideau Club. Both Sir Wilfrid Laurier and the Governor-General, Earl Grey,* spoke at the unveiling ceremony. It remained for Mackenzie King to do a final honour to his friend by publishing a memoir.

But there are two characters in *The Secret of Heroism*, the subject of the memoir and the author. Harper is exhibited as an idealist, a patriot, a man bearing the burden of the world's bewilderment, a nature lover, a student, an ardent friend of the working classes and no enemy of the wealthy except those capitalists who are mean and wastefully opulent. As depicted by Mackenzie King, Harper appears as a painful prig who suffered from a mild form of hysteria. But he frequently gave expression to notions widely held by the English-speaking Canadian middle-class. For example, he loved his parents, a fairly safe and common sentiment, but he loved them more ardently and in a better prose style than the average Canadian burgher is capable of doing. He worked hard. When he was down on his luck he had faith in the future. He was suspicious of too much amusement. He believed in progress. He thought of the other fellow. He liked Keats but was just a bit doubtful about Shelley. He was above all a Tennyson man. And he disliked New York.

A fair proportion of *The Secret of Heroism* was devoted to

Harper, but none of it to the exclusion of Mackenzie King. Mackenzie King is identified with all that Harper said, thought and did; but always Mackenzie King is the leader of the two. Mackenzie King brought Harper to Ottawa. Harper tells all to Mackenzie King. Harper holds the fort in Ottawa while Mackenzie King goes out to tame the raging passions of the wild British Columbians. In the final chapter the spotlight is shifted completely away from Harper and plays directly upon Mackenzie King. Two of Harper's letters are used to focus the whole light on the author of the memoir, not its subject. The second letter concludes:

> "The Canadian Manufacturers' Association to the contrary not-withstanding, your work is neither superficial nor ephemeral. It is of the very essence of a force which is calculated to prove a strong lever in regulating the labour movement, and indeed other movements as well, in Canada. It is my happiness to be associated with you in that work. I think I comprehend its nature and its importance, immediate and even prospective, and I trust I may prove true to its demands and purpose."[1]

It is not surprising that Mackenzie King later took to spiritualism, for he chose as his first election agent a man beyond the grave. When Marjory MacMurchy (later Lady Willison) reviewed *The Secret of Heroism* for the Toronto *Globe* she referred to it throughout her article as *The Secret of Success*. Readers thought she was being maliciously candid about Mackenzie King's first book, but she always asserted that she did not intend the mistake. She claimed that she was under the honest impression after reading the book that it was meant to further the author's career, and that she gave it a mistaken title quite unintentionally, in response to her unconscious.

The Secret of Heroism appeared in January, 1906. In August, 1906, the Executive Committee of the Trades and Labour Congress requested the Minister of Labour to send Mackenzie King to England to discuss the emigration through fraudulent representations of men destined for strike-breaking work. Thus, a civil servant was being openly preferred to his political superior for the conduct of certain business. Thus was an indentification of a civil servant with a policy being established.

Simultaneously another kind of honour came his way in the

---

[1] King, *The Secret*, etc., pp. 159–160.

form of an appointment as a Companion of the Order of St. Michael and St. George. At this time Canadians were still appointed to the British orders of chivalry. Sir Wilfrid Laurier had not yet committed the Liberal Party to opposition to titles, and his offer to make a bonfire of ribbons and orders was still twelve years in the future. In 1906, a C.M.G. was an honour which a Canadian civil servant valued highly. The appointment of Mackenzie King to the Order, in 1906, before his thirty-second birthday, precipitated a fight among the other deputy ministers who owed their appointments to the Liberal Party. The spirit of jealousy was aroused, but so also was that of inquiry. The voice of envy suggested that Mackenzie King had got the appointment directly upon the recommendation of the Governor-General, Earl Grey, without ministerial recommendation and that Mackenzie King had rendered no public service worthy of a C.M.G.

The voice of envy may not have been so very far from the truth. In the Willison Papers there are several letters from John King to the proprietor of the strongly imperialist Toronto *News* enclosing speeches of Earl Grey heavily loaded with Grey's famous lucubrations on imperialism. "The boy" had asked his father to pass these along for publication. In *The Secret of Heroism*, too, Grey's imperialist sentiments were prominently displayed. Grey did not know Harper, but he thought he must be like "another young civil servant of the Crown" who, before he was carried to his grave "in the Matoppos of Rhodesia", said, " 'Well, it is a grand thing to die for the expansion of the Empire'—that Empire which, in his mind, as in that of Harper, was synonymous with the cause of righteousness."[1] And so, perhaps, Mackenzie King *was* decorated for a service. Henceforth the letters C.M.G. appeared after his name on the reports he wrote.[2]

A Governor-General cannot make a minister, however. The creation of this animal requires other magic, which Mackenzie King revealed he possessed. The problem was to interest Laurier. Identifying himself with a policy was a help to this end, but more was required, i.e., for practical politicians to prove to Laurier that Mackenzie King could be elected as a Liberal. To

---

[1] King, *The Secret*, etc., p. 17.
[2] e.g. *Report of the Royal Commission on the Dispute between the Bell Telephone Company of Canada Ltd. and Operators*, (Ottawa, 1907)

effect this manoeuvre Mackenzie King worked through the Toronto *Globe* staff. His first step was to offer F. A. Acland,* the news editor of *The Globe*, a job in the Department of Labour on the understanding that Acland would get the Deputy Minister-ship, if Mackenzie King got something better. Thus, Acland's and Mackenzie King's interests were rendered parallel, and, indeed, identical. What Acland was able to do which started *The Globe* working for Mackenzie King we do not know, but we have the testimony of the business manager and treasurer of *The Globe*, J. F. Mackay, that he "took some small part at the time of his (Mackenzie King's) entrance into public life" and that "he had as high hopes as to his future as anyone".[1]

Another former employee of *The Globe* who participated in the Mackenzie King campaign was named Hamilton. Just at the moment when the political butterfly was about to burst from its bureaucratic chrysalis Hamilton, with Acland, prepared an article, under Mackenzie King's direction, extolling Mac-kenzie King's merits and his exploits. But the lard was unfor-tunately spread too thick, and a case of political indigestion followed. In his enthusiasm Hamilton and his ghostly prompter lamented the inferior quality of the Ministers from Ontario in Laurier's Cabinet—which weakness, it was inferred, would be corrected by Mackenzie King's elevation. A great eructation followed the appearance of the article. Laurier was obliged to inquire. Mackenzie King denied that he had taken any part in suggesting the article and asserted that it was a product of the mistaken enthusiasm of his friends. Laurier accepted Mackenzie King's disclaimers, but dryly remarked that Mackenzie King should pray to be delivered from his friends.

Mackenzie King's friends on *The Globe* organized for him a publicity campaign during the election of 1908 such as no new-comer to politics had ever known before. Between September 5th, 1908, when Sir Wilfrid Laurier opened the electoral cam-paign at Sorel, Quebec, until October 26th, when the election was held, Mackenzie King's name was never absent from the pages of the principal English-language Liberal newspaper. For days before the young civil servant accepted the party nomina-tion in North Waterloo, *The Globe* created an atmosphere of anticipation about the advent of the "brilliant young adminis-

[1] *Laurier Papers*, J. F. Mackay to Laurier, 6 March, 1911.

trator" with "the splendid and uniformly successful record in Ottawa". When finally, on September 21st, Mackenzie King accepted the invitation to contest his native constituency in the Liberal interest, as much of the front page (and more of the whole newspaper) was given over to recounting his policies, his exploits, his sacrifice, his moral courage and his mental powers, as was devoted to Sir Wilfrid Laurier's great meeting in the neighbouring county. A two-column box was put under Mackenzie King's picture on the front page of the edition of September 22nd bearing the legend: "No Moral Decay Here." Beneath the legend was set forth Mackenzie King's message of acceptance. When Sir Wilfrid visited North Waterloo on September 24th a front page headline and story was devoted to the news that "Labour is to Have Separate Portfolio". Sir Wilfrid was reported to have described his new disciple as "a man of the future". No single politician of either party, including Sir Wilfrid Laurier himself, was the subject of so many leading articles in *The Globe* as "this versatile young man of affairs".

As the election campaign drew to a close the editors of *The Globe* discovered the high point in the struggle to consist in "the clean, manly fight" before an audience of 6000 people in Berlin, Ontario, between Mackenzie King and Alexander Wright. The unfortunate Mr. Wright was put up by the Tories to demonstrate that the Conservative Party had sponsored the legislation which made trade unions legal in Canada, that Conservatives, too, had investigated the sweating system, and that they had also established a "Labor Bureau" in Ottawa, and that in doing these things they had anticipated Mackenzie King by some years. The ex-civil servant brushed Mr. Wright's history aside with nimble ease. He depicted the horrors of the sweating system and he told of seeing garments intended as uniforms for government employees scattered about on the beds of sick children in the homes of harshly sweated mothers. "Mr. King then gave a jocular demonstration of what had been done in the Labor Department by setting up volume by volume eight annual volumes of *The Labor Gazette*, each fatter than the last . . . and he made a big hit when he pointed out that each copy of *The Labor Gazette* bore the union label. . . ."[1]

When the election was over *The Globe* burst into song on

[1] *The Globe*, Toronto, 22 October, 1908.

Mackenzie King's behalf. On October 28th the work of an anonymous poet, "X.Y.Z." made its appearance in the columns of *The Globe* under the title "To William Lyon Mackenzie King C.M.G., Minister of Labor". Like other poets "X.Y.Z." had the faculty of pre-vision, for Mackenzie King's appointment as Minister of Labour was still eight months in the future, and Parliament had not yet created the office as a separate entity. "Hail to thee, Labor's first Minister!" cried the poet: "In love we twine thee a wreath of bay."

And he concluded:

> "Thrice welcome, then, O wise, beloved Son!
>   May voice of conscience make thy pathway clear;
>   May fuller deeds of greatness, year by year,
>   Speak to the world of duty nobly done!
>   The cause, to which thy cause is linked anew,
>   Has given thee thy proudest WATERLOO!"

But this proudest Waterloo was not only a tribute to the publicity of *The Globe*. Mackenzie King himself demonstrated agility as a politician. He stated that his love of the Liberal cause was the powerful motive which caused him to sacrifice "a $5,000 appointment at Ottawa"; but before his nomination it was reported that "Mr. King has already been promised the support of a number of influential Conservatives in the riding if he will consent to run".[1]

In dealing with the Conservative candidate Mr. Reid, a former teacher of his, Mackenzie King was careful to appear his friend. Mr. Wright supported Mr. Reid with two arguments: that the Conservative tariff policy had made jobs for industrial workers, and Conservative legislation had enabled workers to organize legally and bargain. Mackenzie King agreed with Mr. Wright. He claimed that he supported even more whole-heartedly than Mr. Wright the right to organize, and he also believed that "the National Policy (of high tariffs) had built up Canadian industries".[2]

Indeed on serious points of policy he never challenged the Conservatives. His attack was limited to trading arguments about which party was the least corrupt or which had increased most the national debt. He appealed to his followers "to make

---

[1] *The Globe*, Toronto, 21 September, 1908.
[2] *The Globe*, Toronto, 22 October, 1908.

this contest clean from the beginning to the close of the poll'',
but this did not prevent him from declaring that the sitting
Conservative Member for North Waterloo, Col. Joseph Sea-
gram, employed yellow labour in his racing stables and that he
ought to fire his Chinese stable hands and give the jobs to white
men.[1]

The essence of his appeal was to Labour because, he said, he
was working on labour's behalf. But he appealed to the employers by saying he wished to create industrial peace and bring
prosperity. In fact, as it had been observed during his first
years in Ottawa, "King had something for everybody."

How much more went into the translation of Mackenzie
King we cannot say. Acland got his Deputy Ministership
shortly after Mackenzie King became Minister of Labour.
When Mackenzie King resigned from the Civil Service, Acland
prepared an elaborate address from the officials of the Department of Labour in which they could not

> "but feel that the qualities which have enabled you already to
> achieve so much for the advantage of Canada and the spirit that
> prompts you now at no slight personal sacrifice to make deliberate
> choice of the hazards of public life, will permit you to render yet
> more distinguished services for our country. . . ."[2]

Some element of doubt, however, appears to have been at
work either in Acland's mind or else in the staff, for the address
concluded with the hope that the idealism of Henry Albert
Harper would, "through life, temper your aims and ambitions
with the principles of the soundest patriotism and religion."

And so Mackenzie King departed from his desk in Ottawa.
Thus far, ideas had not embarrassed nor ideals obstructed the
even flow of his career. A party of his colleagues accompanied
him to the station to see him off to the political wars. In the
party was the poet Wilfred Campbell. After the train had
pulled out of the station the party fell to discussing Mackenzie
King. The poet was one of his admirers. "Gentlemen," he said,
"we have seen history made to-night."

---

[1] *The Globe*, Toronto, 21 October, 1908.
[2] Quoted in Rogers, *Mackenzie King*, pp. 37–38.

CHAPTER V

Working on the Railroad Workers

Mackenzie King was Minister of Labour from June, 1909, until the resignation of the Laurier Administration, following its defeat at the polls in September, 1911. During the interval between his election to the House of Commons in October 1908 and his appointment as a Minister, he was employed by the Government, at the suggestion of the Governor-General, as a special representative to do business with and on behalf of the British Government. He visited India and surveyed the system for preventing the immigration of Indians to Canada. He conducted a negotiation with the Chinese, and also acted as a British representative on an International Commission set up to regulate the opium traffic.[1] As a Minister responsible for an aspect of the Government's policy, he had a modest record: one of which he had nothing to be ashamed, save his handling of the strikes of workers in British Columbia, Alberta, and Nova Scotia, but more particularly on the Grand Trunk Railway System in 1910, and nothing to warrant his selection as Leader of the Liberal Party. The most important piece of legislation which he fathered was the Combines Investigation Act of 1910, and the most dramatic and, in some

[1] The genesis of Mackenzie King's concern with the opium traffic (an interest which could safely be opposed) is worth relating. Following his investigations of the anti-Asiatic disturbances of 1907, it was decided that the Government should pay compensation for property damaged during the riots. One of the claimants for compensation was the owner of a large opium factory. It was then discovered that Canada possessed the largest opium boiling plant in the British Empire, and that British Columbia was in a fair way to becoming the opium metropolis of the world. The objects of the Opium War were then reversed, and war on the opium trade declared.

respects, consequential act of his term of office was his intervention in the Grand Trunk strike. He played a prominent part in several politically advantageous but minor matters such as the Committee on the Eight-Hour Day and the legislation to prevent phosphorus necrosis.

His manner as a Minister gave the impression of business-like competence in the presentation of any case he had to make. In spite of his long practice, he never became an accomplished orator or even a moderately interesting speaker (as late as 1919 Laurier spoke of him as "improving"),[1] but he seldom failed to have a careful mastery of any brief he was required to present, and he obviously possessed an unusual gift for sensing the nuances of meaning in any discussion carried on by a committee, by the House of Commons, or in a political meeting. His demeanour was distinguished by a formal courtesy and a gentlemanly bearing. His physical appearance evoked simple, descriptive adjectives, like plump or short or youngish, but the total appearance of the man left no distinctive impression upon his contemporaries. He could be written up, but he could not be described or caricatured or photographed with success. The innocent moon face of his youth had gone. The white piping on the waistcoat, affected by men of ministerial rank in Canada, appeared more often, and when he campaigned he sometimes wore the knee-length jackets which Sir Wilfrid Laurier had preserved from the 1870's.

The Combines Investigation Act of 1910 may be regarded as a major piece of legislation, not on account of what it accomplished, but because it represented an attempt to deal with a difficulty which had long excited tension in North America, i.e., the transfer of wealth among group interests by devices such as trade agreements, contracts for price maintenance, monopolies, mergers and all those schemes which are considered "restraints of trade". Belief in the efficiency and justice of free competition was an essential part of the folk-lore of America. It was not, perhaps, as fundamental a belief among Canadians as it was among the citizens of the United States, but it was a dogma which was received with extensive credulity. Unfortunately this dogma was contradicted by both the character of the economy

---

[1] *Laurier Papers*, Laurier to Domville, 14 January, 1919.

and the content of legislation. The terrain of Canada, the nature of its resources and the difficulties of moving across its vast expanses, required the development of enterprises on an enormous scale, frequently at a cost so great that only the State or the very wealthiest private citizens in combination with each other and fortified by foreign investment could undertake them. Technology, too, dictated the scale of Canadian enterprises, and that scale was more often large than small. Competition, free enterprise, small units of production and the higgling of the market are alien to Canadian history and the Canadian environment.

Not only were circumstances favourable to gigantic units of production but, in the sphere which technology and the character of the market reserved for small units of enterprise, they lent their assistance to conspiracies in restraint of trade. The isolation of Canadian centres of population, the high cost of transport, enforced by distance and sometimes by the acts of the transport interests, tended to create in Canada a number of small markets for certain commodities, rather than one large fluid market. Either that, or there was one large market for a very few producers. As a result, coal dealers, undertakers, egg dealers, watch-case manufacturers, binder-twine makers, oatmeal millers, stove producers, barbed-wire manufacturers and insurance underwriters early discovered that it was relatively simple to rig the market in their favour. The complaints occasioned by alleged high prices led to an investigation of these practices by the Canadian Parliament as early as 1888. In 1889, Parliament legislated, but in such a way that persons engaged in restraint of trade had first to be found guilty of an offence against the common law and the criminal code. In spite of this difficulty, the Canadian courts tended to interpret the common law doctrines and the criminal code with respect to restraint of trade in a manner favourable to the maintenance of competitive conditions, in so far as the devices of law could undo the facts of environment and business organization.

The legislation of 1889 was directed to the solution of a fairly small and simple problem. The economic progress of Canada during the period of the Laurier administration had changed the situation so that, by the time Mackenzie King came to deal with it, the problem was of a new magnitude. The situation was briefly this. Laurier had come to power in 1896, advocating traditional Liberal panaceas: separation of Church and State, freedom of thought, and freedom of trade. In his handling of the Manitoba School question and the institution of a unilateral system of Imperial Preference which did not interfere with Great Britain's system of free trade, he exhibited a mild inclination to translate his principles into practice. But the golden age of the Canadian manufacturers was too much for him. When Harper was wrestling with Mackenzie King for his soul, Sir Wilfrid Laurier in a higher sphere was surrendering first to one interest group and then another: the Roman Catholic Church, the Canadian Manufacturers' Association, the railway promoters and the architects of imperialism in London. As the western Liberal editor, John W. Dafoe,* put it, Laurier hung on to office "by placating various powerful interests at the expense of the general public".[1]

Laurier's capitulation to business provided the opportunity for the would-be tycoons. Simultaneously with the boom there developed the "merger movement". As a means of ensuring technological adaptation and progress and the economies of large-scale production and management, this movement had much to be said for it. Not unexpectedly, it was taken over by financial racketeers whose "motive lay in the possibility of selling the bonds and stocks of the greatly over-capitalized new companies formed".[2] The consumers, the investors, the small business man and the wage-earners had ample reason to complain; for it was only out of their pockets, their muscles and their brains that there could be found the means to provide the financial racketeers with the profits and the power which their manipulations had won for them.

On the whole the Canadian courts were sympathetic to suitors who sought to upset arrangements which had the effect of raising prices. In 1905 the United Shoe Machinery Company, which leased but did not sell its products to shoe manufacturers, sought an injunction in the Superior Court of Quebec to prevent a lessee of its shoe machinery from using machines other than those leased from them in accordance with the terms of the leases. The case dragged through the Canadian Courts,

---

[1] Quoted in W. L. Morton, *The Progressive Party in Canada* (Toronto, 1950), p. 26.
[2] O. D Skelton, *General Economic History of Canada* (Toronto, 1913), p. 260.

where a decision was rendered in each instance for the defendants on the grounds that the leases, which the United Shoe Machinery Company were endeavouring to maintain in all their particulars, were instruments for the restraint of trade and the prevention of free competition. Finally, in 1909, the case reached the Judicial Committee of the Privy Council in London. The courts of Great Britain were at this time extremely tender towards restrictive agreements. Lord Atkinson, on behalf of the Judicial Committee, ruled that,

> "if the monopoly established by the appellants and their mode of carrying on their business be as oppressive as is alleged (upon which their Lordships express no opinion), then the evil, if it exists, may be capable of cure by legislation or competition, but in their view not by litigation. It is not for them to suggest what form the legislation should take, nor by what means the necessary competition should be established. These matters may, they think, be safely left to the ingenuity and enterprise of the Canadian people."[1]

The Combines Investigation Act represents the ingenuity and enterprise of Mackenzie King and Parliament in dealing with the situation created by Laurier's long retreat and by the steady and rapid rise in prices during the years 1897–1911. Like the Sherman Anti-Trust legislation in the United States, it was constructed out of the folk-dreams of the farmers and small business men who are politically as important in Canada as they are in the American Union. It was based on the supposition that there is such a thing as a normal, free, competitive market, and that such a market can be maintained by investigating the practices of large-scale business enterprises. Mackenzie King did not, however, go so far as the American legislators in leading an assault on bigness as such. He acknowledged, realistically, that big undertakings might be beneficial, and he argued that "this measure seeks to afford the means of conserving to the public some of the benefits which arise from large organizations of capital for the purpose of business and commerce". Lest the proposed Bill seem to interfere with the current trends in business organization, Mackenzie King assured the House and the men listening in Montreal and Toronto that "this legislation is in no way aimed against trusts, combines and mergers as such, but rather only at the possible

[1] Quoted in J. A. Ball, *Canadian Anti-Trust Legislation* (Baltimore, 1934), p. 32.

wrongful use or abuse of their power, of which certain of their combinations may be guilty".[1]

In the debates Mackenzie King sharply condemned the difficulty of undertaking prosecutions under the laws as they existed. His plan was to permit anyone who felt aggrieved on account of the business practices of an alleged combine or monopoly to apply to the courts for the establishment of a board of investigation. If the applicant could make out a *prima facie* case the court would order the establishment of a board according to the formula established for the formation of Boards of Conciliation under the Industrial Disputes Investigation Act. Mackenzie King attached enormous importance to the publicity which such Boards could give to business practices either to ensure condemnation or approval. The Act, in fact, did not provide for any penalties except in cases where those involved refused to give evidence, or otherwise obstructed the operation of the Act. Mackenzie King expected, however, that prosecutions would be undertaken for breaches of the Criminal Code depending upon the facts disclosed by investigation by Boards.

Abstract justice, and a better running economy were not alone the objects which Mackenzie King sought. After the passage of the Act he wrote to Laurier about the New Year's gift he had prepared for the shoe manufacturers: "I much hope that our Combines Investigation Act may be the means of bringing some relief to the shoe manufacturers of this country and the Province of Quebec in particular".[2]

The Combines Investigation Act of 1910 received some favourable publicity in the United States as an example of an improvement on the Sherman Anti-Trust Act. The improvement was purely theoretical, because only one investigation was undertaken under the authority of the Act. This involved the United Shoe Machinery Company, whose legal victory had precipitated the legislation originally. The lawyers of the Company challenged the inquiry in the Courts, and held up proceedings for eleven months. It required another eleven months before a report was brought in. The Board was divided two to one against the Company, but the minority report was an able defence of the Company's policies. In fact nothing

---

[1] *Debates of the House of Commons*, 1909–10, Vol. II, p. 2057.
[2] *Laurier Papers*, King to Laurier, 31 December, 1910.

happened as a result of the entire investigation. No further investigations were undertaken. The Act remained on the Statute
Books until 1919, when it was repealed.[1] The legislation did
nothing more than still for the time being the complaints and
fears of a variety of Canadian interests adversely affected by
the trusts, whose conquering course in the United States was
now directed across the Canadian frontier. The ineffectual
character of Mackenzie King's Combines Investigation Act,
considered in conjunction with the growing Liberal interest in
reciprocal free trade with the United States, and their ardent
desire to attract American capital into Canada suggest, indeed,
a general policy which would have opened the way for an
enlargement of American control of Canadian business—a
control which, by 1911, already embraced approximately a
quarter of all Canadian manufacturing enterprise.

The Grand Trunk Railway strike of 1910 was an event
which might have destroyed, or seriously crippled, the career of
a less adroit politician than Mackenzie King. Had he been a
man of sensitive philosophic disposition, it might have changed
the course of his whole life. As it turned out, Mackenzie King
succeeded in transforming an acute embarrassment to the
Liberal Party, and one of the major points in the indictment
of the Government placed before the voters by the Opposition
in 1911,[2] into evidence of his abiding love of labour and his
resolute devotion to justice. As late as 1935, in the midst of
depression and labour unrest, his loyalty to the displaced
strikers of 1910 and his friendship with one of the strike leaders,
James Murdock,* was produced as a reason why Mackenzie
King should have the support of the wage-earning interest.[3]

The issues of the dispute were fairly simple. The Railway
Brotherhoods of North America (i.e. in Canada, the United

---

[1] According to Ball, *Canadian Anti-Trust Legislation*, p. 50: "Publicity and expense
to the applicants plus the tediousness of the one investigation were powerful factors
in discouraging public use of the facilities of the Act." Towards the end of 1919
anti-trust legislation in the nature of two Acts, the Combines and Fair-Prices Act
and the Board of Commerce Act was passed by the Government. This new legislation soon found itself in difficulties, and by the end of 1921 the Privy Council had
asserted that it was invalid. In June, 1923, a new Combines Investigation Act was
guided through the House of Commons by Mackenzie King.
[2] *The Liberal-Conservative Handbook*, 1911, pp. 182–85.
[3] Rogers, *Mackenzie King*, pp. 43–44.

States and Mexico), and in particular the Order of Railway Conductors and the Brotherhood of Railroad Trainmen, were engaged, during the prosperous years 1909–11, in effecting a continent-wide arrangement by which their members would be paid for the miles they travelled in the course of their work; and wages and rules would be as nearly uniform as possible having regard to differences in operating in the several regions of the continent. The rules governing payment on a mileage basis were of very great importance because railway technology was improving rapidly at this time. Improvements in gradients, the flattening of curves, the installation of heavy rails, improvements in motive power, handling equipment and the bearings on wheels were some of the factors in making it possible for train crews to operate trains farther and faster than hitherto. Payment on a mileage basis meant that the workers' share of the nation's income would tend to increase, or at least maintain itself as productivity increased. Time rates, on the other hand, meant that the worker did not share so easily in the benefits of technological improvement and better ways of trans-porting goods and people by rail.

The Brotherhoods tackled the North American continent region by region. The companies in the United States west of the Mississippi River agreed to standard rules and rates first: then the railway companies of the south-east, then of the north-eastern United States. The Canadian companies were tackled last, in 1910. They offered some resistance. The men made it clear that, should conciliation fail, they would strike. In ac-cordance with the provisions of the Industrial Disputes In-vestigation Act the railway companies and the Brotherhoods applied for the establishment of Boards of Conciliation. Hearings were held in May and June, and the majority reports were generally favourable to the Brotherhoods. The Canadian Paci-fic Railway Company and several lesser companies eventually accepted the findings, and proceeded to negotiate new agree-ments with the unions, establishing the standard rules and rates of pay considered appropriate to Canadian conditions.

The Grand Trunk Railway Company chose to seek another course. The Grand Trunk system covered a substantial territory in the provinces of Ontario and Quebec, with connections with the railroads of the United States where, in fact, it had lines of its own. In 1910 it was about to extend its connection into the Canadian West and thus create a continental system by joining with the Grand Trunk Pacific Railway Company running across the prairies and the mountains. The financial history of the Grand Trunk had been full of disappointments for the shareholders. The officers of the company in 1911, and particularly C. M. Hays,* the newly-elected President, were ambitious to score a triumph in terms of financial success. A factor in this success was the wage system of the company, which in the case of conductors and trainmen was based on monthly payments. By 1910, there was a 38 per cent differential between the incomes of men working for the C.P.R. and men doing the same jobs and running the same mileage on the Grand Trunk. This can be explained in part by the mileage system of payment in force on the C.P.R. It is easy to see why C. M. Hays and his fellow officers were reluctant to accept the findings of a Board of Conciliation, the majority report of which called upon the Company to adopt the system of payment and the higher rates of wages paid on the C.P.R. and on the other railways of North America.

The Grand Trunk Railway Company had a very close connection with the Liberal Party. Sir Wilfrid Laurier readily hearkened to its every appeal. The tender regard for the Grand Trunk on the part of the Liberal leaders was the factor upon which President Hays relied to find a way out of the situation confronting him as a result of the majority report of the Board of Conciliation. Hays seemed to have in mind several courses which he considered desirable and for the effecting of which he required and expected the help of the Liberal Cabinet.

The first course was to accept the findings of the Board of Conciliation and to shift its cost to the public. "Repeatedly in the course of his conversation Mr. Wainwright [one of Hays' assistants] referred to what it would cost the Company to grant the demands of the men," Mackenzie King told Laurier, "and repeatedly mentioned that if the Company was receiving what other Companies were receiving for the carrying of the mails, it might be possible for them to meet the demands made upon them."[1] If a hidden subsidy from the public in the form of increased mail rates was not possible, Hays wanted to delay the implementation of the Board's findings until such time as

[1] *Laurier Papers*, King to Laurier, 19 July, 1910.

the Company could extract the necessary funds from the people of western Canada. "The Management", Mr. Hays wrote,

> "will pay the same standard of wages as the Canadian Pacific Railway as soon as the Grand Trunk Railway Company through its relations with the Grand Trunk Pacific Railway Company, is in a position to participate in the higher rates obtaining, on the traffic in the North-west, by reason of the completion of that road and the obtaining of through-mail connections . . . which should be accomplished within two years."[1]

Failing these alternatives, Hays could endeavour to break the power of the Brotherhoods and preserve the traditional wage structure. The possibility of finding the necessary funds out of the surpluses of the Company never occurred to Hays or to members of the Liberal Administration.

Each of the possible courses open to Mr. Hays, save that of agreeing to the findings of the Conciliation Board, depended upon the co-operation of the Federal Government with the Company. If the issue between the conductors and the trainmen of the Grand Trunk and their employers was a matter of great financial concern to Mr. Hays and the directors of the railway, the development of a strike in an industry as important to the community as the Grand Trunk system, bore the potentiality of disaster for the Liberal Party, for the Liberal Minister of Labour and for his much publicized "solution" of industrial conflict—the Industrial Disputes Investigation Act. If the Liberal Cabinet were lured into a course of strike-breaking, they would lose votes in nearly every constituency in central Canada and the Maritime Provinces, for Grand Trunk workers were an organized interest of extensive dimensions. If, on the other hand, the Cabinet sat back and waited until the undoubted power of the men had brought the Company to its knees they would lose much of the financial assistance upon which the Liberal Party relied for its organizing work, and the support of the powerful employers' interest would melt away. A clear victory for the Brotherhoods might, in addition, transform the Canadian labour movement. Should this happen the Liberal Party might disappear forever, or be compelled to undergo an inner transformation so serious that its existing leaders would know it not. These dreadful possibilities were hidden within the

---

[1] *Labour Gazette*, Vol. XI, 1910, pp. 195–6.

tension growing between the Grand Trunk executives and their men.

Mackenzie King, as Minister of Labour, was a central figure in the drama unfolding in June, 1910. His June mood was a complacent one. He seemed to think that the acceptance of the standard rules and rates by the C.P.R. made acceptance of the majority finding of the Board by the Grand Trunk almost automatic. Writing to Laurier from Berlin, Ontario, on June 20th, 1910, he was optimistic. His friend, Joseph Atkinson,* the proprietor of the Toronto *Daily Star*, had been chairman of the Board, and Mackenzie King told Laurier that "Mr. Atkinson feels that to ask the men to accept less than has been granted would not be an approach to justice". On June 21st, Laurier congratulated Mackenzie King on his success and remarked that "The Grand Trunk have to agree willingly or unwillingly, but probably willingly. They would place themselves in a very false position if they were to refuse. The contrast between them and their competitors will be more damaging than the increase would cost them."[1]

Within ten days this optimism was severely shaken. It became evident that Mr. Hays was determined to achieve something no other railway president in North America had accomplished, i.e., to come out of a collision with the railway Brotherhoods with his net surpluses on revenue account intact and the Brotherhoods in retreat. He seems to have accurately assessed the fortitude of the Liberal Party and the character of its leaders. Thus he had the courage of their lack of conviction.

Early in July, as reports reached him of the tempestuous discussions between Mr. Hays and the Brotherhoods, Laurier began to worry. He was away from Ottawa on a trip in western Canada, and many of his ministerial colleagues were off on holidays. His Minister of Labour was preparing to leave for Europe. As the storm signals began to go up Laurier wrote to Mackenzie King ordering him to remain in Canada. Mackenzie King assured him that such a directive was unnecessary and that he was planning no strategic withdrawal to Europe.

Situated in his lonely command post in Ottawa, behind the front lines in Montreal, Mackenzie King began to plan his policy. His first move was traditional: to attempt to satisfy

[1] *Laurier Papers*, Laurier to King, 21 June, 1910.

both the company and the Brotherhoods by transferring the burden of a settlement to the general public. On July 16th, 1910 he wired to Laurier:

"Probabilities are I will be asked by Mr. Hays to personally intervene today to prevent general strike over Grand Trunk System on Monday. It is possible only thing which may save situation will be an assurance that Government will grant Commission to enquire Mail service rates. If as very last resort this step necessary to save situation would you authorize me to give assurance on condition that Company succeed in averting strike. Lemieux en route Gaspé says he cannot give an answer at this juncture because Council agreed to defer till full meeting. If authority given you can rely on my not using it unless only possible effective way of averting calamity."[1]

This was too indelicate a proposal for Laurier. From Winnipeg he wired his reply the same day:

"Your telegram means that Company willing to defer to demands of men provided increased mail mileage is promised by us. Company should not make such request at this juncture. I am willing to use my influence with Council to have Commission appointed on my return first week of September and I am sure that with this Council will agree. Company ought to be satisfied with that and should not press us to break understanding adopted at last meeting of Council that nothing but routine business would be taken up during vacation."[2]

In response to this snub from Sir Wilfrid Laurier, Mackenzie King tried to explain that the suggestion of a government subsidy by way of increased mail mileage was an idea of his own and not a specific proposal of the President of the Company. This seems to have been the case. In the first fortnight of July President Hays appears to have come to want more than simply an increased mail subsidy. He was seeking the whole-hearted co-operation of the Government in forcing a capitulation upon the Brotherhoods. To do this he proposed that the Railway Labour Disputes Act, which had been superseded by the Industrial Disputes Investigation Act, be revived; that the Government appoint a Board of Investigation and Arbitration under its terms without consulting the Brotherhoods and, indeed, in spite of them. If the Brotherhoods refused to co-operate, this would tend to put them in the wrong with the public on the

---

[1] *Laurier Papers*, King to Laurier, 16 July, 1910.
[2] *Laurier Papers*, Laurier to King, 16 July, 1910.

score of disobeying a government order; if they did co-operate the new Board might well find a solution more advantageous to the Company. In any event, Hays' proposal had the advantage, from his point of view, of putting the Government in the position of compelling the Brotherhoods to do something under legislation, which they rightly believed had been superseded by the much advertised Industrial Disputes Investigation Act.

Hays had already considered this manoeuvre before the Board of Conciliation had reported. Late in May, he sent an emissary to Sir Wilfrid Laurier suggesting such a course. Laurier had dismissed the suggestion since its acceptance would have meant an arbitrary suspension of the Government's existing system of dealing with labour disputes established by the Industrial Disputes Investigation Act. After the findings of the Board of Conciliation were published, Hays' emissary appeared again in Ottawa with the same proposal. This time he saw the Minister of Labour, who "expressed [his] willingness to go to Montreal . . . with a view of seeing whether the men might be induced to arbitrate should Mr. Hays desire. . . ."[1] It was not, however, "Mr. Hays' wish that the men should be consulted at all. . . ." In the Minister's opinion Hays wished "to throw an additional onus upon [the men] in the event of the strike taking place".

Sir Wilfrid Laurier was instinctively anti-union. He loved the people. He loved the workers, provided they were not organized and determined to assert their claims. In this instance, he thought "the men very wrong to strike".[2] But Laurier was also instinctively a political campaigner and a counter of votes. To shy away from a course of strike-breaking was no evidence of an orientation in the direction of labour. It was simply common sense, which Laurier had the candour not to embellish and to exhibit as proof of a love for labour. His Minister of Labour, however, saw the propaganda possibilities in this initial position, and he wrung from it every drop of political advantage he could. What followed revealed, however, that an alliance with the Brotherhoods was not his policy, nor was simple neutrality of the kind which Laurier appears to have favoured.

---

[1] *Laurier Papers*, King to Laurier, 4 August, 1910.
[2] *Laurier Papers*, Laurier to King, 2 August, 1910.

The refusal of the Minister of Labour to force arbitration upon the Brotherhoods left President Hays once more in the position of having to accept substantially the same terms as those to which the Canadian Pacific Railway and other companies had agreed, or to fight a strike. He decided upon fighting the strike. The officers of the Brotherhoods sent out the strike order. At 9.30 p.m. on July 18th, 1910, the conductors, brakemen, switchmen and baggagemen of the Grand Trunk system everywhere in Canada and the United States came off the trains and went home. Within twenty-four hours between 8,000 and 9,000 men had been affected by the strike order.[1]

In order to understand properly what had happened it must be borne in mind that the second largest concentration of workers in the second largest enterprise in Canada at that time had ceased to work. The Grand Trunk Railway ran through the most populous regions of the most highly industrialized and the richest agricultural areas of the country. The failure of its trains to run for many days inevitably meant dislocation in industry, hardship to individuals and a growing paralysis of the economy. The situation created was bound to provoke the question of the government's competence to govern. It was, too, a situation which the Minister of Labour had asserted was unlikely to occur under the wise legislation passed upon his inspiration.

The forces lined up against each other were fairly evenly balanced. The 4,250 men of the railroad who obeyed the strike call were not the whole work force of the Grand Trunk system. The locomotive engineers and firemen were still at work under their contracts of employment with the company. And so were the maintenance men in the workshops and round houses of the company. ". . . It is to be remembered," wrote Mackenzie King,

"that our Industrial Disputes Investigation Act, by requiring men to submit their differences to a Board before going on strike meant a tremendous handicap to the men and a no less equal advantage to the company. But for this Act the other railway brotherhoods might have struck instantly in sympathy; some of

[1] This is the figure Mackenzie King gave in a debate in the House of Commons on 21 March, 1911, p. 5786. It was not the same figure he supplied elsewhere, e.g. *Labour Gazette*, August, 1910, p. 196, where the figure given is 4,250 men. In the House of Commons when he was under attack Mackenzie King gave lower figures, e.g., 3,450, *Debates of the House of Commons*, 1910–11, Vol. I, p. 1075.

them would probably have done so and brought the company instantly to its knees."[1]

Thus, the Industrial Disputes Investigation Act assured Hays of one position and protected him from the possibility of a sympathetic strike. Whether he could build upon the basis thus assured him by recruiting a force of strike-breaking conductors, trainmen, switchmen and baggagemen depended upon several factors: his ability to find the men, his ability to protect them at their work, and their ability to do the jobs involved. If Hays was able to keep his trains running, undoubtedly he would win.

But the Brotherhoods had certain advantages. Train conductors, brakemen, switchmen and baggagemen require, for the satisfactory performance of their duties, considerable training and long experience of the complexities of the system they operate. They cannot be recruited off the street. The rules of the Brotherhoods governing apprenticeship and seniority had insured that there were few or no unemployed men with the requisite experience. Furthermore the long course of railway expansion in Canada had insured that the market for labour of this sort was in short supply. Hays might have found a sufficient supply of strike-breakers had he been able to comb the United States and Europe, but the Canadian laws against the importation of strike-breakers were an obstacle, if they were enforced. In fact, when the strike commenced the Canadian Government proceeded to enforce its laws against the importation of strike-breakers. On the other hand the local authorities called out the militia in many centres to protect the Grand Trunk system whenever their trains were running.

After the strike had been in progress for a week it became evident that President Hays' side was the weaker. The acting Prime Minister, Sir Richard Cartwright,* ordered the agencies of the Government to report on the situation through local inquiries addressed to the Customs Houses, the Chambers of Commerce and the Boards of Trade across Canada. This inquiry revealed that within seven days of the strike order the Grand Trunk system as a means of transporting goods and people had come to a stop.[2] The value of the Company's

---

[1] *Laurier Papers*, King to Laurier, 4 August, 1910.
[2] *Laurier Papers*, Cartwright to Hays, 27 July, 1910.

securities was daily depreciating in England and abroad; the Company's system was paralysed; according to Mackenzie King, "its losses occasioned through the crippling of its business was mounting up to the million dollar mark and over...."[1]

This being so, one would have expected President Hays to make the best he could of his misjudgment, to attempt to resume negotiations with the Brotherhoods, and to make such a deal with them as the circumstances and his own folly would permit. This expectation seems to have been at the root of the Cabinet's action when they met on Tuesday, July 26th. Sir Richard Cartwright wrote to President Hays on July 27th, telling him that the evidence in the hands of the Government showed he was beaten and that the time had come to negotiate a settlement or to arbitrate. Sir Frederick Borden,* the Minister of Militia, was given the letter for personal delivery to Mr. Hays in Montreal.

At this stage Mackenzie King rushed into action with his favourite notion that mediation between two equal forces is the path to salvation. This was a most fortunate conception for Mr. Hays; because the forces in the situation on July 28th, 1910, were not equal. The Brotherhoods were in command of the field, and Mr. Hays was in retreat. "... I felt," wrote Mackenzie King to Laurier, that "... the public were strongly enough at my back to permit of my going down to Montreal and sizing up the situation with a view of giving the public a clear-cut statement as to who was in the right and who was in the wrong...."[2] The question was no longer who was right or who was wrong, but who was obstructing the settlement which the circumstances required.

Accounts of what followed vary considerably. The account in the *Labour Gazette* tells one story; another story is that presented by Mackenzie King in response to questions in the House of Commons; a third story is that told by Mackenzie King to Laurier in confidential letters and telegrams exchanged before, during and after the strike. None of these accounts exactly agree either in details or in general meaning. According to the *Labour Gazette*, "the Minister of Labour left for Montreal ... and was joined there by the Hon. Sir Frederick Borden."[3]

[1] *Laurier Papers*, King to Laurier, 4 August, 1910.
[2] *Laurier Papers*, King to Laurier, 4 August, 1910.
[3] *Labour Gazette*, Vol. XI, 1910, p. 207.

In the report to Laurier based on Cabinet documents Mackenzie King apparently gave a more accurate report of what happened. Sir Frederick Borden, who was intending to go home to Nova Scotia, received a commission by the Cabinet to deliver to Hays the Cabinet's letter informing him of their judgment of the situation and their advice to reach a settlement. Borden saw Hays, "who was very pleasant". Borden believed a settlement should not be difficult of achievement. So certain was he of this that he was preparing to leave Montreal for Nova Scotia. He only stayed his course upon receiving from Mackenzie King an urgent request to remain in Montreal until the Minister of Labour arrived upon the scene.

The saviour of the situation appeared determined to bring the parties together in accordance with the requirements of his theory of social relations. The Cabinet, on the other hand, appear to have considered it prudent to leave the parties to settle their difficulties themselves. Sir Frederick Borden's conduct both before and after Mackenzie King's arrival in Montreal suggests this. Unfortunately the Cabinet's course would have left Mackenzie King out of the picture. He would have had nothing to save, and hence could not emerge as a saviour. And so he stepped to the centre of the stage. He had arranged this with a prompter.

> "To strengthen my position as much as possible I arranged, by letting [the men] know of my willingness to do so, to have a communication sent me by the men asking my personal intervention. . . . I requested the men over the long distance telephone to keep their communication to me confidential. I was fearful lest knowing I had been requested to come by the men, it might embarrass Sir Frederick. . . ."[1]

It might also have angered Sir Frederick and the rest of the Cabinet.

Once Mackenzie King arrived, President Hays appears to have realized that he was no longer obliged to deal exclusively with the Brotherhoods but also with a politician with irons of his own in the fire. In this fact Hays seemed to have glimpsed the hope that he might, in spite of his predicament, extract some advantage for himself out of a situation otherwise disastrous; that, in fact, his original judgment of the Liberal politicians

---

[1] *Laurier Papers*, King to Laurier, 4 August, 1910.

with whom he had to deal was not, perhaps, wrong. Hays saw plainly that he would be obliged to concede all the main points recommended by the Board of Conciliation, but he hoped that he might be able to punish the strikers in some way and to demonstrate to them the power of the company to maintain discipline by depriving men who went on strike of their seniority rights, their pensions and perhaps their jobs. Quite naturally the Brotherhoods were determined not to permit the victimization of individuals for withdrawing their work in the course of a dispute.

From the first moment of his intervention in the negotiations in Montreal, Mackenzie King encouraged Hays, by his suggestions and his conduct, to believe that he could achieve objectives in negotiation through the Minister of Labour that he could never attain in negotiating directly with the officers of the Brotherhoods. As soon as Mackenzie King arrived in Montreal and had had dinner with Sir Frederick Borden, he and the Minister of Militia went to see Mr. Hays. They sat talking on Hays' verandah until midnight. Then Mackenzie King went to see the men and stayed with them until three o'clock in the morning. At ten o'clock in the same morning he was once more in conference with the men. After lunch he went to see Hays and his subordinates. Thus, the parties were kept apart instead of being brought together. Neither party knew exactly where it stood in relation to the other party, or even what the other party was being promised or encouraged to think by Mackenzie King. It was out of this technique of playing both ends against the middle that the Grand Trunk strike developed into a disaster for the Liberal Party and became a major factor in their defeat by the Conservatives in the election several months later.

The Brotherhoods knew they were in a winning position and they were prepared to be magnanimous. They would arbitrate all matters, or they would accept the findings of the Board of Conciliation and leave all disputes as to meaning to the sole determination of the Chairman of the Board, or they would settle any differences of view about the findings of the Board by direct negotiation. They were even prepared to accept a rate of pay offered by Hays. They were so conciliatory that even Sir Frederick Borden began to soften in his hostility toward them.

Mackenzie King took their offer to Hays. Hays wanted to know whether Garretson* and Lee,* the international presidents of the Brotherhoods, agreed to the offer. Mackenzie King discovered that this was the case. Then Hays produced his joker. He would agree to everything, but he could only undertake to take back the men on strike "as soon as possible" and only those who were not guilty of disorderly conduct. In short, Mr. Hays was proposing to take back whom he pleased when he pleased and would retain his right to hire, fire and suspend employees for any reason he thought sufficient. He was determined to teach Grand Trunk men that they could not strike with impunity, even to enforce the findings of a Board of Conciliation.

Instead of dissociating himself from these suggestions, which he must have known no serious trade unionist could ever accept, Mackenzie King went to the men and told them

> "very plainly that I thought they had made a mistake in not agreeing to arbitration at the very onset, that in this they had not been true to the principle which their Brotherhoods had always professed . . . that as they had struck without arbitrating Mr. Hays had been forced to take on men to fill their places, it was only reasonable that they should allow him some time to get rid of strike-breakers he had employed, and to maintain the position which the business community generally would expect him to maintain; that the words 'as soon as possible' saved him in the eyes of the public. . . ."[1]

Mackenzie King must have had marvellous powers of persuasion because he induced the officers of the Brotherhoods to agree "that if Mr. Hays would give his word to Sir Frederick and myself that by 'as soon as possible' he meant not longer than thirty days, the strike might be declared at an end. . . ."[2]

Mackenzie King needed an agreement desperately, for the whole policy on which he had based his career was in jeopardy. He achieved this agreement by various means, but primarily by misrepresentation. Hays was not concerned about the employment of strike-breakers. His subsequent conduct revealed that their fate was the least of his worries. His object was to take back only those men whom he needed to run his trains, to fire all those whom he considered disorderly and to maintain

---

[1] *Laurier Papers*, King to Laurier, 4 August, 1910.
[2] *Laurier Papers*, King to Laurier, 4 August, 1910.

his prerogative to decide what the word disorderly meant. Telling the men that Hays was concerned with strike-breakers and not with strikers constituted one element of misrepresentation in Mackenzie King's method of getting agreement. The other is interesting.

According to the story he told Laurier, Mackenzie King approached one of the members of the Canadian Committee of the Brotherhoods early in the negotiations and obtained from him, "in his own handwriting, a statement which he thought would cover the ground, the men having met me at that time by agreeing to the use of the words 'as soon as possible', provided it would be understood that they did not mean a time longer than thirty days." When the officers of the Brotherhoods assembled with the Minister of Labour and Sir Frederick Borden, after reaching an impasse in their negotiations with Hays, Mackenzie King reported that he "took out of [his] pocket and showed to Messrs. Garretson and Lee [the International Presidents of the Brotherhoods]" the statement in the handwriting of the Canadian officer. He then told the officers that he, Mackenzie King, felt justified in suggesting the words "as soon as possible" to Mr. Hays because he had this agreement with one Canadian officer of the Brotherhoods. The Minister of Labour boldly stated that he had informed Hays that he was "committed to this extent" as a result of getting a handwritten document signed by one leader who either did not know with whom he was dealing or did not fully grasp his responsibilities.

Having extracted a promise from the representative of the men, Mackenzie King then returned to see Hays. Hays offered some objections, and Mackenzie King immediately gave way by stretching thirty days into ninety days, "as giving him (i.e. Hays) ample time to reinstate all the men, and also affording some measure of punishment to those who may have been offenders in milder ways."[1] Hays still refused to put any specific time for reinstatement in a written agreement, and Mackenzie King consented to this. An agreement was then drawn up and presented for Hays to sign. As Hays was signing he began to complain about the hard lot of the Grand Trunk. Mackenzie King immediately responded to this with a blank

[1] *Laurier Papers*, King to Laurier, 4 August, 1910.

cheque to the effect "that we would certainly be only too
pleased to represent to our colleagues anything he might do to
help out the present situation. We thought they (i.e. the
Cabinet) would not be lacking in goodwill toward him for
anything he might do." Hays immediately jumped at this
offer by suggesting that the Government ought to help him by
taking some responsibility for employing the men he did not
want to employ. "He said he supposed work could be found for
them on the I.C.R. [Intercolonial Railway] or if not on the
I.C.R. provision might be made in some other way." Mackenzie
King immediately agreed to this proposal believing, as he told
Laurier, that Hays meant the government should employ the
strike-breakers. Hays then asked Mackenzie King for a memorandum clarifying this undertaking by the Government.
Mackenzie King wrote one out immediately in which he
promised on the Government's behalf to employ the strike-
breakers for whom Hays could not provide employment. Hays
listened to the proposals in this confidential letter as Mackenzie
King read it to him. His first reaction was to try a little pressure.
He said that he did not like the word "reinstate" as it was being
applied to men on strike. Mackenzie King responded with an
immediate agreement to change the word. What would Mr.
Hays suggest? "Take back," suggested Hays. Very well, agreed
Mackenzie King.

The nuances of this situation were very fine, but Hays was an
artist in their apprehension. He saw that Mackenzie King was
still betraying the men, that he could still be pushed. With a
flash of inspiration Hays turned on the Cabinet Ministers. "This
is not my undertaking at all;" he declared. "You are to
look after the men out on strike; I am to take back as many of
them as I can, and any whom I do not take back you are to
provide for."[1] "Sir Frederick and I were dumbfounded,"
Mackenzie King told Laurier. Sir Frederick Borden wrung his
hands and pleaded. Mackenzie King reported him as saying,

> "We have done all as members of the Government, that it is in our
> power to do to relieve this situation. We have gone down on our
> knees (or words to that effect) to you in our endeavour to make it
> easy for you in every particular to do what is in your own interest,
> as well as what the public are demanding. You have blocked

[1] *Laurier Papers*, King to Laurier, 4 August, 1910.

proceedings at every turn. For this strike and all that has grown out
of it and may grow out of it, the responsibility must rest with you;
yes, with you."

According to Mackenzie King, "this took Mr. Hays a little
by surprise, and he said, 'Sir Frederick, you should not speak
that way.' " Apparently Sir Frederick was getting under Hays'
guard, when Mackenzie King stepped into battle. This is his
account: "I drew up in front of him and said: 'Mr. Hays, I may
be a young man, but I happen to be another member of the
Government, and as another member of the Government of
this country, I repeat to you every word that Sir Frederick has
uttered.' "[1]

Borden wanted to have done with talk, and bade Hays
good-bye, "without adding any words." Mackenzie King,
however, had a store in reserve.

> "I turned and said: 'Mr. Hays, I am not going to say goodbye, I
> shall be back to see you again; this is really too unfortunate; you
> must surely see that this is getting very serious. Can you not think
> of Sir Wilfrid Laurier and what is owing on the part of your
> Company to the Government; it will never do to have any kind of
> a breach between the Government and your Company. Won't you
> think it over and see, if on no other ground, at least for the sake of
> Sir Wilfrid and all that this may mean to him and to his Govern-
> ment, you can find a way to settle this difficulty?' "

Hays was a graduate of American big business. He was a
"tough baby". With the fine-drawn, hard cynicism of a man
used to buying and selling politicians, he replied: "It will be
too bad if there has to be a break with the Government, but I
do not see wherein I can change my position."

This plain statement by Hays of his determination not to
change his position provides an interesting commentary on the
subsequent behaviour of Mackenzie King. The Minister of
Labour's next move was to meet the officers of the Brotherhoods
at their hotel where he told them that Hays' undertaking to take
back the men "as soon as possible" meant that all the strikers
would be taken back within ninety days with the exception of
those guilty of violence or damaging the Company's property.
He asked the men whether an undertaking by Hays that "as
soon as possible" meant ninety days would cause them to bring

[1] *Laurier Papers*, King to Laurier, 4 August, 1910.

the strike to an end. They said, "Yes." Unfortunately for truth
Mackenzie King neglected to tell the union leaders that Hays
had no intention of consenting to ninety days or any fixed time,
and that the words "as soon as possible" were the only ones to
which he would consent, because they left him an opening to do
what he in fact did, i.e., refuse to re-employ in the Grand Trunk
system men who in his opinion were too militant in their devotion to the union. Thus, the men's consent to a course of action
was obtained by Mackenzie King's suppression of the realities
hidden in the four little words "as soon as possible" as well as
in the words "take back".

It was Mackenzie King's opinion at this stage that:

> "There were two alternatives left to Sir Frederick and myself, one
> to draw up a brief statement which would make clear to the
> public the point to which negotiations had brought us and the
> reason why they did not result in settlement. This meant dis-
> closing everything, with all of possibility (sic) it carried with it to
> Mr. Hays and his Company, to say nothing of other possible con-
> sequences. The other alternative was to make still another
> attempt to save Mr. Hays from himself. I prepared a brief state-
> ment in accordance with the first alternative. . . ."[1]

The plan to rouse the public against Hays and the Grand
Trunk Railway Company remained on tap. It was never put to
Hays. Instead, Mackenzie King read it to Hays' vice-presidents,
Biggar and Wainwright. This appears to have frightened them,
and they said, according to Mackenzie King, that it might mean
civil war. This over-dramatizing of the situation does not appear
to have affected Hays, who regarded his subordinates as a
collection of "nervous Nellies", but it did provide an excuse for
Mackenzie King to abandon a plan so fraught in his mind
with revolutionary possibilities. How did he envisage his role?
As the Canadian Robespierre? Or perhaps the Canadian
Mirabeau? In fact the situation was not revolutionary at all:
only dangerous for the Liberal Party. It was obviously a case of
having to invent sin in order to sell salvation.

The actual proposal which Mackenzie King and Borden put
to Hays directly was a guarantee given, it seems, without
Cabinet authority that

> "we [i.e. the Government] are prepared to say, that if at the end

[1] *Laurier Papers,* King to Laurier, 4 August, 1910.

of three months' time there should be still in your employ any men whom you may have engaged since the strike commenced and retained in virtue of the terms of an engagement at present existing, the Government of Canada will relieve you of such responsibility as you may be under in view of contractual relations by undertaking to find suitable employment for such men".

We are bound to conclude from what followed that Hays had decided that a Government which would provide jobs for strike-breakers would do anything. He met every proposal with an alternative which left him more area of manoeuvre. Mackenzie King himself recognized this. "I saw at once," he told Sir Wilfrid Laurier, "that here again was a new device to enable Mr. Hays to carry out one of the only two possible intentions in his mind, whether to have no settlement at all, or to settle only on the basis of not taking all the men back." In spite of this impression Mackenzie King went to the Canadian officers of the Brotherhoods and asked them for a blank cheque, after telling them how "the Government of Canada was standing by them in an endeavour to see fair play and get justice in the present situation". What is justice? Messrs. Berry and Murdock of the Conductors and Trainmen did not stay for an answer. They are reported by Mackenzie King to have said, in terms highly unlike those of experienced trade union negotiators: "Mr. King, whatever you do, whatever you ask or whatever you say, we will approve of your course."[1]

Mackenzie King had arrived in Montreal in time for dinner on Thursday evening, July 28th. By Sunday, July 31st, he had so impressed Hays by his continued capitulation "on behalf of the men" or "in the public interest" that the President of the Grand Trunk could only treat him with complete contempt. On Sunday afternoon, Mackenzie King threatened Wainwright and Biggar, Hays' assistants, with public exposure, and put them into a panic. By evening he had veered to the other extreme, having prepared an agreement by the terms of which

"it should not be obligatory upon the Company to take [the men] back in the order of their seniority, but that there should be lee-way within the three months to enable them to take back the men in any order so long as at the end of three months all had back their former positions. This . . . [gives] ample room for discipline, and

[1] *Laurier Papers*, King to Laurier, 4 August, 1910.

[enables] the company in the eyes of the public to appear to have had entirely its own way in the settlement of the dispute."[1]

The Minister of the Crown took this around to Hays' home on Sunday night. Hays was getting ready for bed, and sent down word that, "unless it was important he would be glad to leave matters over until the morning." If he wished, Mackenzie King could come upstairs and see the President of the Grand Trunk "in his dressing-gown". Mackenzie King consented to attend this *lit de justice*. Hays received the proposal, told Mackenzie King he would give him an answer in the morning, and went to bed.

True to his word Hays replied in the morning by letter. He said that

"while we are not entirely in accord with you in the meaning you attach to the clauses [about reinstatement] quoted, where room exists for a different opinion, there should be no difficulty in arriving at some mutually satisfactory settlement, should occasion make necessary, and with this understanding your proposition is accepted".[2]

Mackenzie King declared that this letter obviously meant nothing. Not at all. It was an invitation to capitulate still further. Hays introduced a new suggestion designed to weaken the men. Let the Minister of Labour make an agreement covering only the Canadian employees of the Grand Trunk. The American employees were no concern of theirs. "I could not help feeling," Mackenzie King told Laurier, "how fraught with truth were the words 'patriotism is the last refuge of a scoundrel'." But scoundrelly or not Mackenzie King faithfully placed before the men Hays' suggestion that the Canadian employees of the Grand Trunk settle for themselves and leave their Yankee fellow employees in the lurch. They told Mackenzie King politely that they could not agree to this. The limits of the men's patience were being reached. Mackenzie King sensed this. He adroitly told them that "as Canadians I would be mistaken in them if I thought they would take any other stand and that as men I would be ashamed of them".[3] This bit of well-timed flattery prompted them to renew their blank cheque on an account by now heavily overdrawn.

[1] *Laurier Papers,* King to Laurier, 4 August, 1910.
[2] *Laurier Papers*, Hays to Borden and King, 1 August, 1910.
[3] *Laurier Papers,* King to Laurier, 4 August, 1910.

In as much as the men had refused to accept this new capitulation and were still harbouring the delusion that everyone would be *re-instated* within *thirty or ninety days*, Mackenzie King could do nothing but attempt to extract from Hays an undertaking of some sort. Hays sat tight. His subordinates were "visibly agitated", but he refused to budge. Mackenzie King was obliged to pack his bags and leave Montreal with no agreement, and conscious that Hays had in his possession an undertaking by the Minister of Labour to employ strike-breakers on Government railways or in the Government service.

Before he left, however, Mackenzie King had hinted to Wainwright and Biggar that he was prepared to capitulate still further to the President of the Grand Trunk.

> "Before leaving I turned to Mr. Biggar and Mr. Wainwright and said: 'I see only one faint glimmer of hope which can save all. It means more in the way of responsibility than I can take on my shoulders, but perhaps my colleagues knowing the situation, will help to carry it with me, to save this country and to save Mr. Hays.' They asked me what it was. I asked Mr. Biggar if the reason Mr. Hays had given for refusing to include all men in his undertaking was because I had limited the Government's obligation to the men in Canada. He replied yes. I said, 'Do you think that if the government were to extend its obligation to include all, Mr. Hays would extend his also.' "[1]

Leaving this question with the Grand Trunk officials, Mackenzie King left Montreal. He arrived back in Ottawa Monday. On Tuesday emissaries came from Mr. Hays. Mackenzie King introduced them to Mr. Brodeur* and Dr. Pugsley,* the only two Cabinet members then in Ottawa. Brodeur and Pugsley did not understand the issues in detail, Wainwright assured them that only a few dozen men were involved in the Government's undertaking, and that "the Company would be opening up new parts of lines, and would be needing extra men before the next three months were completed". After this assurance they consented to Mackenzie King's agreeing on the Government's behalf to employ all the strike-breakers on the Grand Trunk system in the United States as well as in Canada. Then, presenting his blank cheque to the unions for payment, Mackenzie King told them he had the assurance that they wanted and that they could go back to work.

---

[1] *Laurier Papers*, King to Laurier, 4 August, 1910.

In the afternoon of August 2nd, 1910, the strike came to an end. Hays immediately cancelled the pension rights of all the men who had gone on strike, claiming that the law required continuous service in order to establish a pension right. He took back only those men whom he required to run his railway, re-employing them quite often in different and less remunerative posts than those they had held previously. Eight months later there were still at least 250 men denied their jobs, and two years later the dispute was still in progress. Fifteen years later, when the Grand Trunk had ceased to be a privately owned company, the pension rights of the conductors and trainmen were restored.

Hays failed to achieve his original objective because the men were well enough organized to "win" the strike. His secondary objective of punishing the men was achieved with the assistance of the Government, which waved a big impressive stick and talked extremely small. Even Laurier reproved Mackenzie King for making the incredible promise to employ strike-breakers, which contradicted the Government's own legislation. "I certainly regret the action which the Government took as embodied in your confidential letter to Hays, but I will not put my judgment against your own and against the rest of the Council . . . ",[1] he wrote.

Mackenzie King was acutely conscious of having mishandled the entire affair, and of having earned for the Government the contempt of the Company and the hatred of the men. His report to Laurier of August 4th, 1910, covers thirty-eight typewritten pages. "I felt the duty was mine" he concluded the thirty-eighth page,

> "and I was prepared to discharge it, if need be, alone. However, it may be that in seeking to shoulder the whole responsibility myself that any of it might be spared yourself and my other colleagues, I have unwittingly added to the responsibilities of all in the extent to which I have gone, but unless I am mistaken . . . it is a responsibility which will be willingly shared."

Although he was thus conscious of having landed the Government with a burden, his letter contained some adroit manoeuvres to shift the blame and to maintain his character as a "friend of the working man".

---

[1] *Laurier Papers*, Laurier to King, 11 August, 1910.

In his eyes, Hays was transformed from the ordinary, stubborn, hard-headed business executive trying to keep down his costs and maintain his profit margins into a prototype of those "mean" capitalists about whom Harper and he used to worry in the days of their youth. He lifted chunks out of Lincoln Steffens and the muck-rakers to describe Hays: Hays "feared neither God nor man". ". . . Railroading, in the United States," King explained to Laurier,

> "is a business which with a certain school of men is run on certain principles. One is that human life, to say nothing of human feelings, is not to be considered, either as respects its loss through accident or its massacre as a means to an end. The end is the power of money as against all other powers in the world. To admit the solidarity of labour in any industrial struggle is to admit something more powerful than money, and that must not be done, no matter how great or how tremendous the cost. Mr. Hays has seen himself in this struggle as the chief representative of that school. . . . He had only before his mind the one maxim of railroadism of the school to which he belongs,—that a man's price rises as he shows his ability to destroy the strength of other men."

This is fine rhetoric. But if Mackenzie King believed that "the solidarity of labour" was so important and so beneficial for humanity, why did he think it important to keep the public in the dark about what was happening, to provide strikebreakers with jobs and to bring the strike to a close at the moment when the locomotive engineers and firemen were about to refuse to operate the trains?[1] A situation existed after the first ten days of the strike in which a substantial form of labour "solidarity" could have emerged; in which for the first time there was a likelihood of the railway Brotherhoods striking together; and in which there was some prospect of the action of the men having wide public support. President Hays was unimpressed by rhetoric because he had taken the correct measure of the Government, the men who composed it and the man who represented it.

When Sir Wilfrid Laurier read the blast directed at Hays, he hastily despatched a return letter to Mackenzie King.

> "I have just received your report on the strike and am at this very moment engaged in reading it. I notice it is very severe on Hays but perhaps, however, not more than he deserves. He seems to

[1] *Laurier Papers*, King to Laurier, 4 August, 1910.

have acted in a manner which astonishes me, knowing him as I do to be a man of first-class ability. I do not know if it would be advisable to have a report so severe given to the public, and I wish you would keep it in abeyance so that I may have an opportunity of discussing it with you, before it is put on file and final action is taken on the same."[1]

Mackenzie King, of course, agreed with this suggestion. "Had the letter been other than strictly confidential and personal it would have been quite different in tone and expression."[2]

Apart from the denunciation of Hays, Mackenzie King had a solution for the difficulties of the men which he had brought about. He proposed to Laurier that Parliament be asked to legislate to make it possible for Hays legally to pay their pensions, and that the Government should show the Grand Trunk "no consideration" until it did as the Government wished. This was too much for Laurier. "Your suggestion to reach that position [i.e., full reinstatement with pension rights by Parliamentary legislation] . . . would seem to me a very unfortunate one and even a very dangerous precedent."[3]

In spite of having described Mackenzie King's final promise to Hays as a mistake, of having forbidden the publication of the assault on Hays' character, and of having refused a programme of legislation, Laurier still felt his Minister of Labour deserved a pat on the head. "It is evident that it was your action and your action alone which carried the day and nothing could be better than the way in which you forced Hays from position to position until the final conclusion." This is an extraordinary piece of nonsense. The only position Hays was forced from was his initial one of refusing to accept the majority report of the Conciliation Board. But Mackenzie King did not force him from this position. He was forced from it by the fact that he could not run his railroad. The conductors and brakemen were too well organized to permit him to recruit competent train crews. Mackenzie King's manoeuvres Hays treated with the contempt they deserved. As Mackenzie King showed increasing signs of weakness and willingness to smooth the way for the Company, Hays grew increasingly cynical in his interpretation of every

---

[1] *Laurier Papers*, Laurier to King, 10 August, 1910.
[2] *Laurier Papers*, King to Laurier, 16 August, 1910.
[3] *Laurier Papers*, Laurier to King, 11 August, 1910.

undertaking to which he gave his signature. Hays emerges from the episode as a ruthless and determined man, but one who had a consistent line, real courage, and freedom from cant, hypocrisy and deceptive sentimentality where his own interests were concerned. The same could not be said of the two Canadian trade union leaders. No wonder Hays refused to negotiate with the American International presidents, Garretson and Lee, who had efficiently outmanoeuvred forty American railway companies. No wonder he insisted with a shrewd appeal to Canadian patriotism (though he was himself an American) that he would deal only with Canadians.

Laurier's qualified praise put Mackenzie King into a gushing mood. He expressed the extraordinary idea that pleasing Sir Wilfrid Laurier was more important than settling the strike.

> "I cannot too strongly express the gratitude I feel for the all too generous words and confidence which you have expressed. I speak the whole truth when I say that so long as I have not disappointed or embarrassed you, I really care about nothing else, and that your words of commendation mean more to me in the pleasure and satisfaction which they bring, than the settlement of the strike and all that may have grown out of it one way or the other."[1]

The Grand Trunk strike marked the end of the Laurier epoch. Never again did Sir Wilfrid Laurier have command of the situation in Canada. By the time Parliament met in December his Government was on the way out. Much attention—too much—has been paid to reciprocal free trade with the United States as the issue which defeated Laurier's government. The loss of initiative and the breakdown of popular confidence, which appears to date from the Grand Trunk strike, were the real beginnings of the break-up of Laurier's regime. It marked, too, the beginning of the Mackenzie King phase of Canadian Liberalism.

Before Mackenzie King went to Montreal on July 28th, 1910, the Liberal Cabinet, expressing the technique and the policy of Sir Wilfrid Laurier, were playing the game according to the classical Liberal rules. They were prepared to give the Grand Trunk money and privileges of an economic kind, but when it came to a political issue theirs was the strategy of disengagement, of allowing workers and employers to settle their

---

[1] *Laurier Papers*, King to Laurier, 16 August, 1910.

differences by private contract, within the framework of the law. Mackenzie King introduced a new strategy and a new conception of government. He took the government directly into the strike "to save Mr. Hays from himself"; he deceived and split the men, misled them with flattery and sympathetic words and crippled their power to bargain. At first sight Laurier's praise of Mackenzie King is hard to understand, having regard for the difficulties he had created for the government. Perhaps it was the conventional gesture of a politician long habituated to defending colleagues good, bad and indifferent and afraid to make an enemy. Perhaps the praise signified something deeper: a recognition that the new technique displayed by Mackenzie King was becoming necessary. No member of the Liberal Cabinet wanted the men to win. Sir Frederick Borden admitted that he was extremely hostile to the men, and so was Sir Wilfrid Laurier. So were Mr. Brodeur and Dr. Pugsley. The Grand Trunk strike demonstrated, however, that the men could win: they had the members, the organization and the public sympathy. Obviously a strategy of holding the ring was not enough. A new strategy was called for. Sir Wilfrid Laurier was not entirely conscious that such a strategy was needed nor were any of his colleagues, but he was prepared to admit that Mackenzie King was a new kind of player for a new kind of situation.

The new player, however, had thoroughly confused the game as it was then being played. Laurier was alarmed by the commitments Mackenzie King had made to Hays, and even more alarmed by the pressure he was proposing to put on Hays to prevent a wholesale desertion of trade unionists from the Liberal Party. When Laurier returned to Ottawa he began to straighten out the confusion in so far as it would yield to his ministrations. Apparently some aspects of the business were taken out of Mackenzie King's hands. When Parliament reassembled, the Leader of the Opposition ignored the Minister of Labour and addressed his inquiries concerning the strike to Sir Wilfrid Laurier and the Minister of Railways and Canals, the Hon. George P. Graham.* Although Mackenzie King usually answered for the Government, Graham was put up to reply to several key questions such as the rumoured pressure being applied to the Grand Trunk to undo the mischief done the men. Later during the election campaign we find Mackenzie King actually asking Graham to "let me know how far I can go" in his handling of the Grand Trunk question.[1]

Laurier thought that the answer to the Grand Trunk strike was legislation establishing a system of compulsory arbitration. This he proposed to introduce when Parliament assembled. Unfortunately for him, the full consequences of the Government's betrayal of the Brotherhoods were beginning to become apparent by the end of October, 1910. Not only had the men been deprived of their pensions and more than 250 of them fired (or to use Mr. Hays' terminology "not been taken back"), but they were experiencing difficulty in securing what had been agreed to without the Government's interference. On November 4th, 1910, a delegation from the Trades and Labour Council waited upon Laurier and Mackenzie King to express their resolute disapproval of compulsory arbitration of labour disputes. Later in the month Parliament assembled. Then commenced the long, continuous Tory attack on the Government which was to bring it crashing down in the election of 1911.

At that time the Canadian Tories had no fear of organized labour, and little of that kind of hatred of trade unions which their political rivals popularly represent them to have. They at once took up the case of the Grand Trunk men. At regular intervals, in order that the issue might never die, and without the concentrated flamboyance which denotes a false concern and an artificial sympathy, the Opposition put down questions on the Order Paper.

"Did the Government make an arrangement with the Grand Trunk Railway? . . . How many [men] have not been re-instated, and why not? . . . Was the Minister of Labour a party in negotiating and concluding a settlement? . . . Did the Order of Railway Conductors at their annual convention in Florida pass a resolution condemning the conduct of the management of the Grand Trunk Railway and the Canadian Government?"[2]

Most of the questions were left to Mackenzie King to answer. The *Labour Gazette* of August, 1910, was replete with self-satisfied publicity to the effect that the Minister of Labour had gone to Montreal and settled the strike. This publicity had

---

[1] *Graham Papers*, King to Graham, 30 August, 1911.

[2] These are a few examples of questions asked during the period 1 December, 1910–24 May, 1911.

evoked congratulations more unqualified than Laurier's and more useful in making a case for the Minister of Labour's conduct before the House of Commons. The congratulations of August had turned into the sharp criticisms of December. These were not reported in the *Labour Gazette*. In response to the creeping barrage of questions fired from the Opposition side Mackenzie King adopted dodging tactics. In a written answer given to the House on December 1st, 1910, he declared that "the agreement which was the basis of settlement of the recent strike was made between the parties of the dispute and not between the government and the parties."[1] The responsibility for the settlement rested with President Hays and the Officers of the Brotherhoods. Mackenzie King had done nothing more than bring the parties together. "The conference was kept up between the two parties, not between Sir Frederick and myself and the parties to the dispute. . . . That conference lasted from three o'clock in the afternoon of Saturday until about seven in the evening . . . and was resumed again about nine o'clock and lasted until midnight. . . ."[2] The Minister of Labour, according to his statements in the House, had not taken the initiative in seeking to intervene. The men had invited him. He read their telegram of invitation. He did not, of course, tell the House that he had invited them to invite him; that the Cabinet had sent Sir Frederick Borden to Hays twenty-four hours before Mackenzie King had received his "invitation"; that the Cabinet's policy before Mackenzie King's intrusion was one of non-intervention joined with a warning to Hays. According to Mackenzie King, not only were the parties solely responsible for the agreement they had made, but "Sir Frederick Borden and myself were present as *witnesses*".[3]

The Opposition wanted to know, not only who was responsible for the agreement, but also what was being done to get the men off the Company's black list. It was stated in the press and in the House that at least 265 men had been blacklisted in Canada, and many others had been downgraded for striking. Mackenzie King took the line that he was merely a postman conveying messages from the men to Hays and from Hays to the men. Employing the same devices of argument

---

[1] *Debates of the House of Commons*, 1910–11, Vol. I, pp. 654–5.
[2] *Debates*, 1910–11, Vol. I, p. 1074.
[3] *Debates*, 1910–11, Vol. III, p. 4259. (Our italics.)

K

which had served him so well in Montreal he asserted, seemingly in criticism of the Company, that "the government has expressed to the Company in the strongest terms possible its wish and desire that the agreement should be carried out to the letter",[1] but on the other hand he consented to state the Company's position and to approve it. He had advised "each man who had not been re-instated" to write to the President of the Grand Trunk. President Hays had told these men that they were guilty according to the Company's records of disorderly conduct and violence; that in his mercy he was prepared to let each of them appear before a superintendent of the company in order "to prove to the satisfaction of the superintendent that he has not been guilty of such acts. . . ." According to the Minister of Labour it was "not in the interest of the men themselves" to put pressure on the Company to revise this policy.

Robert Borden, the leader of the Opposition, quietly tore Mackenzie King to shreds. "I do not agree with the Minister that it is fair to the men that they should be called upon to prove a negative. . . . It is a rather new rule that the party against whom a charge is made is obliged to prove himself innocent. The usual rule of English law and fair play is. . . ." etc., etc. Hit with this argument Mackenzie King tried to move verbally over to the Opposition side while remaining in fact on the Company's side.

"To have done other than accept the Company's suggestion as to the method of proceeding, would have been to block progress in the interest of the men themselves. I agree with the hon. leader of the opposition that the methods of the company are extraordinary. I think that they might have taken a more liberal way of dealing with the question. But they manage a railway and understand it and I do not."[2]

When Parliament rose for the Christmas recess Mackenzie King and the Government were in a sadly-battered state. There were a few black-listed men in many constituencies across the country. Each group of victims was the centre of organized discontent—plain evidence to a mass of men with votes of the power of the employers and the treachery of the Government. The issue was not big enough and the circumstances were not appropriate for re-commencing the strike, but they were just

---

[1] *Debates*, 1910–11, Vol. I, p. 1075.   [2] *Debates*, 1910–11, Vol. I, p. 1078.

right for an organized political effort against the Liberal Party. As one newspaper put it: "The matter is serious for Mr. Graham [the Minister of Railways and Canals] in whose home town of Brockville some 30 or 35 men are still on the Company's black list. The rest of the railway men sympathize with these men, and the matter is of electoral importance to the Minister of Railways."[1]

During the recess the Government attempted to find a way out. Laurier's fingers had been badly burnt by Mackenzie King's interference and the contradictory promises he had made to each of the parties to the dispute. He did not wish to involve the Government further and yet he could not let the matter drift. It was hinted in the House of Commons that Laurier and Graham had threatened Hays with cutting off the Government construction subsidies for the Grand Trunk Pacific, of which Hays was also President. Employing either persuasion or pressure, the Government was able to induce the Company to appoint at their own [the Company's] expense a Judge of the Ontario Bench to hear the cases of individual men. When Parliament reassembled this crude device was produced as a defence against the rolling barrage which was once again laid down by the Opposition.

But this defence was no defence. The Opposition broadened their front and started shelling the Government from a variety of positions. The question of the men's pensions was raised and thoroughly ventilated. The prolonged strike of miners in Nova Scotia and in British Columbia was charged against the Government, and the free use of the militia in these disputes was subsequently discussed. In the debate on supply the Industrial Disputes Investigation Act itself was attacked. E. N. Rhodes, a leading Conservative from the Maritime Provinces, and member for Cumberland County, told the House, ". . . I have received resolutions from all the lodges in the county calling for the repeal of the Act. . . ."[2]

On February 10th, 1911, Mackenzie King attempted to reply. He employed the technique for which he eventually became famous. His speech was long, extremely personal, heavily loaded with testimonials to his brilliance, his love of labour and

---

[1] *Ottawa Journal*, 10 December, 1910, (quoted in the *Debates*, 1910–11, Vol. I, p. 1079).
[2] *Debates*, 1910–11, Vol. III, p. 3399.

the wide support he enjoyed among trade union leaders. When he finished a member was obliged to inquire of the Speaker whether there was still a quorum. But if he emptied the House, he had put on the record a vast volume of documentary evidence proving that he had been invited by the leaders of the Brotherhoods to intervene, that they had given him a free hand; that they trusted him; that having so committed themselves, they could not desert him. He pinned them down with letters they could not repudiate. Typical of these tactics was the manner in which he dealt with James Murdock, the Canadian vice-president of the Brotherhood of Railroad Trainmen. Murdock, together with Berry of the Conductors, had delivered himself into Mackenzie King's hands by inviting him, at his own suggestion, to intervene in the dispute. In Montreal, they had consented to let Mackenzie King act as a go-between, instead of assuming the responsibility as leaders of their unions for direct negotiation. Finally they had consented to Mackenzie King's guarantee of the meaning of the words "as soon as possible". On February 24th, 1911, Mackenzie King proceeded to read into the record a letter of Murdock's in which Murdock told the Minister of Labour how he had been born into a family of Liberals; how he had voted for the Conservatives for the past 18 years, and how he was now devoted to the Minister of Labour.[1]

Thus was Murdock locked to the Liberal machine. This conservative labour leader became in his turn Mackenzie King's first Minister of Labour and finally a Senator.

Mackenzie King's defence of his record was not a success. When a quorum had been discovered, J. W. Maddin,* the member for Cape Breton South, rose.

"The Minister of Labour in his speech tonight has gone to some trouble to paint a very good picture of the Minister of Labour. . . . I am quite sure that when the distinguished gentleman who occupies the portfolio of labour had finished adorning himself tonight he had such a halo around his head as would astonish Michael the Archangel. He decked himself with a wreath that contained everything from roses to sunflowers. I would like to add to that wreath one thistle. . . ."[2]

He proceeded to insert the thistles. A Liberal member of one of

[1] *Debates*, 1910–11, Vol. III, pp. 4253–54.
[2] *Debates*, 1910–11, Vol. II, p. 3415.

the provincial cabinets had described Mackenzie King as "the boy Minister" who had handled the strike in Cape Breton like a boy, indeed. And so went the debate.

The Opposition were not troubled by Mackenzie King's defence. When a Tory member as reactionary as Mr. G. Taylor,* member for Leeds, was in a position to challenge a Liberal Cabinet Minister "to meet [him] . . . on any platform . . . in any town . . . before the labouring men of this country", to debate their respective attitudes to the use of bayonets in strikes, and the labour problem generally, the Liberals were in trouble.[1] Mr. J. D. Reid,* the Conservative member for Grenville and future Cabinet Minister, summed up acutely the impression which was growing in the community.

> "It looks to me as though the Minister of Labour is working for the employers instead of the men. That has been instanced in cases before this. In these strikes down East, as far as I can judge from the newspapers, the Minister stood by the employers to the injury of the men. The men always seem to come out second best. The same theory applies to the Grand Trunk strike. In that case the Minister wanted to show the employees of the Grand Trunk what a great thing he was doing for them, and the impression that went all through the country was that the interest of the men had been served by the Minister, that they were all to be reinstated, that everything was to be lovely, and that the Grand Trunk had been brought to time. But you see from the reports afterwards that it turned out the very opposite; the men are the ones that are turned down. . . . In every case he has gone to the employer, made a deal with him, and the men have always come out second best."[2]

On March 21st, W. B. Northrup,* the member for Hastings East, moved a resolution condemning the government for failing to avert the Grand Trunk strike, failing to bring it to a satisfactory end, and failing to compel President Hays to carry out the agreement which the government had guaranteed to the men as a condition for ending the strike. The resolution was lost in the House, but the election was lost in the country.

In May the Order of Railway Conductors meeting in Florida passed a resolution condemning both the president of the Grand Trunk and the Canadian Government. As the session drew to a close Mackenzie King was obliged, in response to a

---

[1] *Debates*, 1910–11, Vol. V, p. 10347.
[2] *Debates*, 1910–11, Vol. III, pp. 4244–45.

question, to place this thistle on the record. By July, the heat of Ottawa and the heat of the final barrage against the government were sufficient to produce from Mr. G. Taylor this penetrating gleam of light concerning the use being made of the Department of Labour:

> "The Minister of Labour talks about interfering in politics, but I tell him that his Labour Bureau is nothing but a political machine from head to foot, and every one of his correspondents throughout the country is simply an agent for the government. The *Labour Gazette* is nothing but politics from start to finish. I throw the thing into the waste basket every time I get it, and I would be obliged to the Minister if he would stop printing it at the expense of the country. . . ."[1]

The Grand Trunk strike was only one item in the bill of indictment presented to Parliament by the Opposition. Mackenzie King's failure in the case of the Grand Trunk Railway dispute was merely the most dramatic incident in the general breakdown of the system embodied by the legislation of which he claimed the paternity. During 1910, there had been 67 strikes affecting 19,554 workers. In 1911 these figures mounted to 104 strikes affecting 28,918 workers. The prolonged strike of August, 1909, in the coal-fields of Nova Scotia was followed, in 1911, by a long and bitter strike of miners in Alberta and British Columbia. This commenced in April, 1911. It affected 7,000 men and caused the loss of several million tons of coal. The Minister of Labour proved helpless, and his legislation equally so. In July, the press of the prairie provinces struck a note of alarm about the prospect of facing a winter without fuel. A conference of Western Associated Boards of Trade attempted to do what Mackenzie King had failed to do. As the elections approached the Minister of Labour attempted to apply pressure to both parties in the shape of a threat to admit American coal to the western market free of duty. This did no good. Militiamen were still patrolling the mining towns when the election came on in September.

Cruel economic facts were exposing the unsubstantial character of Mackenzie King's system of conciliation. During the first phases of Laurier's prosperity when prices were rising, and employment and investment opportunities were improving, conciliation was possible on the basis of wage increases. Once prices

[1] *Debates*, 1910–11, Vol. V, p. 9721.

began to rise more swiftly than wages the system of conciliation began to fail.

The word corruption is an almost forgotten word in the political vocabulary of modern Canada. Before World War I it was a familiar word in the idiom of Canadian parliamentary politics. This is readily understandable. One of the supreme objects of the politicians of that age was the feathering of their own nests and those of their friends and supporters. One novel custom of the time concerned the testimonials or gifts offered to politicians of sufficient eminence and power. In 1910, Laurier's Minister of Finance was offered a magnificent *pourboire* of $120,000 by his friends and admirers. The gift was tarnished unfortunately by the allegation, strenuously denied, that a substantial contribution to the testimonial had come from the General Manager of the Farmers' Bank, which had failed, with great loss to the depositors and shareholders.[1]

The Laurier Government was charged with corruption on a colossal scale in the construction of a new Transcontinental Railway across the Dominion. One half was to be built by the Grand Trunk Pacific Railway Company—from Winnipeg to Prince Rupert—and one half by the Canadian Government— from Moncton to Winnipeg—the government portion being entrusted to the National Transcontinental Railway Commission. The Conservatives charged that $40,000,000 might have been saved if the work of construction had been efficiently planned and they made great political capital out of charges of "rake-offs" and "waste" during the election of 1911 in which Laurier was defeated. The Conservatives then pressed home their charges of corruption in the Liberal Party by appointing Royal Commissions of investigation, including one on the railway scandal.[2]

Every so often an instance of public contracts going to the highest rather than the lowest bidder would be discovered. Jobbing in the Civil Service had become the general rule. A growing nation can stand a great deal of corruption so long as the mass of the people do not feel it too severely, and new

---

[1] *Canadian Annual Review* (Toronto, 1900–11), pp. 271 ff.
[2] *Canadian Liberal Monthly* (henceforth cited as *The Liberal Monthly*), March 1914, Vol. I, No. 7, pp. 76–8; April 1914, Vol. I, No. 8, pp. 91–2; July 1914, Vol. I, No. 11, p. 127; July 1915, Vol. II, No. 11.

individuals are all the time experiencing its delights. But this had ceased to be the case in the last years of the Laurier regime. Mounting prices, low wages and the rapid gobbling up of small businesses by the great corporations were at the root of popular unrest. During the years 1909–11 there were 39 industrial mergers involving a capital of $334,978,266, and 196 companies disappeared as a result. In February F. D. Monk,* a leading conservative member of Parliament with close connections among the nationalists of Quebec, moved a resolution calling for an inquiry into the merger movement and its effects upon the cost of living, the value of Canadian securities abroad and the granting of credit. Mackenzie King was put up to defend his legislation, the Combines Investigation Act. He maintained that investigation was an adequate weapon. The Leader of the Opposition declared that the people wanted legislation capable of enforcement and not simply investigation.

In this debate Mr. Borden called attention to the merger movement, not only as a Canadian phenomenon, but as a device by which American trusts and big business enterprises were establishing a control over Canadian business enterprise. The capital of Canadian manufacturing enterprises was estimated at $1,500,000,000 by 1911. Of this $234,000,000 was estimated to be owned by American companies in the shape of branch factories, without account being taken of autonomous American investments in manufacturing enterprises and heavy American investments in transport enterprises, mining, commercial undertakings and in land and public securities. The growing Canadian alarm about American penetration was not simply a product of nationalist or British imperial enthusiasm, but a fear concerning the opportunities for small business entrepreneurs and working-class standards and bargaining power.

A problem at once more portentous, and less connected with the daily concerns of the people, related to the naval armaments policy of the Laurier Government. In response to demands heard both inside Canada and across the Atlantic to assist Great Britain in the armaments race among the Great Powers, Laurier had devised a policy which he hoped would appease nationalist sentiment and blunt radical and pacifist objections to Canadian participation in the contest of arms building.

In simple outline this policy, expressed in the Naval Service

Bill of 1910, consisted of a plan to build a Canadian Navy at Canadian expense, and man the ships with Canadian sailors "for the protection of Canada". The Naval Service Bill contained a provision by which, with the consent of Parliament, this navy could be transferred to British command. But Laurier would not commit himself as to how or in what circumstances the Navy would be used. The only firm facts which the Canadian people knew were that Laurier's Government planned to spend money on ships which would be manned by Canadian men. These facts were disturbing to a people like the Canadians, used to a long isolation from the cruelties and expenses of world politics. They began to ask questions about what they were doing and about the future. The issue of the navy was loaded with a charge of political explosive. When the explosion took place it may have blown various people in various directions, but it blew them all indifferently, not least the Liberal Party, and not all to its advantage.

While Laurier and his Ministers were being driven first into one corner and then into another during the meeting of Parliament in November and December, 1910, they were meditating a means of dealing a knock-out blow to the Opposition. While the Tories were ragging Mackenzie King over the Grand Trunk strike, he and his colleagues had been quietly negotiating in private with representatives of the United States' Government a programme of reciprocal free trade, which would open the American market to Canadian natural products and admit American products to the Canadian market under the Canadian intermediate tariff schedule. The Americans had actually proposed complete free trade between the two countries, but the Canadian Government realized that a total exposure of Canadian business to the competitive methods of the American trusts and large industrial corporations would kill the plan to integrate the American and Canadian economies. Thus, a step by step plan was agreed upon. In January, 1910, it was presented to the Canadian Parliament as the long anticipated heart's desire of the Canadian people.

Instead of a means to calm the troubles of the people and the turbulence of Parliament, the Reciprocity bill became a catalytic agent fusing all the forces set against the course of the Government into a vast movement which swept away the

Laurier Ministry. The destiny, not of parties, but of the nation itself, became the concern of the Canadian people.

William Randolph Hearst,* who had helped engineer the overthrow of the Spanish Empire in Cuba and the seizure of the Philippine Islands, was deeply interested in Reciprocity. In the case of Canada he, like President Taft, wished to try diplomacy rather than war to extend the area of the United States. Reciprocity was the only issue in the election, he cabled the New York *American*. Annexation had been introduced to evade the real question, and was the wrong word to use, he said.

"The word Annexation has a certain suggestion of force or compulsion about it and is not even properly used in this connection. In my opinion it should be discarded and some word of clearer and better meaning substituted. I suggest the word 'union' or the word 'admission'. Among citizens of the same general character, with cordial interrelations, the subjugation of either one by the other in this enlightened age is an absurd proposition and not seriously to be considered by anyone."[1]

Mr. Champ Clark, the Speaker of the House of Representatives declared that nine-tenths of the American people favoured annexation of Canada. "I am willing to make this proposition," he is reported to have said, "You let me run for President on a platform for the annexation of Canada, in so far as this country can accomplish it, and let President Taft run against me opposing annexation—and—well, I'd carry every State in the nation."[2]

Words of this kind were not just the loose talk of irresponsible American politicians and journalists. Since before the Spanish-American War, American big business had been thinking seriously about their need to expand their market opportunities, sources of supply and opportunities for the investment of capital. John Hay,* who invented the Open Door Policy in China, had thrown into the public forum the idea of an "Atlantic System" based upon the formation of a triple alliance and close integration of the United States, Britain and France. Canada would be a pledge for British good behaviour in this system.[3] Diplomacy and force were the implements used by American business in its onward and outward course. Britain had been taught a lesson in Venezuela in 1896. Re-

[1] *Canadian Annual Review*, 1911, p. 223.
[2] *Canadian Annual Review*, 1911, p. 270.
[3] M. Josephson, *The President Makers* (New York, 1940), pp. 204–05; 509.

volution had been exported to Cuba, and the Philippine Islands seized. A new "liberal" tactic had been devised for penetrating the curtain of foreign imperialism descending around China.

In the case of Canada the Republican Party of the United States thought of reciprocity opening the way to annexation as just the sort of "free trade" line necessary to dish the Democrats,[1] serve the purpose of expansion and win the votes of all those who approved of the manifest destiny of the United States. From Great Britain, where the business and political classes had much experience of American expansionist policies, came urgent appeals to the Canadian people to beware of the apparent magnanimity of their neighbour to the south, lest they lose their independence entirely. Rudyard Kipling wrote:

> "I do not understand how nine million people can enter into such arrangements as are proposed with ninety million strangers on an open frontier of four thousand miles, and at the same time preserve their national integrity. Ten to one is too heavy odds. No single Canadian would accept such odds in any private matter that was as vital to him personally as this issue is to the nation. It is her own soul that Canada risks to-day. Once that soul is pawned for any consideration, Canada must inevitably conform to the commercial, legal, financial, social and ethical standards which will be imposed upon her by the sheer admitted weight of the United States."

Thus politicians and poets sent warnings—and they were not always unheeded.[2]

The bill to establish Reciprocity had not been long before Parliament when the Canadian people and the Opposition in the House of Commons began to perceive the "clear meaning" so apparent to Mr. Hearst and Rudyard Kipling. By July, the dose intended as soothing syrup had become a bottle of gelignite. Laurier decided to recommend the dissolution of Parliament and an appeal to the electors. But he waited too long.

Everywhere in the country the Liberals had an uphill fight against tremendous odds. Liberal apologists such as Laurier's biographer, Skelton,* have suggested that Laurier and his party were beaten by money and mad enthusiasm excited by mutually contradictory elements in the community.[3] Laurier

[1] Josephson, *The President Makers*, p. 402.
[2] *Canadian Annual Review*, 1911, pp. 219–24.
[3] O. D. Skelton, *Life and Letters of Sir Wilfrid Laurier* (London, 1922), Vol. II, Chap. XVI.

himself floundered among the memories of his youth for an explanation of his disaster. He had been beaten by Protestant fanaticism and clerical spite. But the explanation of the Liberal defeat is more complex than that. Liberal policies had driven everyone to the "left", whether they were wealthy business men afraid of American big business or industrial workers afraid of black-listing and low wages. Canada had become an industrial nation, and every active element in the industrial community had been alienated and threatened by Liberal policy. The Liberals had built a political machine, but the machine had left the road.

Mackenzie King recognized the difficulties his Party faced. He threw himself into the struggle with energy. He spoke two and three times a day in his constituency and elsewhere in Ontario. He manoeuvred sharply and confused issues with skill. He was untroubled by the actual affiliations of the Government of which he was a part. These he dropped, and moved far over to the left where the Tories were working and the votes could be garnered. He played on three themes: that he loved labour and labour loved him (some important Trades Councils endorsed the Liberals); that the Tories were anxious to build a navy to fight in imperialist wars; and that reciprocity could cut the cost of living of the people. As a counterpoint to these themes in his 1911 symphony, he assured the manufacturers in his constituency that there would be no further reduction of tariffs and that reciprocity opened to them the largest protected market in the world.[1]

In June, he prepared a pamphlet on labour as a weapon in the Liberal arsenal. But, "I must confess," he wrote to Graham, "as foreseen by yourself, it is by no means the strongest end of the case"[2] of the Liberal Party. Murdock, Berry and someone named Maloney made themselves available to fight for labour's friend, but they could not give Mackenzie King great help. The most they could do was "volunteer the statement that they thought we could count on the railway vote in St. Thomas".[3] This cold comfort only spurred Mackenzie King on. He extracted a letter of gratitude and support from high officers of the International Brotherhood of Locomotive Engineers,

[1] *Canadian Annual Review*, 1911, pp. 204 ff., 216, 227 ff.
[2] *Graham Papers*, King to Graham, 12 June, 1911.
[3] *Graham Papers*, King to Graham, 4 August, 1911.

"which you are at liberty to use in any way you please."[1] One of the officers of the Telegraphers agreed to speak in support of the Minister of Labour. By the end of August, Mackenzie King was able to organize what he hoped would be a great labour meeting in Berlin. Murdock and Campbell consented to speak. "They are both going to back you and me and the Government very strongly," he told Graham. Mackenzie King wanted to make the meeting a matter of significance throughout the province of Ontario.

> "This meeting should do us untold good through the whole of the province. Having it on Saturday night it should be possible to have it well reported for Monday's papers, and Monday being Labour Day, time will be given for working men throughout the day to peruse the speeches. I have phoned Inwood to send up a first-class shorthand man, and what I think should be done is that the speeches made by Murdock, Campbell and others should be taken down verbatim and later we could get up a leaflet for distribution in the railway centres. This to my mind is very important. Knowing these two men, I feel that the way they will speak here will be sufficient to influence hundreds of votes throughout the province."[2]

The testimony of labour leaders was not Mackenzie King's sole action for the purpose of removing the embarrassment of the strike. At his big meeting he was planning to announce a policy which he believed would please everybody: the workers, the management of the Grand Trunk and even the farmers.

> "I should like to be able to say publicly at the meeting here, that our Government had absolutely refused to pass any legislation for the Grand Trunk Railway at the last session, or do any business with the Company one way or the other until their men were reinstated. Can there be any objection to my saying this? *The Grand Trunk could hardly object, because from their point of view, it would show how determined they were in their stand against the men, which is what they are interested in having known as a means of preventing future trouble.*[3] On the other hand there may be reasons which you and Sir Wilfrid may have, which would make it inadvisable for the statement to be made as broadly as I am putting it here. Please write or wire me at once how far you think I can go. I believe that the statement made boldly that all that has been done for the men and final reinstatement has come about by the Government letting the Railway understand clearly that they need not look for any

---

[1] *Graham Papers*, King to Graham, 5 September, 1911.
[2] *Graham Papers*, King to Graham, 30 August, 1911.
[3] Our italics.

consideration of any sort until they carry out the agreement which was made in the presence of Cabinet Ministers, would do us no end of good with the common people all over the country, farmers as well as working men. Let me know how far I can go?"[1]

Well might Mackenzie King ask his older colleague how far he could go, for he had already committed a very embarrassing indiscretion outside his own field. Speaking to an audience largely composed of Germans or descendants of Germans, who abounded in his constituency, he attempted to introduce German nationalist sentiment into a discussion of defence policy. He is reported to have said:

> "Mr. Borden was prepared to take from the Treasury of the country, and would have taken it if he had been at the head of the Government, enough money to build two Dreadnoughts, to send that money to England telling them to sink it in warships. The amount of money he (Mr. Borden) was prepared to send there, to take out of the Treasury to build warships to fight Germany, was more than was being spent on the whole service which the Liberal Government was constructing and which, when built, would remain around our shores as a protection and not as Jingoes might want to use it."[2]

The Conservative press immediately took up this statement by a Cabinet Minister. No responsible British statesman, and certainly no follower of the Liberal British Prime Minister, Asquith, was proposing "to fight Germany". The Liberal Party was already heavily burdened with the charge that its policy of Reciprocity was a step in the direction of incorporation of Canada into the United States. The suggestion from the lips of a Cabinet Minister that its defence policy would be of potential assistance to a possible enemy of Great Britain was playing squarely into the hands of the Opposition which already had the advantage of exploiting both national and imperial sentiment as well as working class resentment against betrayal.

In the election of 1911, the electors may not have known what they were voting for, but they knew what they were voting against: against incorporation into the United States, against involvement in imperialist rivalries, against the enemies of labour organization and rights; against continued economic

---

[1] *Graham Papers*, King to Graham, 30 August, 1911.
[2] Toronto *News*, 22 August, 1911.

and covert political colonialism; against clerical pretensions; against corruption. The Liberals seemed finished as a force in Canadian history. The Tories had no positive alternative to the Liberals to offer, but they knew how to win. In the industrial centres of Canada the Liberals were all but wiped out. Only the farmers—separated mentally and economically from industrial society—remained faithful in large numbers to the Liberal Party.[1] The Liberals lost the election; Mackenzie King lost not only his Cabinet office but also his seat in the House of Commons.

The young hero's career was apparently in ruins. But his ruin was not complete. That he was able to recover may be attributed to several factors. The failure of the Opposition to uncover his promise to employ strike-breakers was the first element in his recovery. Had this agreement been ferreted out he would never again have been able to pass as labour's friend or to enjoy the confidence of Cabinet colleagues who take their own legislation seriously. The second element in his capacity to recover was the magnitude of his Party's defeat which obscured, completely, his own failure. The third element was the new and seemingly unimportant position he occupied in the Cabinet. Had the Department of Labour enjoyed the status of the Department of Finance and attracted as much attention, incompetence and failure such as Mackenzie King's would have destined him for the Senate in spite of his age. As it was the Opposition jeers about the "boy" Minister provided him with an excuse. He was like Johnson's dog walking on his hind legs. The professionals at the top thus did not feel his shortcomings as sharply as the election agents in the constituencies. Finally, Mackenzie King did not fail in the way Laurier and Fielding had failed. He failed trying new methods appropriate to the age in which he lived. The age of Laurier was over. His colleagues were merely regretting. Mackenzie King was learning, and he was teaching.

[1] As O. D. Skelton described it (*Laurier*, II, p. 380): "In Ontario the Conservative victory had been beyond precedent—72 seats to 14. In Quebec the Liberal majority had fallen from 43 to 11. ... The central prairie provinces had gone strongly Liberal, but Manitoba and British Columbia nearly balanced them." Cf. *Canadian Annual Review*, 1911, p. 265.

CHAPTER VI

For Hire

W e have been told how Mackenzie King spent the time during the last meeting of Sir Wilfrid Laurier's Cabinet, industriously writing to his mother and father about the manner in which his life had been "enriched and strengthened by the lessons learned at the great chief's knee".[1] In the letter, it has been reported, he expressed to his parents the uncertainty he felt about his future together with the conviction that he would return again to the Cabinet room in a position of authority. There is nothing incredible about this letter, for it noticed truly the real condition of his personal circumstances, while expressing what we can begin to see was his abiding ambition and the driving force of his life.

His personal circumstances must have been worrying enough. For him, the years between 1911 and 1919 were his age of anxiety. This anxious time—or at least the better part of it —he depicted to his fellow citizens at a later date as one of personal distress, of family misfortune, of death, of near poverty and of unremitting labour.[2] He considered that during this period in the Roxborough in Ottawa he suffered with all humanity.

"As I look back upon those years, so full of poignant suffering for the whole of mankind, I cannot but experience a sense of gratitude, that in the world ordeal it was given to me to share, in

---

[1] Hutchison, *The Incredible Canadian*, p. 33.
[2] *Debates of the House of Commons*, 1920, Vol. CXLI, pp. 1405 ff.

so intimate a way, the sufferings of others, and with it all, so large a measure of opportunity to do my duty, as God gave it to me to see my duty at that time."

The mortality of his family—the death of his father, and then his mother—he regarded as an aspect of the crucifixion of the human race, and he strove to convert the sorrows which come to every man into things extraordinary, making himself thus a symbol of the tragedy of the people.

In so far as his anxiety during the years after 1911 was rooted in social and political circumstances, it had a sufficiently real foundation. The conduct of his office, during the Grand Trunk strike until the election of 1911, had created so many embarrassments for the Government and had been the source of so much popular revulsion against the Liberal Party that Sir Wilfrid Laurier felt little concern about his young colleague's defeat. King's career had reached a point of crisis more serious than the loss of office and of a constituency to represent. Putting the best face upon things Mackenzie King declared at a banquet in his constituency, a month after the debacle of the Liberal Party, that he "had been offered a seat from Ontario but would not probably re-enter Parliament at present".[1] George P. Graham was in fact the only defeated minister from Ontario for whom a seat could be found in 1912. This required such a struggle that it seems likely that Laurier was dealing out seats only to those he felt he really needed and wanted in Parliament.

It would be profitless to debate whether at this stage of his career Mackenzie King stayed out of Parliament on his own volition or because he could not find a way back into the Commons. The hard fact is that he turned quickly from Federal to Ontario Provincial politics. The Conservative Government of the Province of Ontario decided to take advantage of the strong Tory tide running in the Province and in the nation. A dissolution was recommended, and an election in December, 1911, was announced. The Liberal Opposition found themselves in an unhappy condition, afflicted as they were by a party split between big business elements in Toronto and the agrarian and small business interests of the rural areas. Added to this,

---

[1] *Canadian Annual Review*, 1911, p. 308.

the provincial Liberal leader, A. G. MacKay,* was the object of an unfounded campaign of personal vilification. MacKay was considered a "little man's" leader, and for some reason the alleged personal imperfections of this class of politician have always been easy of discovery in Canada.

Mackenzie King was soon at the centre of the situation created by the dissolution of the Legislature and Mr. MacKay's reputation. Early in October rumours about the possible successor to the Liberal leader in Ontario were flying round. At first only three names were mentioned: N. W. Rowell, K.C.,* a young Toronto lawyer closely connected with metropolitan big business, H. W. Mowat, K.C., another of the same type and J. Walter Curry, K.C., with similar connections. Towards the end of October, there were heard suggestions "in certain quarters that Hon. W. L. Mackenzie King would be an admirable nominee for the position".[1] On October 31st, 1911, the Ontario Reform Association, 300 strong, met to consider Mr. MacKay's resignation. A compromise was reached: the Association expressed great confidence in Mr. MacKay and accepted his resignation. He emerged from the meeting with his reputation and without the leadership. A Committee was appointed to select a new leader.

While the Committee was at work the Association listened to an appeal to increase the preference for British goods in the tariff schedules and to fight more thoroughly against the Liquor Demon. Then a new slate of officers was elected. Mackenzie King secured the presidency of the General Reform Association. Obviously he had failed to get the leadership. The Committee reported to the Association that Newton Wesley Rowell had been selected to lead the Party in the Provincial Legislature.

Newton Wesley Rowell was one of the important *dramatis personae* of Mackenzie King's career: a figure both to imitate and to avoid. He was a few years older than Mackenzie King. He possessed mental powers equal or superior to those of the new president of the Reform Association. He was, however, a better articulated example than Mackenzie King of the Ontario bourgeois, generated by the commercial and industrial expansion of that province. Rowell had an acute mind; he was technically accomplished; and he wanted utterly in imagina-

[1] *Canadian Annual Review*, 1911, p. 461.

tion, human sympathy and warmth. He was a prohibitionist. "Rowell is a man of eminent parts and abilities," Laurier once wrote, "but his personality does not seem to have gone deep into the community. What he has of influence seems to arise from the fact that the big interests have pinned their faith on him and push him; and in return he will be the champion of the big interests. . . ."[1]

For the ordinary purposes of campaigning, Rowell was well equipped. He and his new lieutenant, Mackenzie King, threw themselves into the election with enthusiasm. Rowell appears to have borrowed some weapons from his lieutenant's arsenal, for he talked freely about the need for social reform. When pressed to define his terms he revealed that he meant by social reform the closing of bars and the corking of bottles. Mackenzie King, on the other hand, abandoned his high line about composing the tensions in society. Instead, he broadcast grass-roots propaganda. His speech at Whitby, Ontario, affords us a fair sample of his work during his withdrawal from the federal scene.

> "I want to refer to the Prime Minister's (Sir James Whitney's) statement that we could not find any flaws in his Administration with a microscope. It doesn't take a microscope to discover over 1,000 teachers in this Province teaching without certificates. It doesn't take a microscope to see that there are 75,000 fewer farmers on the lands of this Province than there were ten years ago. It doesn't take a microscope to see that the cost of living has gone up in consequence. . . . It doesn't require a magnifying glass to discover 2,000,000 acres of land given away to the Canadian Northern Railway."[2]

The combined fury of Rowell and Mackenzie King was insufficient to dislodge the Ontario Tories. They won the election. The ex-Minister of Labour had almost become an ex-politician with no office, no profession and no official income.

The lack of a substantial salary was probably disturbing to a man so long used to one of the higher incomes provided from the public purse. When he had abandoned his civil service post for open political activity in the parliamentary arena, he appears to have given some thought to an alternative profession. Shortly after his election as the Member for North Waterloo in

[1] *Laurier Papers*, Laurier to Graham, 22 February, 1918.
[2] *Canadian Annual Review*, 1911, p. 469.

1908, he wrote to Harvard about the possibility of receiving his Ph.D. degree, the preliminary work for which he had performed nine years previously. A Ph.D. degree is of little use to a Member of Parliament, but it is all but indispensable for anyone seeking a place in the higher ranges of the North American academic hierarchy. When Mackenzie King was out of office this flirtation with academic life did not ripen into a liaison with any university. He was mentioned as a possible Principal of Queen's University at Kingston in 1914,[1] but tactics *à la* Wilson never unfolded themselves.

He later described himself during this period as "a journalist at present [who] takes an interest in public affairs".[2] He contrived to keep himself in the public eye rather more than the average journalist, however. In February, 1912, the Liberals found they had to put up a hard fight to seat the Hon. George P. Graham in the constituency of South Renfrew. Four former Liberal Ministers went into the constituency on Graham's behalf as well as a platoon of Liberal Members of Parliament. Finally, on February 19th, Sir Wilfrid Laurier appeared at Eganville, the principal town in the constituency. Mackenzie King appeared, too, on the same day. The ex-Minister of Labour was, of course, invited to mount the same platform as Laurier. Graham just managed to win the by-election.

When he heard the final result of the election of 1911, Robert Borden, the leader of the victorious party, described the sharp swing of electoral support away from the Liberal Party as "a triumph of the Canadian people rather than of any political party".[3] There was more wisdom than conventional propaganda in this statement; for it revealed Borden's grasp of the fact that there existed among the Canadian people a movement of opinion, which had neither been manufactured by nor was in the control of either of the traditional political parties. Borden was beset from the moment of his victory by two general classes of problem. The more immediate and personally troublesome were created by the pressure of various interests anxious to put their agents into key posts such as that of the

---

[1] *Willison Papers*, King to Willison, 12 November, 1914.
[2] *R.C.I.R.*, p. 713.
[3] *Canadian Annual Review*, 1911, p. 265.

Department of Finance.[1] The more profound and long range ones concerned the general response of the Conservative and Nationalist victors in the election to the seismic movement within Canadian society. On the manner in which the Conservatives and Nationalists adjusted their thinking and constructed their policies depended the future of the Conservative Party—and the Liberal Party no less.

Borden's response to the election of 1911 was initially very intelligent, and pregnant with the promise that in him Canada had found a new prophet uncompromised by Mammon and Moloch. The perilous and bitter strike of miners in Alberta and British Columbia was brought quickly to an end, to the temporary satisfaction of both parties. The new Minister of Labour, the Hon. T. W. Crothers,* kicked the Grand Trunk management until they moved in the matter of taking men off their black list. In the House, Mr. Crothers declared,

> "that the time is not far distant when it would be the duty of this Parliament to provide means whereby a quasi-public institution like the Grand Trunk Railway Company can be compelled to treat its employees fairly and decently and to carry out the agreements they make with those employees, just as one individual is compelled to carry out his agreement with another individual."[2]

Instead of orating on the responsibilities of labour to capital and the need for industrial peace in the style of Mackenzie King, Crothers stressed in his public utterances the right of labour to organize. The working class had just as much right and as much need to organize as the middle class. "Lawyers are banded together, of course, for the benefit of their clients" he declared sarcastically; "doctors are a close corporation to promote the health of their patients; Manufacturers' Associations exist—for the advantage of the consumer . . . and even ministers of the Gospel have established a minimum wage and a retiring allowance! And is the working man to be seriously told that he is to be deprived of the advantage of organization?"[3]

During the first session of the new Parliament action was taken to dismantle the Liberal Party machine in the Civil Service, to replace it with a non-partisan service based on merit,

---

[1] See W. S. Wallace, *The Memoirs of the Rt. Hon. Sir George Foster* (Toronto, 1933), Chapter XIII, for an account of the prolonged jockeying of the interests.
[2] *Debates of the House of Commons*, 1911–12, Vol. IV, p. 6574.
[3] *Canadian Annual Review*, 1912, p. 194.

and to transform the Civil Service Commission from a promise of neutrality and competence into a reality. A Board of Grain Commissioners was established to introduce some degree of rationality and justice into the marketing of cereal grains. A vain effort was made to take tariff issues out of politics by appointing a Tariff Commission. Springtime promise sweetened the new Parliament. The blight and drought were yet to come. But these were matters of comparatively minor importance when placed beside the portentous and genuinely political questions facing the Borden Government.

The increasing momentum of the Great Powers in the direction of war, generated the gravest anxieties in the Canadian people. The Liberal Party, assuring the people they must defend themselves amid the perils of which they were not the authors, had embarked the nation upon a course of participation in the armament race of the Great Powers. The Liberal Party had been repudiated. Giving too much credit to the obscurantist, Nationalist elements of Quebec, Liberal apologists have depicted the resistance to Liberal policies as the work of a narrow clique of French-speaking fanatics cynically financed by wealthy Tory business interests.[1] This was far from being the whole case. The anxiety concerning the armament policy of the Liberal Party and the resistance to it had spread, by 1911, far beyond the confines of Quebec. In 1911 and 1912, the number of pacifist and socialist resolutions before the annual meetings of the Trades and Labour Congress greatly increased, and in 1912 the Congress appealed to the British labour movement to stop the drift towards war. Expressions of concern were as outspoken and as frequent in the farmers' movement in western Canada.[2] Henri Bourassa* spoke no more clearly and no more decisively against involvement in the armaments race and war than many other Canadians.

Borden and some of his chief lieutenants, such as Sir George Foster, were willing personally to accept and to carry out the policy of building a Canadian Navy as provided for in Laurier's Naval Service Act of 1910. They recognized, however, that no

[1] e.g. Skelton, *Laurier*, Vol. II, Chapter XV, and A. R. M. Lower, *Colony to Nation* (Toronto, 1946), pp. 449 ff., etc.
[2] Paul F. Sharp, *The Agrarian Revolt in Western Canada* (Minneapolis, 1948), pp. 75 ff.

part of Laurier's policy had been more strongly repudiated by the electors than his Canadian Navy and that some alternative had to be found. Carrying out the general will of the people was one alternative, but the Conservative Party was not a people's party. In any event Robert Laird Borden and his colleagues were as little equipped to discover the general will as Sir Wilfrid Laurier. Borden's Minister of Trade and Commerce once summed up the duty of a politician as men like the Conservative leaders understood it: to "impress the men he must lead to victory or defeat, and the masses who are to be moulded".[1] That being their conception of duty, it is not surprising that in place of attempting to discover the real will of the Canadian people, they attempted to discover a compromise between the men they had to lead and the masses they had to mould.

This compromise required a long time to devise. Those elements in society in the grip of the dynamic towards war were strong in both the Liberal and Conservative Party. Those with the most foresight, surveying their needs and interests and the best methods of achieving them, were inclined to the policies of Laurier. A defence in depth was the Empire's need. It was, as Mackenzie King expressed it at Belleville in April, 1912, a policy of "building up a real Empire with Great Britain as the centre, but all the parts establishing centres of naval strength". To the Liberal Senator, Lieut.-Col. James Domville,* its principal attraction was the provision of men it made to the armament of the Empire; for Britain had money and ships or shipyards but might well be short of manpower in time of crisis.[2] But the chief attraction of Laurier's naval policy, according to the Liberal Leader in the Senate, Sir George Ross,* was the fact that it habituated the Canadian people to the idea of armaments and fighting; it "blooded" them. And it was good for business. ". . . A comprehensive scheme", he wrote to the Conservative leader in the Senate, Sir James Lougheed,* "for the development of a Canadian Navy would make a fresh appeal to the people of Canada in every annual estimate taken for its maintenance, in every shipyard built for its construction and in every ship launched for national defence."[3] Leading

---

[1] Wallace, *Memoirs of . . . Foster*, p. 171.

[2] *Canadian Annual Review*, 1912, p. 65.

[3] Quoted in H. Borden (ed.), *Robert Laird Borden: His Memoirs* (London and Toronto, 1938). Vol. I, p. 418.

Conservatives like Borden and Foster did not disagree with these views. In Great Britain, such views were warmly entertained by Winston Churchill, then First Lord of the Admiralty.

The advent of the Conservative Party to office created alarm in the ranks of the Liberal imperialists. Sir Wilfrid Laurier preserved silence, waiting to see what the Government would do. But Prime Minister Borden preserved silence too. In February, the Haldane Mission to Berlin in search of German consent to British naval superiority returned empty-handed. In March, the new German Naval Bill was announced. The anxiety felt in Great Britain soon communicated itself to Canada, and the English language press in Montreal and Toronto began to blossom forth with war scares. The Government still said nothing, although rumours began to seep through the red baize doors of the East Block on Parliament Hill that the Government intended to abandon Laurier's policy.

In April, Mackenzie King was apparently put up by the imperialists to denounce the Government. At Belleville, he attacked Prime Minister Borden for doing nothing, and called attention to the many excellencies of Sir Wilfrid Laurier's naval policy. Pressure of this kind and attempts to arouse the electorate against the Government produced no result. The first session of the new Parliament came to a close without the Prime Minister showing his hand. Early in the summer he and three Cabinet colleagues set out for Britain in an endeavour to discover there some wisdom or some excuse.

By the mid-summer of 1912 it was becoming plain to the imperialists in the Liberal Party that Laurier's naval policy was in danger, and that Prime Minister Borden might have to adopt a less satisfactory policy under pressure from his Nationalist colleagues and out of an affectation of popularity. They proposed to help Borden out of his difficulty. On August 7th, 1912, Mr. J. Frank Beer, a Liberal industrialist of Toronto, issued an invitation to a private dinner party. Sir Edmund Walker, of the Canadian Bank of Commerce was invited, so was Senator R. Jaffray,* the proprietor of the Liberal Toronto *Globe*. The editor of the *Globe*, Dr. J. A. Macdonald,* also attended. J. E. Atkinson, the Pulitzer and Harmsworth of Canada, who owned the Toronto *Daily Star*, was likewise invited. Newton Wesley Rowell was, of course, there. And there were pork-packers and railway-promoters. After an abundance of food, water and talk the dinner party resolved,

> "(1) that in the existing international situation it is desirable that the Naval policy of Canada should be a national policy supported by all parties; (2) that in order to achieve this result the Prime Minister and Leader of the Opposition should be asked to meet, before any public announcement of the Government policy is made, and discuss whether an agreed policy cannot be submitted to Parliament and the nation."[1]

Some of the diners, such as Dr. J. A. Macdonald, refused to support the resolution, but the majority did. A memorial[2] embodying the idea of a "non-partisan" armaments policy was devised. An inspector of one of the big Canadian Banks was deputed to spread the gospel of armaments in western Canada. Eventually a mixed company of bishops, newspaper editors (including the Liberal, J. W. Dafoe), provincial politicians, stock-brokers, meat canners, and half-pay officers were induced to sign the memorial.

Meanwhile Prime Minister Borden was making his inquiries in Britain. According to the late Dr. O. D. Skelton,[3] Borden was subjected to a series of temptations while he was in Great Britain, and he yielded. It is a peculiarity of the provincial mind to believe that innocent Canadians, when they visit metropolitan centres like New York or London, are liable to lose their virtue. The sight of "towering battleships, hovering aeroplanes" and the "ducal banquets and royal garden parties"[3] are the apples which cause our fall. Undoubtedly Robert Laird Borden was, in the phrase employed by one of his colleagues, "a sucker for a duchess", but he was also a shrewd and canny politician.

He went to Britain seeking from the British Government some confirmation of the danger proclaimed in the popular press. In a meeting of the Imperial Defence Committee, Sir Edward Grey did not reveal what Borden subsequently learned, namely, that in certain circumstances Britain was committed to go to war in alliance with France. Churchill was prepared to

---

[1] *Canadian Annual Review*, 1912, pp. 44–45.
[2] The part played by J. W. Dafoe in drawing up this document is shown in his correspondence with Atkinson during this period. See *Dafoe Papers* in the Public Archives, Ottawa.
[3] Skelton, *Laurier*, Vol. II, p. 396.

give Borden a statement in writing that the situation was serious from Britain's point of view, but when the Admiralty produced a document for Borden and the Canadian Cabinet it turned out to be a routine piece of information based on the assumption that the Canadians ought to do their duty and mind their own business. Borden told Churchill that this document was entirely inadequate. Churchill agreed to give him something better, and just before the Canadian Prime Minister sailed for home he "received from him a confidential memorandum respecting the naval situation which had been prepared with great care and illustrated his wonderful ability".[1] Whether this document represented the seduction of Robert Laird Borden is difficult to say.

At home in Canada, Laurier was attempting to devise a policy adequate to the circumstances in which he found himself after the election of 1911. Until the imperialist wing of his party put a gun to his head in August, 1912, he had been content to wait for something to turn up. He had no policy on labour, and apart from relegating his Minister of Labour to provincial politics did nothing to repair the damage done to his Party in this quarter. Reciprocity he proposed to play with the soft pedal jammed down hard. He described his policy thus:

> "After the election of 1911, I found myself surrounded in the House of Commons by very thinned ranks. My associates were Graham, Guthrie,* Pardee* from Ontario; Macdonald,* McKenzie,* Sinclair, Pugsley and Carvell* from the East; and from the West Oliver,* Turriff,* Thomson, Buchanan* and the whole group of western Liberals. There was immediately a line of cleavage between them: Graham, Guthrie, Pardee, Macdonald holding that we should drop Reciprocity; the others still clinging to their former views. I took the ground then that we should not give up Reciprocity, though at that time there was no reason to ostentatiously putting (sic) it forward, and that policy maintained all through the last parliament."[2]

If Reciprocity and integration in the American orbit were buried with slow music, the obsequies of his naval policy were delayed. Mistakes were going to be made and Laurier wanted Borden to make them. But the imperialists in his own party compelled him to embark upon the slow and painful process of making a decision.

[1] Borden: *Memoirs*, Vol. I, p. 365.
[2] *Laurier Papers*, Laurier to Smith, 24 September, 1918.

Following the dinner party of August 7th, 1912, Laurier summoned to him some of his English-speaking colleagues: the Hon. Sydney Fisher,* the Hon. Charles Murphy* and the Hon. Sir Frederick Borden. On August 16th, 1912, the Liberal organ in the capital, *The Ottawa Free Press*, announced that Sir Wilfrid Laurier had decided that he would take no part in a conference on naval policy with Prime Minister Borden. This decision was probably the most important in the history of the Liberal Party in the last half century. It marked its resurrection.

At first Laurier gyrated, as if the very sharpness of his vision had affected the delicate mechanism of his brain. A few days after taking the decision not to meet the Prime Minister he veered sharply towards total pacifism. "Thank God," he declared in Ottawa, "Canada shall never go into it [the armaments race] to settle her differences. In England you think of armaments and war; in Canada we think of Canals and Railways and Public Works." A few days after making this statement he veered back to "a navy for the Empire". "We want a Canadian Navy, but if England were in danger every Canadian would assist the Motherland."[1] In September there was a by-election in the constituency of Hochelaga in the province of Quebec. In the presence of the electors of Hochelaga he played his cards very close to his waistcoat, declaring that he did not wish to propose any policy on armaments until he had learned the intentions of the Prime Minister.

These intentions were made known to the public in December. Prime Minister Borden's compromise between the anxieties of the Canadian people on the question of armaments and the demands of the supporters of arms took the form of a flat contribution of $35,000,000 for the provision of three dreadnoughts, which the British Admiralty would build, man and dispose of as the Lords Commissioners saw fit. Henri Bourassa had charged that "to a tribute of gold Sir Wilfrid Laurier wished to add that of blood".[2] In his eyes the merit of Borden's policy consisted in the fact that Borden did not "desire to fill these Dreadnoughts with human cargoes as food for guns". None of the Parliamentary politicians—Borden, Bourassa or Laurier—were willing to fall into line with the

---

[1] *Canadian Annual Review*, 1912, p. 41.
[2] *Canadian Annual Review*, 1912, p. 43.

popular sentiment. They all were seeking a palatable form for the dose the Canadian people were being asked to swallow. Of the proposals made, those of Borden appeared upon analysis to be the most limited in their scope and the least helpful in their probable consequences to the cause of Empire. They certainly did not appear to be the product of a great imperialist seduction, an abandonment of Canadian autonomy and a humble submission to the dictates of London as the Liberal propagandists sought to make out. The vast and rapidly changing inconsistencies of all the parties to the argument derived from one source: the common unwillingness of them all, whether Liberals, Nationalists or Conservatives, to do simply the majority will of the electors: to abandon attempts to join in the game of power politics and "to mind Canada's own business".

Before the electors, dismayed by the cost of armaments and the prospect of bloodshed, Laurier and the Liberal Party found it advantageous to speak in accents of pacifism underlining their wholesome love of peace and constructive activity. These were the things they said while "moulding the masses". But in talking seriously among professional politicians in Parliament neither Sir Wilfrid Laurier nor his colleague, Sir George Ross, who led the Liberal Party in the Senate, criticized Borden for doing too much on behalf of imperialism. There, and in their private correspondence and discussions, they emphasized the reality of Borden's policy: that it was a policy less helpful to the Empire than Laurier's; that it had serious drawbacks as a policy of mobilizing the full resources of the Empire for war. ". . . If England were on trial with one or two or more great powers of Europe, my right honourable friend might come and ask, not for $35,000,000, but twice, three times, four times $35,000,000. We would put at the disposal of England all the resources of Canada. . . ."[1] Sir George Ross offered to pass the Conservative bill through the Senate if Borden would consent to the creation of a Canadian navy in addition to a gift of $35,000,000. The supreme defect of Borden's policy in Ross's view was the establishment of so weak an imperial connection as a cash link "which exalts British protection against Canadian self-reliance, the outcome of which will be that a Canadian spirit will grow

[1] Quoted in Skelton, *Laurier*, Vol. II, p. 400.

up to assert its entire independence of Imperial support and thus weaken the Imperial connection. . . ."[1]

Laurier, too, was both an imperial statesman appealing to men with power and a politician moulding the masses. In this latter capacity he recognized the advantages to be derived for his party from a refusal to help Borden realize the policy of which he himself was the author and advocate, i.e. arming Canada. Instead of joining forces with Borden to isolate the nationalists, socialists and pacifists and to create a Canadian Navy, he chose the course of inviting Borden to fight the nationalists and anti-imperialist elements in his own Party or to hang on to that Party's flanks. He kept for himself a free hand: freedom to engage in anti-imperialist policies. The preservation of this freedom constituted the resurrection of the Liberal Party. It was the work of Sir Wilfrid Laurier. In the moment of his agony of decision he had called to him followers such as Fisher and Murphy whom he could rely upon to give the answer he wanted and to support it. Looking back upon this decision and the events which followed it we can see that it set the course of the Liberal Party once more in a popular direction and enabled it to resist successfully the "union government" movement in 1917 and to come through the election of 1921 with increased strength. Since August 1912, the Liberal Party has never made another serious or important decision so capable of affecting its destiny or its opportunity for manoeuvre.

It was this which largely prevented the growth in Canada of a popular anti-imperialist party uniting together nationalists, socialists, radicals and pacifists around a Canadian flag. The more Borden and his colleagues were obliged to carry the burden of responsibility for armaments and war, the more the Liberal Party was able to appear before the people as their undefiled saviour. Thus an economy of enterprise was worked out by which the Liberals got the votes and the Tories the blame, while both pursued a policy so identical as to be indistinguishable. The difference, perhaps, was that the Liberal policy involved a more shrewdly conceived and thoroughgoing mobilization of the Canadian economy and people for war.

[1] Quoted from a letter of Sir George Ross printed in Borden: *Memoirs*, Vol. I, p. 419.

While Sir Wilfrid Laurier was devising this last stroke of high political strategy Mackenzie King was off stage. He had developed a singular talent for turning up where he thought history was being made. He had managed to secure an invitation to Washington, while the official Canadian delegation was in conference with President Taft preparing the abortion of Reciprocity. Now he turned up in London just as Prime Minister Borden and his colleagues were departing to present to the Canadian people their ill-fated compromise on imperial armaments. He appeared in London in response to an invitation to discuss conciliation legislation and its enforcement. He circulated around the drawing rooms as well as the settlement houses. The season of royal garden parties had passed by the time of his arrival and the duchesses were in the country. By the Skeltonian calculus he was safe. But he was himself bent upon being seduced; for he desired nothing less than graduation to the British House of Commons. Some years later the Hon. Charles Murphy, Laurier's Postmaster-General, described this event as follows:

"While the Liberals under Sir Wilfrid were in opposition and King was out of Parliament, he resolved to shake the dust of Canada off his shoes, and let others rebuild the party. Accordingly he sought a new political job in England. There he interviewed Sir Donald MacLean, the then Liberal leader of the British House of Commons, as to his prospects of getting a seat at Westminster, but he failed, as Sir Donald saw through him at a glance. Narrating their conversation Sir Donald stated that King had called on him at the House of Commons and said: 'Our future in Canada seems very uncertain. I am inclined to seek Liberal fortune in the Old Country. What do you advise me to do?' Sir Donald's advice in substance was to go back to Canada and work."[1]

When Murphy related this episode he hated Mackenzie King most cordially, but his account is quite credible because he possessed probably the most intimate connection of any Canadian politician with the British Liberal leaders of the time, such as Asquith's Chairman of Committees, Sir Donald MacLean. Murphy was an Irish Home Ruler whose papers reveal a long, intimate and confidential relationship with a section of the British Liberal Party, and it is unlikely that he

[1] *Murphy Papers*, Murphy to Quinlan, 24 May, 1932.

simply invented the incident, although his hatred may have embroidered the conversation.

For some reason which we have been unable to discover Mackenzie King was, during 1912, very unhappy about his place in Canadian politics and about the general nature of their development. Writing to Laurier in 1917, A. C. Hardy* told Laurier, cryptically: "King . . . and I were betrayed in 1912."[1] Something happened in the Liberal Party in 1912 about which the word "betrayal" was freely used by a variety of people, often of the most opposed inclinations and ideas. The nature of the betrayal is not clear from the correspondence. Unfortunately it was always spoken of in such recondite language, that persons unacquainted with the private language of the Liberal back rooms find it difficult to translate their exchanges into understandable English. In 1918 Alexander Smith,* a lawyer, lobbyist and Liberal organizer of Ottawa (the author of the myth that "the Old Chief looked beyond the incidents of the moment and had the future very clearly in view when he chose Mackenzie King to be his Minister of Labour")[2] wrote a long letter to Laurier complaining about the "old gang", "the Committee you surrounded yourself by after 1911."[3] Smith was a Party friend of Mackenzie King. In so far as he condescended to speak plainly to Laurier on the subject of "old gangism" in language comprehensible to third parties, he referred to the "old gang's" responsibility "for the great offence caused by the Liberal Information Office", of which Mackenzie King was appointed the director in 1912. On the other hand, the Hon. Charles Murphy, who was apparently a member of the "old gang", referred bitterly to "Rowell and his gang . . . who betrayed the Party, not only once but twice, namely in 1911 and again in 1917".[4]

There are many at present inexplicable aspects of this free use of the words "betrayal", "old gangs" and treachery in connection with the inner history of the Liberal Party during 1911–12. Laurier himself professed to know nothing about the trouble. Replying to Smith's accusations of "old gangism" Laurier asked Smith to particularize. For his part Laurier

---

[1] *Laurier Papers*, Hardy to Laurier, 21 December, 1917.
[2] O. E. McGillicuddy, *The Making of a Premier* (Toronto, 1922), p. 54.
[3] *Laurier Papers*, Smith to Laurier, 23 September, 1918.
[4] *Murphy Papers*, Murphy to Carr, 22 March, 1927.

knew of only one split in the party in 1912: the division of sentiment on the subject of Reciprocity.[1] To the conspiracies of the imperialist wing of the Party, he chose to turn a blind eye in discussions with Smith, who was a protagonist of something called "Ontario management" without which, according to Smith, the Liberal Party could never flourish. For some reason Laurier always refused to be drawn into a discussion involving Mackenzie King's long-standing difficulties with the personalities among the Ontario Liberals.

As far as we can ascertain, Mackenzie King's appointment as director of the Liberal Information Office some time in 1912 brought him into the centre of an inner party controversy. Apparently it was a controversy not directly about policies but about the control of the second level of the party leadership. Laurier was a man of extraordinarily great power over his Party followers. But he was an old man by 1912, and in the nature of things a struggle for the succession was in the making. To capture the second level of command, to hold the strategic position between the leader and the rank and file was obviously a matter of great importance to the various and often divergent elements within the Party. The evidence seems to suggest that the interests centred in Toronto, which had pushed Rowell into the Liberal leadership in Ontario, were working hard to establish a parallel centre of power in Ottawa with the object of selecting Laurier's successor without reference to the Old Chief's views.

Perhaps the sharp repudiation of the diners of August 7th by Laurier was the occasion for Mackenzie King's autumnal despair concerning Canadian Liberalism. Whatever the occasion and the cause, Mackenzie King was obliged to return to his native land in late November, 1912, and to take up once more the struggle for a career. The situation required the delicacy of a ballet dancer and the same ease of turning. Rowell was denouncing Borden for not giving men as well as money to Britain. "I cannot but confess my own great regret", he told a Montreal audience, "that Canada is not manning and maintaining, as well as giving, these dreadnoughts."[2] Mackenzie King, however, pirouetted to the left. Speaking also in Montreal he said the same thing as Rowell, but he said it in a more ambiguous

---

[1] *Laurier Papers*, Laurier to Smith, 24 September, 1918.
[2] *Canadian Annual Review*, 1912, p. 41.

fashion employing phrases which might have been picked from the speeches and writings of Henri Bourassa. The Government's policy he described as one of "tribute which would lead to the ruin which befell the Roman Empire". It was "fraught with infinite danger". The speech left the impression that he was opposing Borden from the left; an analysis of his imagery, however, reveals that he was opposing him because Borden was not mobilizing sufficiently an overseas dominion of the Empire. When we examine Mackenzie King's activities in 1912, we can readily understand how it was that, in 1918, Senator Sir George Ross, Senator Domville, A. C. Hardy and Alexander Smith became his advocates in the presence of Sir Wilfrid Laurier.

In the spring of 1913, Mackenzie King took a step along the road of return to federal politics. In March, he received the Liberal nomination in the constituency of North York, which his grandfather had once represented. In his speech of acceptance he revealed the first signs of movement away from support for Rowell's argument that the times required of the Canadian people money, materials and men. He told the Liberals of North York there was no defence emergency and he implied that nothing need be done. But he claimed to be very "loyal", and charged that Mr. Borden "has handed himself over body and bones to a group of men in England who say that when men leave the old land and go to the Colonies to build homes for themselves their loyalty cannot be trusted".[1]

This renewal of a formal connection with federal politics together with his directorship of the Central Liberal Information Office in Ottawa brought Mackenzie King more directly under the influence of Laurier and the men immediately about him and removed him in some degree from the influences of the "Ontario management". While he was director of the Information Office and in charge of its day-to-day work, the Office was under the control of a committee consisting of Laurier, Fisher, Graham, Lemieux, Murphy and himself. In the preparation of certain material such as an omnibus pamphlet on naval policy, another committee of Liberal members of Parliament was associated with Mackenzie King in the work of composition and editing. Working thus, surrounded by men expressing the fine

[1] *Canadian Annual Review*, 1913, pp. 282–3.

M

differences on policy of the top leadership of the Liberal Party, but removed from the bold differences freely emphasized in Toronto by men like Rowell, Mackenzie King was obliged to develop a delicacy of touch and a capacity already considerable for combining in one package serious contradictions of policy.

The first activities of the Office in 1912–13 consisted of publishing, in pamphlet form, the thoughts of the Liberal leaders or detailed accounts of notorious Conservative scandals. Altogether fourteen pamphlets were published between the establishment of the Office and the commencement of the publication of *The Liberal Monthly* in September, 1913. The first was a speech of Sir Wilfrid Laurier delivered ten years previously, setting forth the harmonious ideals of the Liberal never-never land. The second dealt with a more concrete subject: Newton Wesley Rowell's advocacy of an armaments policy for Canada. "In the matter of naval defence the time for talking is past," Rowell argued,

"the time for action has come. We should be ashamed to permit the people of Great Britain—financially burdened as they are and continue to be in working out great measures of social reform for the benefit of the masses of the people—to not only bear their own burden of naval defence, but to bear ours as well. Our action should be prompt, not because of any so-called 'emergency', but because action is overdue, and our own self-respect will no longer permit us to let the mother country bear our responsibilities. Our action should be adequate, commensurate with our ability and our share of the burden. Our policy should not be the product of a momentary enthusiasm or of unworthy fear, but as part of a permanent and well-considered plan whereby Canada will undertake her share in the defence of the Empire. Let our policy not be formed by or shaped in response to the spirit of militarism. Our Navy is not for aggression, but for the defence of our coasts and the protection of our trade routes; for the maintenance of the traditions and ideals for which our British system of government and our flag stand."[1]

Twelve of the fourteen pamphlets and leaflets published by the Central Information Office were devoted to aspects of the armaments policy, and ten of them advocated Rowell's brand of "nationalist" imperialism; of armaments adorned with

[1] N. W. Rowell, *Liberals and the Empire*, Publication No. 2 of the Central Information Office of the Liberal Party of Canada.

garlands of maple leaves. The flow of "information" of this description finally provoked an explosion on the part of one member of the committee in charge of the Office, the Hon. Charles Murphy. Murphy was both a liberal and a Liberal. He hated imperialism in the style of an Irish Home Ruler with all the intensity of his Catholic ancestors. He hated both the people who used the big battalions and the fruits of their work. In June, 1913, he wrote to Laurier:

> "The other matter which I wish to bring to your notice again is one I spoke about during the Session. It is this:—that when we are proclaiming Canadianism in the House, another branch of the Party should not be professing in our names, an objectionable brand of Imperialism in the country. So far as that is done by newspapers calling themselves Liberal we may be without remedy, but they do not speak in your name, and consequently their views bind nobody. And besides they would soon drop the role if they found they were the only ones playing it. But the case is different when letters or literature go out from the Central Office apparently under your authority (but not really so) which contain much about Imperialism and little or nothing about Canadianism. Criticism on this score is not by any means confined to Catholic Liberals. I have heard it many times from English Protestant Liberals whose names I could give you. In point of fact the McLarens, the Campbells, the Daws, the McArthurs, the Craigs and hundreds of other Scotch Presbyterian Liberals in my County have expressed exactly the same views."

Murphy was not satisfied with the business capacity of the management of the Information Office. "After reading thus far," he continued,

> "you would be quite justified in asking me how do I propose to remedy these things as you have no time to attend to them, and in any event should not be asked to do so. My answer is—hire the $10,000 a year man we have discussed so often and haven't yet found. It is true some enquiries have been made but as Sir Frederick Borden remarked in your room one day, 'nobody has ever put on his hat and coat on a Monday morning and said—'I am going to find that man before Saturday night.' That's the situation exactly. The enquiries made have been in a haphazard way and generally in the wrong place. To repeat my opinion of what such a man ought to be:—He should be a Liberal, a Canadian, a Protestant, a business man with organizing capacity, and a judge of human nature so that he may choose his staff wisely. Such a man would see that there was complete harmony between the Party's policy in the country, and he could give the

Party in the country the individuality you have given it in the House. Once I named Murray of the Manufacturers' Association as the man. For some reason, never made clear to me, he wouldn't do. . . .

"As an earnest of my desire to engage such a man, as well as my belief in what such a man can accomplish, I will, in the event of a proper man being secured, undertake to collect $2,500.00 per year from the date of his engagement until the date of the next general election—such amount to be applied in part payment of his salary."[1]

This explosion did not blow Mackenzie King out of the Central Information Office nor did it at once dislodge his friends nor the "Ontario management". In September, 1913, the first number of *The Liberal Monthly* appeared. Mackenzie King was the editor. Unlike the *Labour Gazette*, *The Liberal Monthly* did not spread his name conspicuously in the foreground. Indeed, his name did not appear anywhere to advertise his connection with the central propaganda organ of the Party.

By the time of the appearance of *The Liberal Monthly* the Borden Government had been in office for nearly two years. These two years had witnessed many changes. Prosperity was waning rapidly. Unemployment was growing steadily, while the long price rise of the Laurier epoch continued. The number of strikes began to increase. On the other hand the question of armaments was temporarily shelved by the Senate's rejection of Borden's naval policy. Anxiety about absorption by the United States had all but disappeared. The only attack which the Liberals could make upon the Conservatives was from the left. This they proceeded to do.

Laurier ceased to fight for his naval policy. The Leader of the Liberal majority in the Senate had offered Borden to pass the Government legislation to give Great Britain $35,000,000 for three dreadnoughts, if Borden would promise to build a Canadian Navy in addition to "buying" dreadnoughts for Britain. Borden had replied that he would seriously consider such a course if Sir Wilfrid Laurier would back Sir George Ross's offer. This Laurier refused to do. Thus, the way was clear for Laurier to move leftward and to attack the Tories as an "imperialist" government and a tool of "the big interests".

The Liberal Monthly was a political organ of an extremely low

[1] *Murphy Papers*, Murphy to Laurier, 20 and 21 June, 1913.

intellectual level. As propaganda it was, however, not without merit. The articles were short, clear and within the limits of their banality often amusing. The cartoons were badly drawn, but their points were made beyond mistake. Golf was popularly regarded at that time as a game played by decadent anglophiles. Therefore, Mr. Borden was frequently depicted as a golfer, or reports of his latest visit to the links were published. When he visited New York and spoke at the Lotus Club on a Sunday evening, the pious provincials of Canada were slyly advised to note that the Tory Prime Minister was in New York; that he had visited a club with an interesting and decadent name; that he had spoken on Sunday; that an English actor had dined with him there. What the Prime Minister actually said was misquoted and misinterpreted. Likewise, when the Minister of Defence visited England a complete enumeration of his entourage was reported including the information that he was accompanied by two lady secretaries.

Under Mackenzie King's editorship *The Liberal Monthly* stressed the high cost of living, unemployment, and the corrupt alliance between the Conservative Party and "the big interests". War and armaments were discussed along two lines: war and armaments were a racket of the big interests,[1] and the threat of war was a Tory bogy. Peace was, in fact, just around the corner. But there were a number of interesting subthemes harped upon in the first volume of *The Liberal Monthly*. The Minister of Labour, the Hon. T. W. Crothers, was singled out for attack. If Mr. Crothers travelled he was attacked for junketing about the country at the expense of the taxpayers. If he stayed at home, he was attacked for neglecting his duties. "Meanwhile," wrote the anonymous editor of *The Liberal Monthly*,

". . . the report of the Royal Commission on Technical Education and Industrial Training, appointed under the Laurier Government at the instance of Hon. Mackenzie King, is blandly pigeonedholed by Mr. Crothers. The report of the Commission gives the groundwork for the most important piece of constructive legislation in the interests alike of Labour and Capital that any statesman of vision and courage holding the portfolio of Labour could desire. Mr. Crothers and the Government are willing to send thirty-five millions to London for Naval defence but unwilling to

[1] "Toryism and Militarism", *The Liberal Monthly*, October, 1913.

spend an equal amount for a far more practical and enduring form of National defence which rests on the development of industrial efficiency and which meets 'the German peril' at its very basis."[1]

This stress upon the peaceful constructive intentions of the Liberals became the main feature of their propaganda from mid-1913 until the outbreak of war the next year. During the by-election in South Bruce in Ontario Laurier swung far over to the left, and Mackenzie King swung with him. The policy of the Borden Government was depicted as provocative of war. "No nation can take offence at Canada building ships for Canadian waters in Canada's defence," Mackenzie King told the electors of South Bruce, "but for Canada to deliberately place Dreadnaughts in European waters is to invite antagonism."[2] Other Liberal speakers talked about the merchants of death and the agents of Krupps at work behind the scenes in Canadian politics. Added to all this was a slogan "Vote for free food", by which was meant a policy of reducing import duties on food products. The swing left produced the results for which Laurier had hoped. The Liberal candidate, R. E. Truax, was returned with a comfortable majority in a constituency which had returned a Tory candidate in the two previous elections.

We cannot speak with any final authority upon the development of Mackenzie King's ideas during the years 1912 and 1913. All we can detect is a tendency rapidly to shift his ground in discussing a number of subjects. On labour policy, for example, we find him in March, 1912, spinning wildly leftward on the subject of the British coal strike when addressing an American audience at Lynn, Massachusetts. He praised in extravagant terms the "amazing and far-reaching" results of the strike. "There has been demonstrated as never before what is meant by the 'solidarity of labour'," he declared to the members of the Lynn Twentieth Century Club,

"as never before it has been seen how in the last analysis labour and nature are the forces which create all wealth, as never before men have learned how those who live on the top of the earth are

---

[1] *The Liberal Monthly*, October, 1913.
[2] *The Canadian Annual Review*, 1913, p. 288.

dependent on those who work beneath it, and how all industry, all trade, all human existence in fact is made possible by the silent and ceaseless effort of those who toil."[1]

But American middle-class audiences admire other people's struggles for freedom more than such commotions in their own country. Within a year Mackenzie King was talking to the "No Strike" Association of Cincinnati, Ohio, telling them how to overcome organized labour.

Similarly, on the subject of foreign policy and armaments we find him gyrating from north to south, from east to west, like a magnetic compass in the vicinity of a cyclotron. He was "a well-armed Empire" man early in 1912. By the spring of 1913 he was appealing to the Canadian Club of Toronto in these terms:

> ". . . let us begin in a modest way, not seek to surpass the nations of Europe, Germany, France, Britain and all the other nations on earth in our paraphernalia of war. I say we should have a higher ideal than that! There are other ways of helping the Empire! My mind does not run in the lines of war; my mind runs rather along the lines of peace. (Applause)."[2]

A few months later he wanted arms, but not sufficient of them to provoke Germany. With the passage of time from 1913 to 1914 we can discern a steadying of his course in the direction of propaganda for peace. The by-election in South Bruce in October had demonstrated that peace and opposition to armament manufacturers was a popular line. Mackenzie King took it up. As he did so he began to move away from the specifically British imperialists towards the Americans.[3]

Early in 1914, we find him organizing, with the help of American money supplied by the Trustees of the Carnegie Endowment for International Peace, a peace front of his own bearing the name "The Canadian Association of International Conciliation". This was an offshoot of an American organization with a similar name under the chairmanship of Nicholas Murray Butler of Columbia University. Mackenzie King was the Canadian Chairman. His purpose, he told prospective

---

[1] *Canadian Annual Review*, 1912, p. 265.
[2] *Proceedings of the Canadian Club, Toronto, for the Year* 1912–13, Vol. X (Toronto, 1913), p. 221.
[3] He took an active part in the work of a committee preparing the celebration of one hundred years of Canadian-American peace.

members, was to build up a Canadian organization "of persons
of prominence . . . who are known to be desirous of maintaining
and furthering friendly relations between nations".[1] ". . . The
loose form of organization adopted has been purposely
selected", he explained,

> "with a view of avoiding adherence to any particular set of views or
> the propagation of any individual line of peace propaganda. The
> object is, rather, to frankly admit the possible divergence of views
> being assured only of the integrity of purpose, the experience and
> the influence of those who make up the membership of the Associ-
> ation."[2]

Although he approached Tory imperialists like Sir John
Willison with an invitation to join, the men who actually joined
were nearly all Liberals. The only outstanding Conservative
was Borden's Minister of Trade and Commerce, the Hon. (later
Rt. Hon. Sir) George E. Foster. The rest were prominent
Liberal politicians and ex-politicians, wealthy business men,
prominent divines, university presidents, journalists and
members of the bar and bench. Several of the diners of August
7th, 1912, were members, including N. W. Rowell, Joseph Atkinson and Sir Edmund Walker. But J. S. Ewart,* K.C., was also a
member. He was an extremely anti-British opponent of imperialism with respectable professional connections.

While he was bringing his peace front to maturity Mackenzie
King was busily engaged in two other activities. The first, and
most time-consuming, was preparing for and fighting the
Ontario Provincial election of 1914. The second was a secret
and delicate negotiation with John D. Rockefeller which
would enable him to withdraw temporarily from the Canadian
political scene.

The Ontario Provincial election of 1914 was his second opportunity to exhibit his talents as the manager of a Party machine
in action. The Ontario Reform Association of which Mackenzie
King was still the president, possessed money and organization.
Unfortunately the Liberals did not possess a policy. They
borrowed phrases freely from the vocabulary of American
politics to describe the Tory government. It was an exponent
of "stand-pattism". It was machine-ridden. It was a tool

---

[1] *Willison Papers*, King to Willison, 10 June, 1914.
[2] *Willison Papers*, King to Willison, 21 July, 1914.

of the liquor interests. They talked in general about the reform of justice, agriculture, finance and labour, but the only subject upon which they were positive and forthright was prohibition. Their covert enmity to the Hydro-Electric Power Commission of Ontario and the principle of public ownership, already so conspicuously beneficial to the manufacturers, farmers and householders of Ontario, was well known, and their connections with American big business were suspect. When the votes were counted the Liberals were beaten again. *The Liberal Monthly* consoled its readers with the thought that it now had 27 seats instead of 17 in a legislature of 95 members. But, wrote the editor, "the winning of elections is not the chief business of Liberalism . . . With Mr. Rowell the main thing has been public service and practical humanitarianism."[1]

Mackenzie King's part in the Liberal defeat is not entirely clear. He stated in another connection, in 1915, that during the provincial election he "had an engagement to speak every night for a month",[2] and he implied that he had thrown himself whole-heartedly into the election. Newspaper sources do not, however, leave this impression. Compared with his conspicuous display of energy in the Provincial election of 1911, Mackenzie King's part in the election of 1914 appears a muted one.

There is much evidence, in the circumstances of 1914, to suggest some reasons for this. We know that as early as June 3rd, 1914,[3] and perhaps earlier, he was considering an offer of employment in the United States. But the wealth and power of the Rockefellers were not alone the decisive factors in the situation which confronted Mackenzie King in 1914. The Liberal Party was splitting seriously beneath the surface as Canada became increasingly engulfed in the new world of great industrial powers. Laurier and "the old gang" were moving more and more in a popular direction. In this movement they appeared to have abandoned loyalty to the rich and the powerful with whom they had co-operated so freely in the days of competitive freedom, when men contended for innocent objectives like control of railways and the price of wheat. Rowell and the "Ontario management" with whom Mackenzie King

---

[1] *The Liberal Monthly*, July, 1914.   [2] *R.C.I.R.*, p. 8792.
[3] *R.C.I.R.*, p. 8788.

was intimately associated were being placed in a difficult position. Rowell understood politics only as they manifested themselves in Ontario, and he thought of policy only in so far as it
served the men he knew and respected in downtown Toronto.
These men had failed in Ontario in 1911, and again in 1914.
The leader of the Party in federal politics was embarked upon
courses which were emotionally fearful, intellectually incom-
prehensible and politically, it was believed, dangerous. Mackenzie King saw beyond Rowell, and his ambition was greater.
He was being rapidly driven to a point where he might have to
declare himself either for one position or for another. The crisis
of the British Empire was becoming his crisis, and it was natural
that he should seek a way out.

In the course of his negotiations with the Rockefellers
Mackenzie King depicted himself as a close associate of Sir
Wilfrid Laurier. ". . . Just now I am with Sir Wilfrid most of the
time,"[1] he told John D. Rockefeller, Jr.* Testifying in Washington in 1915, he asserted that in June, 1914, Laurier was preparing "to make a tour of the Dominion—the last political
tour he probably would make through the whole of Canada,
and he was kind enough to say he would like me to be a member
of his party and go with him, and that he intended to make the
trip during July, August and September."[2] When, many years
later, one of the "old gang" read Mackenzie King's letter to
Rockefeller and his testimony in Washington, he frothed with
rage. "Note the statement", Senator Murphy bitterly wrote
to Senator Lemieux,

> "that the Old Man was to make a tour in 1914 that would last
> three months, and that the witness had been invited to join
> him. You and I were in Parliament at that time and the witness
> was not. You and I were in constant touch with the Chief and the
> other gentleman was philandering in different parts of the United
> States and Canada. As I never heard of the trip mentioned, I
> doubt that you ever heard of it.
> "Then with regard to the second amazing statement, note what
> this fellow says in his letter to Rockefeller of August 6th, 1914, in
> which he declares he is 'with Sir Wilfrid most of the time'. This
> conveyed to Rockefeller the impression that Sir Wilfrid derived

[1] G. P. West, *Report on the Colorado Strike*, United States Commission on Industrial
Relations (Washington, 1915), p. 160, King to Rockefeller, 6 August, 1914.
[2] *R.C.I.R.*, p. 8793.

all his inspiration from this bucko, who was not in Parliament, and who, to my recollection, was not in Ottawa at the time. He gave Rockefeller the impression that he was a Pillar of Parliament and a Pillar and Solomon of the Liberal Party and that Sir Wilfrid made no move except after consultation with him. ... Then note the statement that the Western trip 'has been called off owing to the war'. Without going too far afield in my investigations I am satisfied that this witness was lying when he made these statements."[1]

This opposition of recollections and impressions concerning Mackenzie King's relationship with Laurier between the defeat of the Liberals, in 1911, and the outbreak of World War I, was a product of many factors, some personal and some political. It would be profitless to attempt to sort them out. Rather, we propose to examine the evidence concerning Mackenzie King's connection with Laurier during these years. Was he the chosen brave of the Old Chief as he suggested he was to Mr. Rockefeller, and as his biographers have since suggested to the public? Or was he the rank outsider depicted by Murphy?

Immediately after the election of 1911 and as a result of his extensive contribution to that debacle, Mackenzie King appears to have been almost completely excluded from a place in the councils of the federal Liberal Party. After the threatened split of August, 1912, and after his own return from Great Britain in November, 1912, he embarked upon a course of rehabilitation in federal politics which brought him physically and politically into closer contact with Laurier and his entourage. In the Central Liberal Information Office he was working in an organization over which Laurier had a direct control and for which he was responsible. The management of the Liberal Information Office and its works did not meet with the unqualified approval of all Laurier's colleagues during 1913 and 1914, but the fact remains that Mackenzie King continued in the position to which he had been appointed, and attacks upon him as a traitor to "Canadianism" and as an agent of "Rowell and his gang" by men like Murphy did not achieve the objective of dislodging him.

But the fact of his survival is no proof that Laurier especially loved Mackenzie King or liked his views. The English-speaking Party leaders for whom Laurier reserved his affection were old

[1] *Murphy Papers*, Murphy to Lemieux, 23 April, 1927.

Liberal fighters, more his own age and politically of his own epoch and his own class: men like George P. Graham, the small town journalist, the happy-go-lucky comedian of the smoking rooms, amiable, shrewd, unscrupulous towards his enemies and loyal to his friends; or Charlie Murphy, the son of poor Irish immigrants, who loved, hated, and schemed with narrow, provincial intensity; or Fred Pardee and Allen Aylesworth,* men from Ontario whom a habitant lawyer could really like. Laurier's correspondence suggests, from the few exchanges between the Liberal leader and his young follower, that their meetings were formal and infrequent. They may have been so close that they seldom wrote to each other, but this is hardly suggested by the dry and official tone of their letters—the one respectful and pompous, the other lacking in those few warm words amid the formal inter-Cabinet courtesies, which reveal affection. In his letters to third parties, discussing or mentioning Mackenzie King, Laurier was never unqualified in his admiration, except on one occasion. In a letter to Lord Minto quoted[1] by Dr. O. D. Skelton in his biography of Laurier written shortly before Mackenzie King appointed Skelton to the Under Secretaryship of External Affairs, Laurier did speak of Mackenzie King with some enthusiasm, but that letter was one exception to a number which contained either important qualifications or an undertone of dry ambiguity.[2]

Mackenzie King knew so little of Laurier's personal life, his manner of doing business and his tastes and disposition that some years after the Old Chief's death he addressed an inquiry to Laurier's personal stenographer asking her

"to write out for me your recollections of how Sir Wilfrid Laurier used to carry on his work from day to day, dwelling more particularly on the following points: (1) How much of his work did he do at the House. . . . (2) What amount of time did he give to personal reading. (3) What time did he take off in the year for holidays . . . ' etc."[3]

This pathetic inquiry suggests the longing to establish in death an intimacy he never knew in life. It is, perhaps, part of the explanation of his later spiritualism; the endeavour of the outsider to establish by psychic means the contacts he never

---

[1] Skelton, *Laurier*, Vol. II, p. 354.   [2] See below, Chapters IX and X.
[3] *Laurier Papers*, King to Miss Yvonne Coutu, 28 January, 1929.

William Lyon Mackenzie King at an early age.

King's birthplace in Kitchener, Ontario. The photograph was taken in 1922, on the occasion of a visit by King to the house, named "Woodside".

A portrait of King as a boy taken by a photographer in Preston, Ontario.

Mab Moss, a friend of King's, photographed in 1893.

King on his seventeenth birthday, December 17, 1891.

King (*standing on the left*) pours tea at a gathering in his room during his time as a university student.

King *(second from the left)* stands at the unveiling in 1905, of a monument depicting Sir Galahad dedicated to the memory of King's friend Henry Harper. Immediately after his appointment as deputy minister of labour in 1900, King invited Harper to join him as his assistant in Ottawa. Harper drowned in December 1901. Sir Wilfrid Laurier and the Governor-General, Earl Grey, spoke at the unveiling ceremony.

King (*sixth from the left in middle row*) on his 1908 mission to China when he negotiated with the Chinese government a draft agreement restricting the entry of Chinese into Canada. Soon after the successful completion of this mission, he resigned and ran for office to become Minister of Labour.

King in India during the 1908 world trip.

King on an election platform during the campaign in 1908, where he ran successfully as the Liberal candidate in Waterloo North, with the enthusiastic support of the Toronto *Globe*.

Minister of Labour William Lyon Mackenzie King in ceremonial dress, December 1910. The suit can be seen amongst the Mackenzie King memorabilia at Laurier House in Ottawa.

Liberal Demonstration at Simcoe, Aug. 15, 1911
Hon. Mackenzie King
Gordon Photo, Port Dover

King campaigning in the reciprocity election of 1911 in which the Laurier government went down to defeat and King himself lost his seat.

King (*middle*) and John D. Rockefeller Jr. (*right*) dressed to enter one of Rockefeller's Colorado coal mines during the 1915 public relations campaign which was mounted by Rockefeller on King's advice after the notorious Ludlow massacre during which eleven children and two women were burned to death by militiamen. On the left is Archie Dennison, described by the Toronto *Star* of the day, as "representative of miners, chosen after implementation of the scheme developed by King for company unions in the mine."

During this same visit, Rockefeller made a point of going to a party and dancing with miners' wives. Asked much later in his life whether this was his idea, King replied: "I did have something to do with the dance at Colorado and for starting him, whether for good or ill, a little on that path."

A group photographed in Colorado in 1915. In the front row, from left to right, King's long-time personal secretary Fred McGregor, King, John D. Rockefeller Jr., and an unidentified person.

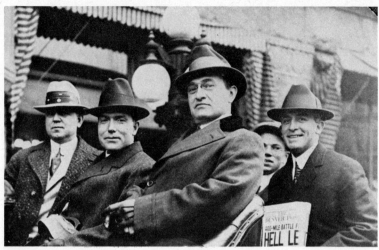

Also in Colorado in 1915. Rockefeller is in the middle in the front row, and McGregor is on the right behind.

The Public Archives caption on this curious photograph is: W.L. Mackenzie King and girl, Colorado, 1915.

King and John D. Rockefeller Jr. in Washington, D.C. in 1915, when King was acting as Rockefeller's labour and public relations adviser.

King and friends at Kingsmere in 1916.

King politicking at the National Liberal Convention in Ottawa held in August, 1919, where he was chosen leader of the party.

King with Sir Wilfrid Laurier. It was Laurier's death in February 1919 that led to the convention later that year where King was elected party leader.

had (and by the nature of his personality and his political out-
look never could have) with a man like Laurier whose life had
been shaped by different forces than those of a lonely dweller in
the waste land of industrial society.

Either on account of the strain involved in his situation in
Ottawa, inside the machine but outside the leadership, or for
prudential reasons, Mackenzie King began to meditate upon a
withdrawal to the United States as a solution of his personal and
political dilemma. During the years 1911–14, he was back and
forth between Canada and the United States speaking in New
York, in Massachusetts and in Ohio. But his connections on the
highest level in the United States date much earlier than this
period.

While he was still a Deputy Minister, Mackenzie King invited President Eliot of Harvard to speak to the Canadian
Club in Ottawa. During the decade before World War I, Eliot
was in the midst of his late prophetic period when he undertook
to teach the people of the United States how to end class conflict. He was closely connected with the most influential business-
men of America and the friend of the most powerful members
of the Republican and Democratic Parties. He came to
Ottawa in February, 1907, and addressed the Canadian Club
on "The Competitive Arming of Nations".[1] He had already
been instructed on the subject of Mackenzie King's solution
of class conflict. He praised Mackenzie King lavishly in
his speech, and he paid some attention to the Industrial
Disputes Investigation Bill, which Mackenzie King had prepared for Parliament during the Christmas season lately
passed. When Eliot returned to the United States he published
an article on the Canadian legislation in *McClure's Magazine*[2]
praising it as an example worthy of American imitation. Eliot
was privately criticized for this article by a member of the
National Civic Federation, who declared that the claims advanced for such legislation were unsubstantiated and much
exaggerated. Eliot passed this criticism on to Mackenzie King
for comment. The Deputy Minister of Labour recognized that
the biggest fish he had yet landed might jump off the dock

---

[1] C. W. Eliot, *The Road Towards Peace* (London, 1915), p. 8.
[2] *McClure's Magazine*, Vol. 30, March, 1907.

back into the water. He poured out an eleven-page letter to Eliot defending his handiwork.[1] After the Royal Assent had been given to the Industrial Disputes Investigation Act fifty copies of the Act were despatched to Eliot. From this time forward Eliot became a convinced advocate of Mackenzie King. In June, 1909, Eliot invited the new Minister of Labour to speak at the Commencement Dinner at Harvard. In September of the same year he wrote another article in *McClure's*, "The Best Way to Prevent Industrial Warfare".[2] Mackenzie King was beside himself with delight at this praise. Everything of importance he put in print went to Eliot.

He received a certain amount of publicity in other quarters in the United States. One of his assistants in the Department of Labour published an explanatory article on the Industrial Disputes Investigation Act in the *Journal of Political Economy* in 1908. In 1910 F. A. Acland, his Deputy Minister, published a considerable article on the subject in the *Annals of the American Academy of Political and Social Science*. In 1911, the *Twentieth Century*, a popular journal, published an article telling the American people how their "rugged northern neighbours are ahead of us in banking and labour legislation" and in "scientific law making" on subjects such as the investigation of trusts.[3] In 1912, Mackenzie King himself told the influential readers of the *Annals of the American Academy of Political and Social Science* about the Canadian Combines Investigation Act.

In April, 1914, he was invited to appear before the Commission on Industrial Relations, appointed by the United States Congress, as an expert witness. On the stand he told the Commission how the Industrial Disputes Investigation Act had "more than justified itself".[4] A few days after his appearance there occurred in Colorado a massacre of miners and women and children which shook the United States. Within a space of days the Rockefeller interests, whose holdings in Colorado were the centre of this serious industrial civil war, approached Mackenzie King with an offer to work for them.

Mackenzie King told the Commission on Industrial Relations, when he was subpoenaed as a witness in 1915, that "the

---

[1] Harvard University Archives, *Eliot Correspondence*, King to Eliot, 21 April, 1907.

[2] *McClure's Magazine*, Vol. 33, September, 1909.

[3] Quoted in Ball, *Canadian Combines*, etc., p. 43.   [4] *R.C.I.R.*, p. 717.

only person I had spoken to or intimated to what had come in
the way of this proposition was Sir Wilfrid Laurier, in whose
cabinet I was. . . ."[1] According to his testimony Laurier replied
to this suggestion of withdrawal with an invitation to accompany him on a tour. In Liberal circles an invitation to tour the
country with the Leader was a conventional expression of confidence and was considered a signal mark of favour by the
leader. One man who had been so invited included it among
his honours in his biography in *Who's Who* and lived for years in
the expectation of succeeding Laurier as Leader of the Party.
Perhaps such an invitation was an outward and visible sign of
an inward and spiritual disposition on the part of the Leader.
But was the sign made to Mackenzie King at this time?

In May and June, 1914, Laurier was engaged in seeing to its
close a ragged session of the Canadian Parliament in which
there had been one of those acrimonious hunts for corruption so
congenial to politicians without ideas to discuss or issues to
fight. He was tired, being seventy-three years old. When Parliament rose in June, he left Ottawa for his summer home in
Arthabaska to relax and rest in rural Quebec villages among
the people he loved. He and Lady Laurier never moved from
Arthabaska during the rest of June, nor during July. On the
afternoon of August 3rd, 1914, Laurier commenced his return
journey to Ottawa. On the evening of August 4th, he issued a
press statement announcing the support of the Liberal Party
for the declaration of war on Germany. "In view of the critical
nature of the situation", he concluded his statement, "I have
cancelled all my meetings." There was no reference to a tour.
There is nothing in Laurier's correspondence to suggest that
on this topic his biographer is anything but accurate in his
account of Sir Wilfrid Laurier's activities and intentions during
the summer of 1914.[2] The invitation to Mackenzie King appears
to have been a vague and general expression without much
concrete and definite meaning.

The plain inference from the facts is that Laurier put no
obstacle in the way of Mackenzie King's departure. On August
6th, 1914, Mackenzie King wrote to Rockefeller giving him
specific advice about his problems created by the massacre in
Colorado. He had already visited New York three times at

---

[1] *R.C.I.R.*, p. 8793.　　　　[2] Skelton, *Laurier*, Vol. II, p. 426 ff.

Rockefeller's expense.[1] His formal appointment as a director
of research for the Rockefeller Foundation was not made until
October 1st, 1914, but he had already sketched out to the
Rockefellers a plan of action for Colorado.[2]

If he withdrew to the United States, Mackenzie King made
sure that a door was left open for his return to Canadian
politics at an appropriate time. He insisted that as a condition
of his employment by the Rockefellers he should be allowed
to maintain his Canadian residence, and that he should be free
to continue his connection with Canadian public affairs. Indeed, he persuaded the Rockefellers not to take him on the
strength of their Foundation until some months after he had
commenced advising them. In the interval between June 3rd,
when he first began negotiating with the Rockefellers, and
October, when he was formally employed, he was doing two
jobs, one for Laurier and the Liberal Party and one for Rockefeller. In the end he chose Rockefeller.

His last big piece of work for Laurier was the preparation
of the August number of *The Liberal Monthly*. With the outbreak of war Laurier abandoned his approaches towards pacifism and his opposition to armaments. "I have often declared," he said in his press statement of August 4th, "that if the
mother country were ever in danger, or if danger ever
threatened, Canada would render assistance to the fullest
extent of her power." In the spirit of the diners of August, 1912,
Mackenzie King produced a number of *The Liberal Monthly*
which proclaimed the unity of the parties. In the cover cartoon
Laurier is shown dropping two slips of paper, one labelled
"Holiday Plans" and the other "Party Differences", the better
to enable him to grasp Prime Minister Robert Borden to his
bosom. A beneficent female looked on, equipped with a shield
bearing a Union Jack and the legend "United Canada", and
she fluttered what looked like wings and extended what were
unmistakably arms. The letterpress of the number was a
scissors and paste job placing the full responsibility of the war on
Germany. Militarism and Autocracy in Uhlan's helmets were
depicted slapping the faces of women and children labelled
British Liberty, Democracy and Humanitarianism. For the

[1] *R.C.I.R.*, p. 8162.
[2] G. P. West, *Report on the Colorado Strike* (Washington, 1915), p. 160 ff.

benefit of those Liberals who wished to follow the military operations, a large map was included.

Mackenzie King's analysis of the international political relations which had brought war was a simple, clear statement of the mechanics of power politics. France had been weakened by the Franco-Prussian War and Russia by the Russo-Japanese War. The relative weight of Germany and Austria-Hungary had increased. Therefore, in accordance with the ancient principle of the Balance of Power, Britain was obliged to support the weaker side. But in the closing paragraph, Mackenzie King (for he wrote the entire August number)[1] concluded:

> "While the Armageddon of Europe fills the thought of man with indescribable horror, the tragic vision is, even now, not without episodes which the world's memory would unwillingly forego. One is the common patriotism which cemented in an hour domestic differences that had brought the peoples of the British Isles to the brink of civil war; another is the sublime heroism of a neutral nation prepared to sacrifice its entire manhood rather than allow its honour to suffer a stain, or a sister country to endure a wrong; and a third is the spectacle of the young free nations of the British Empire rising with one accord, on all the continents of the globe, to strengthen with the vigour of youth, and even before the call of duty, the arm which has protected them through the years, and which at this moment is raised in self-defence at home, and stretches forth to deal a blow at arrogance and aggression abroad."[2]

These words would appear to represent an unambiguous decision to abandon the near-neutrality and near pacifism of the years 1913–14. Other evidence, however, compels the student to make different deductions. The words of *The Liberal Monthly* may have come from Mackenzie King's pen but they flowed either from the brain and heart of another person or from another person within the corporeal frame of their author. On September 4th, 1914, Mackenzie King wrote to William Jennings Bryan, the Secretary of State of the United States, on the subject of international politics. Bryan was the principal and, indeed, the only exponent of strict neutrality in the Cabinet of Woodrow Wilson.[3] He was also a friend of Dr. J. A.

---

[1] We have this information from Mr. Fred MacGregor, his Secretary at the time.
[2] *The Liberal Monthly*, August, 1914, p. 152.
[3] S. F. Bemis, *A Diplomatic History of the United States* (New York, 1942), Chapter XXXII; T. A. Bailey, *A Diplomatic History of the American People* (New York, 1946), pp. 614–15.

N

Macdonald, editor of the Toronto *Globe*.[1] The letter itself is a complex document written with all the verbal subtlety for which its author became famous. The opening paragraphs appear at first sight to consist of a clever argument designed to involve the United States in the European War. The movement of society in history, argued Mackenzie King, is exactly as Sir Henry Maine had described it: from status to contract. "Sir Henry Maine has made it clear", he wrote to Bryan,

> "that what distinguishes modern progressive societies from archaic communities is the recognition given to agreement and contract, as opposed to power or position, in determining relations so far as these affect the property of individuals. Is it not true that transitions similar to those which have taken place between men in their individual relations, have followed in the relations between communities and nations? And may it not well be, that History, viewing the awful struggle in Europe today, will reveal it as one of those painful transitions which make for progress in the world's affairs?"[2]

But Mackenzie King did not go on to discuss the breach of an international contract by the German invasion of Belgium. Instead, he endeavoured to strengthen Bryan's will to neutrality. Strict adherence to the "contracts of neutrality" was, according to Mackenzie King, the best device by which the United States could save the cause of progress in world affairs and "greatly further its own diplomatic ends". "A universally accepted interpretation of neutrality", he wrote

> "very properly prevents the United States of America from taking, or appearing to take, any side in the present struggle. On the other hand, the standards she has set for herself and for other nations would seem to make it impossible for her to be indifferent to an attitude towards belligerents, higher, and more far reaching than that which a mere recognition of the generally-accepted rights of Neutrals would permit her to take. This the Administration has already recognized by allowing it to be known that the Government would not view with favour the exercise of the right of loans being made by American citizens to the government of one of the belligerent Nations,[3]—a right the exercise of which is per-

---

[1] A. Bridle, *Sons of Canada* (Toronto, 1916), p. 279.

[2] *Eliot Papers*, King to Bryan, 4 September, 1914, a copy of which is enclosed with King to Eliot, 9 September, 1914.

[3] This refers to the intimation given to the firm of J. P. Morgan & Co. by the U.S. Government in the form of a telegram from Bryan on 15 August, 1914, that a loan to France, although legal, was inconsistent with the "spirit of neutrality". See Bailey, *op. cit.*, p. 621.

fectly legal, and wholly compatible with a strict neutrality. No one familiar with American public opinion will ever for a moment believe that this view of the Administration has been taken through any desire to lessen the power of France in the present struggle. On the contrary, it is, I believe, everywhere recognized that it is but a part of that higher sense of obligation in international affairs which has been the fruit of educational effort in recent years on the part of some of your most distinguished citizens. The doctrine that wars might be averted were the Nations of the earth to refuse credit to any country that engages in war without first submitting the question at issue to the Hague Tribunal, has, while failing thus far of acceptance, nevertheless, made itself felt to the extent of enabling the Administration to take the stand it has in this particular, and in causing other Nations to respect the stand thus taken.

"May it not be assumed that as respects all other questions which may arise, a like attitude will command a like respect? In maintaining the higher ground, and continuing to view with open disfavour other acts that a strict interpretation of neutrality might permit, but which may serve to prolong the European conflict, may not the United States be the means of advancing the whole basis of world civilization, and, at the same time, in the sum of things, greatly further its own diplomatic ends?"

President Eliot was an unfortunate choice of person for such confidences as these. Eliot did not like the "higher ground" occupied by Secretary Bryan and the object of Mackenzie King's admiration. He had already told President Wilson that the situation in Europe and the prospect of a German victory justified "the abandonment of Washington's advice that this country keep out of European complications".[1] Like Wilson, Eliot, too, wanted to see the universalization of the American Revolution and the American constitution. "The best issue of this War", he wrote to Mackenzie King, "can hardly be more than the abolition of permanent executives having power to make war without action on the part of a representative assembly, and the reduction of militarism. . . ."[2] But Germany was plainly in the wrong, according to Eliot, and must be beaten before there could be any thought given to an exploration of millenary schemes for world peace. "In my opinion, no attempts at mediation should be made by the United States", concluded Eliot, "or any combination of neutral states or any

[1] E. M. House, *The Intimate Papers of Colonel House* (London, 1926), Vol. 1, p. 294.
[2] *Eliot Correspondence*, Eliot to King, 16 September, 1914.

self-selected league, until Germany says she is ready for the cessation of hostilities."

After this exchange, Mackenzie King never corresponded further with Eliot on the subject of international policy. Mercifully, the character of the new business on which he was engaged delivered him from the necessity of such explorations along the perilous path of foreign politics. Three weeks previous to his letter to Bryan the Trustees of the Rockefeller Foundation, meeting at 26, Broadway, in the City of New York, resolved to appoint the Hon. William Lyon Mackenzie King director of an investigation into problems of industrial relations at a salary which he and the Foundation always resolutely refused to disclose, even under the threat of proceedings for contempt of the Congress of the United States.

As the armies began to assemble across the Dominion, Mackenzie King prepared the way for his withdrawal from Canadian politics. On October 1st, 1914, his appointment was announced by the Rockefeller Foundation. On November 27th, he presented his resignation to The General Reform Association of Ontario and he delivered to them his last presidential address. It consisted of a strong appeal to oppose a federal election until the war was over.

What was Mackenzie King's position in Canadian politics at this moment of strategic retreat from the realities of Canada into the orbit of American power? He was cordially disliked by a great many of the Liberal leaders around Laurier (and by none more than the ex-Minister from Ontario) and their allies in the Liberal machine. But he was for all this well connected with a variety of influential organizations and people. He was intimately tied to some of the most powerful men in Canadian business and politics. He was a close friend and a colleague in the Ontario Reform Association of J. E. Atkinson, who long remained the man in Toronto whom Mackenzie King never failed to see or to telephone whenever he visited the Ontario capital.[1] Atkinson controlled the most widely circulated daily and weekly newspapers in Canada, and he understood, and

---

[1] Mackenzie King stopped doing this when he learned that Atkinson was supporting the Co-operative Commonwealth Federation party privately. He then discovered that Atkinson's growing deafness was an obstacle to extended telephone conversations.

sympathized with the cosmopolis which was being produced in every Canadian city by immigration and industrialization. Atkinson and Mackenzie King shared many political ideas. They talked much of social reform, and Atkinson was far in advance of Mackenzie King in what he was prepared to see adopted in the shape of old age pensions, unemployment insurance and family allowances.[1] And both these social reformers were hard bargainers when dealing with labour.

If he had this intimate connection with the new journalism of the mass circulation dailies, he remained in close contact with the old journalism of the Toronto *Globe*. The *Globe* staff had long been part of the apparatus of his personal machine. The former Presbyterian clergyman, Dr. J. A. Macdonald, who edited the *Globe*, was one of the principal advocates in Canada of the affiliation of Canada with the United States, and he had "sold" President Taft on reciprocity in 1911. Through 1915 and 1916, he devoted much personal attention to publicizing in Canada Mackenzie King's work for the Rockefellers.

Then there was P. C. Larkin,* the "tea king of America" whose life was reputedly the most heavily insured in Canada. He had invented the metal foil tea package for the retail trade, and had been the Treasurer of the Liberal Party in Ontario. He was a heavy backer of the Liberal cause and a generous patron of individual Liberal politicians. Larkin was one business prince in Toronto who always stuck close to Laurier in spite of the fact that Laurier does not appear to have liked or trusted him. He operated on the simple-minded principle that Laurier had brought him prosperity and he ought, therefore, to support Laurier. Unlike many of the rich in Toronto he saw the benefits of waging fights on behalf of free speech and against the oppressing of the "respectable" wage-workers.[2]

Mackenzie King, too, was a colleague of Rowell, a friend of Senator Sir George W. Ross, a friend of the lobbyist Alexander Smith, who had proclaimed him Laurier's successor the day he became a Minister.[3] Senator James Domville thought well of him. He had friends in the offices of the Trades and Labour Congress. These were the kind of people to whom Mackenzie

---

[1] *Laurier Papers*, Atkinson to Laurier, 8 March, 1916.
[2] *Laurier Papers*, Larkin to Laurier, 20 January, 1919.
[3] *The Herald*, Montreal, 5 June, 1909.

King was close. They made and unmade politicians because they had money or the means of publicity in their hands. All that he lacked was a connection in Quebec. Laurier was cool, and without Laurier no English-speaking Liberal could hope to have the confidence of the Party in Quebec.

With an Ottawa address on his notepaper he wrote from Wilkes Barre and Denver and New York about the business of the Rockefellers. From the Roxborough he kept his irons hot in the Canadian fire. But he had no Quebec iron to heat in the years 1914–17, while he was serving a new apprenticeship with American big business.

CHAPTER VII

The Liberal Way

It is a comment upon the Parliamentary opponents of the Liberal Party of Canada that no careful and comprehensive examination of Mackenzie King's connection with the Rockefellers has ever been undertaken. Mackenzie King's own account of this connection—its character and the circumstances of its establishment—appears to have been accepted alike by his friends and his opponents with few reservations and little comment. And yet, Mackenzie King's part in the great industrial disputes in Colorado in 1914 reveals the fundamentals of his political position and explains much that happened in Canada after he became leader of the Liberal Party in 1919. When he consented to work for the Rockefellers, Mackenzie King became the servant of the biggest concentration of private capital and the most widely ramified concern in the United States and, indeed, in the world.

In October, 1919, three months after Mackenzie King's election to the leadership of the Liberal Party, Tom Moore, the President of the Trades and Labour Congress of Canada, alluded, critically, to some aspects of the new Liberal leader's work in connection with the so-called "Rockefeller Plan". Mackenzie King was present at this meeting, and he took the opportunity to explain his relationship to the Rockefellers.

"I was asked," he said,

"four or five years ago, by the Rockefeller Foundation of New York if I would make a study of industrial relations with a view of helping if possible to disclose those principles which applied to industry would make for better relations between employers and employed. I was named for that work by President Eliot, of Harvard University, who was one of the trustees of the Foundation. . . . I had scarcely started on this study when my attention became directed to one of the most serious industrial conflicts that has ever taken place on this continent; I mean the strike in the coal mines of Colorado, in which, as persons here know, through differences between the militia and the workers, about one hundred women and children lost their lives and hundreds of families were left famished and starving. I said to myself: What is the sense of making a theoretical study to present to the people of this continent when there is a practical condition that requires looking into? And, without being requested by any person so to do, I went out to the State of Colorado myself to use that particular State as a laboratory in which to demonstrate what could be done as a result of applying certain principles in which I firmly believed. . . . The question was one mainly of recognition of the union. . . . When I had gathered all the information that I could get together, I came back to my residence here in Ottawa, examined that material, sifted it carefully, and drew up what seemed to me some of the outstanding principles that should be recognized if there was to be industrial peace in Colorado in the future. . . . So I sent my impressions to him (J. D. Rockefeller, Jr.) and said in effect: I think this is what is needed in Colorado. I think that to settle the troubles in Colorado, the companies must agree to allow their men to belong to unions."[1]

Now, it may be argued that what happened in Huerfano County, Colorado, between 23 September, 1913, and 10 December, 1914, is of no importance in Canadian history. Perhaps. But Huerfano County was, in fact, a laboratory in which a Canadian politician was tested, and for this reason what happened there should be known. About what happened, there is no dispute. The facts are on record, and neither of the parties to the dispute in those rugged and frank days before World War I tried to deny the facts. Indeed, both the workers and the employers took the facts for granted and did not try to give them any other interpretation but that of class warfare of a brutal and unsophisticated kind.

The desire of various groups in North America for the investigation and discussion of the presumed thoughts and activities of University students, teachers, clergymen, civil servants and trade unionists has never extended to embrace the ideas and activities of Prime Ministers. For this reason, presumably, what Mackenzie King told the Trades and Labour Congress of

[1] *The Daily Star*, Toronto, October, 1919.

Canada in October 1919, has been accepted by the politicians, the journalists, and the biographers. Fortunately, the task of inquiry was undertaken by the Congress of the United States. What that inquiry[1] revealed is told in the ensuing pages. It contradicts both the story told by Mackenzie King and the impression he sought to create.

In the canyons of southern Colorado there were a number of coal mines operated by three large companies and a number of smaller proprietors. The largest organization was the Colorado Fuel and Iron Company employing about 6,000 of the 30,000 men working in the industry. This organization was controlled by John D. Rockefeller and his son John D. Rockefeller, Jr., who owned 40 per cent of the stock and appear from their correspondence, *sub-poenaed* by the Congressional investigating Commission, to have had strong influence over the higher personnel of the company. The coal companies in Southern Colorado exercised an absolute control over their properties and their workers. They owned the mines, the houses in which the workers lived, the shops where they bought their food, drink and clothing. They hired and fired their employees at will. The employers, according to their testimony before the investigating commission, believed that a free labour market existed because any man with his family was free to leave the mining camps if he did not like the conditions under which they lived. They were free to go back where they came from.

The belief in this freedom of choice is one of the gigantic self-deceptions of American democracy. Men and women in company towns could not go back whence they came. They could not go back to Greece, to Mexico, to Italy, to Croatia, to Poland, to the Ukraine, to Ohio or to Kentucky. They had been lured to America and lured into the mines by the assertion that in the bounteous and peaceful atmosphere of the United States, where the streets were paved with gold and no one was ever conscripted into the army, men and women who worked would be rich, free and good. In the company towns of Colorado men and women were none of these. They worked indeed: longer than the hours prescribed by the laws of Colorado and harder

[1] Report of the United States Commission on Industrial Relations (Washington 1915).

than the laws prescribed by Nature. They were mutilated and killed in spite of the safety regulations of the State of Colorado.

To get the coal, the miners first had to remove rock debris with their hands; but they were not paid for doing it. They did not have mechanical coal cutting machinery in 1913, and three years later in 1916, after Mackenzie King had brought new light into the darkness of the Colorado mining camps, a mule was still a luxury a miner was denied. Mules got killed, and mules cost money.[1] After a miner had cleared away the rock debris he hewed coal. He was paid for this; paid according to weight. But who is to say what is a ton of coal? The check-weighmen of the companies were known to differ from the miners on the subject.[2] If a miner thought a ton of 1200 pounds rather light, he might be thought a trouble-maker. There was a way of dealing with trouble-makers. They could be given the worst coal faces. If they persisted in their trouble-making they could be fired out of the mining camps, which meant no house and no food in one of the most desolate and remote parts of the United States. Trouble-makers were sometimes beaten up, especially if they talked not only about the abstract question of how much a ton of coal weighs, but about the more concrete questions of union organization.

For the most part a miner could not argue. Even if he had courage worthy of a Congressional Medal of Honour, he very frequently did not know enough English to argue, let alone organize, negotiate and place his case before the people for interpretation in accordance with the general will. In the idiom of the time, the poor immigrant was told to "speak white".

But miners were paid something. A man with cash in his pocket is a free man. But not in a company town. He must spend it in a company store. No one obliged him to do so, but oddly enough the company store was the only place within a day's journey where he could buy food, clothing, drink and tobacco. He had a company house. An improperly drained, tar-papered shanty was his defence against the winter temperatures of below zero Fahrenheit and the cold nights at an altitude of 4,000 feet above sea level. It kept off the mosquitoes in

---

[1] *American Federationist*, November, 1916.

[2] This was of course not peculiar to the Colorado coal mines. The identical condition obtained in British mines before the union checkweigh system was established in 1887 by the Coalmines Regulation Act.

summer. That is why a miner thought twice about being evicted from a company house fifty miles from nowhere, even if his wife and children had twice as much chance of dying of typhoid fever there, as elsewhere in the United States. A job was a job—particularly in 1913.

The constitutions of the United States and of the State of Colorado guarantee all citizens government of the people by the people. But not in a company town. In a company town the camp marshal ruled. He maintained a police and espionage service, and he passed the sentence, "Down the canyon with you!" upon trouble-makers. The camp marshals ran the elections and they appointed the juries. The Congressional investigation revealed, for example, that a bartender named Baldwin was virtually a permanent jury foreman on cases in the area. It revealed more than this. The political and judicial apparatus of those counties of the State of Colorado in which the large firms operated, was controlled by and worked in the interests of the coal operators. People easily went to Hell in company towns. They could take refuge in every vice which promises an escape: liquor, whores, treachery towards their fellow workers and dreams of heaven beyond the grave. Even the Word of God was brought into the service of the coal operators, for Ministers of religion were hired and fired according to the same principles as judges or mine guards. Inarticulate, disorganized and brutally exploited, the miners' lot might seem hopeless. But men are men, and they retain a capacity—strong in some and perhaps non-existent in others—to resist tyranny, injustice and discrimination and to build a better life.

There had been strikes in southern Colorado in 1883, 1893 and 1903. Each strike was broken by violence and by the importation of strike-breakers. The breakers of one strike became the strikers of the next episode. Late in 1912, and early in 1913, the situation began to mature in accordance with its past pattern of development. The United Mine Workers of America had long been worried by conditions in Colorado, but at this time their treasury was much depleted following a series of strikes elsewhere in the United States. Organizing in northern Colorado alone had cost about $800,000 during 1913.[1] In spite

[1] B. B. Beshoar, *Out of the Depths* (Denver, 1943), p. 43.

of this difficulty the executive of the miners' union decided to
send organizers into southern Colorado, in order that the blind,
inarticulate movement of the men and women there might lead
to an agreement with the operators—an agreement effected by
the experienced skill of union organizers, and guaranteed by
the whole strength of their 400,000 members in the United
States and Canada.[1]

The companies' answer to the United Mine Workers'
efforts to negotiate an agreement was an armament programme.
Well over three hundred Baldwin-Felts "detectives" were
hired. An armoured car, nicknamed by the men the "Death
Special", was built in the machine shops of the Colorado Fuel
and Iron Company. In August, 1913, a company "detective"
shot down a United Mine Workers' organizer in a street of
Trinidad, Colorado. The Governor of the State was then asked
to disarm everyone in the mining camps. This he failed to do.
In their anxiety the Federal Department of Labour sent a
special representative to see Mr. Rockefeller. Rockefeller refused to see him.

The union then wrote to the operators asking for a meeting.
Only two small operators replied.[2] On September 15th, the
union drew up seven demands, which are worth keeping in
mind in the light of Mackenzie King's story that union recognition was the principal issue. They were: (1) Recognition of the
union, (2) 10 per cent increase in tonnage rates and a day scale
comparable to that in Wyoming, (3) The eight-hour day prescribed by the laws of Colorado, (4) Payment for all dead work,
(5) Election of check-weighmen, (6) The right to deal at their
own stores, to choose their own boarding houses and their own
doctors, (7) The enforcement of the mining laws of the State of
Colorado. Recognition was, of course, a fundamental point, but
it was not the only issue. Recognition meant that the operators
were prepared to deal with representatives of the men experienced enough and strong enough to ensure the essential
minimum conditions which the workers felt they required.

[1] The best short account of conditions in Colorado is S. Yellen, *American Labor
Struggles* (New York, 1936). We have relied for our account on G. P. West, *Report
on the Colorado Strike,* and the United States Commission on Industrial Relations
(Washington, 1915), which gives extensive documentation. See also Upton Sinclair's
King Coal and B. B. Beshoar, *Out of the Depths* (Denver, 1943).

[2] One of whom was to become an Assistant Secretary of the Treasury in F. D.
Roosevelt's first Government.

On September 23rd, at least 9,000[1] miners moved out of the camps into tent colonies established on land leased for this purpose by the United Mine Workers of America. 9,000 miners thus challenged collectively the principle that "if you don't like it here you can get out". But they had not moved on. They sat down outside the company towns to demonstrate that the mines where they had worked were as much their mines as those of the stockholders like John D. Rockefeller in Tarrytown, New York; that they had an alternative to what they termed the slavery of individualism; and that they would stay until the companies, and the miners who had remained at work, realized that men and women were not obliged to live in the manner appointed by the coal companies.

The companies were confident. The officers of the Colorado Fuel and Iron Company regarded the situation as favourable to themselves. From New York John D. Rockefeller, Jr., was encouraging them with his praise. "You are fighting a good fight," he wrote to Superintendent Bowers of the Colorado Fuel and Iron Company on December 8th, 1913, "which is not only in the interest of your own company but of the other companies of Colorado and of the business interests of the entire country, and of the laboring classes quite as much."[2] They were well armed. It was suggested that only forty per cent of their miners had moved out. The Union's funds were low. The state militia had been ordered into the area. The Colorado Fuel and Iron Company claimed to be operating at 70 per cent capacity which was supposed to be sufficient to supply the market, at that time rather depressed.

In the tent colonies the situation was difficult. To resolve to live in a tent through the winter in Colorado is itself an act of heroism. To do so is something more. The miners and their wives and children dug holes in the earth beneath their tents. In these they could keep warm and dry so long as the snow was cleared away from their tents. They had some food supplied by the United Mine Workers. They appointed their own camp marshals to keep order and provide leadership. And so a winter of strife wore on. The strike was in fact a form of civil war fought between miner-guerillas and mine guards.

The members of the State Militia soon became anxious to get

[1] J. R. Lawson estimated the number as 12,000 men, in addition to families. *R.C.I.R.*, p. 8005.

[2] Quoted in Yellen, *American Labor Struggles*, p. 220.

back to their ordinary employments in Denver, Pueblo and Colorado Springs. As the militia men applied for leave and were dismissed, company "detectives" were enlisted in their places. Spring was coming on and the miners were still in their camps. They had managed to survive the winter. They were still there, inviting the miners yet at work to join them. They had demonstrated at the cost of many lives an alternative to tyranny.

All these facts seem to have enraged the company guards. During the morning of April 20th, 1914, a company of militiamen, with rifles and machine-guns, occupied a height above the strikers' camp at Ludlow. They entrenched themselves, and shooting broke out. The women and children in the camp took shelter in the dug-outs beneath their tents. The miners answered the fire, but only feebly for they had few rifles and no machine guns. After prolonged firing during most of the day and a night, which silenced the miners, the militiamen charged. Paraffin was thrown on the tents and fire set to them. In one dug-out eleven children and two women were burned to death. Three of the camp leaders were seized and shot—one, Louis Tikas, after being knocked unconscious with a rifle butt by the Lieutenant in command.[1]

At once the American public were aroused. Even the *New York Times,* harsh critic as it was of the American labour movement, sounded the alarm. Denouncing the United Mine Workers none the less, it asked the question: "When a sovereign state employs such horrible means what may not be expected from the anarchy that ensues?"

It was not easy to unload the blame on the State of Colorado. In April, 1914, shortly before the bloody events at Ludlow, J. D. Rockefeller, Jr., was questioned by the House Committee on Mines and Mining. Among other things, he stated then:

> "We believe the issue is not a local one in Colorado. It is a national issue whether workers shall be allowed to work under such conditions as they may choose. . . . Our interest in labor is so profound and we believe so sincerely that that interest demands that the camps shall be open camps, that we expect to stand by the officers at any cost. . . ."

When asked whether "you will do that if that costs all your property and kills all your employees?" Rockefeller replied: "It is a great principle."

[1] B. B. Beshoar, *Out of the Depths,* p. 177.

Q. "And you would do that rather than recognize the right of men to collective bargaining?"

A. "No sir. Rather than allow outside people to come in and interfere with employees who are thoroughly satisfied with their labor conditions. It was upon a similar principle that the War of the Revolution was carried on. It is a great national issue of the most vital kind."[1]

The bloodshed at Ludlow compelled the Rockefellers to change, not their objectives, but their tactics. Pickets were posted at the Rockefeller offices on lower Broadway and the Rockefeller home in Tarrytown, New York. For many years, the Standard Oil Company had been the object of bitter attacks by disgruntled and frightened members of the middle class. Now a coalition of wage-earners and middle-class elements was forming against the Rockefeller interests which threatened to undo all the effects of years of philanthropy and "scientific" public relations, and to revive all the old memories of the "octopus". What to do? John D. Rockefeller, Jr., and his legal adviser, Starr J. Murphy, were quick with an answer: put out a smoke screen of words and get experts to do the job. These experts were Ivy Lee,* the public relations genius of the Pennsylvania Railroad, and Mackenzie King of Canada.

Ivy Lee was approached directly, and he was shortly engaged in flooding the pipe-lines to the middle class with accounts of the way the executives of the United Mine Workers of America exploited the people. For example, the mere fact that on one occasion the annual wages and expenses of an official were described as for a nine-week period, did not trouble Ivy Lee.[2] He knew what the middle class wanted to hear, and he told it to them. They wanted to forget Ludlow; Ivy Lee helped them to do so.

Ivy Lee being thus put in charge of fabrication, King was given the responsibility for design. His account of this activity, as he told it in 1919, was the one we have related: he was engaged to make an academic and scientific study of labour relations in general; but his disposition, being at once scientific, passionate and practical, prompted him to study the situation in Colorado and to make suggestions for binding up the

---

[1] Quoted in the *New York Times*, 7 April, 1914; and in Yellen, *American Labor Struggles*, p. 221.

[2] See Yellen, *American Labor Struggles*, p. 239.

wounds of the community and for insuring that such social distress never again afflicted that unhappy state. In so far as the Commission on Industrial Relations appointed by the Congress of the United States was able to get the facts, they do not support this story.

Mackenzie King was approached in June, 1914, seven weeks after the massacre at Ludlow, by Jerome D. Greene,* the secretary and a director of the Rockefeller Foundation. Greene was a friend of Mackenzie King whom he had met at Harvard, when Greene was secretary to President Eliot. Lord Grey, when he was Governor-General of Canada, had also introduced Mackenzie King to Greene. In a letter dated June 3rd, 1914, Greene wrote:

> "Through the Rockefeller Foundation we are already planning some economic and social studies which may have an ultimate bearing on the solution of the labor problem; but it has seemed to us that, if, *in our purely corporate capacity as owners or directors of large industries*, we can work out, *on a basis compatible with sound finance*, any substantial improvements in the relation of capital and labor, we shall be, perhaps, doing a greater social service than we could render through any of our strictly philanthropic expenditures. It is with reference to a wise approach to this great problem that I am now asking your aid."[1]

Mackenzie King was *sub-poenaed* by the Commission on Industrial Relations and put on the witness stand. There he attempted to interpret this letter as an offer of employment for academic and scientific purposes, and to argue that the invitation was unconnected with events in Colorado. His recollection of his interview with John D. Rockefeller, Jr., was to the effect that Rockefeller had only mentioned Colorado as an example of the need for such studies. According to Mackenzie King,

> "he said, 'I will explain to you why I am asking this question (about labor relations) now, and why I am asking your advice. This situation in Colorado has brought home to me'—I am not using his exact words, but this is the substance of it—'has brought home to me an aspect of the industrial trouble that I had never comprehended to the degree that I now comprehend'...."[2]

Between Frank Walsh,* the chairman of the Commission, and Mackenzie King a great argument developed about the meaning of the words "in our corporate capacity". Fortunately, the Commission *sub-poenaed* not only Mackenzie King but his

[1] *R.C.I.R.*, p. 8788, our italics.   [2] *R.C.I.R.*, p. 8790.

correspondence, and we need not depend upon a mere interpretation of Greene's letter of invitation.

Following the invitation from Greene, Mackenzie King
visited New York, where he met Greene, John D. Rockefeller,
Jr., and Starr J. Murphy. Mackenzie King's version of this
interview, as he told it on the witness stand, suggests that all he
did on this occasion was engage in some general discussion
about labour relations. Colorado was mentioned in the way
we have described. His main suggestion was that Sydney Webb,
among five or six others whom he mentioned, should be invited
to direct the study of labour relations for the Foundation. What
Sydney Webb would have made of Colorado we can only sur-
mise. According to Mackenzie King, Rockefeller spoke of the
situation as if he did not quite understand the issues. "The
question, as I understand it [this is Mackenzie King's version
of Rockefeller's words] is the recognition of a particular union . . .
as long as the question remains one of recognition, I suppose the
struggle will go on."[1]

One of the baffling features of Mackenzie King's mind was
its capacity to discover useful half-truths among the multitude
of pressures bearing upon him in a particular situation. In this
instance he was able to deceive others and, perhaps, even himself not only with the ambiguity of his objectives, but also
by the very conflicts among the men inviting him to undertake
work with the Rockefellers. On the one hand, there was ex-
President Eliot of Harvard, one of the Trustees of the Rockefeller Foundation, urging him to undertake "the most important work which the civilized world now offers—more
important than any immediate question of war, insurrection,
political constructions, or domestic or foreign trade. . . ."
Eliot believed that the events in Colorado were symptomatic of a death rattle at the heart of capitalist civilization,
which he declared to Mackenzie King, "cannot survive the
existing morbid condition of city life and the factory system
. . . the plain wage system has reached its limit of usefulness;
another great invention for the co-operative use of both capital
and labor must now be made."[2] On the other hand, there were
the Rockefellers themselves and their attorneys demanding an

---

[1] *R.C.I.R.*, pp. 8791–92.
[2] *Eliot Papers*, Eliot to King, 13 July, 1914.

o

immediate plan for stilling the public outcry, for getting the mines back into operation at full capacity and for baffling the United Mine Workers of America. Thus, by reading his correspondence, Mackenzie King could find evidence that he was both a disinterested prophet and an interested servant of profit; both a scholar and a hack adviser.

Eliot pressed him one way and Rockefeller and his attorneys pressed him another. Eliot, more candid and far-sighted than anyone else interested in the Colorado situation, believed that the task there required the services of a construction engineer, rather than a paper hanger. "The Rockefeller Foundation proposes to work out, and put in practice", Eliot told Mackenzie King,

> "all the available means of hearty co-operation between employer and employed, and is to bring about that goodwill on both sides which is the surest promoter of efficiency. You doubtless realize what an extremely complicated problem that is. The solution will utilize profit sharing, co-operative management, sickness and death benefits, accident insurance, co-operative stores and good housing, and each house to have a garden."[1]

Eliot's influence was never continuous, however. When Mackenzie King's work was nearly over, Eliot was still telling him that an economic solution finally would have to be found. What Mackenzie King was doing was only a beginning. "The supplement, I suppose," he wrote, "to be profit sharing."[2]

By August, 1914, Mackenzie King had got down to cases about Colorado. This is revealed in one of the most illuminating letters of Mackenzie King which has yet seen the light of day, and one which Mackenzie King himself realized could have been damaging to his political career if properly used by his Parliamentary opponents.[3] The letter dated August 6th, 1914, was in response to one written by Rockefeller on August 1st, in which Rockefeller reported to Mackenzie King in detail the situation as it then was in Colorado, and in which he enclosed a letter from the company president. Rockefeller's letter contradicts Mackenzie King's statement on the witness stand that there was no particular discussion of Colorado. But no matter what they discussed in Tarrytown, in this letter Rockefeller

---

[1] *Eliot Papers*, Eliot to King, 13 July, 1914.
[2] *Eliot Papers*, Eliot to King, 10 December, 1915.
[3] *R.C.I.R.*, p. 8794.

invited Mackenzie King to submit a plan for "developing some organization in the mining camps, which will assure to the employees the opportunity for collective bargaining."[1] Clearly such an organization could be an alternative to recognition of the United Mine Workers of America.

To this request, Mackenzie King replied as follows (6th August):

"Coming to the Colorado situation: I agree with you in believing it to be extremely unlikely that the United Mine Workers of America will call off the strike. They might be willing to drop open active support by degrees, but I am inclined to think that where recognition has been the principle for which they have been fighting, they will not openly abandon the struggle with anything short of what they may be able to construe as such.

"It may be, however, that organized labour in the United States will realize the opportunities and handicaps likely to come to certain industries through the changed conditions of Europe [i.e. World War I] and will be prepared to cease hostilities where industrial strife at present exists, in order that on the one hand labour may reap with capital a fuller measure of the harvest, or, in industries that may be differently affected, protect itself against consequences that are certain to arise. . . . Looking at the ultimate, rather than the immediate effect, there is, speaking generally, going to be a large amount of unemployment as a consequence of this war, and once the war is over, thousands of men and their families in the Old World are going to seek future employment here in the New. In certain industries it is going to be easy for employers to find all the labour they desire, and unions will be confronted with a new problem. Recognition, simply for the sake of recognition, is going to be seen to be less pressing as an immediate end than that of maintaining standards already existing, and may rightly come to regard as their friends and allies companies and corporations large enough and fair enough to desire to maintain these standards of their own accord. . . ."[2]

This letter reveals much about Mackenzie King. It shows, for instance, that he did not become interested in the Colorado situation after his work with the Rockefeller Foundation had begun, but *before* he took up his engagement there. He did not "go out to the State of Colorado [himself] to use that particular state as a laboratory", but also because Rockefeller wanted him to do so; and perhaps even because his chance of establishing a connection with Rockefeller turned on his ability to provide a

[1] West, *Report on the Colorado Strike*, p. 159.
[2] West, *Report on the Colorado Strike*, p. 160 ff.; also *R.C.I.R.*, pp. 8449–52.

means of reducing the tension (so dangerous to the Rockefellers) following the Ludlow massacre.

Of more consequence is what is revealed about his understanding of labour's needs. ". . . It was charged," he said, "that I, who had been representing (*sic*) labor in Canada for years, had sold out, or something to that effect."[1] Assuming that Mackenzie King ever had "represented" labour, this letter would certainly seem to support the charge. In it he treats union recognition as a species of fetish, which trade unionists madly pursue at the expense of the substance of decent wages and conditions of work. With some cynicism he suggested that labour and capital (if labour is clever enough) can reap the rich harvest of war. Peace after war, on the other hand, will bring unemployment in its wake, and this, too, will keep labour in line. Mackenzie King did not, of course, specifically approve of war and unemployment, but he noticed their effects upon the political relations of employers and employees and saw in them a means of muting the importunities of the wage workers.

Discussing the concrete situation in Colorado, Mackenzie King supplied Rockefeller with the plan Rockefeller wanted. To meet Rockefeller's requirements, a plan must achieve three things: (1) avoid recognition and negotiation with the United Mine Workers of America; (2) provide some means of keeping in touch with the mine workers to replace the system which had obviously broken down and had provoked a public scandal; and (3) restore the public reputation of Rockefeller. That Mackenzie King thought he should try to achieve these three objectives, is indicative both of his understanding of the relations between capital and labour, and of his position *vis-à-vis* the wage earners.

Mackenzie King had only briefly, and not very comprehensively, contemplated a system of labour relations based upon compulsion, and in that case the compulsion was to be employed by the state and it was intended that it should operate according to a pattern of law. He never believed at any time in labour relations based on armed company police such as characterized the regime in Colorado, which the officers of the Colorado Fuel and Iron Company euphemistically described as the open shop or "freedom to enjoy conditions of one's own

[1] *R.C.I.R.*, p. 8794.

choosing". He pointed out to Rockefeller three possible systems of more civilized labour relations: (1) individual contracts binding employers and employees, (2) collective bargaining between employers and employees on a plant or company basis, (3) collective bargaining between employers and employees through union organizations. To Mr. Rockefeller he recommended the second method, i.e., the method of company unionism.

Before a company union could be established in the plants of the Colorado Fuel and Iron Company the strike in southern Colorado had to be broken. In the manner predicted by Mackenzie King in his letter to Rockefeller of August 6th, 1914, the war in Europe began to affect the industrial situation in the United States. Prosperity once more began to seem "around the corner". The strike in Colorado was costing the high command of the United Mine Workers enormous sums of money, at a moment when it seemed possible to participate in prosperity elsewhere in the United States, by new agreements with coal operators who had already recognized them and were long used to union bargaining. Frank J. Hayes, the International Vice-President of the union most concerned with Colorado, appears to have begun to lose his determination in the autumn of 1914, and he sought for a way to cut his losses in Colorado. President Wilson provided him with his opportunity.

On December 1st, Wilson announced that he had secured the consent of certain eastern coal operators, and of the United Mine Workers, to the appointment of a commission representative of both the operators and the union, under the Chairmanship of the Hon. Seth Low,* a former mayor of New York. This Commission would attempt to find a solution of the situation in Colorado. Upon the promise of the President thus to "find a solution" the officers of the Union recommended that the strike be declared at an end. On December 10th, 1914, the strike was over. The men on strike were left wet and cold on the plains and in the canyons of Colorado. Some left the State, others were obliged to beg for their jobs again from the coal companies. The time was propitious for Mackenzie King to bind up the wounds of the industrial community.

The task of getting the Union to accept a union which was not a union, and then to get such a union accepted by the mass of miners in Colorado, required extraordinary skill. On January 27th, 1915, officials of the United Mine Workers of America were invited as individuals to an unofficial meeting in the Rockefeller offices at 26, Broadway, New York City, with Mackenzie King, Starr J. Murphy and John D. Rockefeller, Jr. The Union officials present were Jim Lord, Frank J. Hayes and E. L. Doyle, Secretary of District 15 (Colorado) of the United Mine Workers. John Lawson, the principal field commander of the Union in southern Colorado, was invited but could not attend. The meeting lasted three and a half hours. Mackenzie King tried hard to win some assent for his plan of company unionism. He made no progress. As the meeting broke up and the Union officers were leaving, Mackenzie King took Doyle aside and said to him

"that whatever plans he put into effect would ultimately lead to recognition of the union if Lawson and [he] conducted [them] selves in the future as [they] had in the past. [He, i.e. Doyle] made no reply to this as [he] doubted his sincerity when he made the statement to only one man instead of bringing it up at the meeting . . . just adjourned."[1]

Mackenzie King's words to Lawson and Doyle were remarkable, because those two men were the heart and brains of the strike, and they had to be expelled from the Union before the United Mine Workers could liquidate their obligations in Colorado. As it was, Lawson was meditating at the very moment of Mackenzie King's kindly flattery an attack upon the flatterer. Two days later, as a witness before the Commission on Industrial Relations, Lawson declared,

"And who is the man chosen to conduct this million-dollar investigation into industrial unrest? One Mackenzie King, an alien, whose contribution to the industrial problem is a law that prescribes a jail sentence for the worker who dares to lay down his tools. If labor had any doubt as to his real intent that doubt was removed by the letter read at this hearing. Under date of August 6th, 1914, Mackenzie King wrote to John D. Rockefeller. . . ." etc.[2]

Lawson was not able to obstruct for long. On February 15th, 1915, he was charged before the District Court in Trinidad,

---

[1] Edward L. Doyle to one of the authors, 24 May, 1953.
[2] *R.C.I.R.*, p. 8007.

Colorado, with murder. Ten others were charged jointly with him, and 191 other miners were arrested on various charges. On May 2nd he was found guilty and sentenced to life imimprisonment.

With the leaders in Colorado safely under lock and key, it was possible to seek the consent of the men to the Rockefeller Plan. The Plan itself was the result of a compromise among Rockefeller's executives in Colorado, Superintendent Bowers of the Colorado Fuel and Iron, F. G. Welborn, President of the Company, and Mackenzie King. There was a danger that Mackenzie King, in his tactful liberalism, might give too much away in his charter of industrial freedom. It was necessary to demonstrate to Rockefeller and the Company officials that concession was not dangerous. Clause 3 of Section III under the Plan reads: "There shall be no discrimination by the company or by any of its employees on account of membership or non-membership in any society, fraternity or union."[1] Thus, a miner was free to join the Rover Scouts, the Kiwanis or the United Mine Workers of America. But the plan provided no opportunity for the men to employ the services in negotiation of skilled and experienced bargainers not dependent for their incomes upon the Colorado Fuel and Iron Company.[2]

The Rockefeller Plan was democratic. It required consent. A ballot was taken. Edward L. Doyle described the election thus to a friend:

"The Rockefeller union which was put into effect while that gentleman was here is certainly a farce. The officers of the company are the labor leaders of that organization, and the agreement was given to the press before the convention was called with the statement that it was adopted by a convention and reported to the miners for a referendum vote which has to be a secret vote, and this is how they voted: Each miner was given two slips of paper, one red and the other white. On one was printed the word "for" and the other the word "against" and the miner chose which he desired to cast as his ballot destroying the other, and when approaching the ballot box a company superintendent or representative was present to see the color of the ticket voted.

[1] J. D. Rockefeller, Jr., *The Colorado Industrial Plan* (1916), p. 75.
[2] J. D. Rockefeller, Jr., *The Colorado Industrial Plan*, p. 95, gives a diagram of the structure. The only *external* referee was the State of Colorado Industrial Commission, which could intervene only when asked and under certain conditions.

Secret ballot, HA! HA! Of course it was necessary that this method be used because the "ignorant miners" might not know how to cast their vote unless the ballots were already printed and of different color, so they could vote as they desired, without making a mistake even if they couldn't read, and while the reported vote showed eleven to one in favor of the agreement. "Fremont County" ran about two to one, so you can see that the men of your old camping ground are still of the same mind as on the twenty-third of September, 1913, and the Rockefeller union will, if they have their way of it, finally be christened the United Mine Workers of America, and new officers elected to succeed the company officials who now pass as officers of a later union."[1]

The Plan was accepted by an overwhelming "popular majority of eighty per cent of the miners".[2]

The last stage now followed. After the Plan had been accepted, the President's Commission, consisting of the Hon. Seth Low, Mr. Charles W. Mills, a coal operator, and Mr. Patrick Gilday, an official of the United Mine Workers from Pennsylvania, visited Colorado. The wreckage of 1913–14 had been cleared away by November 1915. Gilday had his doubts about the plan: ". . . if the men cannot select their own delegates with freedom, on any proposition that comes up, then they are to me far better without it [the Rockefeller Plan]."[3] But if Gilday had his doubts he also had his orders from the Union executive. They were determined to wind up the Colorado strike. Lawson and Doyle were silenced when they attempted to report their objections against the President's Commission to the international convention of the United Mine Workers at Indianapolis in January, 1916.[4] Finally they were expelled from the Union, in spite of the overwhelming support they received in the election for officers in District 15. Gilday signed the report which stated that

"the plan is . . . something more than a means of escaping from dealing with the union. . . . Representation in the first instance has been achieved by a part of the body politic only; but time has inevitably broadened such representation till all are included. . . . Your Commission cannot believe that a body of

[1] *Doyle Correspondence*, Doyle to Felix Pogliano, 14 October, 1915.
[2] Rogers, *Mackenzie King*, p. 55.
[3] Extract from the testimony before the Federal Commission on the Labor Difficulties in the Coal Fields of Colorado, p. 71.
[4] Beshoar, *Out of the Depths*, p. 352.

American men granted such rights as the Colorado Fuel and Iron Co.'s employees now enjoy under this plan by formal contract can permanently be deprived of those rights."[1]

The science of public relations required that in Colorado Mr. Rockefeller, Jr., himself, should appear in overalls in the morning and in a dancing suit in the evening. When he was a very old man, President Eliot wrote to Mackenzie King for a clarification of one point in the Colorado episode. "Did you advise him [i.e. Mr. Rockefeller, Jr.]", he asked, "to enter upon that campaign in Colorado when he danced with as many of the miners' wives and daughters as possible?" Mackenzie King, also older and wiser, replied, "I did have something to do with the dance at Colorado and for starting him, whether for good or ill, a little on that path."[2] The dance soon ended and the organizers of the entertainment departed again for New York.

In January, 1916, Mr. Rockefeller was able to report in the columns of the *Atlantic Monthly* that a new era had dawned in Colorado. Labour and Capital were now partners. Each now understood its true interests; and they understood each other. All were now equal citizens in the "Republic of Labour". Of course,

> "The problem of the equitable division of the fruits of industry will be always with us . . . [but] assuming, as we must, the fundamental fairness of men's purposes, we have here possibly a medium through which the always changing conditions of industry may be from time to time more closely adapted to the needs, the desires and the aspirations of men."[3]

Mr. Rockefeller had discovered "morale"; that an indispensable factor in high productivity is the establishment of the conviction in the mind of the man at the machine or on the end of a shovel that he is a human being and accepted as such. The era of the labour relations expert had dawned.

Mackenzie King painted the lily rather more than Rockefeller. He spoke of the new Colorado: "happy and prosperous communities, assuming the aspect of garden villages . . ."[4] in

---

[1] Quoted in *I. H.*, pp. 445–46.
[2] *Eliot Papers*, Eliot to King, 28 July, 1925; King to Eliot, 11 August, 1925.
[3] *Atlantic Monthly*, January, 1914, quoted in Rockefeller, *The Colorado Industrial Plan*, p. 31.
[4] *I. H.*, p. 446.

place of the tar-paper towns and armed tent colonies of the past.

When Mackenzie King was called before the Commission on Industrial Relations sitting in Washington in May, 1915, he was examined concerning this character of his plan for industrial relations. The Chairman of this Commission was a Democratic politician named Frank Walsh of Missouri. Behind a mask of seeming stupidity Walsh was a shrewd, sharp and cynical realist. His stubborn adherence to the dogma that a politician, and indeed any human being, can occupy only one of two positions—either *for* labour or *against* it—was useful in eliciting the views of witnesses. He acted like an acid which decomposed the personalities of witnesses and exposed their elements to the public gaze. For this reason Mackenzie King was frequently at odds with the Chairman and as frequently driven into a defensive position.

Cutting through the elaborate organization of boards involved in Mackenzie King's plan, Walsh asked this question: "The plan you proposed to Mr. Rockefeller the first time you ever had a talk with him was that the men selected to prevent the grievances should be men actually inside the industry and not called from the outside. Is that correct?" "No!" was Mackenzie King's first answer, but Walsh read him some sentences from his own correspondence. Then he asked whether it was not the case, "that all members of such boards [proposed by Mackenzie King] excepting possibly persons chosen as chairmen, referees, or umpires, should be persons actually employed in the industry, or connected with it in some way, not persons from outside?" The witness made an evasive answer. Then Mackenzie King burst out: "You do me a great injustice—I want to make this plain—you do me a great injustice if you try to infer that this was any attempt not to recognize the union or any attempt to evolve machinery which would prevent the union getting recognition."

Walsh ignored this outburst, and put an even more precise question: "That is what I am asking you as directly as possible; under that [plan] could these men have chosen Frank J. Hayes, or Mr. McLennan, or any other of the members of the United Mine Workers of America?"

To this Mackenzie King replied:

"Mr. Chairman, you are a lawyer; when you are called in to advise in regard to a particular situation, you advise with regard to the situation put before you. I was, as an expert, asked to advise as to a particular situation, and I took the situation as presented to me, and I gave advice within the restrictions placed upon me. Any attempt to construe that advice to in any way show prejudice against labor unions is something I think would be dishonorable in the highest degree, and I want to make it most emphatically plain, *both for my own sake and for—for the sake of my own reputation* and for the sake of the reputation of this commission, that any effort of that kind is doing one of the greatest acts of injustice to any man that can possibly be done."[1]

This outburst refutes Mackenzie King's story that he was an impartial, academic research worker of a scholarly foundation who happened to use Colorado as a laboratory subject. He had become a professional labour relations expert working for the Rockefellers for the objectives which they had set him.

Walsh was unperturbed by the outburst itself. He told Mackenzie King that he would continue to ask questions to which the witness could answer yes or no, and that the Commission itself would judge him. King then denounced the way in which witnesses were cross-questioned as "disgraceful". After he had calmed himself Walsh asked: "You did not like it from the very start the way I have conducted the hearings?" To this Mackenzie King replied:

"I regret it deeply, from the standpoint of labor, and anybody that wishes labor as much good as possible does so. This is a commission that has a possibility of rendering one of the greatest services to industry, and I regret that it has been managed in such a way that I fear such possibilities are gone."[2]

Walsh let this pass, and asked: "What salary do they pay you?" Mackenzie King exploded again, "That is a matter you do not have a right to inquire into," etc., etc. ". . . I think it is just as well that matters that are private should be kept private. . . . If you think I am the sort of man that is going to be influenced by the salary I receive, if you will say so, I will answer the question." To this Walsh rejoined with the candour of a native American long accustomed to the cash nexus. "I do not know the sort of man you are, but if you ask my opinion I will

[1] *R.C.I.R.*, p. 8796; our italics. [2] *R.C.I.R.*, p. 8797.

say that my experience in life, covering a good many years, is that a man who accepts remuneration from another man for work to be done naturally feels very much beholden to that man." "That may be your way; it is not mine," replied the future Prime Minister,[1] too modest to reveal the measure of his temptation.

The Commission did judge Mackenzie King and his plan, and so did history. The interim report on the situation in Colorado reads:

"Mr. Rockefeller's responsibility has a significance beyond even the sinister results of his policy in Colorado. The perversion of and contempt for government, the disregard of public welfare, and the defiance of public opinion during the Colorado strike must be considered as only one manifestation of the autocratic and anti-social spirit of a man whose enormous wealth gives him infinite opportunity to act in a similar fashion in broader fields. . . . The nation-wide significance and importance of the Colorado conflict and the company's ruthless policy of suppression are emphasized again and again. By June, 1914, Mr. Rockefeller had formulated something like a definite plan for a nation-wide campaign. The most highly paid publicity expert in the country had been borrowed from a great eastern railway, to be taken over later as a permanent member of Mr. Rockefeller's staff. A 'union educational campaign' is to be conducted, and the country is to be flooded with articles by college professors and others bitterly denouncing trade unions. And at the very time when he prepares to circulate Professor Stevenson's intemperate and amazing defence of industrial absolutism and tirade against trade unions, Mr. Rockefeller enlists the aid of Mr. W. L. Mackenzie King, expert on industrial relations, to devise specious substitutes for trade unions that will deceive, mollify and sooth public opinion while bulwarking the employers' arbitrary control."[2]

But Commissions of Inquiry can be biased. Was there any other tribunal before which Mackenzie King and his plan were judged? The plan was inaugurated in the plants of the Colorado Fuel and Iron Company, and the Colorado Legislature was induced to establish by law a system of compulsory investigation, conciliation and arbitration of industrial disputes. Both the plan as established in the Colorado Fuel and Iron Company and the system of conciliation in the State of Colorado have

---

[1] *R.C.I.R.*, p. 8797.
[2] West, *Report on the Colorado Strike*, pp. 152–53.

been carefully studied by academic students of industrial relations. Examining the labour relations of the Colorado Fuel and Iron Company during the period 1915–22, B. Selekman and M. Van Kleek, in their book *Employees' Representation in Coal Mines*, found that the plan did not bring industrial peace to the company, although it appears to have diminished bitterness. In seven years there were seven major strikes in Colorado and four of these were in plants of the Company. Rioting had, however, diminished, although troops were still called out. The importation of strike-breakers diminished, and union meetings were frequently permitted (although Selekman and Van Kleek do not say of which unions). This hardly represents a new heaven and a new earth. Indeed, the plan seems to have achieved what it was intended to achieve—the separation of the workers into those organized in the company union and those organized in real unions. In 1938, under a new political dispensation, the National Labor Relations Board heard the case of the unions against the Colorado Fuel and Iron Company, and after an investigation, pronounced the "industrial councils" to be company unions, ordered them dissolved and ordered free elections to be held in the plants of the Company.

The judgment of history on the system of industrial conciliation set up in the State of Colorado is hardly better. C. E. Warne and M. E. Gaddis studied the system in 1927, after it had been in operation for eleven years. They believed it could be said for the system that it had tended to diminish bitterness and to enable small employers and their employees to iron out their differences. In large disputes the system did not work, and "the strategic power of labor has been materially reduced by law".[1] This, again, was the intention of its authors.

In considering Mackenzie King's part in the events we have described, it is not necessary to believe that large trade unions are everywhere and at all times indispensable to the welfare of wage-earners. The organization of production and technological excellence may for some time contribute to the economic well-being of wage-earners as much as or more than, skilful trade union negotiation. But it still remains a fact that in the circumstances which obtained in North American industry at

[1] C. E. Warne and M. E. Gaddis, "Eleven Years of Compulsory Investigation of Industrial Disputes in Colorado," *Journal of Political Economy*, XXXV, 1927, p. 682.

any time from the Civil War to World War I industrial employers, egged on by financiers like Rockefeller, were consciously
seeking to prevent the organization of wage-workers in a way
which would enable them to bargain on equal terms with their
employers. Negotiation is a skilled business, yet the open shop
philosophers wanted either not to negotiate at all, or to limit
the negotiations to discussions with men at the plant level, who
were engaged full time in industrial employment and could be
dismissed from their employment at any time by the employers
with whom they were negotiating. Rockefeller never moved
except among a platoon of experts: his attorneys, his public
relations experts, his labour relations advisers and so on. Yet
he expected the miners in Colorado to negotiate (when public
opinion finally forced him to consider this policy) with his
superintendents without the aid and counsel of anyone outside
the mines. This was the essential feature of Mackenzie King's
plan for industrial peace, and this is the feature of the plan
which Commissioner Walsh, to Mackenzie King's great indignation, so unfeelingly exposed. By any process of *a priori*
reasoning the scheme appears unjust and disadvantageous
to the wage-earner; and what reason suggests, actual facts have
proved. Company unionism of the kind recommended by
Mackenzie King has never benefited wage-workers generally.
Generally it has been a device for promoting paternalism and
sapping the spirit of independence of labour.

The evidence printed in the Report of the Commission on
Industrial Relations constitutes a convincing refutation of the
story of Mackenzie King's part in the Colorado troubles, which
he told to the Trades and Labour Congress of Canada in
October, 1919. But this evidence, in so far as it concerns Mackenzie King, is not complete. A representative of the employers on the Commission on Industrial Relations, Commissioner Harriman, attempted to give Mackenzie King an
opportunity to develop the point that his "scientific" inquiries
had embraced all parties to the dispute in Colorado.[1] Mackenzie
King seized the opportunity and suggested that he had had
talks with the officers of the United Mine Workers of
America. When he was telling his story to the Trades and
Labour Congress of Canada in October, 1919, he even went to

[1] *R.C.I.R.*, p. 8812.

the length of alleging that the officers of the United Mine
Workers had told him they approved of his plan for labour
relations because it was the best compromise which the circumstances would allow.[1]

What are the facts about Mackenzie King's relations with
the United Mine Workers of America during these events?
Did he, the social scientist, study this union as a factor in the
situation? Or did he negotiate with it as a labour relations
expert employed by the Rockefellers? Did he gain qualified
support from the United Mine Workers for the plan of labour
relations which he drew up for the Rockefellers?

In attempting to discover whether or not Mackenzie King was
the impartial investigator he purported to be, Chairman Walsh
asked Mackenzie King whether he had attempted to see the
officers of the United Mine Workers of America in Colorado or
the officers of the State Federation of Labour. Mackenzie King
was evasive. "I refuse to disclose any of the interviews I had in
Colorado. . . ." he said. When he was pressed to answer, he
angrily declared,

"I do not intend to disclose the names, and I do not intend to let
the impression go abroad that I avoided seeing anyone, not for
one minute. If the president and secretary and treasurer and
those other men you speak of were interested in seeing me, they
knew exactly where I was staying, and there was no one that was
refused an interview who asked for it, and I was most anxious to
see them and most solicitous. If there was any keeping away, they
were the ones that kept away and not me. . . ."[2]

At this point Commissioner Harriman attempted to help
Mackenzie King out of his difficulty by asking him whether he
had seen the senior officers of the United Mine Workers. The
witness replied that he had seen them several times. Where? In
New York. The Chairman returned to the question. Had
he seen Mr. Doyle, the District Secretary of the United Mine
Workers in Colorado? Yes, Mackenzie King had seen Mr.
Doyle, but did not have a lengthy interview with him. "You
say you saw him in Colorado?" "Yes," answered Mackenzie
King, "I did."[3] Chairman Walsh then produced a telegram:
"Wire relative to Mackenzie King consulting officers of United

[1] *Daily Star*, Toronto, indecipherable date, October, 1919.
[2] *R.C.I.R.*, p. 8811.   [3] *R.C.I.R.*, p. 8812.

Mine Workers or State Federation received. Mr. King did not call on or consult any of the officers of the United Mine Workers or the State Federation of Labor while he was in Colorado." This telegram was signed by E. L. Doyle and W. T. Hickey.[1]

Caught, Mackenzie King attempted to get out of the trap.

"I met Mr. Doyle one afternoon when I was calling on 'Mother' Jones. I talked with him in the same room in which I talked with 'Mother' Jones. I engaged to see Mr. Doyle at a future time . . . when your communication [the *sub-poena* to attend the Commission] came . . . I had to shorten many of the interviews I was to have had in Colorado . . . [the interview with] Mr. Doyle was one of that number."

It is plain from this testimony that Mackenzie King did not make any serious attempt to see one of the main parties to the dispute in Colorado. His discussions with the officers of the United Mine Workers in New York were not fully investigated by the Walsh Commission, but our study and the evidence we have been able to discover suggests that these discussions were not designed to disclose what the Union wanted, but whether the officers could be split or could be induced to accept a company union. What part Mackenzie King had in the manoeuvring which led to the report of the Seth Low Commission and the expulsion of Doyle and Lawson from the United Mine Workers, we have been unable to learn. All we can conclude is that Mackenzie King was hardly the "student in public affairs" depicted by his admiring biographers.

It has often been supposed that Mackenzie King was one of those politicians who make up their minds by counting heads and headlines; that as a politician he was froth on the surface. This is quite a mistaken view. His part in the Colorado episode and his conduct before the Commission on Industrial Relations reveals the penetrating way in which he was able to assess the strength of the forces at work, and how he was never misled by public passion and majority opinion.

When he joined forces with Rockefeller the indignation about the Ludlow massacre was immense. The Congress of the United States, reflecting this indignation, referred this matter to its Commission on Industrial Relations which was, in the

[1] *R.C.I.R.*, p. 8812.

main, bent on exposing Rockefeller and his associates and little disposed to conceal their shortcomings. Even the most anti-labour newspapers had been forced by the brutalities in southern Colorado to fall back on the defensive after many years of vicious anti-union propaganda.[1] And yet Mackenzie King was not deterred by mere public indignation from joining the unpopular side. He understood the realities of power.

At one stage of the inquiry in Washington Commissioner Walsh thought it likely that Mr. Rockefeller, as a director of the Colorado Fuel and Iron Company, would have some influence upon Mr. Rockefeller as a director of the Rockefeller Foundation; and that Mr. Rockefeller's interests as a business man might influence his policies as the director of a charitable foundation financing scientific studies of industrial relations. Mackenzie King flatly denied this possibility. "There is", he said, "something deeper than a man's mentality—his conscience and his own heart. If Mr. Rockefeller got a report from me saying a thing meant social justice, I don't care what board he was on, he would stand for it."[2] In spite of the evidence in the record, Mackenzie King depicted Mr. Rockefeller as a great friend of labour. "I would say," he declared,

> "that a man with as great wealth as Mr. Rockefeller has should use it to improve conditions not only as far as his own employees are concerned, but for the benefit of his fellow men generally. . . . Mr. Rockefeller has done that very thing. That is the very thing he is seeking to do. He is trying to do it in all sincerity, and I humbly submit, Mr. Chairman, that no one who strives to destroy an effort of that kind, to frustrate it, is a true friend of labor, irrespective of who he may be."[3]

Mackenzie King sought to show that in his love of labour, Mr. Rockefeller surpassed the executive of the United Mine Workers of America, Commissioner Walsh, President Wilson and the Congress of the United States. Indeed, these men were actually the hidden enemies of labour, obstructing the efforts of Mr. Rockefeller to uplift and reward the men in Colorado who foolishly went on strike, and, with continuing folly, were to do so again and again. When questioned about what he had

---

[1] The *New York Times* was calling for company unions at the time Mackenzie King appeared on the scene. See *New York Times*, 30 July, 1914, also Rockefeller to King, 1 August, 1914, *R.C.I.R.*, pp. 8440–41.

[2] *R.C.I.R.*, p. 8788.   [3] *R.C.I.R.*, p. 8814.

P

actually discovered in Colorado, Mackenzie King refused to talk. "No, Mr. Chairman, I have said I do not desire to discuss the Colorado situation."[1] And he did not. In the end Commissioner Walsh and the labour representatives of the Commission recommended to the House of Representatives of the United States that Mr. J. D. Rockefeller, Jr., and Mackenzie King be summoned before Congress and compelled under oath to answer questions.[2] But this never happened.

In most men's lives there must be some area of certainty; some person or principle which is good and right beyond question. In Mackenzie King's life the Rock of Ages was Rockefeller, *sans peur et sans reproche*. He represented the perfect conscience at once pure and omnipotent. Nothing ever shook Mackenzie King's confidence in Rockefeller. John D. Rockefeller, Jr., reciprocated by describing Mackenzie King as the man to whom he owed most in his life next to his father, who made the Rockefeller fortune. From Mackenzie King, John D. Rockefeller, Jr., received admiration when others reviled.

Mackenzie King's behaviour in the Colorado affair poses a number of psychological problems. Having viewed the whole gruesome business of Ludlow did he callously decide to fight on the stronger side? Was he willing to do anything for the sake of power? Had the desire for power so completely corrupted him that the sympathies of his youth were dead in his heart?

The process by which the youthful fighter against sweat shops was transformed, first, into a hired labour relations expert and finally into a Prime Minister was a complex and unheroic one. Rockefeller seems to have appreciated that Mackenzie King might go sour if he were fully confronted with the facts before him. Writing to Welborn, the president of the Colorado Fuel and Iron Company, on August 11th, 1914, after Mackenzie King had agreed to undertake the work but before he had had an opportunity to see the situation with his own eyes, Rockefeller said,

"If there is any man available who could be helpful in working out such a plan as this, I believe Mr. King is the man. My thought would be for him to go to Denver in an entirely private and unofficial capacity as your guest, without its being generally known that he was there. I should not expect him to undertake to visit

[1] *R.C.I.R.*, p. 8815.   [2] *R.C.I.R.*, pp. 267–69.

the coal properties of the company, but rather simply to confer with you gentlemen in your own office."[1]

Mackenzie King seems to have fallen in with this design to keep his inquiries on a bureaucratic level, where human realities, sweat and tears were invisible. He wished to forget the past or to avert his eyes from it. "Do you believe from your investigation in Colorado," he was asked by Chairman Walsh, "that a condition of industrial freedom existed in Colorado in 1913 prior to this strike?" King would not answer this question straightforwardly.

> "As to that I would say that the impression I gathered while I was in Colorado was that the people in that state were mostly desirous that bygones should be bygones and that men should work together constructively to build up Colorado rather than to perpetuate a memory of the strife that has been going on there. . . ."[2]

Chairman Walsh asked him if it was not important to get the facts. He agreed that the facts were worth having, but he denied that it was any use putting them to the American people. Chairman Walsh suggested to him that the reporting of the facts to the American people was essential in order to bring to an end the conditions existing in Colorado. "Is that not the way to do it—to put it into the minds of the people—before the people?" To this question Mackenzie King replied, "I do not know that that is the way to do it, and I don't know that you honestly think it is. The way to do it is to get hold of the forces controlling the situation, and if they are wrong, to remedy it."

Chairman Walsh asked, "Is there any force in the American people?" To this Mackenzie King replied, "We are playing in words." Chairman Walsh's comment was, "No, I am not. Is there any force to control the Rockefeller interests in Colorado to do the right thing if they are not doing the right thing, except the ordinary people in America?" Then Mackenzie King revealed his trust in the relative powers of wealth and democracy. "If you are speaking of the immediate force and immediate influence," he said, "I think that the conscience of young Mr. John D. Rockefeller is more powerful on that, and will effect social justice in Colorado quicker than any other single force that you could bring to bear. . . ."[3]

Mackenzie King's policy seems, indeed, to have been based

---

[1] West, *Report on the Colorado Strike*, pp. 167–69.
[2] *R.C.I.R.*, p. 8816.   [3] *R.C.I.R.*, p. 8816.

on self-deception, purposeful forgetting of the facts, an un-democratic theory of politics, a powerful ambition and the need for a job. But Colorado was only a beginning. As American industry expanded in response to the demand created by war Mackenzie King worked on the construction of machinery by which employers and workers reaped the harvest vouchsafed them by Providence. Industrial councils, commonly known as company unions, were installed in the plants of some of the largest industrial enterprises in the United States.[1] By 1919 Mackenzie King enjoyed a reputation for leadership in big business circles in New York. By one of the curious ironies of chronology, it happened that the very week when Mackenzie King was explaining his zeal for union recognition to the Trades and Labour Congress of Canada in Ottawa, in Washington John J. Raskob of the United States Steel Corporation and a famous Wall Street figure was describing the Canadian Liberal leader as "one of the foremost men in the world today in the introduction of the so-called shop industrial councils" as an alternative to trade-union organization.[2]

Under Mackenzie King's leadership Canada moved with ever increasing momentum into the economic and political orbit of the United States. The Liberal Party under his direction resumed the path towards a policy of step by step integration into the American economic and political system, which it had been obliged to abandon by the election of 1911. That the Rockefeller interests subsidized the Liberal Party directly or indirectly or received any benefits from its victories is extremely unlikely. The Mackenzie King–Rockefeller connection was a more tenuous and sophisticated relationship than that of poli-tician and paymaster. Interests such as those of the Rockefellers require not favours but social stability.

All the same, Mackenzie King's connection with the Rocke-fellers was a devastating answer to suggestions that he was a dangerous radical. His connections with big money during his days as a Deputy Minister and Minister (Sir William Mulock was hardly a penniless man) are relatively unknown. After the

---

[1] A small selection of companies includes, General Electric, The Youngstown Sheet and Tube, International Harvester, Standard Oil.

[2] *Proceedings of the First Industrial Conference (called by the President)* 6–23, October. 1919, (Washington, 1920), p. 214.

establishment of the Rockefeller connection Mackenzie King never wanted for friends among the very rich in Canada. Masseys, Larkins, MacConnells and McCarthys were his good friends. Indeed, one of the first suggestions to Laurier that Mackenzie King succeed to the leadership of the Liberal Party came from the St. James's Club in Montreal.[1] But the Liberal Party never became the rich man's party. Mackenzie King would have seen no advantage in that.

After Mackenzie King retired from politics John D. Rockefeller, Jr., presented him with a birthday gift of $100,000 worth of shares "with a heart full of admiration, devotion and affection to ease any financial problem I might have in the years that lay ahead".[2] It is a measure of Mackenzie King's success as a politician that a gesture, which thirty years previously might have ruined his career, was regarded by the public, when it was made, as evidence of the Rockefellers' generosity and Mr. Mackenzie King's high standing.

We cannot neglect the serious contribution Mackenzie King made to the development of the American industrial community. On the eve of World War I the United States was heading towards internal difficulties, of which the Ludlow Massacre was only a sign. The revulsion against Rockefeller in the spring of 1914; the outcry in the press and the anger expressed Congress were manifestations of a growing turbulence in American society. An answer had to be found. To this situation Mackenzie King made a contribution in the shape of encouraging a new policy for American Big Business.

The practitioner of "soft" tactics taught the most important single business man in the United States the wisdom of company unionism. "John D., Jr., accompanied by William Lyon Mackenzie King . . . visited his Colorado coal properties, and with the assistance of Mr. King, set up the first of America's company unions. . . ."[3] This is the opinion of Edward Keating, the editor of *Labor* (Washington, D.C.) and a U.S. Congressman for Colorado in 1913–14. Mr. Keating regarded Mackenzie King's creation as a "fake organization", but it served its purposes for over twenty years. Philanthropy and "labour

[1] See Chapter X.
[2] Paragraph 57 of Mackenzie King's will printed in *The Canadian Liberal*, September, 1950, p. 56.
[3] Beshoar, *Out of the Depths*, p. xviii.

humanism" in the style of Rockefeller and Mackenzie King developed into one of the two major policies of anti-union employers in the United States. It came to compete with "Fordism" —the policy of high wages for intense work in open shops—as a means of securing high productivity in an atmosphere of industrial peace. Mackenzie King was not, of course, the first man to believe that problems of labour relations are susceptible of solution by such a policy, without any degree of economic or social change. But he was the first man to convince a key business man of its desirability as an answer to the troubles which the suppression of union activities had brought to the United States by the winter of 1913-14. To have designed a policy of such great importance, and to have brought it into operation in collaboration with the wealthiest man in the greatest industrial nation in the world, was no mean contribution to the economic and political history of North America.

CHAPTER VIII

La Poudre Aux Yeux

The transformation of a labour relations expert for American big business into a Canadian Prime Minister is not as remarkable a feat as one might suppose, but in this instance it was a complicated process possessing not only its own intricacy but its peculiar drama. By 1916, Mackenzie King seemed lost as a Canadian politician. He was out of office, out of Parliament, and out of the country. He was engaged in an unpopular and a fundamentally unsavoury business. In January, 1916, his political circumstances resembled those of Mohammed in August of the year 1 of the Hegira. But in his heart was the true faith in himself and his ambition.

When Mohammed departed for Medina he did not give up his spiritual residence in Mecca. Nor did Mackenzie King give up his residence in Ottawa when he set out for New York and Colorado. His abiding ambition was still the highest office in Canadian politics. In the Rockefellers he had found a new and powerful aid to this end, but they could never be the principal or decisive means. His connection in Canada had to be maintained in a lively condition. Following the near disaster for his career, which he had experienced in 1911, he discovered that the recovery of strength and, indeed, its increase, depended less upon a constant and conspicuous place in the public eye than upon an intimate and steady connection with important men in the driving seats of the political machine. During the years from August, 1914, until July, 1917, and again during 1918, we find Mackenzie King much withdrawn from the

Canadian public eye and yet at the same time warily active in Canadian politics, while engaged in other activities in the United States.

The perils of his situation—working for the Rockefellers in the United States while aspiring to office in Canada—were demonstrated to him within a few weeks of his formal appointment by the Rockefeller Foundation. In November, 1914, a Conservative newspaper in Toronto, *The News*, owned by his father's old friend, Sir John Willison, described him as a "high-priced labor sleuth". This description excited the indignation of the Kings, both father and son. First one and then the other tackled Willison. "What most concerned me", Mackenzie King wrote to Willison,

> "was not any injury to myself which I thought the heading on the article might bring, but the distinct feeling of disappointment it produced in the hope I cherished with respect to the announce- ment of the intention of the Rockefeller Foundation in setting apart a portion of its income for the purpose of helping to improve if possible the relations between capital and labor. It seemed to me that the designation of myself as a 'high priced labor sleuth' could not fail . . . when associated with the Rockefeller name . . . to add to the prejudice that in some labor circles exists against it, and to that extent help to frustrate what I know to be my own purpose in accepting the appointment of Director of Investigation of Industrial Relations, and the point of the trustees in offering it to me."[1]

This was Mackenzie King's characteristic response at this stage to public criticism: to eschew public polemics and to appeal privately to influential people to appreciate his activities. Another response was to withdraw further from the public gaze and to work more unobtrusively than he had done in his days as a civil servant. A fortnight after the appearance of the story of the "high priced labor sleuth" Mackenzie King resigned the presidency of the General Reform Association of Ontario.

During the next year he was almost continuously absent from Canada. In the spring of 1915, he was called before the Commission on Industrial Relations first in New York and then in Washington. His correspondence with the Rockefellers, including the highly significant letter to Rockefeller of August 6th, 1914, was made public. This occasioned him the gravest

---

[1] *Willison Papers*, King to Willison, 12 November, 1914.

anxiety. He prepared a specially printed explanation of the
letter of August 6th for circulation in the event of a too extensive
discussion in Canada of its cynical realism. Mackenzie King
described this explanatory material as

> "a printed document that I had printed for my own convenience
> . . . it was not issued as a public document. . . . During the hearings
> of the Commission in New York there was a letter I had written
> to Mr. Rockefeller read into the testimony. I thought, as I
> listened to the questions there, that a very unfair inference was
> being drawn from a certain paragraph. I am a man in public
> life, and I have to protect my reputation. . . . One of the gentlemen
> who testified . . . drew inferences—there were others also who did
> —that I thought were unfair. Now, that part of the inference was
> telegraphed to Canada and published by the opposition press of
> that country with a view to doing me political injury . . . some
> parts of this . . . were telegraphed and inserted in the Conservative
> press—a large part of it—from one end of Canada to the other
> . . . it was charged that I, who had been representing labor in
> Canada for years, had sold out, or something to that effect; and
> I expect when I take up my next political contest to have to face
> such problems as may come from false inferences, and so I printed
> the documents to have them ready to circulate if that subject is
> brought up."[1]

But the subject was not brought up in Canada in the way
Mackenzie King feared it might. The tactic of withdrawal was
yielding its benefits; for by May, 1915, Mackenzie King was so
out of the public eye, and this organ was so engaged with a
view of other and more exciting prospects, that little political
capital could be made from thrashing a minor Liberal ex-
Minister who appeared to have quit Canadian politics.

From time to time, through 1915 and 1916, there were petty,
malicious references to Mackenzie King in the Canadian press.
The Ottawa *Citizen*, for example, referred to him as "W.L.M.
King of the Rockefeller gold belt". Such references worried
him. He did not fight back in the open. Instead, he continued
to complain and to plead with the Tory newspaper proprietor,
Sir John Willison, whom at this time Sir Wilfrid Laurier had
felt obliged publicly to rebuke for his extreme antipathy to the
French-speaking part of Canada. "With what you know of me
personally and of my purpose in private and public life,"
Mackenzie King wrote,

[1] *R.C.I.R.*, p. 8794.

"perhaps you will be agreeable to saying a word which may help
to make it plain to the writer [of a particular article] just what the
exact nature of my connection with the Rockefeller Foundation is,
and just what have been the motives which have actuated me in
accepting the opportunities of useful work which connection with
the Foundation afford. . . ."[1]

By July, 1916, when Mackenzie King dictated these words,
the strains of Canadian political life were beginning to affect
personal relations. Willison was apparently unsympathetic to
his young protégé. He expressed "a doubt as to the possibility
of earning an income in the United States and serving in the
Canadian Parliament".[2] In response to this doubt Mackenzie
King offered a simple-minded defence. He needed money to help
his family. He was really living in Canada. Look at the letter
head of his stationery; and do not be bothered by the post mark.

> "It is true that part of my income comes to me in the form of
> cheques from New York, but it has never occurred to me that in
> accepting remuneration in this way I was differently circum-
> stanced from any persons living in Canada who might have in-
> vestments in American securities, or who might be selling their
> produce in American markets."[3]

During most of 1915 Mackenzie King was too busily at work
with Ivy Lee and Starr J. Murphy in repairing the public
relations of the Rockefellers, to give much attention to Canadian
affairs had he so desired. By January, 1916, the Rockefeller job
was done, and he had the leisure afforded him as an officer of
the Rockefeller Foundation to look over the irons he had in the
Canadian political fire. How hot were they?

The evidence available of his activities during 1916 strongly
suggests that Mackenzie King was cautiously and privately
renewing his association with leaders of the Liberal Party. Early
in March he wrote a letter to Laurier on the innocent and in-
nocuous subject of industrial museums. Then a few days later
he followed this up with some information about his work for
the Rockefellers. Laurier advised his ex-minister to publicize
this information in the Liberal press, and Mackenzie King promised to have J. D. Rockefeller Jr.'s book on the Colorado Plan
sent to "every paper in the Dominion".[4] A publicity campaign

---

[1] *Willison Papers*, King to Willison, 21 July, 1916.
[2] *Willison Papers*, King to Willison, 28 July, 1916.
[3] *Willison Papers*, King to Willison, 28 July, 1916.
[4] *Laurier Papers*, King to Laurier, 11 March, 1916.

concerning the Rockefeller plan was arranged with the help of Dr. J. A. Macdonald of *The Globe*. In June, more information about the Rockefeller plan was sent to Laurier, and he replied that he was glad to notice that "attacks against you have ceased".[1] Shortly after this Mackenzie King was writing to Laurier about a patronage question in the constituency of North York where he hoped to serve as Liberal candidate.

On the policy level he was feeling his way cautiously during 1916. In April, he submitted a report to the National Liberal Advisory Committee on the subject of "Industrial and Technical Education" at the same time that his friend Joe Atkinson of the Toronto *Star* was pressing Laurier to adopt a generous welfare programme embracing old age pensions, widows' pensions, unemployment insurance, a system of workmen's compensation, a minimum wage and maximum hours, and a system of local wage boards.[2] But industrial museums and technical education were not subjects of public controversy. The political fires burning in Canada by 1916, cast a glow upon the scene which blotted out shadows thrown by these little finger tricks.

One last public political act of Mackenzie King, before he departed to the United States in 1914, consisted of an appearance on a public platform in Ottawa with the Governor-General, Sir Robert Borden, Sir Wilfrid Laurier and Sir George Foster in which a joint appeal was made for money to support an all-out war effort. This was in September. In November, he returned to Canada briefly for the purpose of resigning the presidency of the Reform Association. On that occasion he pleaded with the Liberals for support for the war and with the Government to abstain from an election during the period of hostilities. Thus, Mackenzie King took his departure from the public stage while the political unity precipitated by the first shock of war was still something of a reality.

With the declaration of war the leaders of Canadian society— leaders in the church, politics, business and the professions— were united in one enthusiastic body eager to fight and win. Even those professional politicians whose principal stock of political capital consisted of pacifism and petty nationalism were

[1] *Laurier Papers*, Laurier to King, 15 June, 1916.
[2] *Laurier Papers*, Atkinson to Laurier, 8 March, 1916.

enthusiastic. Henri Bourassa declared his zeal with nearly as much warmth as Sir Wilfrid Laurier, Newton Wesley Rowell or Sir Sam Hughes.* Employing the arguments of his racial philosophy, Bourassa thus declared for war:

> "Canada, an Anglo-French nation bound to England and to France by a thousand ethnic, social, intellectual and economic ties, has a vital interest in maintenance of the prestige, power and world-wide action of France and England ... [it is Canada's] national duty to contribute in the measure of her resources, and by means of an appropriate action to the triumph, and above all, to the endurance of the combined efforts of France and England."[1]

The murmurings of criticism, the first sign of a rent in the seamless cloak of war enthusiasm, appeared from the labour ranks. J. C. Watters, the President of the Trades and Labour Congress of Canada greeted war with no warmth. On August 4th, 1914, he told a newspaper reporter in Sydney, Nova Scotia,

> "You can quote me as saying that England should hang her head in shame at an alliance with barbaric Russia against the country most highly civilized in all the world. . . . The policy of the Labour party is to make war against war, and we are proud of Keir Hardie's* proposal that there should be a great international strike against war."[2]

Pacifism was strong among an element in the Canadian labour movement, and hardly less strong was the democratic pacifism communicated from the United States. Writing amid the tensions of the late war period, J. Castell Hopkins* described the situation as it dwelt in his capacious memory: "The country had to pass from a condition of extreme Pacificism to one of continuous war-thought and an organized action. . . ."[3]

The spreading of enthusiasm for the war throughout all classes of the community was easier and more successful during the first year of the conflict than at any later time. The dimensions of the struggle could not yet even be guessed. Victory would, it was popularly supposed, come quickly. The fact of widespread depression and unemployment during part of 1913 and 1914, and well into 1915, did not render more difficult the task of recruitment. In the first three weeks of the war absolutely

---

[1] Quoted in M. P. O'Connell, "The Ideas of Henri Bourassa", *The Canadian Journal of Economics and Political Science*, August, 1953, p. 374.

[2] *Canadian Annual Review*, 1917, p. 417.

[3] *Canadian Annual Review*, 1917, p. 472.

more men enlisted in the Canadian armed forces than enlisted in the United States Army during the first three weeks after the American declaration of war in 1917, in spite of the numbers of Canadians being 8,000,000 and Americans being 100,000,000.[1]

The problems of morale were from the first months of the war among the most important facing the government of Sir Robert Borden. He and his colleagues had to decide how far to lead the Canadian people into the war, and by what means. The task of assembling the new and larger armies which the nature of the war demanded, was soon to run into difficulties. Partly through absence of leadership on the part of the government, partly as an expression of the instinctive prejudices of minorities, a discussion commenced in 1915 of the general questions of citizenship and its obligations.

This discussion was centred around the question of bilingualism in the schools of Ontario.[2] It had long been the policy of both the community and governments of Ontario to preserve bilingual education where the French-speaking population predominated. Owing to inadequate attention to the problems of bilingual education, it had given way in some districts to education exclusively in French or even to no education at all. In 1912, the Ontario Department of Education endeavoured through the famous Regulation 17, to enforce the long-established policy of the provincial authorities. This effort disturbed some French-speaking politicians who made a speciality of racist agitation, but before the outbreak of war few serious and fair-minded persons ventured to charge that the Conservative Government of Ontario sought to suppress French as a language of instruction in the schools.

Unfortunately for Canada there existed in its midst a group of people whose notions of politics did not appear to be far removed from the Plantation of Ulster. The Orange Order flourished. Its general ideas, if not its more extreme views, were widely accepted by both men who called themselves Conservatives and some who called themselves Liberals. With the energy and lack of imagination which characterizes the Calvinist tradition, a substantial body of English-speaking

---

[1] But Canada in 1914 was a depressed country, and U.S.A. in 1917 was prosperous.

[2] For a full account, see *Canadian Annual Review*, 1915, pp. 502–17; and 1916, pp. 524–32. See also Skelton's *Life and Letters of Sir Wilfrid Laurier*, Vol. ii, pp. 468–90.

people came forward willing and determined to transform the educational policies of the Ontario Government into a means of suppressing the use of the French language. Quite naturally the French Canadians regarded such a move as the start of a process which, if unopposed, would eventually undermine their characteristic way of life in all its aspects—economic, cultural and religious. The whole course of their history taught them to see this possibility. Not unexpectedly they resisted by a variety of means. By the spring of 1916, an issue which liberal-minded people had long considered settled had become the subject of controversy in the federal Parliament.

Thus, the feelings of the great majority of Canadians concerning the catastrophe of war became confused with racial questions, in a way which afforded many opportunities to blind-alley prophets like Henri Bourassa and Armand Lavergne* or Sir John Willison, Newton Wesley Rowell and John W. Dafoe.[1] These men, crying aloud for racial justice or alternatively for "equality of sacrifice" and the "rounding up of slackers", gave to the community an appearance of racial cleavage. But underneath this apparent cleavage, among the farmers of Western Canada[2] and Ontario as well as the peasants of Old Quebec and in Trade Councils across the country, resistance to the necessities of war became a real problem for the Government.

This problem was intensified by the vast but inconclusive bloodshed of 1916, beginning with the slaughter of Canadian troops in the Ypres salient.[3] On the western front, the Somme and Verdun revealed at the cost of 2,000,000 men killed, wounded and missing that victory for either side was not in sight. On the Italian front nine battles had been fought on the Isonzo. The vast Russian drive into Roumania had collapsed. The German surface fleet failed at Jutland to open the way for an invasion of Britain, but, underseas, German submarines were bringing starvation closer to every British home. The battle of the Somme was declared over on November 18th, 1916. President Wilson tried to arrange for peace talks in December, and in January, 1917, appealed for peace without victory.

But there was no real basis for peace negotiations, and

---

[1] There is some evidence of this spirit of racial bigotry in the *Dafoe Papers*.
[2] P. F. Sharp, *The Agrarian Revolt in Western Canada* (Minneapolis, 1948), pp. 75–6, 95–8.
[3] See Mason Wade, *The French Canadians* (London, 1955), pp. 693–94.

Wilson's appeal failed. Before March, 1917, had run its course, the decision to fight to victory had been made on both sides. On April 6th, the United States declared war on Germany. That month German submarines sank 875,000 tons of allied shipping and exceeded the expectation of the German military leaders by 275,000 tons. A renewed attack by the Allies on the German western front failed in the summer. The eleventh battle of Isonzo saw the Italians still moving towards Trieste at the rate of five miles a year, a prelude to their collapse at Caporetto in October, 1917.

The renewed intensification of the war in 1917 was followed by widespread war-weariness on both sides. After the battle of the Chemin des Dames in May, there was mutiny in the French Army. A Socialist peace congress met in Stockholm in May. In July the Reichstag discussed a peace resolution, and in October there were mutinies in the German fleet. In July the Russian Government of Prince Lvov began to fall apart. On August 1st, the Pope issued his appeal to the powers to come to terms. "In the summer of 1917," writes Professor Langer, the American diplomatic historian, "peace no longer appeared to be far in the future. The inability of both sides to win a decision on the battlefield and the victory of the revolution in Russia led to a widespread of defeatism, pacifism and socialism."[1]

Against this background of events in Europe, the response of the people of Canada to the decisions of Spring 1917, to renew and intensify the war, was not dissimilar. The Government of Sir Robert Borden was forced to move away from the voluntary system of fighting the war. Step by step it moved towards the system of compulsion and discipline necessary to produce the men and materials to fight. By the early summer of 1917, the Canadian community had reached the point where it must break with its past and embark upon a course of strong government devoted to war and victory or a conservative course of participating but not totally fighting.

The problems created by the decision to intensify the war effort were most acute in the matter of manpower for the armed forces. By the end of 1916, the voluntary system had produced 400,000 men for the armed services. But the rise in prices of food products had made farming a hopeful business, and farmers

---

[1] W. L. Langer (ed.), *An Encyclopaedia of World History* (Boston, 1948), p. 941.

were anxious to keep their sons and hired men at their tasks. Booming industry had created more jobs than men (although mounting prices did not improve the lot of the industrial worker). Well-founded rumours of corruption in the letting of war contracts, the emergence of a class of conspicuous wasters and war profiteers, the blood-letting and the hysteria all combined to reduce the enthusiasm which induced men to enlist in large numbers. At the beginning of 1916 men were enlisting at the rate of 30,000 a month; by the year's end the rate of enlistment had fallen to 6,000 a month.[1]

The decision to resort to conscription broke the traditional structure of Canadian politics. Until 1914, the Borden Government had been less committed to an armaments policy than the Liberal Party. Although they were accused of subservience to London and smeared with the charge of imperialism by Liberal propagandists, the Government of Sir Robert Borden had actually devoted a far smaller proportion of Canadian resources and manpower to preparation for war, than would have been the case had Laurier's policy of armaments been brought to fruition and increased from year to year. But entry into the war had precipitated a crisis in the Conservative-Nationalist Coalition. Borden's nationalist colleagues in the Cabinet continued to co-operate so long as the voluntary system was maintained, but as opposition to the war appeared, the nationalist propagandists like Henri Bourassa and Armand Lavergne moved more and more away from the Government in the direction of an alignment with popular sentiment.

A similar precipitation was to be observed in the ranks of the Liberal Party. At the outset all the Liberal leaders were enthusiastic about the war and prepared for a bipartisan policy of fighting until victory. As war-weariness developed the Liberal Party, too, began to split. Those elements which had endeavoured to establish a bipartisan armaments policy in 1912 moved increasingly closer to the war enthusiasts in the Conservative ranks. Rowell, the Liberal leader in Ontario, beat the drum more zealously than the Conservative Premier of the province, Sir William Hearst, and when the race issue was raised over the matter of bilingual schools, he boldly abandoned

---

[1] In February, 1917, 6,800 men enlisted, and there were 22,000 casualties that month. See Mason Wade, *The French Canadians*, Chapter XII.

the course of Mowat, of sympathetic regard for French-speaking Canadians, in favour of a policy loaded with over-tones of racial bigotry and appeals to Anglo-Saxon race pride. Sir Wilfrid Laurier, on the other hand, began to exhibit less and less enthusiasm for the war as he watched the growth of anti-war sentiment. When the decision of the Government was announced to conscript men into the army, Sir Wilfrid Laurier's enthusiasm for the Government's policy was finally extinguished by the flood of evidence of popular opposition. "My correspon-dence satisfies me", he told Rowell, "that in every province there is amongst the masses an undercurrent that will be sore and bitter if at the present moment a conscription law is forced upon them."[1]

Sir Wilfrid justified his course by several arguments. Some of them were in a measure sentimental, such as his belief that conscription is fundamentally illiberal and opposed to the ideals of his youth. But his principal argument was an appeal for sympathy on the grounds that, by remaining on the popular side, he was performing a higher service. "If, at the present time," he wrote to Hardy, "anybody can restrain and face the extremists, I think I am the man. Were I to flinch at all in the position which I always maintained, my usefulness would not only be gone, but my self-respect would be gone with it."[2]

Laurier, of course, had no intention of bringing Canada's participation in the war to an end. He made this as plain as he did his opposition to conscription.

"Should I be called upon to form a Government I would hope to include in it representatives of business, of labour and of agri-culture, of the men whose sole object in dealing with affairs of the country will be to devote the whole resources, wealth and energy of the country to the winning of the War. . . . I would hope to have a Government representative of the masses of the people—the common people—whose guiding principle should be to defend them against organized privilege . . . the supreme end is to assist in the tremendous struggle in which we are engaged, to maintain the unity of the nation, to avoid the divisions and discords which, for many years kept in check, are now unfortunately again looming up dangerous and threatening."[3]

[1] *Laurier Papers*, Laurier to Rowell, 2 June, 1917.
[2] *Laurier Papers*, Laurier to Hardy, 23 May, 1917.
[3] From Laurier's election manifesto quoted in *Canadian Annual Review*, 1917, p. 599.

Q

If his intentions were not different from Borden's, Laurier's course of action was. He began to move rapidly left, as the Administration moved reluctantly towards the perils of strong government. From Winnipeg Laurier received the report that "there is a considerable body of anti-conscriptionist sentiment among the Socialistic element of the working men . . . [and that there is] also . . . a small but active group of pacifists who hold the views of the independent Liberal party in England. . . ."[1]

Well might Mr. Dafoe thus write to Sir Wilfrid. Three days previous to the writing of this letter a member of the Manitoba Legislature, F. J. Dixon, told a large meeting in one of the churches in Winnipeg that, "as far as fighting goes, I prefer to do mine here, and if I have to shed my blood I prefer to shed it here where I know it will be for freedom."[2]

Organized labour on the west coast declared against conscription, and demanded a referendum on the subject. Three thousand miles away on the Atlantic coast, the Halifax Labour Council demanded a referendum and stated that "no form of conscription should be submitted to the people unless it carries with it provisions for the nationalization of food supplies, the conscription of surplus wealth, the control and operation by the Dominion of Canada of all industries essential to the carrying on of the war". In the House of Commons Alphonse Verville,* a Liberal-Labour member from Quebec and an officer of the Trades and Labour Congress of Canada declared: "Organized labour has notified the Government and the country in that respect. When they say that they will use all the means at their disposal to oppose compulsion I want this Parliament and the country to know that means a general strike. . . ."[3] The 33rd annual meeting of the Trades and Labour Congress which met in September, 1917, demanded conscription of wealth, immediate repeal of the Military Service Act, increased pay for soldiers, a more liberal policy with respect to Oriental immigration, the establishment of a Workmen's and Soldiers' Council, "to protect the interests of the soldiers and workers in all contemplated adjustments of our present systems."[4] J. C. Watters, the

---

[1] *Laurier Papers*, Dafoe to Laurier, 30 May, 1917.
[2] *Canadian Annual Review*, 1917, p. 419.
[3] Quoted in *Canadian Annual Review*, 1917, p. 487.
[4] *Canadian Annual Review*, 1917, p. 422.

outspoken opponent of war, was unanimously re-elected president. The only officer willing to co-operate with the Government was P. M. Draper, re-elected secretary-treasurer.

Following the passage of the Military Service Act late in July, 1917, outbreaks of violence commenced. Lord Atholstan's home in Cartierville was blown up on August 9th. The plotters who committed this act of violence declared that they intended to blow up the offices of the conscriptionist newspapers, the Mount Royal Club and the home of Senator Beaubien. Supporters of the Government could not gain a hearing in Quebec. Meeting after meeting was brought to a close before it began by revolver shots, barrages of eggs and stones and mass shouting. On August 30th seven persons were seriously injured in a riot in Phillips Square in Montreal. Attacks commenced upon the clergy. One agitator declared that Canada had "been sold body and soul by the capitalists to the Empire."

"The situation here calls for great discretion and caution," wrote Sir Clifford Sifton from Ottawa to his Editor in Western Canada who was leading the campaign for military service,

". . . As it stands now it appears to be quite impossible for Laurier to go in [i.e., to join Borden in forming a Union Government] on a policy for conscription. The opposition to conscription in the French-Canadian population seems to be intensely strong and the opposition in labour circles is also very strong. I do not know what the attitude will be with a population of foreign origin, but it will be hopeless to expect any enthusiastic support. Apart from this there is no indication of any enthusiastic support in the villages and rural districts of Ontario.[1] In the letters which the Members are receiving on both sides, the people who say that they are in favor of conscription invariably elaborate the scheme which they are in favor of. Needless to say it is carefully drawn up so as to exclude themselves and their employees. . . ."[2]

Given such a response to a policy of intensifying the war effort, the Government was obliged to call upon every resource in order to maintain its capacity to govern. In May, 1917, Sir Robert Borden had returned from consultation with Lloyd George, determined to implement a policy of conscription. His

---

[1] For the leading role of certain Liberals in promoting the movement for Union Government, see the Dafoe Papers for this period. Cf. Senator Norman P. Lambert, Memorandum on *The Winnipeg Convention of 1917.*

[2] *Dafoe Papers*, Sifton to Dafoe, 5 June, 1917.

first move consisted of an invitation to Laurier to join with him in the formation of a coalition government. The coalition would pass the legislation necessary for conscripting men, and then, he proposed, the coalition would seek a mandate from the people. Sir Wilfrid Laurier recognized the madness, from his own point of view, of this policy.[1] He refused to cut himself off from "the common people" and "the masses" so frequently mentioned in his correspondence. When the Military Service Act was introduced into Parliament in June, 1917, the Liberal Party split and so did the Conservative-Nationalist Coalition. The diners of August, 1912, came into their own. A large group of Ontario and Western Liberals deserted Laurier and voted with the Government. A *bloc* of nationalists voted against the Government.

Laurier was saddened by the effect of this upon the Liberal Party. Sir Wilfrid was a man of warm affections and he possessed in the highest degree the feeling that a political party is not just a mere organization for the convenience of business but something in the nature of a church, a fellowship or a *Kämpferbund*. As the Tory appeal to patriotism, fear, and class and race hatred developed, Laurier's old companions-in-arms deserted him one by one.

"Yesterday it was Pardee, and today it will be Graham!", he cried out, "Graham and Pardee as dear to me as my own brothers. Do not, however, think hard of them, for I do not. . . ."[2] Even his old comrade, Sir Allen Aylesworth, wavered over conscription. Perhaps it was necessary. Laurier wrote to his "dear . . . old and sincere friend". Aylesworth ceased to waver. "I stick by you no matter what happens, and there are thousands upon thousands of Grits all over Canada who will say the same thing and will always say."[3]

Finally, there came the defection which hurt most: that of the Rt. Hon. W. S. Fielding* who had served as his Minister of Finance from 1896 until 1911, and to whom he had proposed to transfer the leadership in 1908. Fielding had worked until long after the passage of the Military Service Act to find some way by

---

[1] The story is told with sufficient accuracy in Skelton's *Life of Laurier*, Vol. ii, Chapter XIX. In the *Laurier Papers* one can follow the hourly negotiations with the Conservatives and amongst the Liberals.

[2] *Laurier Papers*, Laurier to Aylesworth, 22 June, 1917.

[3] *Laurier Papers*, Aylesworth to Laurier, 21 June, 1917.

which, when he was obliged to speak out (for he was not in Parliament at that time) he would speak the same words as his Leader. In the end he could not, and on November 7th, 1917, when Laurier reached home with the pain of Fielding's defection burning in his heart, he went to the quiet of his library, and there copied on to one of the fly leaves of his Bible the bitter cry of David from the fifty-fifth Psalm:

> "For it was not an enemy that reproached me, then could I have borne it: neither was it he that hated me that did magnify himself against me, then I could have hid myself from him. But it was thou, a man mine equal, my guide, and mine acquaintance. We took sweet counsel together, and walked unto the house of God in company."

Laurier's Parliamentary moves against the Government consisted in moving for a referendum on the Military Service Act. He believed that the majority would not support the Government policy. And so, apparently, did the Government. Sir Robert Borden refused to put the Military Service Act to a popular test. Instead, he offered seats in his Cabinet to some Liberal deserters and reformed his Government under the label "Unionist". Then his Cabinet devised the War Time Elections Act. This was a simple work of genius which revealed the Government's confidence in the popularity of its policies. Its object was to disenfranchise as many as possible of those who might be expected to support Laurier: people naturalized since 1902, conscientious objectors, and Quakers; and to enfranchise and get control of the votes of as many as possible who might be expected to fall for the specious argument that conscription would bring the boys home by Christmas, e.g., the female next of kin of men in the armed forces, and the soldiers overseas. Once the War Time Elections Act was passed Sir Robert Borden called an election. The only thing which remained to be done was to give to the farmers of Canada an assurance on the eve of the election that their sons would not be conscripted and, by implication, that the wage-earners of the towns would pay the tribute of blood and high prices which victory required.

During these stirring times Mackenzie King cut no conspicuous figure before the public. He kept to the back rooms seemingly undecided as to what course to take. In so far as

Laurier's correspondence is any guide to his activities he appears to have dropped his connection with Laurier during the later part of 1916. It was not until December that we find him writing to Laurier, and then not about Canadian politics but about himself and his work for the Rockefellers. He reminded Laurier that he still lived in Canada. As if to underline the reminder he sent Laurier a Christmas gift. In 1910, he had presented Laurier with the *Life of Disraeli*; now he chose the *Life of Botha* as an appropriate offering.

During the first half of 1917, Laurier was corresponding in great volume with his old friends in the Liberal leadership, but not with Mackenzie King. His mind was occupied with conscription and his heart with the defection of Pardee and Graham and the wavering of the deaf old fighter, Aylesworth. Sometime during this period, King sent Laurier an undated telegram telling him of a meeting of Liberal politicians in Toronto which was unanimous in support of Laurier's leadership of the Party. But it seems obvious that Mackenzie King was not conspicuously in the thoughts of the Liberal leader. In July, 1917, while the Military Service Act was being debated in Ottawa, Mackenzie King wrote to Laurier a letter longer than any since his thirty-eight page effusion following the Grand Trunk strike. It was concerned with a projected deal involving the sale of a Montreal newspaper *The Mail*. One of the participants in the deal was a Liberal bolter named George Lindsey, one of the leaders of the Liberal-Conscriptionist movement of Ontario, for whom Mackenzie King seems to have been acting as a go-between in approaching the Old Chief. Laurier was short with his correspondent.

"I have yours of the 9th inst. enclosing George Lindsey's letter, which I now return. I am sorry to say that at the present time it is not possible for me to even consider Nicholls' [editor of *The Mail*] suggestion. The party is somewhat disorganized now and until harmony is restored and such erring brothers as George Lindsey come back to the fold, nothing can be done. This must be obvious to George."[1]

If this letter betrays a trace of coldness, it is understandable, for Laurier was at the moment of his life's crisis when he was standing up against the heaviest onslaught he had experienced

[1] *Laurier Papers*, Laurier to King, 11 July, 1917.

since the bombardment by the bishops in 1895–96. It was hardly an appropriate moment to attempt a deal with the jelly-fish elements in the Party.

Early in September the War Time Elections Act was sprung on Laurier. An election was obviously in the making, and Mackenzie King was prepared at last to say something and do something. On September 16th, 1917, he wrote to Laurier with the happy tidings that a plough manufacturer in North York was supporting him as Liberal candidate. "I sum up the proceedings," he wrote,

> "when I say that the meeting was solidly and *without exception* for a Laurier Liberal and no one else. This I am sure will delight you the more when I tell you that among the strongest speeches delivered were one by the Hon. E. J. Davis, who opposed us in the Reciprocity campaign, and one by William Fleury, who, as you know, is a manufacturer of ploughs and farm implements and along with the Davis's and Canes one of the three leading manufacturers of the riding."

Apparently North York was an exception to the rest of Canada, where the plough manufacturers and their friends were deserting to the Tories. This was good news, indeed, from North York, but as Laurier read on he came upon the joker. "They were quite prepared to accept from you a statement," he read,

> "that if returned to power, to assist in the winning of the war with men and resources would be the first duty of your government; that they were quite prepared to believe a new administration formed under your leadership would be able to find the men necessary by voluntary enlistment without the necessity of resorting to conscription. It seemed the general opinion that, the Conscription Act having been passed, the Liberal Party should allow it to remain on the Statutes, and in no way give a pledge to its repeal, but the party might very properly take the position that the Act had never been necessary and would not be enforced so long as the requirements of the situation as indicated after conference with authorities in Britain and the United States could be met without its provisions.
>
> "There was a very strong feeling . . . they believed that Canada's part in war would be more effectively prosecuted by a government formed by you than any government formed by Sir Robert Borden. . . ."[1]

This is vintage Mackenzie King. We shall keep the Military

---

[1] *Laurier Papers*, King to Laurier, 16 September, 1917.

Service Act on the statute books; that will get the plough manufacturers on our side. Then advocate the continuation of the voluntary system; that will get the rank and file. All that remains is to provide a logical way out for the opposites voting for us. And so we say we shall be governed by the advice of experts in Great Britain and the United States. We can win the election. We will not be responsible for any policy; and we will be in office and we will do what we think we can get away with.[1]

Laurier replied dryly that the "news . . . is certainly very gratifying. I have had similar expressions from many quarters. . . . I would like to know when you expect to be in Ottawa".[2]

Well might Laurier refuse to comment on this letter. He was probably following the advice he had given Mackenzie King in his youth to pray for deliverance from his friends. Laurier appreciated the volume, if not the causes, of the indignation about conscription, and he was not prepared to deceive himself or others with such a policy as Mackenzie King's. Parliament had passed the Military Service Act. He advised the people to obey the laws passed by Parliament, but he was determined if returned to office to put the Military Service Act to the people and let them vote. If the people supported the Act, he would enforce it; if they rejected it he would recommend Parliament to repeal it. In October the Toronto *Globe* recommended a line to Laurier similar to that of Mackenzie King, except that it lacked the sinuosity of the original but was embellished with lures like a promise of free trade in food-stuffs and farm implements with the United States. Laurier replied sharply and clearly. "My motion (for a referendum) did not mean that, were we to come to office, this would involve repealing the Act, but it involved that no action should be taken upon it until submitted and approved by the people. Those are my views well considered, carefully thought, and I can see no reason to change them."[3]

Mackenzie King appears to have appealed to a wider constituency of manufacturers than those resident in North York.

[1] See in this regard, J. W. Pickersgill, "Mackenzie King's Speeches", *Queen's Quarterly*, Autumn, 1950, for an analysis of what the author describes as Mr. King's "passion for accuracy".

[2] *Laurier Papers* Laurier to King, 18 September, 1917.

[3] *Laurier Papers*, Laurier to Houston, 23 October, 1917.

A manufacturer, A. K. Cameron, long an intimate friend of Sir Wilfrid, wrote to Laurier in October, 1917, from Montreal urging the summons of all Laurier Liberals in Ontario to a convention. "It would seem to me," he wrote, "that there are two men in Ottawa at the present time who are specially fitted because of their position and training to take charge of the handling of such a gathering, namely—the Honourable Mackenzie King and Mr. Alex. Smith."[1]

Laurier cautiously replied: "If the matter is to be taken up it should come from our friends in Ontario. I will speak to King about your suggestion, but if you could take action yourself, it would be all the better. In the state of disorganization in which we are now, I have nobody around me whom I could entrust with that work."

A few days before writing this letter Laurier was busy getting the movement against the government under way in Toronto. Mackenzie King was a Toronto man who intended to run in a constituency which embraces some of the outer suburbs of that city. But this is how Laurier wrote to his principal organizer in Toronto: "Could you form a grand committee in the city of Toronto in which you would bring in as many of the big men as possible: Aylesworth, Dewart, Larkin, Bowman and as many others as you can think of, with Aylesworth as Honorary Chairman to take charge of matters generally and to give a lift to public opinion?"[2] Laurier either forgot to mention his ex-Minister of Labour, or else he purposely omitted his name.

Rumours have circulated and suggestions have been made that Mackenzie King tried to find a place in the "Union" Government in 1917. According to Sir Robert Borden, "I was told in the summer of 1917 by an intimate friend of King that he [King] was ready to join the proposed Union Government."[3] He appears to have had some discussion of the subject. In a letter to Laurier of October 17th, 1917, he told his leader about a conversation he had had with Rowell, by this time a minister in the "Union" Cabinet.

". . . I asked if in a contest I were to stand for the principle of

[1] *Laurier Papers*, Cameron to Laurier, 19 October, 1917.
[2] *Laurier Papers*, Laurier to Harding, 15 October, 1917.
[3] Borden: *His Memoirs*, Vol. II, pp. 995-96.

Union Government and for the Conscription Act as passed, would I be permitted by the government to run against Armstrong, who has received the Tory nomination, without any interference by the government, or would I have to support the present government of Sir Robert Borden."[1]

The purpose of the question, Mackenzie King told Laurier, was to discover the hypocrisy of the "Unionists". Rowell's reply to his question was "conclusive as to the government not having been formed on grounds of principle, but for purposes of power and office". What this letter proves is not at all clear. Was Mackenzie King making overtures to Rowell, which he wished to explain away to Laurier, or was he simply seeking for information from his opponents? Although there is insufficient evidence to answer these questions, the impression cannot be avoided that Mackenzie King was engaged in some kind of negotiations with the Tories and "Unionist" Liberals during the summer of 1917. Some substance is given to the impression by Laurier's failure to invite Mackenzie King to any of the meetings of leading Liberals, called in Ottawa and Montreal during the spring of 1917, for the purpose of discussing Sir Robert Borden's invitation to form a coalition. One of Sir Wilfrid's closest associates recorded privately that rumours were about in the middle of 1917 that Mackenzie King was willing to join the Union Government; and that at one stage Laurier despatched his maid-of-all-work, Walter Mitchell, to persuade Mackenzie King to remain loyal to him. Mitchell concluded a species of non-aggression pact by the terms of which Mackenzie King would appear before the electors as a Laurier Liberal, but would not be expected to compromise himself by speaking on Laurier's behalf outside his own constituency.

Laurier's mistrust of Mackenzie King, evident enough in his correspondence, the "left Unionist" line Mackenzie King was pushing, his association with outspoken Liberal conscriptionists like Lindsey, his long intimacy with Rowell and his subsequent friendship for him after he became Prime Minister—all these things point to some undefined relationship with Laurier's enemies. On the other side of the argument are his power of calculation, his belief in loyalty to a leader as a constituent in

---

[1] *Laurier Papers*, King to Laurier, 17 October, 1917.

political success and his habitual preference for appearing to be a man of the left.[1]

Whatever the purpose of his questions to the chief Liberal bolter, Rowell, he proceeded in his letter of October 17th, 1917, to develop a plan of campaign which he recommended to Laurier. First he analysed Canadian opinion in a way which suggested that Sir Robert Borden was right and Sir Wilfrid Laurier was wrong.

"Canadian opinion is, I believe, overwhelmingly one in regard to three things:

"(1) That Canada is vitally concerned in the issues of the war, and that her utmost endeavour must be that of lending every assistance possible to see it brought to a speedy and successful termination;

"(2) That a non-party government should have been formed at the commencement of the war, and that a non-party government is preferable to a strictly party government so long as the war continues;

"(3) That the Canadian soldiers at the front should know that they have the strong support of the government at home . . . that Canada will continue to provide such resources and men as conference with the British, American and other allied authorities disclose as needful.

"To allow the present government a monopoly of any one of these positions would be unfair to Liberal opinion as it would be disastrous to the future position and well-being of the party. . . ."

Mackenzie King then suggested an approach to each of these positions. About the righteousness of the war there could be no doubt. The United States had entered the war, and the twin voices of London and Washington were now compulsive in a way that the voice from London had never been. He simply echoed the Wilsonian simplification of the issues. ". . . It is a question for Canadians, in common with all free peoples,

---

[1] There is another interesting interpretation of these events printed in the London *Times Literary Supplement* of 4 December, 1953. The anonymous author states: "Sir Robert Borden told a friend, when he was Prime Minister and when King had not become Leader of the Opposition, that King would leave his party if Borden would give him a seat in his Government. Borden was not disturbed about this lack of political loyalty (incidentally, it is most improbable that King ever made such an offer) but felt King's abilities were so limited that he would make a thoroughly unsatisfactory Minister. Borden realized that King might become the Opposition Leader (largely due to distaste of Fielding, the natural successor of Laurier, through his war policy) and felt that such an appointment would be of the utmost value to the Conservative Party."

whether democratic or autocratic principles are to triumph in government, whether nations that have won freedom are to remain constitutionally free or become degraded to the level of a militarist civilization. . . ."[1]

On the second topic Mackenzie King did not care to elaborate. Instead, he concentrated on the iniquities of the War Time Elections Act which violated all the canons of representative, responsible government. This was true enough, but conscription and war were the issues in the public mind, and not the incidental crimes of the government.

On the third topic, of reinforcing the army overseas, Mackenzie King tried once more to interpret Sir Wilfrid Laurier to himself in a way calculated to win the support of "the men who have been the leaders in organization, [who] are the ones who are holding back".[2] "Does not the position you have already taken", he asked Laurier,

> "imply that you are willing to allow the Conscription Act to remain, to sanction what has been done under it, and that if the needed number of men cannot be secured voluntarily, they will nevertheless be secured, which means that Conscription in such an emergency would be a necessary resort? If this is a true interpretation of your position and any other would mean that though you were satisfied men were needed you would not be willing to have them provided, which is what your opponents seek to have the people believe but which your friends know to be false—would it not be possible to make this position clear in the first statement you issue? It is the uncertainty that exists in the minds of many of our candidates as to the position of the party on this point that is causing them to hesitate between continuing their support and coming out in favour of the union government led by Sir Robert Borden. . . ."[3]

In short, Mackenzie King wanted Laurier to adopt the policy of Sir Robert Borden, qualified by a promise (designed to win the votes of the rank and file) that conscription would be continued only if Britain and the United States thought it should be. Inasmuch as conscription was already in force in Britain and the United States, there can be little doubt what British and American experts would have advised, had they been so foolish

---

[1] *Laurier Papers*, King to Laurier, 17 October, 1917.
[2] *Laurier Papers*, King to Laurier, 7 November, 1917.
[3] *Laurier Papers*, King to Laurier, 17 October, 1917.

as to attempt to make decisions properly the responsibility of the Canadian Government.

To Mackenzie King's 3,000 words of advice, Sir Wilfrid Laurier replied: "My dear King, Here is a letter I commend to your attention. Yours faithfully, Wilfrid Laurier."[1] It is not completely clear from Sir Wilfrid Laurier's Papers what letter was commended to Mackenzie King's attention, but it would seem to have been a letter to Laurier from Professor O. D. Skelton reporting to Laurier the volume of discontent with the Military Service Act and the growing scepticism about the war.

Three weeks later the political situation crystallized in Mackenzie King's proposed constituency of North York. The "Union" Government sent a message to the Liberals of North York to the effect that they would withdraw the Tory candidate in favour of a "Win-the-War" Liberal. Two names were proposed as a suitable Liberal of this type; a soldier serving in France and N. W. Rowell. After the go-between from the Government had finished making this proposition to the "fifty leading Liberals of the riding" Mackenzie King spoke. "I addressed the meeting after Urquhart," he told Laurier,

"and came out four-square as a supporter of yourself and of your manifesto in its entirety. The meeting was overwhelmingly with me, and a motion by Urquhart that a committee of five should be appointed to meet with the Conservatives of the riding to discuss the nomination of a win-the-war candidate had only five or six supporters. Unfortunately this number includes some of our best friends here."[2]

Laurier may have neglected to mention Mackenzie King as a member of the "Committee of Big Names" in Toronto, and he may have been lukewarm about Mackenzie King as an organizer of Laurier Liberals in Ontario; but he was anxious to exhibit Mackenzie King in Western Canada as an answer to the Tory propaganda that the opponents of the "Union" Government were all disloyal French-Canadians, "cockroaches of the kitchen of Canada," as one Tory professor of McGill University so elegantly put it. There were three Liberal ex-Ministers from Ontario who were still supporting Laurier: Sir Allen Aylesworth, the Hon. Charles Murphy and Mackenzie King. Aylesworth was very deaf and he had been much withdrawn

---

[1] *Laurier Papers*, Laurier to King, 20 October, 1917.
[2] *Laurier Papers*, King to Laurier, 7 November, 1917.

from public participation in politics for some years. Murphy was a good platform performer, a skilful politician and a loyal supporter of Laurier; but he was an Irish Catholic with a strong sympathy for Home Rule and, on that account, a man who might arouse controversy on issues extraneous to an already complicated situation. There remained Mackenzie King: young, white, Protestant, a Liberal, in possession of all his faculties. Accordingly, Laurier invited him to accompany him to Winnipeg.

Early in October, Mackenzie King had excused himself from meeting Laurier in Toronto on the grounds of his mother's illness. "Meanwhile, please let me assure you that I would not allow any circumstances except the one I am mentioning to prevent me from being in Toronto while you are there."[1] Now he felt obliged to refuse the invitation to another tour, which was not being cancelled this time. "Last night", he explained to Laurier,

> "I spoke to one or two of the men who are wholly reliable and mentioned it to them that you might wish me to go with you to Winnipeg next week, and asked if they did not think such a mark of confidence on your part would be more helpful to me in the riding than remaining here to get the organization into shape. To my disappointment I found they were unalterably opposed to my leaving the riding at this juncture if it could be at all avoided."[2]

Laurier replied: "Your present duty must be to your own riding. Do not think any more of the western trip."

A week later Laurier wanted Mackenzie King to venture into Quebec in the cause of the Laurier Liberals.

> "Our friends in Sherbrooke are very insistent that you should give a meeting to McCrea at your own time and selection during the contest. You made such an impression when you went there, that they feel satisfied you would bring back a few voters who are lukewarm towards us.   .
> Let me know what day would best suit you, so that I may have the matter arranged at once."[3]

This time neither his mother's chest condition nor the state of organization in North York stood in the way of answering his leader's appeal. Sherbrooke was a long way from North York, he told Laurier, but he seems to have realized that this argu-

---

[1] *Laurier Papers*, King to Laurier, 7 November, 1917.
[2] *Laurier Papers*, King to Laurier, 7 November, 1917.
[3] *Laurier Papers*, Laurier to King, 15 November, 1917.

ment would not carry conviction. "There is one other consideration I think I should mention, and that is that going into the Province of Quebec to speak during this contest would, I think, be a mistake from the point of view of Liberal interests in this province."[1]

Laurier did not reply to this evasion. On November 21st Mackenzie King was back at his old endeavour to get Laurier to promise not to touch the Military Service Act.

> ". . . I am certain that a clear cut definite statement from you on this point, leaving no doubt one way or the other, would not cost us a single seat in Quebec, while it might help to gain for us dozens of seats elsewhere. With this handicap removed, I think I shall have pretty clear sailing in the riding. Without it I am going to lose some of our best friends and many of the other side whose support I otherwise would gain. . . . I think, too, you should in all your speeches emphasize the supreme issue, namely to keep a united Canada, and to avoid the sort of thing that has happened in both Ireland and Russia."[2]

In reply to this Laurier sent the last letter he wrote to the candidate for North York before the election: "I did not say I would repeal the Act, but that I would suspend it. Repealing would be undoing everything that has been done. Suspending would be conserving what has been done, but prevent any further enforcement. These arguments are too obvious for me to repeat them. . . ."[3]

In spite of mass enthusiasm Laurier did not win the election, nor Mackenzie King his seat. The policy of conscription was adroitly used by the "Unionists" to play upon the war-weariness of the Canadian troops. They were induced to believe that conscription could bring a quick end to the war, and would enable them to shift the burden on to the shoulders of the slackers who had let them fight so long. The selective body of women voters were appealed to in the same way. The exclusion of naturalized citizens from the franchise, the activities of Mackenzie King's old friends in the trade union movement such as Gideon Robertson of the Telegraphers and Calvin Lawrence of the Locomotive Engineers, and the unrestrained use of racial agitation combined to restrict to the province of Quebec the

---

[1] *Laurier Papers*, King to Laurier, 16 November, 1917.
[2] *Laurier Papers*, King to Laurier, 21 November, 1917.
[3] *Laurier Papers*, Laurier to King, 22 November, 1917.

electoral expression of opposition to the war and to the Government.

Quebec returned 62 Laurier Liberals in 65 constituencies. This overwhelming parliamentary victory for anti-conscription and anti-war feeling in Quebec has served to obscure the very considerable strength of this sentiment elsewhere in Canada. Excluding the vote in Quebec, more than 500,000 people in the non-French-speaking provinces cast their ballots against the Government compared with a pro-Government civilian vote of 780,000. The Conservative Party as such lost the election. Only the "Unionist" Liberals saved the Government. Propaganda cleverly designed to capitalize on war weariness, together with masterly organization and an electoral law which distorted the voting process, were sufficient to achieve this result.

In this contest Mackenzie King made his political fortune. Laurier doubted his loyalty. In the election he had pushed a line so like that of the Government that only in refinements of emphasis could the differences be detected. He had refused to travel to Western Canada or to Quebec with Laurier lest the people see him with his leader and he be obliged to say too much. But, in spite of all this, he appeared to have been loyal to Laurier, and Laurier appeared to have been loyal to Liberalism and the General Will of the people. Out of these appearances Mackenzie King was to construct, anew, his career. He turned from the electoral fray to build for himself a platform to the taste of the times: *Industry and Humanity*.

CHAPTER IX

"Industry and Humanity"

Prior to launching himself on his Parliamentary career Mackenzie King had written a book, *The Secret of Heroism*. It had been an indispensable part of the whole launching process. He had built his political machine in the civil service, the press and the labour unions. Then had come the message to the people contained in *The Secret of Heroism*. In the pages of this book the dead Harper had witnessed to the wisdom of Mackenzie King, to the ideals they shared and to the hope they jointly entertained concerning the harmony of labour and capital to be brought about by the ministrations of the Deputy Minister of Labour. They had stood firm for the great things of life about which the community agrees: mother, idealism, kindly religious sensitivity, social peace and work.

In December, 1917, Mackenzie King was engaged in a new and more ambitious launching than the enterprise of 1906–08. Another book was in preparation: something grander, less personal, more general and more in accord with the social anxieties of 1917–18; a message to the people, and particularly to the right people, who had the power to make and unmake Prime Ministers. Ostensibly the Director of Research of the Rockefeller Foundation was working on "a statement of underlying principles . . . which should obtain in all efforts at reconstruction".[1] (pp. ix–x.) In July, 1917, Mackenzie King had told Laurier for the first time about his project. "I have moved

---

[1] All page references are to W. L. Mackenzie King, *Industry and Humanity, A Study in the Principles Underlying Industrial Reconstruction* (Toronto and Boston, 1918).

out to my cottage here at Kingsmere", he wrote, "and am working away on my book for the Rockefeller Foundation to have it out of the way in the event of a contest."[1] The book was, he said, his "own property". (p. x.) He was, however, "grateful [for] the opportunity of study afforded [him] by the Rockefeller Foundation". (p. xi.)

The impression Mackenzie King gave, and the expectation he aroused, that he was writing a learned work on industrial relations similar in manner and in content to the *Principles of Labor Legislation* produced by J. R. Commons and J. B. Andrews a few years previously, was at the root of the disappointing reception accorded the book by learned critics. The only learned journal in North America which ventured to give *Industry and Humanity* publicity in the shape of a notice was the *American Economic Review*.

"Dr. King", said the reviewer,

"brings to his study of the principles underlying industrial reconstruction an unusual preparation along both academic and practical lines. His experience as Minister of Labor in Canada and his connection with the Rockefeller Foundation together with travel and observation world-wide in extent should give unusual concreteness, vividness, and value to anything he might write on the labor question. One finds, however, a certain diffuseness of statement and indulgement (*sic*) in generalities, and at times an avoidance of the main issues."

The reviewer summed up the book: "Dr. King in this book (like some economists at times and most college professors all the time) is primarily a preacher, and his ideals and hopes for industry are at least good enough to come true."[2]

Although the *American Economic Review* did not appreciate the purpose of the author of *Industry and Humanity*, its reviewer was correct. *Industry and Humanity* is not a book about technical problems of labour relations. In its pages Mackenzie King was a preacher, preaching a gospel to those groups in Canada which could make him into a Prime Minister. His ideals and hopes for industry may have been good enough to come true. Their utility consisted in being good enough to win the leadership of the Liberal Party.

---

[1] *Laurier Papers*, King to Laurier, 9 July, 1917.
[2] *The American Economic Review*, Vol. IX (1919), p. 582.

Industry and Humanity is a long book of nearly 150,000 words together with 9 annotated charts setting forth in diagrammatic form their author's picture of the cosmos.[1] In this *magnum opus* Mackenzie King essayed to describe the dilemma threatening man and society, and to suggest a way out. In a succession of chapters he put himself in accord with the great positive features of the General Will about which few sane men will disagree: the desirability of peace, health, work, democratic representation, education and freedom of opinion. *Industry and Humanity* is not specifically concerned with Canada; indeed, none of the particular problems of Canadian society were considered, and Canada was mentioned only here and there as the scene of Mackenzie King's labour or as an illustration of the great truths he had to teach. One of its first Canadian readers felt strongly that in thus neglecting to write specifically about Canadian experience in an attractive manner Mackenzie King had done himself a disservice. This reader told Laurier that he felt he ought to admire *Industry and Humanity*, but he found another contemporary work on Canadian politics by W. H. Moore easier to read. ". . . The one has the arts of popularity, [Mackenzie King] lacks them entirely. The one is intensely human, the other machine-like."[2]

After the publication of *Industry and Humanity*, Mackenzie King soon realized that the book itself did not possess the clarity required for a successful message addressed even to a small but influential public. During the spring of 1919, following its publication shortly after the Armistice, Mackenzie King produced a boiled down and spiced version of *Industry and Humanity*, which he used as the text of a series of public addresses to audiences at luncheon clubs in Montreal, Toronto and other centres of industry and commerce in Ontario and Quebec.[3] In *Industry and Humanity* he had worked out a political line. That

---

[1] These cosmic maps were regarded by President Eliot as absurdities. Tactfully, he wrote to King, "I know there is a distinct tendency to the diagrammatic method in all sorts of subjects; but I have also observed that they repel many readers who receive from them the impression that their author is not a practical man. The diagrams you showed the Rockefeller Board the other day produced that impression on at least four of your auditors. . . ." The author, however, did not take Eliot's advice. *Eliot Papers*, Eliot to King, 31 May, 1916.

[2] *Laurier Papers*, Congdon to Laurier, 24 January, 1919.

[3] An example printed in W. L. Mackenzie King, *The Message of the Carillon and Other Addresses* (Toronto, 1927), pp. 191 ff., is his address to the Empire Club, Toronto, 13 March, 1919.

was the essential value of the book to its author. It was his personal platform on which to campaign for the leadership of the Liberal Party and upon which he stood in appealing for power.[1]

If *Industry and Humanity* was ignored or unkindly considered by the critics, and unread by the public, was it a failure? Is it unworthy of attention? Is it a proof that even successful men have their failures upon occasion? Not at all. *Industry and Humanity* was the first and remains the only book on politics of a classical character produced by a Canadian. Oecumenical in its purposes and its proportions, it is an examination of the foundations and dynamics of politics, a statement of the objectives of the State and a plan for their realization. Apart from the fact that it was written, published and republished on the eve of elections by one of the most successful parliamentary politicians in history, *Industry and Humanity* commands attention as one of the most generalized and most skilful examples of political thinking in the period of change in which the world has lived since 1914. Certain aspects of his thought anticipated by some years attitudes and modes of understanding of men as diverse in their immediate interests and as similar in their final concerns as T. S. Eliot and James Burnham.

That *Industry and Humanity* has remained largely unread is not surprising. It is unlikely that Mackenzie King ever intended his book to be popular. In its manner and its matter *Industry and Humanity* was ill-suited to the Canadian taste of that time. It was nearly as little adapted to understanding in the United States, where studies of government abound and books on politics are practically non-existent, save the classic works of Madison, Jay and Hamilton. Old-fashioned modes of expression and bathetic sentimentality of tone rendered it likewise objectionable to Europeans who, like its reviewer in the *Times Literary Supplement*,[2] might have better grasped the significance of the book had they not been repelled by the style.

Both the style and the matter of *Industry and Humanity* were aspects of the author's purpose. He had long appreciated that a

[1] *Murphy Papers*, Haydon to Murphy, 7 October, 1920, states: "The meetings have been great. The enthusiasm as never before—so they say themselves—new interest, new vision—new efforts to get together. The people have a hunger for the story, and the war feeling is not all over. *Industry and Humanity* appeals take much more than you think. . . ."

[2] 26 June, 1919.

politician in a parliamentary democracy is obliged to employ several modes of discourse according to the section of the community to which he is appealing. The mode of discourse he employed in the pages of *The Liberal Monthly* differed greatly from the mode of *Industry and Humanity*. In *Industry and Humanity* Mackenzie King was addressing himself to the four centres of power which he considered to exist in an industrial community such as Canada: the owners of capital; the managers who organize production; the labour interest and the community. Because he was a Canadian politician aspiring to power in a community harbouring racial philosophers like Armand Lavergne and religious enthusiasts like H. C. Hocken, the Grand Master of the Loyal Orange Order, he carefully avoided discussion of evocative or confusing words like race, language, imperialism and nationality, and excluded the problems connected with them from consideration. But he did not exclude them from discussion for prudential reasons alone. He did not consider them of fundamental importance. He realized that, for success as a politician, he must clearly and unambiguously state a position agreeable, not to a narrow following in the Liberal Party, but to the basic elements and institutions in the community. These may differ in particulars, but they agree in all being essential parts of the social system of Canada in the twentieth century.

In the manner of a prophet or classical political philosopher of the seventeenth century, Mackenzie King recognized the central question of politics as one which entered into the lives of every human being who had seen a brother die or human life maimed by the cruel working of a society made up itself of human beings. This central question is: why are human beings inhuman? Why does humanity destroy itself? Why is life loaded with death? And what is the way out of the dilemma of man? Politics as a subject is not finally about party programmes nor is it about the preservation of old nor about the creation of new ones. This Mackenzie King understood. This lifted him high above contemporary Canadian practitioners of the art. This prophetic quality, too, made him a better master than they.

On the first page of *Industry and Humanity* Mackenzie King directs our attention to the novel, *Frankenstein*, by Mary Wollstonecraft Shelley. This sets the tone of the book which is intended to "cause the truth to make its appeal to the imagination, as well as to the reason, of those who peruse these pages". Man lives in the presence of demoniac powers, and these are of his own creation. Our author gets quickly down to cases.

> ". . . Behold at what cost Industry has been directed to the transformation of the world's resources into instruments of human destruction. Who can say the extent to which the application of scientific knowledge and the inventions of science have been devoted to augmenting and perfecting means of human slaughter, on land, and sea and in the air? Who can estimate the percentage of the world's capital and labor that has been applied to forging the weapons and amassing the munitions which have made possible the awful carnage of our day? Surely, Industry is something other than was intended by those who contributed to its creation, when it can be transformed into a monster so demoniacal as to breed a terror unparalleled in human thought, and bring desolation to the very heart of the human race." (pp. 3–4.)

Thus did Mackenzie King state the human dilemma. This dilemma may not have excited the political scientist who wrote in the *American Economic Review*, but it was very much in the minds of millions of people in the years 1918 and 1919. Two possible general solutions of the dilemma presented themselves both in history and actually in the Canadian community. One general solution of the dilemma is that offered in a variety of forms by the secular philosophers such as Hobbes, Locke, Hume (in spite of certain philosophical reservations), Rousseau, and Marx. The solutions offered by each of these philosophers were based on the belief that man can, by the use of his mind, and fortified by human courage and will, devise social institutions capable of maintaining peace and ensuring the social conditions in which he may live and achieve happiness. Another general class of solutions consists of those which deny man's capacity to control his own destiny. The common element in this class of solution is the reliance upon transcendental, extra-human powers for the restraint of the demoniacal elements at the root of human misery and inhumanity.

With his habitual preference for working both sides of the street Mackenzie King endeavoured in *Industry and Humanity* to place himself in an attitude of seeming preference for both kinds of solution. But he gauged carefully the strength of the institutions of the community to which he was speaking and, in his final decision, he reposed his whole confidence upon the second class and developed his main argument to harmonize with this type of solution.

The social frustration of human endeavour, he asserted, is merely an incident or a visible and passing manifestation of larger forces at work in the universe. Employing the name of Louis Pasteur to lend the authority of Science, Mackenzie King sees the world as a battle-ground between the Law of Peace, Work and Health and the Law of Blood and of Death. Pasteur seems to have meant by the word Law, tendencies at work in society to make use of material resources for life-giving or death-dealing purposes. In Mackenzie King's scheme of things Pasteur's truisms became the keystone of his system and the means by which he "reconciled" liberal social science to the requirements of a community wherein the social authority of clerics is very great.

Before we examine the manner in which Mackenzie King performed this miracle it is necessary to discover something of his approach to the social sciences themselves and particularly to that area of them which was his own field of specialization. Both by training and experience he had a proper respect for the accumulation of facts and for precise detail. Much of what he has to say about the demonstrable relationship between hours of work and the health of workers, between the speed of assembly lines and fatigue, about the benefits of insurance funds is quite unexceptionable and not new. His preconceptions about science and about social science were quite orthodox, and, indeed, were slightly out of date by 1918. He accepted the dogmas of science derived from the physics of Newton and Clerk Maxwell, to the effect that the natural universe is a harmoniously functioning system the motions of whose parts are in accordance with laws capable of rational apprehension. The harmony, which was believed to characterize the natural universe, Mackenzie King quite unscientifically assumed to exist in the social universe: ". . . If", he writes,

> "all material things of the heaven and of the earth are thus related in a perfect harmony which human intelligence is able to grasp; is it conceivable, is it rational to believe that underlying the social relations of men and of nations, an order is not discoverable somewhere, obedience to which will bring us a perfect harmony?"

The answer to this question is, of course, yes. This harmony is not to be found, however, in the social order as it actually exists. This order is shot through with Fears which have banished Faith.

"A careful analysis of the fears which surround the parties to Industry, and especially Labor and Capital, discloses that, almost without exception, they are bred of mutual suspicion for which, it must be admitted, experience has given ample grounds. Deeper than suspicion lies a belief, sometimes consciously, oftener unconsciously, entertained, in *opposed* as contrasted with *common* interests. . . . Labor's attitude of resistance fills Capital with alarm. Capital's attitude increases Labor's resistance. As fears increase, antagonisms develop. A growing class-consciousness conceived in mistrust gives birth to vast organization, leading to intensified fears of Labor, on the one side, and of the monied interests, or Capital, on the other. . . . Thus is commenced and developed the same kind of competitive arming which has proven so fatal between nations, the same kind of alliances on the part of opposed groups, the same inevitable drift toward ultimate disaster to all concerned. Such warfare is surely none other than the working of the Law of Blood and of Death which leads to extermination." (pp. 260–61.)

Where, then, does the harmony of the social order exist if it is so patently absent in the society around us? It dwells where it dwelt in the time of St. Augustine: in the mind of God. "Is not", asked Mackenzie King, "all that Humanity has been called upon to endure, evidence of a wanton departure somewhere from the purpose of God among men?" (p. 152.) Answering this question, he wrote, "We know whence the deviation has arisen. It is in our industrial and international relations. We have turned the dials of human conduct to commercial uses when they were intended as guides to the divinity which lies everywhere about us." (pp. 152–53.)

Although Mackenzie King invited his readers to examine at considerable length his work as a civil servant, a politician and a labour relations expert and to note well the changes in institutional relationships of which he had been the author, or at least the inspiration, he expresses no faith in institutional reform as a means of meeting social needs or, as he would say, "of realizing the divinity which lies everywhere around us". This is the key point at which he departed from the traditions of secular political science. Hobbes, Locke, Rousseau, Marx, even the Hegelians of various descriptions, all had in their particular ways a lively appreciation of man's capacity for self-annihilation and for getting himself into frustrating social difficulties. But, advocating different kinds of institutional reorganization, all have agreed that institutional organization is the way out, and that man either through the agency of individuals, or of the community will, or of class consciousness, or of a professional bureaucracy is capable of controlling his destiny. It is not surprising that the works of philosophers of this order have come under the disapproval of religious authority; for the implication of all secular political science is that Churches are either unnecessary or at best subordinate social agencies.

This was not the view of Mackenzie King. He distinguished between the form of social institutions and the control of them. Form is a matter of indifference. "What so many fail to see", he wrote, "is that large organization of Industry and vast wealth are *in themselves* neither good nor evil." "It is not against the *form*, but against the possible *abuses* of industrial organization, whatever the system, that protests should be uttered." "Clear discernment between a form of organization and possible abuses under it, whether the control be individual or collective, will save much confusion, and make possible speedier adjustment of existing wrongs." (pp. 101–03.)

The rejection of the notion that there is a relationship between the form of institutions and their activity in society opened a further way into the sanctuaries of the church. Institutions are controlled by individuals, but individuals are by their nature incapable by themselves of anything but serving themselves. Mackenzie King does not fall back upon the Church Fathers or upon *Institutes of the Christian Religion* in order to reassert the doctrines of Original Sin and human impotence. He relies, instead, upon some thoughts of William James to the effect that the individual is conditioned by his social function and that this conditioning blinds him to nearly all needs but his own. "Hence the stupidity and injustice of our opinions, so far as they deal with the significance of alien lives. Hence the falsity of our judgments so far as they presume to decide in an absolute way on the value of other persons' conditions or ideals." But Mackenzie King did not follow James to James's conclusions. He took from him what he wanted, and then proceeded to assert that the scales would be lifted from the eyes of the blind, not by disciplined, experimental and historical inquiry but by emotional paroxysms and by turning our attention from the material to the spiritual world. "The universe of spirit," he wrote,

> "not the material universe, needs now to be explored. Matter knows nothing of aspiration and despair, of love and hate, of faith and fear. Yet these are the chords of human sensibilities upon which all the joy, all the passion and all the pathos of human life are expressed. The materialistic interpretation of life has failed to give us progress according to any true meaning of the word. It has brought only death and desolation in colossal measure. We must begin anew with a spiritual interpretation of life, and out of the human service which it inspires seek to reconstruct our dismantled world." (pp. 124–25.)

Mackenzie King was, in fact, a pioneer explorer of the route of retreat from the natural to the supernatural. In *Industry and Humanity* his first seance is in view.

Not content with a general proposition about the importance of the spiritual universe, he specifically points to "the agencies for the cultivation of this field and for garnering its harvests". "In ways undreamed of," he wrote in his final chapter,

> "individuals and institutions may play their part in the solution of industrial and international problems. For example, if women and if the Church could but realize and be true to their special opportunities of service to the world, the vast problems of Industry and of the State would soon be solved. Except to shield them, men have no desire to circumscribe their activities. Men understand the fields of sacred influence which are peculiarly theirs, and, amid the strife of the world, look for sustained inspiration to a devout womanhood and a consecrated church. It is from the reverence for life which men get from their mothers, and from the faith which a religion pure and undefiled imparts, that there comes the spirit of mutual aid through which the material interests of the world make way for the nobler aspirations of the soul." (p. 488.)

Coming from a trained social scientist this passage is at first sight incredible. It reveals, however, Mackenzie King's preternatural sensitivity to currents of feeling running ever so slightly in society. Thus early Mackenzie King recognized the failing faith of the North American middle class in themselves and in their destiny.

A study of *Industry and Humanity* reveals very clearly why Mackenzie King was never a reformer of institutions. Although he held power longer than any previous parliamentary Prime Minister, and in spite of a reputation as a man interested in and capable of social and industrial reform, his record is nearly barren of significant institutional changes. Constitutional reform made no headway. National laws governing labour relations and labour standards are virtually non-existent in Canada. His sole achievements in the sphere of popular welfare were a meagre system of old-age pensions, a system of unemployment insurance and family allowances. In *Industry and Humanity* he quotes with some disapproval a description of conditions in a cotton textile factory in the province of Quebec upon which he himself reported in 1909 (p. 313). But the Royal Commission on Price Spreads reporting on conditions as they existed twenty-five years later, during which time Mackenzie King had been Prime Minister for nine years, found that sweat shops still survived in Canada and that "unemployment and low wages have reduced many workers to a state of abject poverty". But Mackenzie King's policies could have been accurately predicted by a careful reader of *Industry and Humanity*; for he revealed there that he shared none of the traditional beliefs of liberals and socialists in the efficiency of institutional change to secure human well-being.

Mackenzie King's intellectual and political capitulation to ecclesiastical influences may have served him well as an office holder, but it caused him to serve Canada ill as a creative leader. Perhaps mankind was bewildered in 1918, but bewilderment is a permanent condition and need occasion none of the apocalyptic alarms which Mackenzie King and others have sounded and are still sounding. In the presence of bewilderment about man's social condition, the Church is no more qualified than any other institution to offer leadership. Indeed, it is less qualified than many. Churches may appear as the agents of the mysterious powers, but in the material world they are institutions like others, dependent for their existence upon the organizing talents of their professional personnel and the money they can collect to support their organizers. The Churches are, in fact, secular interests as much as industrial corporations or the government bureaucracy. Their officers do not know any more about society, and often less, than the officers of other institutions. With a few notable exceptions occurring rather more frequently in the Protestant Churches than in the Roman Catholic, the clergy, like Mackenzie King, have small faith in either the alteration or the reconstruction of social institutions. The spiritual world, having the greatest and the final significance for man, is the main concern of their lives. To suggest, as Mackenzie King does, that the influence of the Churches can be decisive in ensuring the harmonious functioning of their social and economic institutions and that mere forbearance and brotherly love are sufficient to solve economic and social problems betrays an ignorance of society and history which it would be hard to credit were it not set down so categorically in the pages of *Industry and Humanity*.

The message in *Industry and Humanity* addressed to Canadian business men is not susceptible to simple exposition either of its content or its purpose. Mackenzie King's attitude towards particular princes of business, as we have seen, had varied from the acute personal hostility he evinced for the President of the Grand Trunk to the unqualified devotion and admiration he had for the Rockefellers. This duality of attitude was a long-standing and general one in his mind, and it was not merely a matter of difference in personality among the business men with whom he had contact. In *The Secret of Heroism* he quoted with approval Harper's determination to pursue and penalize the "mean men" among the employing class. Earlier, in his newspaper articles on sweating, we have noticed the distinction he made between the exploiters of sweated labour and the owners of the big, airy factories powered with electricity. Just as his old teacher Taussig had deplored the virile savage, Henry Clay Frick, so Mackenzie King helped Rockefeller oust Bowers, the superintendent of the Colorado Fuel and Iron Company, when the regime of industrial feudalism in Colorado had provoked a public scandal. As an exponent of "soft" tactics in the relationship between employers and employees he deplored the exponents of "hard" tactics, whom he identified in his own mind as Tory types.

The leaders of finance and industry form the most influential group in Canadian society. Given the influential character of the business leaders, Mackenzie King was obliged to formulate an attitude to them, to state it and to prove his reliability by reference to his record. Considered as a message to business leaders, *Industry and Humanity* provokes admiration for the method of presentation if not for the message itself. It is no vulgar appeal to consider the merits of the Liberal Party. Mackenzie King was sensible enough to know, and had enough respect for his readers to know that they knew, that the Liberal Party had no merits apart from its leaders, and that none of its traditional equivocations nor any of its promises would evoke the least response in business men. We cannot be certain, but it seems evident from *Industry and Humanity*, that Mackenzie King never expected to change any votes by what he had to say. His purposes were more long range and more fundamental: they were to state in the most general way the political problems confronting the strongest group in Canadian society, and to propose a solution.

In the execution of this purpose Mackenzie King did not employ a pussy-foot technique. He did not stoop to telling big business men what they wanted to hear. Instead, he told them what he felt they needed to know: viz. that they were threatened with destruction and deserved to be. "Possibly no prejudice has surpassed in intensity that which has been felt against 'Capital- ism'," he wrote.

"Nor are there lacking ample grounds for the prejudice. In the first place the substitution of large-scale organization in Industry for the domestic system, made possible by capitalist direction in the last century and a half, has wrought more change in the social order than the combined forces of many preceding centuries. The transition has been accompanied by inconceivable hardship and injustice. . . . Worst of all, it has occasioned the instability characteristic of modern industrial life, and has rendered in- evitable the commercial depressions, the financial panics, and the violent industrial crises which have become recurring phenomena of our times." (pp. 98–99.)

For the Canadian business class this was probably strong medicine, but it had become quite conventional elsewhere by the year 1918. Europeans had been talking like this since the re- volution of 1830 or earlier, and from the early 1880's it was commonplace enough in the United States among people who read books on the social sciences. A sense of catastrophe and a bad conscience were as much part of an American millionaire's make-up as a propensity to conspicuous waste.

At first sight Mackenzie King appears as a prophetic critic of the capitalist social order. But any group can face a great deal of criticism provided they are not persuaded they are socially useless. Mackenzie King invited his readers to dwell upon the evil disposition of certain capitalists, but not to examine the role of capitalists as a social group—the personally good ones as well as the personally bad ones.

"In abstract theory," we read in *Industry and Humanity*,

> "both Anarchy and Socialism are defended on the assumption that Labor creates all wealth, and therefore that all wealth belongs to Labor. Moreover, the method sometimes suggested of effecting a regime of Socialism is that of forcible expropriation by the State, without compensation to owners, of all private property, which is the method of Anarchy." (p. 408.)

Mackenzie King did not pause long to examine this argument. In his view an industrial product is the result of the co-operative activity of four human factors: the capitalists who make available their wealth for the purposes of production; the managers who organize capital and the work force; labour which, under the direction of managers makes and tends machines or makes products directly; and finally the community which sustains the whole apparatus of production.

While he set up four categories of human factors in the productive process, he suggested that capital and management are generally found together as a combined social force and labour and the community are often, but not always, united against them. "Instead of a fraternal attitude between the parties," we read,

> "there is too often a sort of disguised truce between Management and Capital on the one side and Labor and the Community on the other. They look at each other, as one writer has expressed it, 'across No Man's land,' an area of ever-present possible conflict which, in their common interest, ought to be the ground of joint approach." (pp. 381–82.)

Thus, Mackenzie King appears to accept the concept of a class struggle. According to Mackenzie King this arises, not from any conflict of interest between these opposing groups, but from their misunderstanding of their common interests. Each of the four parties to production has a function, and each of their functions is a necessary part of the whole process.

What, then, are the functions of the four human factors in the productive process? During his active life, up to the time he wrote *Industry and Humanity*, Mackenzie King had to deal frequently with the largest industrial organizations in the world. He very rightly noticed the specialization of function which was developing. Financiers and managers made up a group which for all political and social purposes acted together, as Mackenzie King acknowledged, but which were functionally differentiated. While he endeavoured to justify the existence of both financiers and managers on the basis of their functions, he attached considerably more importance to the managers, whose productive role is an obvious one and whose presence is necessary in any productive system which can be at present imagined. It is significant that Mackenzie King was alert to these new developments and that, while he has much to say in criticism of financiers, he is unreserved in his admiration for managers. While he would bind the other factors in production by rules of mutual interdependence, to the managers he would give a very free hand. "Management is a function", he wrote, "which does not admit of divided authority." (p. 368.) There is no reason why management should not be compelled to operate within a framework of general policy, but Management will often dictate.

> "In the case of Industry, this body [the governing body] would be the Directorate representative of Labor, Capital, Management and the Community, with Management advising, and often dictating to, the other constituent elements, just as under the British Constitution, the Prime Minister and his Cabinet ... dictate to Parliament." (p. 426.)

The fact is, that in spite of an elaborate plan for participation of the four factors, capital, management, labour and the community, in the formulation of policy, Mackenzie King considered a centre of power necessary in industry or in government; and that centre of power, he believed, should be Management.

For the owners of the means of production, Mackenzie King had many censures. "For the preferential treatment Capital has thus far received, there is no defence possible on grounds of

democratic theory or fundamental justice, only an explanation."
(p. 370.) Elsewhere he speaks of the ."undemocratic and exclusive attitude" which is "so congenial to many capitalist
investors and large employers of Labor". (p. 375.) He advised
them at one point to learn from King Albert of Belgium, who,
under the stress of war, stopped talking of "my armies", "my
country" and "my people", and employed phrases like "our
country", "our people", etc. Although he would strip them of
their powers Mackenzie King believed they had a place in the
economic system. Capital is a surplus over and above what is
spent on daily living either on necessities or luxuries. This
surplus will only come into being if individuals have some
inducement to create it. Security of property and the firm fact
of a return on investment are the only practical social devices
for ensuring capital accumulation. He considered the possibility
of socialist organization but rejected it on the grounds that,
while an approximation to socialism is possible in war so long
as men are united against their enemies, in peace human nature
is such that they require material inducements to do what is
socially necessary. Hence, the institution of private property
and the inducement of profit are necessary to bring responsibility into the care and development of the capital and resources required for social well-being. If people took Christianity
sufficiently seriously socialism might work, but this "as yet is
unhappily far from being the main incentive in Industry".
(p. 409.) "Psychologists are agreed that of all instincts, that of
ownership is one of the most deeply rooted, and one of the least
likely ever to be eradicated." (p. 411.)

For the owners of capital Mackenzie King had this social
justification, but he held out to them also the hope that they
would last forever provided they mended their way:

> "Whilst it is unlikely that Socialism in the form of the omnipotent
> and ever-present state, or Industrial Unionism controlling Industry
> in conjunction with a democratized state, will ever permanently
> succeed the present order, it is altogether probable that Collecti-
> vist ideals, and in particular what they represent of the com-
> munity idea and improvement in the status of Labor, will vastly
> expand their influence in the years to come." (p. 419.)

Judged from the point of view of Canadian business men in
1918, Mackenzie King's ideas appeared disgustingly radical.

There are still elements in the Liberal Party who regard Mackenzie King as a troublesome radical element who was only tolerable because he could win elections. Amongst men who were culturally provincial and, on economic questions, intellectually primitive, Mackenzie King's thoughts on capital were hardly calculated to attract support. Actually his ideas were in no way novel. He accepted human nature in its North American form. Of the North American community he was a shrewd judge of the actual. He did not expect the Canadian business men to appreciate this. Instead, he relied upon a trump card which they could neither explain away nor ignore, i.e., that he had worked for John D. Rockefeller, that Rockefeller approved of him, and that Rockefeller gave voice to his ideas.

Mackenzie King's treatment of labour as a social factor in the life of the community consists of two elements: a message to Canadian labour leaders telling them of his position in relation to theirs, and an analysis of the role of labour in relation to other classes.

We have already noticed how, by 1918, the Trades and Labour Congress of Canada had swung around to opposition to the Industrial Disputes Investigation Act, Mackenzie King's principal claim to fame as a "Labour statesman". A Commission of the United States Congress had labelled him a deviser of "specious substitutes for trade unions that will deceive, mollify and soothe public opinion while bulwarking the employers' arbitrary control". This was an opinion expressed in 1915. In 1916, a committee appointed by the President had contradicted this view, and had expressed a qualified approval of the Rockefeller Plan. In Canada Mackenzie King had given the Plan considerable publicity with a view to overcoming his reputation as a "high priced labor sleuth". In spite of these efforts, however, he was still vulnerable to attack by moderate as well as radical elements in the Canadian trade union movement. In *Industry and Humanity* he endeavoured to set at rest the fears of the union hierarchy.

In order to do this he dealt carefully with his record. The Industrial Disputes Investigation Act was depicted as a great step forward which had the support of Canadian labour bodies

s

at the time of its passage by Parliament. In order to defend his part in the Colorado affair he passed boldly to the attack. In Colorado ". . . industry has progressed as never before in its entire existence. Happy and prosperous communities, assuming the aspect of garden villages, in which community activities are being more and more community controlled, speak of the new citizenship. . . ." (p. 446.) Great play was made with the report of the President's Committee and quite naturally nothing was said of the Congressional Commission. Words, however, were unlikely to convince union leaders if in fact the Colorado Plan was dangerous to them. Mackenzie King made great use of the fact that in the Rockefeller Plan there is a provision that "there shall be no discrimination by the company or by any of its employees on account of membership or non-membership in any society, fraternity or union".[1] Chairman Walsh of the Congressional Commission had exposed the joker in this provision,[2] but Mackenzie King pointed to it not as recognition of the union and an undertaking to bargain, which any experienced trade unionist could see, but as a step towards recognition, "and Agreement in the Nature of a Collective Bargain".

With skill Mackenzie King, who had refused to make any comment on conditions in Colorado, who had wished to let bygones be bygones, swung around in *Industry and Humanity* to a denunciation of the company towns of the Colorado Fuel and Iron Company: "Houses and shacks stood in rows unenclosed, or were scattered in clusters about the canyons and prairies. There was little in the way of public control. . . . Pioneering in industry, like all forms of pioneering, is necessarily accompanied by much in the way of autocratic control. . . ." (p. 436.) But John D. Rockefeller, Jr., had changed all this with the advice and assistance of Mackenzie King.

> "To one and all he delivered the same message. 'They tell you,' he said, referring to popular comment on the disturbances of a few months previous, 'that we are enemies. I have come here to tell you that we are not enemies, but partners. Labor and Capital are partners, not enemies. Neither one can get on without the other. Their interests are common, not antagonistic.' " (p. 438.)

This was the sort of thing many of the trade union hierarchy

---

[1] Rockefeller, *The Colorado Industrial Plan*, p. 75.
[2] See Chapter VII, p. 204.

in Canada wanted to hear. In the period 1918–1919, when *Industry and Humanity* began to circulate, the Canadian trade union movement was badly split between those, like the Hon. Gideon Robertson of the Telegraphers, who had entered the "Union" government and helped break the Winnipeg General Strike in 1919,[1] and those like R. B. Russell and R. J. Johns of Winnipeg, who wished to press on from craft to industrial unionism and on to socialism. The triumph of right-wing labour after the smashing of the Winnipeg General Strike by the authorities in June, 1919, made this message about partnership singularly appropriate, especially coming from a politician whose hands were clean in so far as the strike-breaking activities of the Canadian Government, in 1919, were concerned. As Mackenzie King had predicted to Rockefeller in August, 1914, the end of the war had created a situation in which leaders, at least of the old and conservative unions, were coming "to regard as their friends and allies companies and corporations large enough and fair enough to desire to maintain . . . standards of their own accord". To those union leaders Mackenzie King was speaking.

And when he spoke he brought them another comforting message. The socialists, anarchists and syndicalists are all wrong. "Syndicalism", he wrote, "makes its appeal to the ignorance and prejudices of the masses." (p. 407.) Toward socialism he was a little more rational and considerate, but, he asserted, "labor has long since recognized that the Socialist State is based too largely on a conception of human nature which leaves human imperfections out of account." (p. 411.)

Finally, Mackenzie King placed before the Canadian union leaders a scientific justification for reducing the fluidity of the labour market by excluding Asiatics from Canada. The Law of Competing Standards[2] was set forth in all its subtle glory to provide the blessing of Science for racial discrimination. But the Law of Competing Standards was something more. In *Industry and Humanity*, Mackenzie King boldly advocated a plank of the National Minimum.

"In advocating enforcement of this minimum as the necessary basis of any genuine industrial efficiency or decent social order,

---

[1] D. C. Masters, *The Winnipeg General Strike* (Toronto, 1950), p. 78.
[2] See p. 81.

labor fortifies its position by accepting without reservation the Christian precepts that 'No man liveth to himself alone', and that 'We are members one of another'. It applies these teachings to the economic foundations of society." (p. 349.)

Unfortunately the Law of Competing Standards, which he created as a bar to an international minimum, can also be used as an excuse in a nation of federal states and regional differences, like Canada, for doing nothing about a national minimum. Wage differentials between Ontario, Quebec, the Maritime Provinces and western Canada were then, and are still, the foundation of very real differences in material and social standards of life in the various regions of Canada. The Constitution of Canada is an obstacle to the establishment of a national minimum, but a Constitution is nothing if the will is strong. The Law of Competing Standards, however, undermined the will.

His message to the right wing of Canadian labour was the closest Mackenzie King came in *Industry and Humanity* to stating a platform. In a sense this message is the least satisfactory of the whole book. Far more interesting and more instructive is his discussion of labour in relation to the community as a whole and to the other factors in production; for it was upon his conception of labour in this regard that he built the entire edifice of his practical policies. His intellectual conceptions of labour and his analysis of its social role illuminated the path of his life.

Labour is the source of all wealth. This is the starting point of his analysis. "The effort", he wrote,

"necessary to effect the transformation of natural resources into services and commodities is the muscular and mental effort of human beings, aided by the labor of brutes and by natural forces which human beings control and direct, and by tools, appliances and machines, themselves the result of human effort in the past. With the ceaseless expansion of Industry, this interweaving of effort has developed on a world scale, and is shared in by human beings in all quarters of the globe. Industry is thus expressive of activities common to humanity, and its expansion is Humanity's common task. So inexhaustible are natural forces and other resources of Nature that the only limit to the possible development of Industry is the extent and ingenuity of human effort. The extent of human effort is a matter of cooperation between the parties to Industry: ingenuity, a matter of intelligent coordination of functions." (p. 127–28.)

Here we have Mackenzie King's first generalization about the social world. Services and commodities are the product of muscular and mental effort. This effort is the most fundamental of social activities. It is universal. No law of diminishing returns sets a limit to what human effort can accomplish. Given human ingenuity and social co-operation the possibilities of what man can do are limitless. These are the moral and social assumptions of socialism.

His next step leads him along another path. There is a distinction between muscular labour and mental labour so great that each must be regarded as separate factors in production.

> "Whilst some element of directing intelligence is essential to the crudest kinds of muscular effort, and some element of muscular effort is essential to directing intelligence of the highest order, the service rendered by directing intelligence . . . is so different in kind and degree from service of labor that is mainly muscular that the two may be regarded as separate and distinct factors in production." (p. 132.)

Thirdly, production requires not only present effort, but the results of past effort in the shape of capital. Thus, a new category emerges: the owner of capital. The community is the highest common factor of the three elements and is, by a strange logic, itself a factor in the industrial complex. Each of the human factors in production has an indispensable function.

By employing this empirical and functional analysis, Mackenzie King succeeded in ascribing to labour a subordinate role in production, and one likely to become even less important as the need for managerial skill becomes greater and greater. Strong of arm and dull of brain like St. Thomas Aquinas' ideal peasant, the worker ceased in Mackenzie King's scheme of things to be the hope of the world, and became instead an object of pity to whom it is wise to accord justice but never power. The anarchists and syndicalists were forces of which Mackenzie King had a lively appreciation. Their appeal, based upon a faith that the workers can manage themselves without the services of capitalists, he considered to be directed to "the ignorance and prejudice of the masses". (p. 407.)

On the basis of his conception Mackenzie King established his attitude to labour. This was a compound of pity and expediency. In view of the productive powers of society the incomes and living conditions of sections of the wage-earners were in his opinion "unjust" i.e. a product at once of selfishness on the part of their employers and helplessness on the part of the workers. The pity he felt for match girls suffering from "phossie jaw" and telephone operators driven to nervous exhaustion must have created a very strong impression of a deep sympathy for the working class and an involvement in their destiny.

Mackenzie King sensed the importance of labour in the community, and he knew it was growing ever greater. He was sufficiently a political realist to grasp the fact that the importance and the weight of the wage-workers did not depend upon whether they voted or did not vote, but upon the fact of their numbers and their fundamental contribution to the productive process upon which all of human life depends. He never, therefore, stopped to consider the potential power of labour in terms of its constitutional position. Indeed, he was a thoroughgoing and natural democrat of the North American type who could not conceive of government unsanctioned by the process of voting by the mass of the adult population. Bearing all this in mind it is necessary to ask, further, what Mackenzie King conceived the importance of labour to be. Here we encounter the element of expediency in his attitude. Labour is the muscular in contrast to the mental and fundamental element in production. It is, therefore, both a necessary and an inferior element. Just as the body must be fed and exercised in order that the brain may function, so the wage-workers must be adequately fed and properly housed in order that they may the better sustain the managers and owners. In his conception of the role of labour in society Mackenzie King never went beyond this. His attitude and his policies were only verbally different from and often, from the point of view of labour, inferior to those of his Tory opponents whom he delighted to flay.

Mackenzie King recognized that if society has a common faith, all will go well; if it is shot through with fears it will fall apart. This is his view (p. 364), and he directed his whole attention to the creation of faith: a faith in the order of society as it existed when he wrote *Industry and Humanity*. What he failed to perceive was that social and economic developments had, in fact, undermined seriously the dogmas and the faith he sought to strengthen, and that new faiths were coming into being in the world beyond the range of his experience.

For a man who claimed to advocate the rights of labour, Mackenzie King said surprisingly little about the right of labour to organize. He accepted the existence of unions as a matter of course, but he did not say whether by the word union he meant a company union or a real union. He nowhere considered the value or otherwise of unions as a means of educating their members in public affairs and their responsibilities as citizens and as human beings. His main attention was directed to the construction of apparatus for the government of industry which would banish conflicts between the owners and managers on the one hand and workers and the public on the other, and establish a parallelism of interests among the parties of industry. The object of industrial activity is, of course, maximum productivity and efficiency. Mackenzie King ardently worshipped the aim of ever-increasing productivity and efficiency, and he believed that abundant production made possible social manoeuvrability on a greater scale than was possible in poor societies. In order to achieve increased productivity the wage-earners must be accorded two things: status and a personal and material interest in increased productivity.

Upon first reading *Industry and Humanity* the man of 1918 might be persuaded that Mackenzie King proposed a radical reconstitution of the economic system. "The organization of business, its terminology and its spirit, must all change if Industry is to fulfil its true mission and be made to reflect real partnership." What he actually proposed was of a very limited nature which involved nothing more than the stock devices of personnel managers hired by corporations whose directors believed in "soft" rather that "hard" labour policies. On the question of status he had nothing precise to say, and it is indeed difficult to discover what exactly he meant by status. His chapter on government in industry is loaded with rhetoric directed at privilege and autocratic government. He took a very firm line about Prussian aristocracy, plutocracy and militarism. He discreetly hinted, by quoting a British officer wounded on the Somme, that American and British industrialism might bear a trace of the evils so prominently and safely noticed in Prussia. When he descended from the heights to consider the case of workers in industry he could only suggest that owners and managers accept the notion of co-partnership, Round Table Conferences and Whitley Councils as devices for convincing their workers that they are not in fact wage workers but partners in the enterprise in which they work. Calling attention to King John, Magna Charta, Pym and Hampden, Mackenzie King suggested that the principle of responsible government should be introduced into business. But he never stopped to particularize. He implied that the capitalists, the managers, the workers and the community should all share in determining the policy of an enterprise in order to ensure the general well-being, but he never disclosed what form this participation might take. In some way he expected the boards of directors of enterprises to become parliaments made up of representatives of capital, labour, managers and the community. How they might be selected readers were never told. They were assured, however, that "Management need not be robbed of any of its necessary measure of control".

When he came to consider the ordering of industry to ensure the interest of the worker in increased productivity, Mackenzie King was more specific. His remedy for the conflict of interest between worker and capitalist was profit sharing. The piecework system as a method of paying labour commanded his admiration, but he recognized that organized labour had become so opposed to the system that it could not be advocated. For this reason he advocated profit sharing as an alternative in order to interest the worker in maximum efficiency, scientific management and maximum exertion at all times. The by-product of this system at that time—unemployment—Mackenzie King disposed of easily. "Where there is actual displacement of Labor, new opportunities of employment should be found as quickly as possible, and provision of a right and proper kind made for Labor that is displaced." (p. 286.)

The easy ways in which Mackenzie King disposed of the social and economic problems created by the dynamic drive for efficiency and increase of output point to the weakness of his general understanding of economic and social problems. All his thought is directed to the problems of particular firms and how to make them efficient and productive. That there could be economic, social and political problems created by an aggregate of firms all driving for maximum efficiency and maximum productivity he did not attempt to discuss. He accepted uncritically until the day he died the dogmas of equilibrium economics.

As a politician Mackenzie King was necessarily interested in the community, the fourth factor in the productive process. Whether there is such a thing as the community apart from the capitalists, managers and workers, it would be difficult to argue. It was, however, the field Mackenzie King was obliged to cultivate in the interest of his ambition and his destiny. The community is the final authority in establishing the relations of industry. It can only exert this authority on the strength of its knowledge. Opinion must be formed out of knowledge. To this point Mackenzie King's argument was unexceptional liberalism. On first inspection he appears to have attached great importance to undifferentiated knowledge. Information will make the people free; this seems to be his message. But we discover after further study that Mackenzie King was speaking to the controllers of the agencies for informing the public, and that the purpose of knowledge among the people is not to guide their actions but to inspire their faith.

The three agencies to which Mackenzie King was making his appeal were the Churches, the press and the professional politicians. Of the institutions capable of influencing the decisions of people and of determining the patterns of social and, finally, political action, the Churches of Canada are vastly the most powerful. Advertising agencies, schools, universities, newspapers, the radio, do not compare with the Churches either in the social and political importance of their influence or in its extent. Of the Churches the Roman Catholic Church is, of course, much the most influential by reason of its wealth, the organizing capacity of its professional personnel, the vast numbers of its communicants and character of its dogmas which bring to the individual the comfort of certainty. The zeal and ubiquity of the Roman Catholic clergy have checked sharply the growth of the secular mental atmosphere so strong in countries deeply influenced by the Protestant Reformation and revolutions on the French and Russian patterns. The Protestant Churches in Canada have benefited from these activities of the Catholics and they, too, flourish in spite of the fact that their influence is seldom as decisive in any particular community, or nationally as that of the Roman Catholic Church.

It is a commonplace to observe that a century or more ago, when Mackenzie King's grandfather was an active politician, Liberals were anathema to the Roman Catholic clergy. Although this is common knowledge an effort must be made forcibly to recall it in order to understand what Mackenzie King was driving at in some of the more contradictory and high flown passages of *Industry and Humanity*. He was a member of, and aspired to become the leader of, the Liberal Party of Canada. Although not as suspect as it had once been, this party's history of relations with the Roman Catholic Church was still a matter for consideration both in the archiepiscopal palaces in Quebec, Toronto and Winnipeg and in the gathering places of the Liberal politicians. The Liberal and radical movement had been originally, in the time of William Lyon Mackenzie and later in the time of George Brown and Alexander Mackenzie, the work of Protestants, deists and agnostics in the manner, but wanting perhaps in the carefully articulated philosophy, of the English radicals of the Benthamite school. The reformers, as they were known, had as their affiliates in French Canada, a small party which bore the name of *Rouges*. They were anti-clerical, liberal and rationalist in their sympathies. Worse, from the point of view of the clergy, they were the organizers of centres of secular influence known as the *Instituts Canadiens*, where young men and old could read the classics of liberalism from Voltaire to Mill, and enjoy all the mental influences of metropolitan France. Thus, as late as 1896, even the Liberal Party of Canada was something of a liberal party fighting for traditional liberal objectives: representative and responsible (the Anglo-Canadian liberal's version of republican) government, the separation of Church and State, freedom of the press, freedom of opinion, and social equality.

The weakness of the Liberal Party in the years after Confederation was its inability to command a following among French-Canadians sufficiently large to form a majority in the legislature. The Liberal regime of Alexander Mackenzie, returned in 1874 on a wave of revulsion against corruption and depression, was a miserable failure. Almost in despair the

Party accepted as a leader a moderate *Rouge* from the province of Quebec, Wilfrid Laurier. By the time this happened *Rougeisme*, or liberalism, in Quebec had been badly undermined. The ultramontane party in the Church, fighting on two fronts, against old-fashioned Gallican influences to the right and infidelity and liberalism to the left, had succeeded in battering down all opposition. The *Instituts Canadiens* had been forced to close under the threat of mass excommunication and all the practical loss and social discomfort which such a sentence can mean in a community where the mass of the people obey the priests. By the '90's *Rougeisme* had been intellectually and morally emasculated and was incapable of challenging the Church in any serious way.

When Mackenzie King was a young man the liberal movement was faced with a great test and a great opportunity. This was the Manitoba School question. Stripped of all its constitutional and legalistic complications the issue was a simple one of separation of Church and State. The liberal leader, Wilfrid Laurier, succeeded in marrying a growing sentiment of provincial isolationism among French-Canadians with traditional liberal principles. He stood firm in the election of 1896, not for the separation of Church and State, which was the policy of the liberals of Manitoba, but for the independence of the provincial authorities of Manitoba. This refinement the Church would not accept. It hurled its anathemas at Laurier only to discover that in spite of threats of hell fire a considerable body of French-Canadians voted for Laurier and the Liberal Party.

This victory for traditional liberalism as distinct from the Liberal Party was its last. Sir Wilfrid Laurier may have read Voltaire, but he had never done more than enjoy him. In office liberalism became for him a species of opportunism which aimed, not at constructing a society composed of free, rational individuals, but at composing the animosities of bodies as philosophically and practically illiberal as the Roman Catholic Church, the Baptists, and the Seventh Day Adventists. There is a case for the policies of the Liberal Party of Canada, but it is not one based upon the various political and social theories and practice which make up that body of thought which bears the name of liberalism. In fact, Laurier soon made his peace with the Church. When the North-West

Territories were organized as provinces, in 1905, the principle of separation of Church and State in the organization of schools was abandoned completely.

In considering *Industry and Humanity* it is necessary to bear in mind the vicissitudes of the Liberal Party of Canada in its relations with the strongest and most skilfully led mass organization in the country. For a man like Mackenzie King, a Protestant, the grandson of a notorious liberal, a man educated in the secular University of Toronto and the even more republican and liberal institutions of Chicago and Harvard, there was an especial need for a statement of his position if he was ever to hope for office in Canada. The clergy to whom he was speaking in *Industry and Humanity*, whether Roman Catholic or Protestant, were probably not, as a body, distinguished for intellectual sophistication or great critical powers. But among the clergy there were individuals—probably not more than a few but those moving the Churches—of oecumenical experience and powerful critical faculties. We cannot know Mackenzie King's inner thoughts when he wrote *Industry and Humanity*, but on the evidence of the book itself it is plain that he realized that mere lip service to religion would not be enough; that the shallow devices by which Hobbes had failed to deceive the theologians of the Church of England would not serve in speaking to experienced and professional religious leaders.

If Mackenzie King was sensible of the power of the religious leaders he was sensitive, too, to the discontents of the mass of the people with their churches. As a young man he and his friend Harper appear to have meditated much upon the subject of the Churches and religion. They came to the conclusion that the Churches were open to criticism and personal religion was more important than institutional. "On the place of churches in national and social life, I take the ground", wrote Harper, "that the important thing for a man is his religion, what he actually believes regarding his relation to the universe, rather than his church affiliation. The first is individual and real, the latter more or less artificial . . . an institution, machinery."[1] Grown more prudent on the subject of religion Mackenzie King

---

[1] *The Secret of Heroism*, p. 146. Mackenzie King's publication of Harper's mild criticism of churches as imperfect vehicles of religious experience seems to have been a factor in a quarrel between Mackenzie King and Harper's brother, a Presbyterian clergyman.

in middle life acknowledged the faults of the Church by urging them to till the fields and harvest souls more energetically than they were doing, for they alone could in the final analysis create the Faith needed to preserve the fabric of society.

A section of *Industry and Humanity* is devoted to education and opinion. To achieve social peace the Government must mobilize opinion. To do this Mackenzie King wanted the Government "to get the facts" about industrial disputes and indeed, about everything of social consequence. Reading *Industry and Humanity* one might infer that, of all professions, teaching and journalism are the most important. In *Industry and Humanity* he expressed approval for the accumulation of information; in private correspondence, however, he severely defined the term. Advising Sir John Willison about the methods which should be employed in handling news relating to labour questions he wrote:

"I felt this the more keenly, as I had looked for a contrast in this particular in the attitude of the Canadian press towards an impulse of this kind, as compared with the journalism we find so much fault with in the United States. The more I try to discover the source of social unrest, the more does it seem to me that the press generally is one of the factors which contributes materially to it, and this is not so much merely through lack of care in statement of fact and truth as in an avowed and palpable catering to known prejudices and enmities on the part of the less favoured and fortunate members of society. I do not see how this evil, which is fraught with possibilities of disaster to the whole of society, is to be effectively combatted except by a wholly different conception of the responsibilities they owe to society on the part of men who do sensational writing and those responsible for the journals which publish it. . . ."[1]

When Chairman Walsh of the Commission on Industrial Relations suggested to him that only through investigation and the informing of the whole people of the United States about the condition of the working-classes could there be created the opinion and sentiment necessary to remove evils such as non-recognition of bargaining rights, oppression in company towns, industrial espionage and violence, Mackenzie King expressed a greater confidence in the conscience of Mr. Rockefeller than he did in the informed opinion of the American people.[2] He

[1] *Willison Papers*, King to Willison, 12 November, 1914.
[2] *R.C.I.R.*, p. 8816.

denied that a knowledge of the history of the wrongs arising out of the accumulation by rich men of wealth and power was of any utility. Rather than discuss in public what he knew about the particular situation Mackenzie King invited Chairman Walsh "to have a personal, intimate conversation . . . about conditions in Colorado".[1] Let the politicians exchange confidences in private, but by no means let us have public discussion. This was Mackenzie King's practical, as opposed to his published, philosophy of education and information as stated in *Industry and Humanity*.

If Mackenzie King's political career depended upon the attitudes of the churches, the business class, the trade union hierarchy and the press, the possibility of a career as a party leader depended upon the party politicians, i.e., the Liberal members of Parliament and the extra-Parliamentary politicians of the constituencies. It would be painting a false picture of the intellectual interests and the philosophic depth of this important element in Canadian political life to suggest that they carefully scrutinized the pages of *Industry and Humanity* and were influenced by its analysis of the problems of politics and society. But to say this does not mean that *Industry and Humanity*, especially the shortened, simplified version disseminated in public addresses, did not have a powerful influence with the politicians. To the professional politicians two questions were uppermost in their minds when considering a leader. "Who can lead us to victory at the polls?" and "Given a capacity to win who will best protect and advance the interests with which we are connected in the extra-political world of business and organized religion?"

The professional politicians recognized the perils surrounding the Government in 1918 and 1919, and the opportunities which they offered to drive the Tories from office. The volume of discontent in Canada during these years was very great. High prices and post-war inflation had reduced the unorganized workers in many areas to abject poverty.[2] Unemployment added to the misery and insecurity among the people. The threat of renewed war against Russia made many hearts sink, and Sir

---

[1] *R.C.I.R.*, p. 8810.
[2] Masters, *The Winnipeg General Strike*, p. 128.

Robert Borden had been obliged to tell Lloyd George that "public opinion in Canada would not support" the despatch of Canadian troops to Russia.[1] The riotous exultation across Canada in November, 1918, and the bonfires which burned the effigy of the Kaiser were not only jubilation about victory but an expression of relief at the end of a blood letting which had taken more Canadian lives from among Canada's 8,000,000 people than the Americans lost from among the 100,000,000 people of the United States.

The analysis of *Industry and Humanity* was not designed to deal constructively with this discontent nor to build out of it a more rational and humane society, but its rhetoric was well designed for quotation by people who could not, or did not want to understand the book when addressing people who had never heard of it. *Industry and Humanity* was rich in passages tasting of the times and designed to harmonize with the popular mood.

In *Industry and Humanity* an awareness shines forth that World War I was a vast moral catastrophe and that this catastrophe was intimately connected with the greed and the social irresponsibility so abundantly evident in the vitals of Canadian society. Referring to *Frankenstein*, Mackenzie King asked: "What is this weird tale but a parable, all too realistic, of the War that has destroyed so large a portion of mankind? Where, but in the studies of political philosophers, were conceived those ideas which have ... led to the destruction of Humanity on a scale so appalling?" (pp. 2–3.) War does not appear in *Industry and Humanity* as something glorious but as an acute human tragedy. It may have appeared in his letter to Rockefeller of August 6, 1914, as an opportunity for business men to discipline labour, but in 1918 war was depicted as something else more in tune with the times.

If the people were fed-up with poverty and low wages the Liberal politicians could quote this from *Industry and Humanity*. "It is true that while the serf was bound to the soil, the soil also was bound to the serf. In this particular, as well as in the personal responsibility which masters had for the care of their slaves, many a serf and many a slave of former times was better off than some of the toilers in Industry today." (p. 110.) If this reference was too historical the politicians could quote the

---

[1] D. Lloyd George, *Memoirs of the Peace Conference* (New Haven, 1939), Vol. 1, p. 230.

approval Mackenzie King accorded to this statement of a British officer wounded on the Somme: "For the spirit of German Imperialism is too often the spirit of English and American industrialism, with all its cult of power as an end in itself, its coarse material standards, its subordination of personality to mechanism, its worship of an elaborate and soul destroying organization." (p. 399.) Again, "the voice that is heard above the din and confusion of the world today is that of Labor demanding a fuller and freer life." (p. 304.) This was stronger stuff than Sergeant Langdale of the Military Intelligence took down in shorthand at the labour meeting in the Walker Theatre in Winnipeg in December, 1918. J. S. Woodsworth and John Queen were sent to jail for less. Unfortunately they had no one in the St. James's Club, Montreal, suggesting they be made leaders of the Liberal Party.

If the people were restless, Mackenzie King promised them change. He was all for it. "The chaos which, within the past decade, has accompanied the transitions of the ancient absolutisms of China and Russia, reveals the nemesis which sooner or later is bound to overtake resistance to change." (p. 401.)

But if the majority of the Canadians were fed-up, Mackenzie King recognized that they were neither plunged in numb despair like the French nor in revolt like the Russians. A denunciation of War and Greed was all well enough and it could evoke a cheer, but what most Canadians really disliked were political disturbances. They were shaken, but not very far down. Mackenzie King had a draught that just suited: a sedative not a purge.

"It is not alone a new dawn Labor and Capital may summon forth; they can create a wholly new civilization. Let Labor and Capital unite under the inspiration of a common ideal and human society itself will become transformed. Such is the method of creative evolution." "Let Labor and Capital unite under the ideal of social service: the work of continued production will go on; not only will it vastly increase, but the whole complexion of Industry will become transformed. No longer will Industry be the battleground of rival and contending factions; it will become the foundation of a new civilization in which life and happiness abound." (p. 528.)

The phrases which could be picked out of *Industry and Hu-*

manity by the professional politicians to demonstrate to the people that their author was a sympathetic character who could comfort them and yet demanded nothing of them, are not so interesting as the sentences here and there in the book which throw some light on Mackenzie King's conception of the state and the political process. The vein of social realism, so marked in the man, prompted him to adopt an economic interpretation both of history and politics. In spite of the space he devoted to the soul and the importance he attached to the spirit, Mackenzie King never regarded politics as something "pure" in the philosophic sense; something above or beyond economics and the material life of society. Although he is regarded by some Canadian intellectuals as the agent of Canadian national self-realization, as a leader who forged a new national unity and as a statesman who achieved for Canada an independent place in the world community, Mackenzie King, curiously, had practically nothing to say about the abstractions of nationalism or the imponderables of race consciousness. For him the basis of the political order was the economic order. If stability is achieved in the economic order, all will be well in the political sphere; and vice versa. "For if," he wrote, "in all the relations within Industry, there existed perfect adjustment, the habit of mind of communities would be such that, in the domain of politics, variations from the laws applicable to Industry would be unnatural." (p. 162.) "Fundamental beyond all other considerations is the attitude of the parties to Industry toward one another." (p. 140.) The predominant characteristic of the relations among the parties of industry was, in Mackenzie King's view as follows:

"Industry based on its present competitive, profit making system creates and sustains bitter strife between different classes in society. Were our vision sufficiently clear, we should see that this struggle lies at the root of the appalling upheaval taking place at the present moment between the armies of the world." (p. 379.)

This social realism has been shared by the most creative minds in North American politics. Mackenzie King viewed the social organism much as Madison did when he wrote,

"But the most common and durable source of faction has been the various and unequal distribution of property. Those who hold and those who are without property have ever formed distinct

T

interests in society. Those who are creditors, and those who are debtors, fall under a like discrimination. A landed interest, or a manufacturing interest, a mercantile interest, a moneyed interest, with many lesser interests, grow up of necessity in civilized nations, and divide them into different classes, actuated by different sentiments and views. The regulation of these various and interfering interests forms the principal task of modern legislation, and involves the spirit of party and faction in the necessary and ordinary operations of government." (*Federalist*, No. 10.)

Madison, the child of the enlightenment, coldly viewed this cruel social condition as permanent. The poor could be prevented from dispossessing the rich, and rich from robbing one another by constitutional contrivances designed to prevent one faction or interest from gaining power over all. Mackenzie King could not face the jungle quality of society so serenely accepted by the architects of the American constitution; for in place of the multitude of interests struggling indiscriminately with each other he could see the awful contention of one class with another.

The "vast organizations . . . of labor, on the one side, and of the monied interests" were forces too powerful to cancel themselves out without catastrophe.

The political apparatus which Mackenzie King suggested as necessary to deal with these enormous social tensions, however, differs little from that which Madison and his colleagues had designed for an earlier and simpler situation. He nowhere suggests that the State can do more than play the role of a mediator. A statesman is only a superior kind of personnel manager working in a broader field. He put it thus: "The art of establishing relations of confidence between expanding groups in Industry is akin to the highest of the arts of statesmanship. It demands the same order of ability as is required to preserve peace and harmony between diverse elements that compose a nation." (p. 169.) The state and the politician thus have a somewhat more positive role than was ever allowed by the political theories associated with the *laissez faire* school. Mackenzie King attacked *laissez faire* attitudes in politics. "The old *laissez faire* attitude of non-interference with personal rights and private property was based upon the self-interest of a privileged few, supported, through a strong antithesis, by the theory that 'man's self-love is God's providence' ". (p. 350.) Because "men are largely indifferent to the well-being of their fellowmen . . . and selfishness and greed know no bounds" (p. 351), the community must protect itself and assert the principle that man is his brother's keeper.

But Mackenzie King did not pursue very far the idea of the positive state upholding the interests of labour. He attached too much importance to the parties to industry reforming themselves by spiritual insights and influence of the Churches. On the other hand he did not attempt to develop the idea of a strong state directed to the close control of labour and the destruction of its organizations.

The state had a positive purpose much like that ascribed to the sovereign by Hobbes, i.e., the preservation of peace. Mackenzie King did not recommend the civil sword as an instrument of peace, but talk, as device for bringing each party to a dispute to conceive of the general interest and to be guided by it. The statesman's special role is to arrange compromises and to rise above the blindness which circumstances of private interest induce in individuals. The statesman does not merely register the balance of power among pressure groups because he has a function of restraining special interests, and asserting the general interest. Unfortunately Mackenzie King's conception of the general interest was so abstractly moral, so general and so based upon equilibrium economics that in fact the statesman as he conceived him could have no role but that of a middleman among interest groups. Mackenzie King's own practice conformed to the implications of his political theory.

It must be borne in mind that, when Mackenzie King wrote, neither the American nor the Canadian states had a strongly developed repressive organization. This kind of activity was only organized on an *ad hoc* and temporary basis by the public authorities to meet particular emergencies. Before the outbreak of war in 1914 the army, the police and the bureaucracy were all immature and rudimentary in form in Canada and the United States. (By 1918, however, the Royal North-West Mounted Police had begun surveillance of the labour movement as a normal activity.) Mackenzie King exactly expressed, in the inchoate nature of his ideas about the state, the existing character of the actual state in Canada. It is significant too, that, concealed among his "neutralist" and traditionally

North American notions of the state, were several hints that on the industrial level unreserved power of decision and action must be retained by the managers and on the political level the Prime Minister must be able to dictate to Parliament. (p. 426.) The question of power was never sharply raised by Mackenzie King, and he did not, perhaps, wish that it should be; but he was conscious, however, that power in society always resides somewhere.

Many aspects of *Industry and Humanity* have been omitted from consideration in this study. We have not discussed the derivative character of much of the book. Ideas and even literal words of Eliot, for example, were lifted out of his letters to Mackenzie King, and incorporated in the text of *Industry and Humanity*, and its author's dependence on publications such as those of the Garton Foundation was more extensive than his acknowledgements suggest. But taken as a whole and for the purposes it was meant to serve, *Industry and Humanity* can most usefully be considered along the lines of the analysis above.

The evaluation of *Industry and Humanity* is difficult. As a political document designed to establish a programme for victory at the polls it was an extremely clever piece of work finely tuned to the circumstances of the hour; so appropriate to the sickness of society that Mackenzie King was able to republish *Industry and Humanity* with no serious alterations (save one re-interpretation of his personal history)[1] in the depths of the depression of 1930, when poverty and the threat of a new war hung over the world. As a scientific analysis of society it is bound to command interest. We cannot dismiss the analytical parts of *Industry and Humanity*, and merely explain the book away as a clever bit of rhetoric perfected by a shrewd practical politician. Mackenzie King's analysis of society was one of the foundations of his policies and one of his guides to action. He was a successful politician. Why? We believe he was successful because he was a scientific politician; because he understood better than any of his serious rivals in Canada and most of his contemporaries elsewhere the actual forces he had to deal with. He conspicuously lacked the arts of the rule-of-thumb politician. He had a dull personality which compared in no way with the personal

[1] See p. 41.

magnetism of men like Roosevelt or Churchill. He was an impersonal, secretive political technician who depended for his success upon his capacity to understand both theoretically and practically the anatomy of society and the laws of its movement. He never invited men to love him, and very few did. Nor did he invite them to hate him, and very few did. But he knew how to manipulate them, and he did.

Mackenzie King had learned something at second hand from Marx. One of his teachers was Sir William Ashley, and Ashley, influenced by Marx, wrote, ". . . the work of the Economist should be (i) the investigation of economic history—no facts are too remote to be without significance for the present, and both Lasalle and Marx have given a great impulse to investigation in this direction, and (ii) the examination of modern industrial life *in the piece*. . . ."[1] Another teacher, whose influence Mackenzie King acknowledged in print, was Archdeacon Cunningham. Cunningham, too, was a scientific historian who attached the greatest importance to changes in the form of production as factors in the evolution of the social and political life of communities. Differing from Marx on the subject Ashley attached little importance to the class struggle as a phenomenon or as a critical factor in the evolution of society. Cunningham ignored it completely. Unlike his teachers Mackenzie King was closer to Marx on this important element of Marxism; for he attached the highest importance in his analysis of politics to the class struggle. Unlike Ashley, who repudiated Marx's theory of surplus value, Mackenzie King's initial generalization regarding the basic constituents of production was closely akin to that of Marx on the same subject.

Mackenzie King's close affinity to Marxism in some of the basic elements in his analysis of society seems to have been the chief intellectual (as distinct from personal and political) factor in his ability and refusal to pursue the logic of his primary hypothesis. This hypothesis compelled him, just as his experience did, to look into the awful social abyss which he believed the opposition of classes could open up in North American society. He could see no constructive potential in the opposition of classes. What this opposition presaged seemed to him to be simply chaos and the end of civilization.

[1] Ashley, *Life of William James Ashley*, p. 35.

Mackenzie King's message for the churches of Canada may have possessed its prudent element. Little that Mackenzie King did was ever wanting in that ingredient. But there is something deeper than prudence and opportunism in his abandoning of the rational, secular foundations of traditional liberalism and his retreat towards the supernatural and the psychic. The world his analysis revealed was too terrible to contemplate, and he had neither the mind·nor the heart to see and to go beyond it. The dark clouds gathering prompted him to seek a shelter. He fell back first to the comforting hypothesis of a natural harmony in the physical and social universe which had been cherished by the original liberals and scientific thinkers of Great Britain and France. Then he fell back further, for the real facts contradicted the optimistic assumptions of the eighteenth century. Finally, he found himself in the Dark Ages of the supernatural where the material world in which we live assumes a secondary importance. There by faith we can be healed. Form becomes inconsequential. The essence is what must be discovered.

Industry and Humanity is a textbook of political quietism. Nothing is worth doing, because the world of the flesh is nothing. All one can do in the world of the flesh is eat, sleep and win elections. But those activities are purely personal, signifying nothing. This absence of faith in the material world and its institutions, and his contrary faith in faith itself divorced from the world of things, people, energy, atoms and molecules, was at the root of Mackenzie King's total conservatism. In his subsequent career as a Prime Minister he succeeded in doing nothing, or as near to nothing as the exigencies of politics would permit. This, we think, explains his success as a politician in Canada. His unwillingness to disturb anything and his sentimental sympathy for everything; his great sensitivity combined with a want of passion for anything but power; all these combined to make him the friend of every interest in the nation, no matter how contradictory intellectually, morally and politically those interests might be. Mackenzie King possessed tolerance in an enormous measure. Its presence served him well, for it helped him to avoid attempting to make French-Canadians into Anglo-Saxons and Roman Catholics into Protestants. In any case neither of these things are worth doing. Thus, he avoided senseless and suicidal errors in his political life, and he helped to relax social tensions in some degree. Fundamentally he did nothing, however. *Industry and Humanity* plainly promised nothing. In retrospect doing nothing looks better than doing something only because Mackenzie King's more dynamic rivals were so hopelessly bent on fatal forms of activity. Mackenzie King had no policies which lead anywhere, but he had technique. He resembled an engineer in charge of a great powerhouse. Most of the time he did nothing, but he knew how to do nothing and why he was doing it.

Under Mackenzie King the Canadian economy ran its wildly fluctuating course: misery and frustration in one decade; prosperity in another; booms and threats of war in another. Does the holding of office in such conditions represent success?

"For Industry and Nationality alike, the last word lies in the Supremacy of Humanity. 'Over all nations is Humanity.' Of more worth than all else man can achieve is the well-being of mankind. The national or industrial economy based on a lesser vision, in the final analysis, is anti-social, and lacks the essentials of indefinite expansion and durability. The failure to look beyond the State, and beyond Industry as a revenue-producing process, has brought chaos instead of order. To glorify institutions, regardless of men, women and children whose individual existences they were meant to serve, is to negative, not to promote progress." (p. 25.)

No civilized man will disagree with thoughts such as these. In the mouths of men who act on these precepts they could lead to gaol and to exile; in the mouth of Mackenzie King they led to the Prime Minister's office. The only person who glimpsed and publicly stated in 1919 the whole purpose of *Industry and Humanity* was a product of the old and sophisticated political culture of Europe, and he was anonymous. Writing in *The Times Literary Supplement* a reviewer assessed the book, recognized its relationship to events of the hour, and grasped its appeal to those suffering moral anxiety and crying for a way out.

"Mr. Mackenzie King ... speaks with the authority of a singularly wide experience; and though it does not extend to the time when Bolshevism appeared to embitter the strife and heighten the gravity of the issues, his words have significance for the understanding of present Canadian labour difficulties. Unlike the majority of successful mediators and legitimate 'strike-breakers', he does not trust to the universal extension of the devices which he found effectual. . . . The book has obvious failings. Mr. King is not concise. He is a little too theoretical to be always instructive. His special points would have stood out much more clearly had they not been embedded in matter which his readers could sacrifice without loss. . . . All the same the book will appeal to two distinct classes, those looking about for useful practical devices and those who would explain to themselves the causes of the wasteful anarchy, the quarrels and dissensions everywhere to be found."[1]

[1] *The Times Literary Supplement,* 26 June, 1919.

CHAPTER X

The Powerful and the Glory

When Laurier counted his supporters in the House of Commons after the election of December, 1917, he might well have been dismayed. He could see only 82 Laurier Liberals, of whom 62 were from the province of Quebec. Over on his right, politically, were 38 "Liberals" who supported the "Union" Government. Opposite him were a Tory host which outnumbered his supporters nearly two to one. The prospect was not so dismal as a count by the tellers of the House might suggest. When he looked beyond the House of Commons, and surveyed the whole Dominion things looked much better for the Laurier Liberals. The manner of the Tory victory had discredited them, and their truculence as governors flavoured with their expediency as politicians was not calculated to add to their reputation. They commanded the affections of the rich, the respectable and the corrupt, but they commanded nothing else.

Laurier's spirits were high. His experience in the election seems to have revived in him something of the old liberalism of his youth, and he appeared to live again. He had passed his seventy-seventh birthday before the election. He had travelled across the Dominion in bitter December weather during the course of the campaign. Back in Ottawa, he was full of energy and enthusiasm. Indeed, from his correspondence during the last year of his life, one gains the impression of a preternatural sharpness of insight, a cunning and subtle appreciation of the multitude of forces at work around him, and a confidence about the future, clear and undefiled by the disguised despair of *Industry and Humanity*, and the panic of his opponents. As the tide of social discord mounted in the country and throughout the world during 1918, his confidence seemed to increase. Replying to an English friend who, experiencing alarm about the Allied intervention in Soviet Russia, had written to him, he declared:

"It seems more and more that we are on the eve of changes which will be even more far reaching than you suggest. It is a new world that will spring from the ruins of war.

"It would be rash to make predictions, but it seems to me already apparent and beyond doubt that the new world will be based upon a wide sweeping of privileges and a nearer approach to social equality; in other words this means the advent of democracy. In my judgment the advent of democracy will be a blessing, though as everything human not an unmixed blessing, but it will bring to the masses of mankind a greater share of happiness than they have ever had before."[1]

During the year 1918 there was no question about Laurier's capacity as a leader. He had confidence in his policies and in himself. "You tell me that in this election you went against me" he told an army officer who wrote to him from England. "In this, let me tell you frankly, you were wrong, but if it be any consolation to you, you know that you are not the only one . . . you will find, when the war is over, that it will be difficult to undo the mischief which has been done. . . ."[2] If he saw the problems of politics clearly, he saw with equal clarity that he must soon hand over the leadership to someone younger, and stronger physically, than himself. He did not seem to be much worried by the problem of beating the Tories. That would be simple. The real problem was to reunite and revive the Liberal Party.

In most political parties the character and understanding of the leader are amongst the most important factors in the party's role in history. Certainly this is conspicuously so in the case of the Liberal Party of Canada. It is, and it has long been, a party of diverse interests—economic, religious, racial and social—united by the vague, traditional liberal principles of liberty, equality and fraternity. A party so committed to the object of no victory for anyone or anything depends upon its leader in an

[1] *Laurier Papers*, Laurier to W. H. Griffith, 20 December, 1918.
[2] *Laurier Papers*, Laurier to Lt. Col. A. T. Thompson, 18 January, 1918.

extraordinary degree for the determination of what actual victories are won (and in whose interests), and for the formulation of its policies and the arranging of its compromises. Laurier had always been careful to keep all final decisions about policies and people in his own hands, for he realized that his party would soon dissolve into its contentious elements were he to relax for so much as a moment his spring-steel power of command. Even as late as 1915, when a new National Committee was being built up, he made sure that nineteen of its forty-five members were personally selected by himself and that, thus, there would be small prospect of anybody ever dictating to him the course of the party in the exclusive interest of any one of its components.

Thus, for reasons of necessity, there existed in the Liberal Party a tradition established by Sir Wilfrid Laurier of a leadership strong and decisive in relation to the leader's lieutenants in the Cabinet, his Parliamentary following and the backstage managers of the Party. Both the vigour and the power in the party of Laurier, after the election of 1917, made him, as leader, an important factor in the determination of his successor. The prospects of the party, which appeared excellent to those capable of going beneath the surface of politics, made the question of the succession one of the utmost importance to every interest in the nation. For these reasons the selection of a new leader for the Liberal Party became, during 1918 and 1919, the focal point of serious domestic politics in Canada. The man who won the Liberal leadership would have a good prospect of power. Every powerful interest, therefore, became increasingly desirous of securing the elevation of a man who could be trusted, not only to win elections, but also in office to do, or not to do, what the interests concerned required.

Laurier looked at the problem of the succession exclusively from the point of view of the Party's interest in victory. Quite naturally he regarded the victory of the Liberal Party in the future as he had regarded his triumphs in the past, as a guarantee of the social *status quo*, and of the political and social relaxation necessary for the functioning of an industrial economy of continental dimensions. Leadership of the Liberal Party was in his mind simply a matter of skill. Skill consisted of certain obviously necessary talents such as platform manners and the capacity to manoeuvre in the House of Commons, but its most important ingredient was negative; an absence of open commitment to any interest such as a Church, particular business enterprises, a particular region or a particular race. After the election of 1911 Laurier had begun to consider a successor, and the man whom he believed the most likely candidate and for whom he had the most personal admiration at that time was W. S. Fielding, his Minister of Finance. George P. Graham, his Minister of Railways and Canals, likewise enjoyed his confidence and to a greater degree as time went on, his affection. Going over in his mind the events surrounding the selection of Laurier's successor, Sir Allen Aylesworth, Laurier's "dear old friend" wrote: "I know that in 1911 Laurier—fully intending to retire, thought Fielding was the man who ought to succeed him —and it is very likely that in 1919 Lady Laurier thought Fielding as leader would be better qualified than any other man available, but she felt very keenly the defection of 1917."[1]

The defection of 1917! This had disrupted all Laurier's conceptions about his successor. Fielding had not joined the Union Government. Until the very last moment he endeavoured to find a device by which he could stick with Laurier,[2] but when the split on conscription came he felt obliged to desert his leader. Once he had done that he was no longer sufficiently detached from his class, his race and his religion to be a successful Liberal leader capable of commanding support among workers, farmers and industrialists, in both French and English-speaking Canada. Graham, too, had deserted his leader for a moment at the critical hour, and Laurier had loved Graham "like a brother". When the election of 1917 was over Laurier could see no obvious successor in sight.

But there were plenty of candidates. Laurier had hardly recovered his breath after the election before he was afflicted with petitions, advice and correspondence concerning his successor. A few days after the New Year he received a note from an aspirant, E. M. Macdonald, staying in the Ritz-Carlton Hotel, in Montreal, complaining that,

"A gentleman, a friend of yours, told me today that you had said in his presence on Thursday that a seat was to be found for

---

[1] *Murphy Papers*, Aylesworth to Murphy, 25 July, 1929.
[2] *Laurier Papers*, Fielding to Laurier, 31 May, 1917.

Mackenzie King in Quebec and that expressions were used as to his possible future leadership.

"I have no ambition in that way and have always [been] frank as to my position and attitude with you and I am amazed at the statement in view of your ideas as expressed yesterday. . . ."[1]

Laurier was sharp with Macdonald. He told him that he could call at the Ritz-Carlton in a few days, and he invited Macdonald to produce his informant there for a frank talk about what had been said. ". . . You will always find me perfectly frank, and whatever I do or say I can repeat to the whole world. . . ." He stated his policy plainly:

"There never was any mention at all of Mackenzie King's future leadership. I discussed with some friends the possibility of getting seats for Graham, Oliver, E. M. Macdonald and Mackenzie King. The Opposition has been very much weakened by the late election, and I am anxious to bring back to the House our best fighters as soon as possible. I discussed the matter with Graham himself last Tuesday, and besides with Graham with Gouin, Lemieux and Fisher, but very informally. . . ."[2]

Such seems to have been Laurier's policy about the succession: to gather around him as many likely men as he could; to find them places in the House of Commons, and to let them prove themselves prior to a Convention of the Party. He wished to make the selection of the new leader a great popular event calculated to arouse mass enthusiasm for the Liberal Party.

As part of the process of arousing enthusiasm Laurier turned to the task of bringing forward people about whom the public could become enthusiastic and around whom the opposing elements in the party could unite. Graham was brought back into the fold even though, as he told Laurier, he felt ". . . more like running away somewhere and hiding. . . ."[3] W. T. R. Preston,* one of Laurier's confidants, was sent to Toronto for the purpose of sounding one of the judges on the Ontario Bench, W. R. Riddell, who was ". . . clean morally (and) above suspicion politically. . . ."[4] Riddell was tempted and Laurier declared he "would be glad to ascertain your view as to

[1] *Laurier Papers*, Macdonald to Laurier, undated, January, 1918.
[2] *Laurier Papers*, Laurier to Macdonald, 12 January, 1918.
[3] *Laurier Papers*, Graham to Laurier, 10 September, 1918.
[4] *Laurier Papers*, Preston to Laurier, 26 June, 1918.

any action you would take in the reorganization of the party, and the position which you would occupy in it. . . ." Laurier even offered to visit Riddell in Toronto because, as he told the judge, "I say without hesitation that no one is better qualified than yourself."[1]

Laurier was turning over in his mind a winning "combination"[2] of which Riddell appears to have been one of the elements. Who was the other element of the combination? On July 5th, 1918, Aylesworth wrote to Laurier strongly recommending Henri S. Béland,* who was something of a hero. Béland "spoke English perfectly", had "charming manners", and had enjoyed the political advantage, during the controversies of 1917, of residence in a German prison camp. In Aylesworth's view Béland could hold Quebec and, being a bit of a hero, could win support in Ontario. He urged Laurier to forget his bitter belief that no Roman Catholic French-Canadian should ever try to lead the Liberal Party again.[3] Aylesworth would on no account support anyone who had deserted Laurier. "*Some* of the deserters who now support the ragamuffins in power will get back and may perhaps ultimately live down their past to some extent—but never any one of *them* for leader."[4] Laurier was enthusiastic about Béland. "Barring the question of his origin, I am sure no one in the ranks would be more acceptable. . . ."[5]

But Laurier was promising support to no one.

The documentary evidence points plainly to the fact that as late as the summer of 1918, Laurier had no specific person in mind for the leadership. There is, however, the suggestion, derived from the recollections of people who helped to make the choice of leader, that in the privacy of his home during the months before his death, Sir Wilfrid had indicated to his wife that he believed the appointment of W. S. Fielding as his successor would be the best means of re-uniting the opposing

---

[1] *Laurier Papers*, Laurier to Riddell, 4 July, 1918.

[2] *Laurier Papers*, Preston to Laurier, n.d. 1918.

[3] Laurier expressed much the same view about the necessity of a Protestant leader for the Liberals. "The break of 1917 cost me too much to build afresh with Fielding or Rowell or Sifton," he is reported to have said, "But the new leader must be a Protestant. I'd ask no Catholic to go through what I have suffered." See Preston, *My Generation of Politics and Politicians*, pp. 382–83.

[4] *Laurier Papers*, Aylesworth to Laurier, 5 July, 1918.

[5] *Laurier Papers*, Laurier to Aylesworth, 8 July, 1918.

wings of the Party.[1] But he betrayed no evidence of this belief in his correspondence. Until the day of his death he emphasized the necessity of the Liberals coming together to make a free choice.

Less than a week before he died he wrote to Motherwell,* one of the Saskatchewan Liberals who had remained loyal to him:

> "The question of leadership certainly is a subject of anxiety to me, but whenever I lay down the reins, the choice of the party will be absolutely unhampered. . . . The National Liberal Convention cannot take place until late next fall. It should not be summoned until peace has been signed and the slate is clear for action. The first step should not be a National Convention, but provincial conventions all over, and after this has been done the field will be ready for the National Convention. This is my suggestion. I should like to have your views as to the same."[2]

So much for Laurier's policy of selecting a successor. It does not seem to have been agreeably received by at least one of the aspirants.

Mackenzie King did not throw himself into the battles of the Liberal Party with the object of demonstrating his capacities as a field general and a popular captain of the Liberal hosts. On the contrary, he practised once more his strategy of withdrawal. Jealous rivals might mention his aspirations and enemies might plant mines for his hoisting, but he simply disappeared underground. In Toronto someone was trying either to embarrass him, or was showing him a mistaken kindness, by circulating stories in the newspapers to the effect that "Quebec is going to select a leader for them [i.e. the Liberal Party] in the person of Mackenzie King". Murphy reported this to Laurier and said, "If persisted in this will first destroy King, second weaken your influence and power [in Ontario] to re-unite the party, and third further divide the party on issues that should never arise."[3]

His disappearance was very wise. Quebec was seething with discontent as the Government proceeded to enforce the Military Service Act. J. N. Francoeur* announced his intention to propose in the Quebec Legislature a resolution favourable to

---

[1] *Cameron Papers*, Memorandum on the Liberal Convention of 1919. In his book, p.334, Preston states that Laurier "had offered Fielding his old seat in the House next his own", and that Fielding's refusal "had been misunderstood".

[2] *Laurier Papers*, Laurier to Motherwell, 11 February, 1919.

[3] *Laurier Papers*, Murphy to Laurier, 13 January, 1918.

Quebec's secession from the Dominion. At Easter, 1918, riots broke out in Quebec City. The police stood idly by while the rioters burned down Federal Government buildings. Troops were called in to reinforce the Federal police, and the rioters started to answer military violence with rifle fire. An abyss was opening into which members of every interest, English-speaking or French-speaking, were horrified to look. Even Armand Lavergne, the intransigeant racialist, was frightened. To appeals from the civic authorities to head off the rioters he responded with false statements to the crowd that he had obtained an agreement with the military authorities to withdraw troops if the rioters went home and stacked their rifles.[1] The hierarchy of the Church stood by wringing their hands and appealing to Christian sentiment. The Government itself was frightened. Only among the humble and respectable citizens in the constituency of Broadview in Toronto was there much enthusiasm for what the Government had done.

But, if people were frightened by the opening abyss, it was a dangerous thing to talk about. There is no evidence that Mackenzie King had anything to say. We have been unable to trace his movements after the election of December, 1917, until we find him writing to Laurier from an "absolutely fireproof hotel" in Denver, Colorado, on December 1st, 1918. Some of the time during 1918 he was at the Roxborough or at Kingsmere working on *Industry and Humanity*. He seems to have spent a good deal of time in the United States installing company unions in various large enterprises and further building his reputation as a saviour of the war production apparatus of the U.S.A. Whatever he was doing, he was keeping quiet about Canadian politics.

But he was not inactive. In the absence of an opportunity to look at Mackenzie King's correspondence we have been obliged to trace his activities in the correspondence of Sir Wilfrid Laurier. The evidence there suggests that some time during the last half of 1918 a movement was organized in Montreal, Ottawa and Toronto to push him into the leadership by securing Laurier's support for his candidature. The evidence suggests that Laurier died without having delivered to him his fief.

An anticipation of the strategy employed by Mackenzie

[1] E. H. Armstrong, *The Crisis of Quebec, 1914–18* (New York, 1937), p. 229.

King's pressure group was revealed to Laurier four days after the election of 1917, although it is unlikely that Laurier could at that time grasp its full significance. Indeed, this early and isolated instance of a movement favourable to Mackenzie King only becomes meaningful to an observer in the light of what happened later. A few days after the election, Laurier received a letter from A. C. Hardy of Brockville, dated December 21st, 1918. In the election Hardy had stood as a Laurier Liberal but he was a Laurier Liberal of the Mackenzie King variety, i.e., a supporter of Laurier who advocated an acceptance of the Military Service Act. The election, however, had changed his view. He was surprised to find that Laurier's line was popular with labour and with a numerous body in the country in spite of the fact that "unionists" had managed to "win" the election. His letter to Laurier was a combination of overflowing admiration, a petition for forgiveness and a move on behalf of Mackenzie King. "I can frankly say that after my first weeks' campaigning", he wrote,

> "I regretted not having come out straight against conscription.
> . . . If I can do anything, I want you to command me and if any
> small means I can place at your disposal for the Party can help,
> they will be readily and gladly given to the best of our ability—I
> say 'our' because I speak for my wife as well. I hope to be able to
> keep King to the front from now on. He and I were betrayed in
> 1912. . . ."[1]

Thus the unexplained "betrayal of 1912" was introduced into the struggle as a weapon. Whatever Laurier may have been hearing in the lobbies, he does not appear to have had any further representation on the subject of the "betrayal of 1912" until September, 1918. Late that month Laurier received a great blast on the subject from his old friend, Alexander Smith. Smith informed Laurier that Liberals everywhere had been telling him of "their intense disappointment" about the "old gang" which surrounded Laurier, and had held his affections since the defeat of 1911. Liberals, he wrote, "have been looking for better things in vain". East and west, Smith claimed, he found that Liberals were saying, "Laurier, yes. But Laurier and the old gang, never." Smith was sharp. "The Liberals look to you for leadership, but it must be free from 'old gangism'. We will

[1] *Laurier Papers*, Hardy to Laurier, 21 December, 1917.

u

then have real leadership, and can by a combination of that and the efforts of good and true liberals have in addition to this leadership, organization and direction and management." Finally he threatened Laurier. ". . . Whilst 'old gangism' prevails it will not be difficult to reorganize a new Union Government, and so it may go on renewing from time to time until 'old gangism' is suppressed or submerged."[1]

Mackenzie King's name was not mentioned in this letter. Indeed, no one was mentioned by name. The implication was that no one whom Laurier worked with and personally liked was any good. The blast was aimed by implication at Murphy, Pardee and Graham, who had been Cabinet Ministers from Ontario, and were very close to Laurier.

Laurier professed not to know what Smith was talking about. "Let me say at once", he replied, "that the terms of it are altogether too general, and I would ask you to give me some concrete information." He candidly named his associates whom he supposed Smith meant by the "old gang". Mackenzie King's name was not among them. The only cleavages in the party Laurier knew about concerned the question of reciprocity with the United States, which dated back to 1911, and the contemporary issue of conscription. What "old gangism" meant he pretended not to fathom.

Whether Smith ever particularized his charges, we do not know. The blast against "old gangism" was apparently only a preliminary barrage laid down with the object of clearing barbed wire from the field and wounding the enemy in forward positions. The big push was yet to come. The push came partly from outside the Liberal Party.

Industry and Humanity appeared in November, 1918, and so did a similar piece of literature entitled *Industrial Relations*. This was a pamphlet dated November, 1918, published in Toronto by the Canadian Reconstruction Association. The motto of this organization was "Unity, Stability and Prosperity". The Honorary President was the Rt. Hon. Lord Shaughnessy, K.C.V.O., the president of the C.P.R. and the elder statesman of the Canadian moneyed interests. The President was Sir John Willison, the ex-Liberal and family friend of the Kings. The vice-presidents were financiers and industrialists, such as Sir Augustus Nanton

---

[1] *Laurier Papers*, Smith to Laurier, 24 September, 1918.

and Huntley Drummond. A general committee of fifty-two was drawn from the top ranks of both English-speaking and French-speaking wealth in Ontario, Quebec, the Maritime Provinces and Manitoba. Apparently there was no one west of Winnipeg rich enough to include in the Committee, for it was wanting in representatives from Saskatchewan, Alberta and British Columbia.

The pamphlet, *Industrial Relations*, was not only published at the same time as *Industry and Humanity*, but it adopted the same line, contained the same material and even in matters of style exhibited the same tendency towards bathos and sentimentality. It only differed from *Industry and Humanity* in that it framed the threat to the *status quo* more sharply than Mackenzie King's book. In *Industrial Relations* Bolshevism is the danger. "Not a few wild theories and fantastic panaceas have been tested in Russia with consequences of ruin and horror beyond imagination. Yet there are disciples of the Bolsheviki in the United States and even in Canada."[1] The answer to this threat was Mackenzie King's answer. "Love of God and love of man are the bases on which human society rest; they are the final motives of all right conduct. Without them all societies crumble and the world becomes the pandemonium it is today."[2] The Rockefeller Plan was explained with great admiration. Bolshevism could be headed off with "industrial councils" known, in some quarters, as company unions. Whatever else happened, "it is necessary that there should be a better understanding between capital and labour."[3]

Whether Mackenzie King wrote the pamphlet of the Canadian Reconstruction Association we cannot say. The important fact is that he was an exponent of ideas which were recognized as good and the advocate of policies which were recognized as necessary by the Big Interests. They felt the tremors and the earthquakes of the social world; they were preparing for them with skill and subtlety. And they were looking for someone capable of understanding and executing the new policy which they felt to be necessary.

Simultaneously with the appearance of *Industry and Humanity*

[1] The Canadian Reconstruction Association, *Industrial Relations* (Toronto, 1918), p. 4.
[2] *Industrial Relations*, etc., p. 8.
[3] *Industrial Relations*, etc., p. 3.

and *Industrial Relations* the campaign began to secure Laurier's agreement to Mackenzie King as his successor. On November 15th, 1918, Alex. Smith produced the name of his alternative to the "old gang". He simply sent Laurier a copy of a letter he had written to Mackenzie King which read:

"I duly received yours enclosing one draft resolution re a phase of the labor discussion and practical application of the principle involved therein and have to thank you for the same. I was disappointed that you had not time to drop in to talk over this and other matters before you left on your recent trip; for at the same time I intended to discuss with you a proposal urged upon me by Hon. Senator James H. Ross* which briefly is to the effect that you should be induced, and if you cannot be induced, then to be prevailed upon, to take more interest in Canadian public affairs. The Senator urged so strongly that whilst I am but a private citizen I thought it more than courtesy to put clearly before you his views and the outline he suggested for carrying them out.

"I am taking the liberty of sending a copy of this letter to Sir Wilfrid Laurier, but will not discuss with him the essential features until you have an opportunity to get from me the Hon. Senator's outlines."[1]

The campaign had commenced. The pressure on Laurier to induce him to nod in the direction of Mackenzie King was never relaxed until his death.

Within a fortnight of Smith's "invitation" to return to public life, Mackenzie King became active on his own behalf. On December 1st, 1918, he wrote to Laurier from Denver. He told Laurier what he was doing and where he would be during the next two weeks in case Laurier should want to see him. Then he produced a high card to see whether Laurier was able to raise it. "Mr. Rockefeller, Jnr.," he wrote,

"is anxious to talk over with me the trip to England of which I told you. He is anticipating that I shall wish to leave for the Old Country at once, to spend the next few months in the study of industrial conditions there. Not knowing just what the probable political developments in Canada may be, I have thought that, before finally arranging for passage, or, for that matter, before deciding definitely upon the trip itself, I should like to have another talk with you. . . ."[2]

There is no evidence of how Laurier replied to this. Ap-

[1] *Laurier Papers*, Smith to King, 15 November, 1918.
[2] *Laurier Papers*, King to Laurier, 1 December, 1918.

parently he was unwilling to raise Mackenzie King, because we find Mackenzie King writing to Laurier more than six weeks later, still in the United States and still hinting that he will sail to visit Britain at any moment unless a clear, loud bugle call from Liberal headquarters summoned him, post-haste, to save all.

During these six weeks, however, Mackenzie King's friends were not inactive. On January 12th, 1919, Lt. Col. the Hon. James Domville wrote to Laurier from the St. James's Club in Montreal:

"I thought it might interest you to know that we had the Hon. Mackenzie King speak at the Montreal Reform Club last evening on 'Reconstruction'. He made a marvellous speech, clear and gave solutions to some of the economic problems that are confronting Canada at the present time. He carried the crowd with enthusiasm. . . . It gave new life, new thought and new hope to the Liberals of this district. The audience was about half French and half English, and if it was possible your compatriots were more enthusiastic than we—at any rate, he was appreciated, and it was realized by a few of us talking it over, Walter Mitchell [Provincial Treasurer of the Province of Quebec] and others, that if King could carry this message across Canada speaking at the principal centres that it would mean new life to our cause."[1]

Who was Domville? Domville was an old man, rich in money and experience, a prime example of the Canadian upper stratum who from politically bomb-proof shelters in the deep rear order the affairs of the Dominion. In spite of his origins and his military enthusiasms, he stuck by Laurier in 1917, apparently because he was old enough and intelligent enough to realize the idiocy of conscription from the point of view of the interests he represented. Contemptuously he spoke of the "Unionist" victory as a triumph of "Preachers, women, money, mistaken zeal, fanaticism and race cries".[2] Now as he neared the grave, he and men like him were pushing Mackenzie King.

Laurier replied to Domville with a declaration of his intention to do nothing more for Mackenzie King than help him get into Parliament.

". . . I am not at all surprised at what you tell me about Mackenzie King's speech. He is improving all the time as a public speaker

[1] *Laurier Papers*, Domville to Laurier, 12 January, 1919.
[2] *Laurier Papers*, Domville to Laurier, 18 December, 1917.

and carries his audience wherever he goes. The first thing to attend to would be to find him a seat in Parliament, and this is a subject which, I am sorry to say, I have not been able to bring to a satisfactory solution. It may be yet possible, however, to reach that object."[1]

This thrust concerning Mackenzie King's "improvement" was now some ten years old and wearing a little thin. The process of improvement was first noticed by Laurier in 1909, but he was still using this double-edged compliment, as a stereotyped device for not offending Mackenzie King's friends without committing himself to a definite approval of the man.

A week after Domville's letter, Laurier received a piece of crude and threatening advocacy from another quarter. On January 20th, 1919, P. C. Larkin wrote from Toronto:

> "The Hon. Mackenzie King dined with us yesterday, and after he left I was thinking matters over, he having mentioned some of his affairs. I am much afraid that Canada is, at least for some years, going to lose the services of one of her most able men. . . . I think it is such a pity that a seat in the House cannot be found for him for I feel certain that would tempt him to give up work he is now doing in the United States, and even refuse the splendid offer he has recently had made to him."

Larkin had apparently been told that Laurier was dragging his feet in the matter of finding Mackenzie King a seat. He reminded Laurier that he himself had been offered a seat in Parliament, but that Laurier had been "kind and considerate enough not to answer" his request for advice on the subject of acceptance. Then he suggested that he was not going to permit Laurier to treat Mackenzie King in this way. "I mention this", he told Laurier, "because I was thinking of writing to Mr. Mitchell, who is thoroughly conversant with affairs in the province of Quebec and who is a confrère of Sir Lomer Gouin and asking him if he could not find a seat in the Dominion House for the Hon. Mackenzie King."[2]

Laurier was annoyed by Larkin's letter. "It would be indeed a great loss to the country were Mackenzie King to finally make up his mind to use his great ability elsewhere," he wrote coldly.

[1] *Laurier Papers*, Laurier to Domville, 14 January, 1919.
[2] *Laurier Papers*, Larkin to Laurier, 20 January, 1919.

"I have no doubt that he would be in the next House of Commons, if he were to throw himself in the fray at once. He desires to be in Parliament, and I desire it still more than he does. . . . I have always taken a deep interest in King's career, and I can report to you from personal knowledge that he is improving every day, a fact which, I am sure, you have yourself noticed. If he would take my advice, it would be not to wait to get into the limelight for an official recognition such as he would receive from being nominated as a candidate, but to throw himself in the fray at this very moment."[1]

But Laurier began to yield. He assured Larkin he had really been trying to get Mackenzie King a seat, had discussed the matter several times with Mitchell, one of the Liberal impresarios in Quebec, and would try to speed matters up.

Apparently he spoke to the Hon. Rodolphe Lemieux about doing something for Mackenzie King, because Lemieux wrote to Laurier on January 23rd introducing a new complication. In public esteem Lemieux was, next to Laurier, perhaps the most important figure in the federal ranks of the Quebec Liberals.[2] But Lemieux was apparently not anxious to place all his bets on Mackenzie King. He agreed that it was necessary to elect Mackenzie King and it might just be possible to place him in Maisonneuve but "il faut élire Fisher . . . en St. Jean Iberville".[3] Sydney Fisher was a former member of Laurier's Cabinet whom some people spoke of as a possible Liberal leader. Lemieux told Laurier that he ought to have "two lieutenants of the first order": King *and* Fisher.

While Lemieux was writing thus from Montreal, Mackenzie King wrote from the Blackstone Hotel in Chicago. He sent Laurier a testimonial from an unknown admirer, a certain Mr. McColl. He told Laurier about his work with the Standard Oil Company of Indiana, and some American steel firms. Again he played a high card to see if Laurier would raise him. "The work I am doing in this connection", he wrote,

"is so important in its influence upon the future relations of Capital and Labour in America that I have felt, as long as present engagements keep up, I should postpone the trip I had planned to England. The other matter of which I told you in Ottawa is also

---

[1] *Laurier Papers*, Laurier to Larkin, 23 January, 1919.
[2] Lemieux possessed two seats in his own right, having been returned in 1917 for both Maisonneuve and Gaspé.
[3] *Laurier Papers*, Lemieux to Laurier, 23 January, 1919.

causing me to delay my departure. I am to be allowed ample time for consideration of the acceptance of the position I told you of. I am seeking to view the matter wholly from the point of view of the greatest opportunity of social service likely to be afforded and what the attitude of some of my Liberal friends in Canada may be towards effecting adjustments which will make possible an early return to public life in Canada."[1]

Mackenzie King called Laurier's attention to his outstanding performance at the Reform Club in Montreal, and enclosed a testimonial in the shape of an editorial from *Le Soleil*. Then he told Laurier again about the offer made "by the gentleman with whom I have been so closely associated in New York". He was indispensable to that gentleman. Then he told Laurier about "the delight and appreciation" with which he had read one of Laurier's speeches. Finally, he closed with these words:

"It seems to me that very little is needed to rally the progressive forces around the standard of Liberalism at this time, and I do hope that some of our friends will be bold and brave enough to sanction a course which would surmount local fears, prejudices and jealousies, and make possible the beginning of a real reconstruction, industrially, socially and politically in Canada."

Laurier was able to tell Mackenzie King that things were now moving in his favour in so far as a seat in the House was concerned. The pressure was beginning to pay off. ". . . Friends who thought you could not be a candidate in Maisonneuve are now changing their mind. One, who has, I think, a paramount influence in the riding, has told me that he is now a convert."[2] These words were fatal to the career of Rodolphe Lemieux. He had not converted quickly enough. The pressure to bring Mackenzie King back to Canada was too great for Laurier. Laurier asked Mackenzie King to "please come back. . . . I would not yet speak too positively, but it is sufficient to remember that at this period of all periods, things are moving fast".

This letter caused Mackenzie King to give up "thought of going abroad". But he was determined to get something more substantial than the mere promise of a seat before he said no to Rockefeller. "My heart and will", he told Laurier, "are with my own country, and only the lack of opportunity of service

[1] *Laurier Papers*, King to Laurier, 23 January, 1919.
[2] *Laurier Papers*, Laurier to King, 27 January, 1919.

there at all comparable with that which lies before me through the connections I have formed here would lead me to take any step which might mean a permanent severance of my life relations with Canada. . . ."[1]

On February 3rd, Laurier told Mackenzie King that he had seen both Mitchell and Domville. But he had nothing to say about a constituency.

"They . . . informed me that you are going to receive an invitation from the Canadian Club at Montreal to speak towards the end of the present month. They want me to impress on you that you must accept. This desire I share absolutely. Domville wants you also to tour the Dominion in connection with the Fifth Sunday Meeting Association (speaking on Reconstruction), with which you are acquainted. This request I also support. Your speech in Montreal has produced a great impression even more with the thinking man than with the crowd, and the oftener you speak on that line, the better it will be not only for the country, but for yourself also."[2]

During the first week in February, stories began to appear in the American press to the effect that "W. L. Mackenzie King is the most likely successor to Sir Wilfrid Laurier".[3] Out in Saskatchewan W. R. Motherwell came upon one of these stories and wrote hastily to Laurier asking about a certain "mysterious silence".[4] In one of the last letters he ever wrote Laurier told Motherwell that the question of the leadership worried him greatly, but that a National Convention would decide the question, and that the broadest possible constituency of Liberals must be heard on the question. A few days later Laurier received a letter from Mackenzie King agreeing to speak to the Canadian Club in Montreal. About the Fifth Sunday proposition, Mackenzie King was, however, reserved.

"This is something I should like to consider very carefully before coming to any decision upon. . . . I am keeping a perfectly open mind, in the hope that when I get back to Ottawa matters will have so shaped themselves that it will be possible for me finally to determine what course it is going to be best to pursue, and to be in a position, should I decide not to accept the overtures which have

[1] *Laurier Papers*, King to Laurier, 30 January, 1919.
[2] *Laurier Papers*, Laurier to King, 3 February, 1919.
[3] *Detroit Free Press*, 2 February, 1919.
[4] *Laurier Papers*, Motherwell to Laurier, 7 February, 1919.

been made to me from friends on this side [i.e., in the United States whence he was writing] to give to them substantial reasons for the decision finally made."[1]

Laurier's reply to this was a brief statement that he had "nothing to add to what I have already written". Laurier appears to have felt that Mackenzie King would have to clear up his difficulties with the Liberals in Ontario before any further attention could be given to advancing his career at Ottawa. The Ontario Liberals had already held two conventions to which Mackenzie King had not been invited. Laurier had inquired why not. He had been informed that ". . . Ottawa did not want to have him speak here (in Toronto), and that he (Mackenzie King) was detested so much at Ottawa that they would not let him speak at the Eastern Association Meeting".[2] Laurier wished at least to help Mackenzie King to straighten out this entanglement. He told Mackenzie King that there was a meeting of Liberals in Toronto being arranged, and that a date convenient to Mackenzie King would be fixed. ". . . Your presence there is indispensable," Laurier concluded.[3]

Mackenzie King replied that he could attend the meeting in Toronto. He would come to Ottawa and then he would go to New York. Laurier was free to read anything he liked into that statement. "I have had splendid success in the work here (i.e. in Chicago)," he wrote, "which promises to be even more far-reaching than I had in any way anticipated." During the morning of the day Mackenzie King wrote these words in the University Club in Chicago, Sir Wilfrid Laurier had a slight stroke while he was working in his office. He recovered, and went home on a tram-car. When he arrived there, he suffered a devastating visitation. He lived for a day insensible. On Monday, February 17th, 1919, he passed beyond the reach of negotiation and pressure.

Mackenzie King never got his seat in Maisonneuve nor did he receive the blessing of the Old Chief. He was obliged to change his medium for getting into touch with his leader.

If matters had not "so shaped themselves in Ottawa" as

---

[1] *Laurier Papers*, King to Laurier, 9 February, 1919.
[2] *Laurier Papers*, Preston to Laurier, 8 February, 1919.
[3] *Laurier Papers*, Laurier to King, 12 February, 1919.

Mackenzie King had hoped they might, Laurier had done something in approaching Lemieux about a seat which could be interpreted, and may have been so interpreted, as a gesture of approval. He did not, as it turned out, need such a gesture. If the Big Interests thought conciliation, soft answers and the promise of Reconstruction were necessary in November, 1918, by the summer of 1919 such tactics had become the only means of heading off widespread unrest. A few days before Christmas a large meeting in Winnipeg had assembled to protest against interference in the affairs of Soviet Russia. To the enthusiastic audience R. B. Russell declared, "Capitalism has come to the point where she is defunct and must disappear." Sam Blumenberg, a socialist in a red necktie, followed him with this happy inspiration which he put into the mouths "of thousands of men coming back who went over to fight": "We have fought for this country, and by the gods, we are going to own it."[1] But there were soldiers and soldiers. In January, 1919, a gang of soldiers prevented a memorial meeting for Karl Liebknecht and Rosa Luxembourg, and they wrecked Mr. Blumenberg's dry-cleaning shop in Winnipeg. The press fulminated about "aliens".

But in spite of attempts to divert discontent in the direction of "aliens", the movement grew in western Canada and became more and more turned away from a dog and cat struggle among the workers themselves towards a social conflict with economic and political objectives of a serious kind. Away on the Pacific Coast, in Vancouver, the editor of the B.C. *Federationist* observed in January that "everything was going well with the slave class". He meant politically. "It is impossible to demand too much, because nothing short of the whole shooting match is of any use. It is now realized that compromise is impossible, between the working class and the master class. It is a fight to a finish, a fight to the death."[2]

In March, 1919, while Mackenzie King was advocating "soft" tactics to the Empire Club in Toronto, the One Big Union movement was holding a Convention organized by the British Columbia Federation of Labour at Calgary, Alberta. The Convention was a serious affair. "There was a good deal of ability shown in [the] debates," commented the editor of the *Canadian*

[1] Masters, *The Winnipeg General Strike*, p. 4.
[2] Quoted in *Canadian Annual Review*, 1919, pp. 456-57.

Annual Review. The Convention directed its attention to creating a labour organization and leadership capable, firstly, of ensuring the welfare of the working class without dependence upon legislation, "allegedly called Labor laws," and finally, of taking power. "We have got to have an organization", declared one speaker at the Convention, "whereby, when the time comes, when we have reached that point where we are going to take over, [and] operate the wheels of industry—which time we have talked about so long. At that time we will have to have an industrial organization similar to that which has proven of such a benefit in Russia." The Convention decided to clear out of the way the obstacles to working-class progress in the form of the old trade union leadership and organization and to create One Big Union. When the Convention adjourned the delegates reconvened with fresh delegates from other provinces to form the Inter-Provincial Western Conference under the chairmanship of one of the vice-presidents of the Trades and Labour Congress of Canada. Even this convention, more representative of orthodox unionism, agreed to a resolution

> "that the aims of labor as represented by this Convention are the abolition of the present system of production for profit, and the substitution therefor of production for use ... this Convention expresses its open conviction that the system of industrial Soviet control by selection of representatives from industries is more efficient and of greater political value than the present form of government."[1]

The Government's wind was thoroughly up by the late spring. The Royal North-West Mounted Police were working night and day with their shorthand note books in order to discover and to list the leaders of the movement. By April the Cabinet in Ottawa had ceased to believe that it could stand alone against revolution. Sir Robert Borden was away in Paris having a succession of "interesting conversations", learning French, substituting for Lloyd George in the Council of Five, and staying up late.[2] At home his deputy, Sir Thomas White,* was so alarmed he wanted to radio for cruisers. "Council much concerned over situation in British Columbia," he cabled his chief on April 19th, 1919.

[1] *Canadian Annual Review*, 1919, p. 459.
[2] Borden's account of his adventures in Paris is very amusing, if long winded. See his *Memoirs*, Vol. II.

"Bolshevism has made much progress among workers and soldiers there. We cannot get troops absolutely dependable in emergency and it will take a long time to establish old militia organization. Plans are being laid for revolutionary movement which if temporarily successful would immediately bring about serious disturbances in Calgary and Winnipeg where socialism rampant. We think it most desirable British Government should bring over a Cruiser from China station to Victoria and Vancouver. The presence of such a ship and crew would have a steadying influence. Situation is undoubtedly serious by reason of propagandaism from Seattle and workers and soldiers."[1]

Out of range of cruisers the workers of Winnipeg proceeded to create a serious situation not in response to alien propaganda from Seattle, Petrograd or Munich, but because the employers in the metal-working and building trades would not agree to discuss an increase of wages sufficient to permit people to eat and to buy fuel and clothing. When the police arrested a metal-worker of German birth, who was a union organizer, the Winnipeg Trades and Labour Council began to prepare for a general strike. Strikes in particular industries were in progress in Toronto and Vancouver. "Winnipeg", it was stated by R. B. Russell, "must stand firm for the sake of labour everywhere." On May 7th the trade unionists of Winnipeg voted 11,112 to 524 for a general strike. On May 15th, 1919, they went out in a body. When no milk or bread was delivered on the following Friday morning the press of Canada made the startling discovery that women and children were being starved to death in Winnipeg by the Bolsheviks.

The leaders of the strike only talked revolution. When the strike came they limited its objectives to an improvement in wages and recognition of the right to collective bargaining. They tried hard to keep the peace. On the other side a panic view was taken. "No thoughtful citizen can longer doubt that the so-called general strike is in reality revolution—or a daring attempt to overthrow the present industrial and government system."[2] As it was the leaders merely sat still. Meanwhile the authorities, representing the lawyers, merchants and manufacturers, who owned the city, watched the provocation of violence

---

[1] Borden, *Memoirs*, Vol. II.
[2] Quoted from *The Winnipeg Citizen*, May 27th, in Masters, *The Winnipeg General Strike*, p. 66.

and then turned the police loose, once they had been sufficiently reinforced with soldiers who did not know what they were to be ordered to do. The Returned Soldiers Loyalist Association was formed. When the municipal police were dismissed because of their refusal to sign a pledge never to strike in sympathy with other workers, the members of the Loyalist Association were converted into a special police force.[1] This special police force patrolled the streets in a body. A crowd assembled. Someone was hurt. The *Manitoba Free Press* announced: "Young Winnipeg soldiers, recently returned from years of overseas service . . . were yesterday, on the main street of their home town, while engaged in the patriotic duty of protecting the peace, the victims of murderous assaults by riotous aliens."[2] The street disturbances increased as the number of "special police" increased. The leadership of the strike began to seek a compromise. Once they showed this disposition the police descended and arrested twelve of the leaders during the night of June 16–17th. On June 21st the Riot Act was read to an indignant crowd assembled before the City Hall. The Royal North-West Mounted Police were turned loose. Twenty-four civilians were killed or injured. The police had six casualties. The next day the Mounted Police paraded the streets armed with carbines and revolvers, accompanied by trucks mounted with machine guns. Two days later the Trades and Labour Council called off the strike.

The events in Winnipeg suggest the atmosphere and the kind of problems confronting the Canadian people when the Liberal Party was obliged to find a new leader. Even more than conscription, the Winnipeg General Strike and its aftermath posed a real problem for the Government about policy.[3] The Government had "got tough" in order to demonstrate that it could, and would, cow all resistance. Would the Liberals support the Government?

---

[1] All the historian of the strike will say on this point is that ". . . it seems likely he (the organizer of the Loyalist Association) helped to organize the special police who took over the defence of 'law and order' on June 9th."

[2] Quoted from the issue of June 11th in Masters, *The Winnipeg General Strike*, p. 98. Masters takes this propaganda so seriously that he has made an effort to estimate the numbers of "aliens" in the crowd. His research reveals that of the 24 injured and killed, 4 had "foreign" names.

[3] The Winnipeg General Strike is the biggest event in the history of the Canadian labour movement. As yet it has never been studied carefully with the object of discovering the lessons it has to teach with respect to the problem of securing the proper weight of the working class in the Canadian community.

To expect an unambiguous answer to such a question from Liberals is to expect too much. During and after the Winnipeg general strike, J. W. Dafoe, the editor of the *Manitoba Free Press* gave an admirable exhibition of the kind of agility which the situation required. While the strike was unbroken he flamed with wrath against the strikers. But as soon as a disposition to back down appeared among the strikers he was ready with a soft policy. He opposed the Government's policy of arresting the strikers. It was a mistake on the Government's part, not a crime. "This arrest will enable them to pose as martyrs in the cause of the working man," he wrote.[1]

Although the Liberals of Winnipeg like J. W. Dafoe,[2] Premier T. C. Norris and others, carried considerable responsibility for the General Strike, its character and its suppression, the Conservative-Unionist Government in Ottawa were made to bear the blame for all which followed the defeat of the strike. The Federal Government had supplied the soldiers and machine guns (a Liberal politician won a momentary popularity some years later by revealing the Government's official secrets concerning transportation of arms to Winnipeg),[3] they had sent the Mounted Police, they had intimidated the postal workers, and the Minister of Labour (himself a Liberal Unionist, an ex-trade unionist and a friend of Mackenzie King) had advised the authorities in Winnipeg not to negotiate until the strike was declared at an end. But the actual breaking of the strike was performed by Liberals using weapons provided by the Conservative-Unionists. With their characteristic flair for popularity the Liberals were able to flush quickly out of sight the blood they had shed, and to commence pointing the finger of shame at the Conservatives. The strike had been broken but the people were still indignant. In spite of police repression and the arrest of the leaders of the labour movement in Winnipeg, a socialist candidate for Mayor, S. J. Farmer, who stood when the original candidate went to jail, received 12,514 votes compared

[1] Masters, *The Winnipeg General Strike*, p. 105.
[2] Considering the great interest of Sir Clifford Sifton in the question of civil liberty during World War I, the absence of any correspondence on this subject and on the General Strike with his editor during 1919 is a remarkable feature of the edited copy of the *Dafoe Papers* in the Public Archives at Ottawa.
[3] See Masters, *The Winnipeg General Strike*, p. 104, for information about the the "revelations" of Hon. Peter Heenan, Mackenzie King's Minister of Labour, cf. *House of Commons Debate*, 1926, pp. 4006–07.

with the victor's 15,630. In the election of November, the City Council of Winnipeg was split equally between anti-labour and pro-labour aldermen. In this political atmosphere the Liberals manoeuvred to make their fortunes.

Across the whole Dominion the situation during the| summer and autumn of 1919 was liable to resemble that in Winnipeg. Everywhere there was the threat of upheavals, either on the pattern implicit in the Winnipeg General Strike or on the pattern of a nationalist-secessionist movement which flourished in Quebec. In Ontario the Liberals were obliged to compete with the United Farmers Organization and the newly organized Ontario section of the Canadian Labour Party.

The election campaign in Ontario in September revealed all the parties trying to crowd the left side of the road. The Conservative Government offered the voters a minimum wage law, mother's pensions and labour representation in the Cabinet. The Liberals, under the leadership of a Laurier Liberal with strong leftist as well as liquor connections, promised the same thing and added to these promises substantial assurances about the high cost of living. The United Farmers promised to "do something" about the public debt, to fight socialism and the Big Interests, to prohibit more strictly the drinking of alcohol and to stop building concrete highways for the use of speed-mad owners of automobiles living in cities. The Labour Party promised to nationalize all public utilities and banks, to end censorship, to protest against sending troops to Russia, to do what it could to have Eugene Debs released from his American prison. When the smoke of battle had cleared the United Farmers ("camouflaged Liberals" according to Sir William Hearst, the Conservative Premier) had 45 seats, the Liberals 29, Labour 11 and the Conservatives 25. The Liberals had contrived to win 29 seats under their own banner and 45 seats under the flag of the United Farmers. The Tories had been routed.

In Quebec the Conservatives had no hope and there was no Labour Party. But in spite of the absence of a genuine opposition Sir Lomer Gouin, the Liberal Premier of the Province, campaigned during the provincial election on a "left" platform. He pointed to his labour legislation, and he promised more jobs and more opportunities for workers by a policy of encouraging home industries. He told the people how he had prevented the Americans from cutting pulpwood on the Crown lands of the province and was thus forcing the establishment of paper-making enterprises in Quebec. Sir Lomer asserted that no one needed to inquire whether he believed in, and worked for Canada and the Canadians.

"What the future has in store for Canada politically, no one can tell," wrote one of the Liberal-Unionists in the Borden Government. ". . . The influences at work are too overwhelming to allow individuals to stand in the way. In due time these forces will shift their whole course and politicians will have to fall in with the outcome whatever it may be. . . ."[1]

Such, then, was the condition of movement of the Canadian people in 1919. Sir Wilfrid Laurier was dead. Could the Liberal Party find a leader capable of navigating in the swiftly running currents of the times?

When Laurier died the Liberal members of the House of Commons had appointed a Nova Scotia lawyer from among themselves as a temporary leader. His name was D. D. McKenzie; an amiable man with more talent for intrigue than for politics. Under his direction the Opposition soon began to look what it actually was: a carbon copy of the Government. The situation alarmed the only first-class politician among Laurier's "old gang", the Hon. Charles Murphy. In his opinion the Convention which Laurier had planned to call within a year or eighteen months must be called at once. If an able leader were not quickly appointed the public would soon cease to notice any difference between Liberals and Tories, even in their speeches. This might be fatal for the Party.

With the temporary leader Murphy was candid. ". . . The high cost of living", he wrote as the Winnipeg strike got under way,

"is at the root of the present general unrest, and the opposition, in the House of Commons, has not addressed itself to this question as it should have done, and . . . the Government has been allowed to escape the responsibility that devolves upon it for failure to deal with the problem, and to alleviate the burdens from which the working class are suffering. . . . Our friends are stating openly

[1] From the private papers of the Hon. Charles A. Dunning. J. A. Calder to Dunning, 14 January, 1919.

x

that . . . there is no sense in remaining a member of the Liberal Party. . . . This impression . . . is not likely to be removed, except by emphatic action either in the House or at a National Convention."[1]

A few days later writing to a friend in New York Murphy declared that, if he had his will, he would close the House of Commons at once, or, at least, withdraw all the Liberal members in order to prevent them making any more mistakes and blunders "in the absence of authoritative leadership". To this friend he revealed the full extent of his political imagination.

"The Winnipeg strike, which should be debated every day and which our side in the House should not give the Government an hour's peace, is scarcely ever referred to, so perfect is the policy of drift, in which our leaderless group have attained almost as much excellence as the Government and its supporters. Of course, I realize that the moment anybody says anything about it, there will be the usual cries of 'Bolshevist', 'traitor,' etc., etc., but that risk could easily be run if there were proper direction in the House. I realise that you can only do one or two things properly, and . . . I am devoting myself to the Convention and its work, and the party at large will have to take the consequences of what is or is not done in the House."[2]

Through June and July Murphy laboured at the organization of the Liberal Convention. Some people thought he was labouring to pick the new leader. Although he was by far the ablest politician among the Liberals who had belonged to Laurier's immediate entourage, he never for a moment considered himself a candidate. He was an Irish Catholic, a partisan of Home Rule and an admirer of Charles Stewart Parnell, Padraic Pierce and James Connolly. He knew that he had no chance at all. He belonged to a minority, too small and too poor. But he knew how to organize, and he was an advocate of steady plodding work in this field. Indeed, he believed that if Laurier had paid more attention to organization in 1911 and in 1917, he would have won the first election and rendered the second unnecessary. For this reason he was suspected by many as being an *eminence grise*. To one man who wrote to him on the subject, he replied that his lot was nothing but slavery and

---

[1] *Murphy Papers*, Murphy to McKenzie, 22 May, 1919.
[2] *Murphy Papers*, Murphy to Maloney, 26 May, 1919.

drudgery and that he had no idea who would become leader.[1]
Writing to a friend in Nova Scotia, whom he had no motive to
misinform, he declared:

"Answering your enquiry, I may say that the prospects indicate a
large attendance with a considerable diversity of views. Up to the
present there does not seem to be any particular individual for the
leadership. The papers start booms every other day, in which this
or that individual figures for the moment, and then dies away.
While I am too busy with the details of the work to give much
thought to the question of Leadership, it seems to me that there
may be a contest between East and West—a contingency which,
if it happens, I will very much regret."[2]

While the newpapers were starting booms and Murphy was
slaving over lists of hotel accommodation for delegates, Mackenzie King was across the Atlantic in Great Britain supposedly
"studying industrial conditions". After Laurier had died
Mackenzie King appeared to move closer to the Rockefellers,
but not so close that he was out of the Canadian picture. He
agreed to go to Britain on behalf of the Rockefeller Foundation,
but he also consented to make some speeches in Canada. Indeed,
he managed to appear before important middle class and Liberal
audiences at nearly all the key centres in Ontario and Quebec.
In January he addressed the Reform Club in Montreal. His
programme in March was heavy: the Empire Club in Toronto
on the 13th, the Newmarket electors on the 15th, a public
meeting in Quebec City on the 28th, a meeting in Montreal on
the 30th and the Liberals of Toronto on April 7th.

His address to the Empire Club in Toronto affords a fair
sample of his style and matter at this time. His subject was
industrial peace. "I notice", he told his audience,

"that the Minister of Labour informed the House of Commons a
day or two ago that Canada had had fewer strikes in recent years
than any country in the world. If that statement is true, and I
believe that it is, it is because we have on our statutes a law which
makes provision for the investigation of industrial controversies
prior to lockouts and strikes."[3]

He modestly omitted that he was responsible for the legislation.
Over coffee he told the members of the Empire Club how to
fight Bolshevism:

[1] *Murphy Papers*, Murphy to McMaster, 11 July, 1919.
[2] *Murphy Papers*, Murphy to C. Mackenzie, 18 July, 1919.
[3] W. L. M. King, *The Message of the Carillon*, p. 213.

"It is coming to be seen that the control of labour by its leaders is wholly dependent upon its organization into *conservatively directed* unions; that it is among the unorganized and undisciplined workers that Bolshevism and I.W.W.ism recruit their armies of terror and destruction. *In a union of the organized forces of labour and capital, against a common enemy which menaces all human society lies the hope of the future.*"[1]

Then Mackenzie King took a few swings at the temporarily prostrate militarism of Prussia and wound up with a peroration on Humanity's Gethsemane. The members of the Empire Club had seldom heard such a clear, comprehensive solution of the problems of mankind at once so painless and so much in line with their own ideas.

If Canada had fewer strikes than any other nation in March, 1919, by May she had her share. By this time Mackenzie King was out of range of the clamour. He seemed to have an extra-sensory power of not being where trouble was. But his friends were still in Canada working away on his behalf. According to the journalist Preston his team of promoters consisted of Larkin, Lemieux, Sydney Fisher and Preston himself.[2] Apparently Domville and Mitchell had gone to work on Lemieux to some effect, and his shilly-shallying about Mackenzie King was at an end. Perhaps the death of Laurier had removed Lemieux's last means of resistance. In any event the death of Laurier left him on his own, and he was busily engaged, it seems, in digging his own political grave. The involvement of Fisher was equally a clever move on the part of the men who wanted Mackenzie King, for Fisher was the only English-speaking cabinet colleague of Laurier, save Mackenzie King, Murphy and Oliver, who had remained loyal to the Old Chief in 1917. Fisher was not a strong candidate for the leadership, but he was an alternative to Mackenzie King for the devotees of Laurier to follow.

The problem of lining up a regiment of Mackenzie King men in Ontario was solved brilliantly by the Mackenzie King organizers. They could not recruit from among Laurier's old guard or old gang, and all the Liberals powerfully connected in Toronto still bore the marks of their service in the "Unionist" ranks. But there remained one man with great prestige in the Party who had enjoyed the confidence of, and had stuck to,

---

[1] W. L. M. King, *The Message of the Carillon*, p. 218, our italics.
[2] *Murphy Papers*, Preston to Murphy, 21 July, 1932.

Laurier: Sir Allen Aylesworth. The wall of his deafness had isolated him from the din of Party strife and his reputation was unimpaired. He was like a Party hero of the past but fortunately still on earth and able to vote. This was the man the Mackenzie King managers were able to bring back into service for the purpose of raising the standard of battle in Ontario and enrolling at least a battalion of voters at the Convention on behalf of Mackenzie King.

Aylesworth had originally expressed an interest in Béland as a leader. Then he worked on behalf of Fisher, and he continued to do this until very shortly before the convention. But when he came to realize that Fisher could not command wide support, he began to look around once more. At this moment the recruiting agents delivered to him Mackenzie King's commission and he accepted it.

A few days before the Convention assembled in Ottawa early in August, 1919, items appeared in the newspapers suggesting that Mackenzie King was not really interested in the leadership. This may have been so, but he was careful to time his return to Canada to coincide with the assembling of the delegates in Ottawa. He turned up suddenly, alone and without any visible organization working on his behalf. The effect of being young, innocent and unattached just suited the temper of the delegates—or some of them.

This paste-board fig-leaf was the final decoration on the armour of his innocence. In real fact his candidature had been carefully planned by himself, and his machine meticulously constructed and well oiled. According to one source, "In London in 1919 he told a fellow countryman of his hopes and his desires at the Liberal Convention which was to take place later in the year. He had thought out every detail of procedure in advance, nothing was left to chance. . . ."[1]

There were more than 1,200 delegates in attendance, drawn from all over the Dominion and from several social strata. 1,111 possessed balloting rights, and 949 survived the hazards of the Convention sufficiently to cast the first ballot for the candidates. The numbers were sufficiently great to meet Laurier's requirement of an appeal to people in the movement

[1] *The Times Literary Supplement*, London, 4 December, 1953.

rather than an appeal to professional politicians. The delegates were not, however, a product of provincial conventions and the local heart searchings which Laurier had intended. But they were a sufficiently broad cross section of the party that, in order to win their support, Laurier's successor would have to make an appeal in the way Laurier had hoped he would have to do. A leader who could win the delegates might conceivably win an election. And for Canadian Liberals the art of politics consists in discovering someone or some line which will go down with voters; it has nothing to do with leading, or being led by the people, nor with solving the problem of community living. The delegates were to help in the discovery of the right man and the right formula for electoral success. To assist this process a special invitation to send delegates was extended to the Trades and Labour Congress of Canada, the Canadian Railway Brotherhoods, the Canadian Council of Agriculture and the Great War Veterans' Association. With two of these organizations Mackenzie King had had a long and intimate connection and in them many friends.

Five candidates were nominated for the leadership of the Party. They were W. S. Fielding, Laurier's Minister of Finance from 1896 until 1911; George P. Graham, Laurier's Minister of Railways and Canals who had once been for a short time the leader of the Liberal opposition in Ontario; D. D. McKenzie, the temporary leader of the Liberals in the House of Commons; W. L. Mackenzie King, Laurier's Minister of Labour from 1908 until 1911; and Alexander Smith, an Ottawa lawyer, lobbyist and organizer, a friend of Laurier, Mackenzie King and various other people. Alexander Smith was not a serious candidate, and he withdrew before the first ballot. Still another possibility as a candidate was the Premier of Saskatchewan, W. M. Martin.*

Thus, there were before the Convention two candidates— Fielding and Graham—who had deserted Laurier on the issue of conscription but had refused to join and support the "Union" Government. There were two candidates—Mackenzie King and D. D. McKenzie—who had, or seemed to have, remained faithful to Laurier during the fight about conscription.

As the moment of balloting approached all the other issues

which divided as well as united the delegates were merged in the question of past loyalty to Laurier. To a great many delegates—a majority as it turned out—loyalty to Laurier meant the possession of character, principle, genuine liberalism, a hatred of militarism, war, imperialism and the pride of wealth. It meant the love of people more than of things. Loyalty to Laurier meant belief in the Liberal Party as a serious, meaningful social movement, as a means of uniting Canadians and as a promise that no one interest would dominate all other interests in the community. The substantial minority which were prepared to forget a candidate's stand in 1917 were not necessarily the opposite of the Laurier loyalists, but they attached less importance to liberalism as a movement of the Common People against the Big Interests, of minorities against majorities, of weakness against strength. They tended more to think of the Liberal Party as a device for getting power, dealing with issues as they arose and making compromises. The people who attached no importance, or secondary importance, to the events of 1917 were just the kind of people who had deserted Laurier in 1917; the well-to-do, articulate elements in the Party whose desertion Laurier could observe but could not explain. The man who could continue to flutter on both these wings of the Party would be borne aloft to the leadership.

Although in later life they could scarce bear to admit it even to themselves, the two men who most effectively prepared the ground for Mackenzie King's election as leader were the Hon. Rodolphe Lemieux and the Hon. Charles Murphy. Both these men were close to Laurier. Lemieux was a man of cool temper, and he appears to have been governed largely by his head in making the choices he did. Murphy was a hot, passionate man who admitted that in politics he would do for love or hate what he would never do for money. This was a considerable admission for a man who had so carefully priced the politicians and church dignitaries of Canada.[1] Both drew together after Laurier's death in the conduct of a strenuous fight to keep out, if possible, and, as a last resort to limit the influence of all those elements who had betrayed Laurier in 1917. Laurier himself was not as *Laurieriste* as these supporters. He was willing to welcome

---

[1] There is a letter in Murphy's correspondence in which he discusses in some detail the price tag on a famous Archbishop.

back into the party most of those who had deserted;[1] all, in fact, except one—Rowell.[2] Lemieux and Murphy were not prepared to be so generous. They were both representative of minorities, and they had seen what Toronto and Winnipeg Liberals drawn from the ranks of the rich were capable of doing. For this reason they insisted upon the maintenance of the Liberal Party as a *Kämpferbund* of comrades. While they stood guarding the pass against the intrusion of traitors, the regiment of Mackenzie King marched through with its banners flying, Sir Allen Aylesworth at their head and Ernest Lapointe watching the ranks and reconnoitring the ground ahead.

Of the two guardians of the sacred principle of loyalty to Laurier, Lemieux was of much greater political importance than Murphy. This importance was derived from his standing in Quebec politics. It was and still is popularly supposed that Quebec constitutes a herd of voting cattle who run together in any direction, provided it is not in the direction of the racial slaughterhouse; that Quebec does not care how ill fed it may be or whose brand it may bear so long as Quebec has the assurance of survival. The party politician who can put himself at the head of the voting herd from Quebec will thus possess great strength, it is supposed, in the whole of Canada and in any of its parties. To a certain extent this was true in 1919; but Quebec voters are not so insensitive to questions of economic interest, personal well-being and human dignity as most Canadian politicians suppose.

When Laurier died the politicians appear to have supposed that the men most prominent in Quebec politics next to Laurier would naturally take over. These men were Lemieux, and Sir Lomer Gouin, the Prime Minister and Attorney-General of the Province of Quebec. Both were profoundly reactionary and both were intimately connected with powerful business interests in Montreal. Indeed, after his retirement from politics, Sir Lomer Gouin was elected to the boards of more big financial and industrial institutions than any man in Canada. He became Canada's champion company director.

Lemieux and Gouin had adopted a sympathetic attitude towards imperialism before 1914, and Lemieux was outstanding among Quebec politicians for his imperialist sentiments. With

[1] *Laurier Papers*, Laurier to Bulyea, 23 December, 1918.
[2] *Laurier Papers*, Skelton to Laurier, 23 March, 1918.

the development of the war, both shed these dangerous sympathies. Lemieux became a strong nationalist and anti-imperialist; Gouin's police had stood idly by while the rioters burned Federal buildings in 1918. The experience of war had not induced Lemieux and Gouin to revise their social and economic prejudices, however. They remained partisans of Big Business.

Without Laurier to lead him Lemieux soon became bewildered by the situation which confronted him in 1919. Of the two, Gouin soon emerged as the stronger and abler leader. The vested political and business interests of Quebec turned to him. During the provincial election of 1919, Sir Lomer appeared in Laurier's old constituency of Quebec East. The active representative of the great Taschereau dynasty proclaimed to the electors: "Laurier vivait, il serait ici. Il n'y est pas, mais nous avons son successeur et c'est vers lui que nous devons nous tourner pour lui demander de continuer l'oeuvre de Laurier. Son successeur, il est parmi nous. . . ." And he turned, dramatically, to the proposed heir on the platform, Sir Lomer Gouin.[1]

But this was not to be. A young man without the embarrassing connections of Sir Lomer Gouin was hard at work building a new political machine in Quebec. The young man was Ernest Lapointe—a protégé of Jacques Bureau.* Lapointe had entered the House of Commons at the age of 28, in 1904. His English was bad, and he came from le vrai Canada, down the St. Lawrence where the electors of Kamouraska used to give him regular majorities. Laurier had learned to speak perfect English by reading the Bible and Milton aloud. Lapointe employed a gramophone to achieve the ideal of the Abbé Groulx: English spoken badly enough to prove that he belonged still to the French-Canadian countryside. By 1918 he was one of Laurier's advisers from the province of Quebec, a group which numbered among its members Sydney Fisher, Jacques Bureau, Rodolphe Lemieux, A. K. Cameron, A. R. McMaster, A. J. Gauthier and Charles Marcil. Lapointe, however, was a better politician and a less provincial one than Lemieux or Sydney Fisher, in spite of their outward urbanity which contrasted so markedly with the young habitant's heavy rusticity. He would never listen to any nonsense about French-Canada separating from the rest of Canada and he was one of the few Liberals in

[1] J. C. McGee, *Histoire Politique de Québec-Est* (Québec, 1948), p. 173.

Parliament, apart from Murphy, who had the political imagination to express strong sympathy for the workers of Winnipeg during the general strike there. Sir Lomer Gouin was an advocate of policies designed to encourage industrial development in Quebec and compel American consumers of Canadian minerals and woodpulp to buy products manufactured in Canada, rather than raw materials for manufacture in the United States. Lapointe opposed Gouin and, like many other Liberals, sought the support of American Big Business interests and the western Canadian farmers by advocating "free trade". But the essence of Lapointe's genius consisted in recognizing that the people of Quebec are not voting cattle who instantaneously obey their leaders, but politically-minded people like any other, whose leading requires thought and imagination.

In the spring and summer of 1919, however, Lapointe was of more consequence inside the Liberal Party in Quebec than he was inside the Liberal Party of Canada. On the national level Lemieux was still of great importance, and Lemieux working with Murphy was a factor in diminishing the influence of the forces in the party which were willing, and, indeed, eager to support men like Graham and Fielding, and in strengthening the forces which saw in Mackenzie King the right candidate for them. Added to this was the bitterness among western Liberals against the domination of the Party by wealthy land speculators like Clifford Sifton and journalists like J. W. Dafoe. Shortly after the election of 1917, Laurier received a *cri du coeur* from one of those numerous but powerless elements in Manitoba. A certain A. McLeod wrote from Morden, Manitoba.

"We have lost everything in the West except our principles and honour, (but) with these intact we may live to fight another field, and mayhap win. . . . We were fighting big odds—the corporations—the trusts—the profiteers—the grafters—and the professional politicians of both parties, in a word the moneyed interests. But the worst of all in Manitoba was the lack of a newspaper to express the Liberal view. . . . The Free Press simply sold out the Liberals to the Big Interests. . . . We must have an exponent of Liberalism in Winnipeg—even our friends the enemy expect it, and make sure to say that they will do all in their power to make the road as difficult as possible to travel, and I have no doubt they will do their best to put difficulties in our way."[1]

[1] *Laurier Papers*, McLeod to Laurier, 5 January, 1918; cf. *Murphy Papers*, Murphy to Fisher, 6 September, 1907.

The author of these words was typical of many of the people who came to the Convention.[1] So important were] they that a rumour about Clifford Sifton's support for Graham was found to be highly damaging to Laurier's comrade whom he had loved like a brother.

Thus, the work of professional politicians like Lemieux and Murphy, combined with a strong sentiment of suspicion against any one believed to be connected with the Big Interests were sufficient to make loyalty to Laurier a dominating factor in the choice of a leader. Preston, who worked for King, put it this way: ". . . I knew Laurier did not want him (Mackenzie King) as his successor. Sifton, Senator Beith and several old colleagues also warned me, but I had no thought but of his loyalty to Laurier in 1919. . . ."[2]

Sir Allen Aylesworth, who moved the nomination of Mackenzie King later testified to the same compelling element in the the situation.

> ". . . There was, of course, a combination of causes for the election of Mackenzie King as leader at the Convention ten years ago. Some men were influenced by one consideration—and others by other considerations—but I thought at the time and I still would think—that King could never have won if it had not been that both Fielding and Graham had deserted Laurier. In that sense I would think it not far wrong to say that it was 'conscription that defeated Fielding'. For myself at any rate, the one thing that I was bound to do everything I could to accomplish, was to prevent any man who had deserted Laurier in 1917 becoming our leader in 1919 —because such a result I believed would have utterly disrupted and destroyed the Party. I know that a great many who were at the Convention had exactly the same feeling—and I think it was a very powerful factor in electing King. . . . I called to see her [i.e. Lady Laurier] during the Convention week in 1919—and we talked about the leadership. I told her what I was doing, and how I felt about it—and I believe that if she had voted at the Convention she would have marked her ballots exactly as I marked mine—but I agree entirely . . . it [is] pure newspaper 'bunk' that Laurier himself ever designated King as his successor."[3]

Mackenzie King himself did little at the Convention. He moved and A. W. Roebuck of Toronto, an intimate of Atkinson,

[1] One of these, an old radical, has told us about how he came to the Convention determined to support Mackenzie King because Mackenzie King had been loyal to Laurier and "knew something about labour".
[2] *Murphy Papers*, W. T. R. Preston to Murphy, 21 July, 1932.
[3] *Murphy Papers*, Aylesworth to Murphy, 25 July, 1929.

seconded the resolution on labour. His speech moving the resolution contained the choicest and most enriched bits of
Industry and Humanity. "Industry exists for the sake of Humanity
and Humanity for the sake of Industry." The anti-Bolshevism
with which he had delighted the Empire Club in Toronto five
months earlier was left out. Such talk was not popular at the
Convention. An ex-member for the Yukon had remarked in the
debate with crude and uncomfortable realism that Sir Robert
Borden had, for the first time in Canadian history, turned
machine guns on the workers. Denunciation of the Conservative
leader on this account had been greeted by a big cheer. Indeed,
there was practically no criticism of Bolshevism during the entire
convention, in spite of the furious anti-Socialist campaign in the
newspapers. The rank and file of the delegates were sympathetic, rather than hostile, towards the Russian and Hungarian
revolutions.

The resolution on labour "which Mackenzie King himself
largely framed" embraced all the uncontroversial demands of
labour and avoided all the contentious ones. Labour was promised "the introduction into the Government of industry of
principles of representation whereby labour and the community as well as capital, may be represented in industrial
control . . .". Nothing was said, however, about collective bargaining, which was the subject of the general strike in Winnipeg.
Offices for labour leaders were promised in the shape of labour
representatives on federal commissions and the board of the
Canadian National Railways. Japan had been an ally in the
war, and had emerged stronger than ever, while India was in a
ferment. The "more effective restriction of Chinese immigration" was, therefore, recommended as a safe and sane piece of
racial discrimination. Finally a general promise was made of
"immediate and drastic action by the Government with respect
to the high cost of living and profiteering". But the resolution
did not promise to bring down the cost of living or bring profiteering to an end. The *Manitoba Free Press*, no conspicuous friend
of labour, dismissed the resolution on labour as "an example of
political diplomacy . . . inoffensive, and yet at the same time
not without its special appeal . . . [which] evidently has been
successful. . . ."[1]

[1] *Manitoba Free Press*, 11 August, 1919.

Mackenzie King's words on the resolution constituted only forty per cent of his speech. It had been agreed that there would be no appeals by possible candidates for support, but this agreement was honoured rather in the breach by all the rivals for the leadership save Fielding. Mackenzie King abandoned the undertaking completely. When his time was up he appealed to the Chairman for leave to continue and then made a speech on general political problems one and a half times as long as his remarks in support of the resolution he had been asked to move. And it was a good speech—some have said the best speech Mackenzie King ever made. He was compelled to condense his thought and to find the means of expressing the common resentments and anxieties of the Liberals gathered before him. He said a few words of love for Laurier, which were moving because they were short and simple and presented a startling contrast to the loose sentimentality on the same subject of, for example, the Hon. George P. Graham. Then Mackenzie King launched into an attack upon the Tories. They were destroying Parliament and free democratic government of the people, by the people. The Liberals had the duty of protecting democracy. If they did that they could

> "help save the world from further revolution. . . . So I say, having the memory of our great chief and late beloved leader, we Liberals of Canada have reason to be proud that in him we have one whose name will ever find a place on the honor roll of illustrious statesmen—a place with men like Hampden, Pym, Pitt, Bright, Cobden, Gladstone, Lincoln, men who gave their lives battling for the right of the people to control Parliament, and the right of Parliament to control the Executive; and these rights should be observed in the name of freedom."[1]

But this comparison of Laurier with the great Parliamentarians of history was not quite the conclusion of Mackenzie King's oration. He likened Laurier to another great figure of history. He closed with the words of Tennyson on the greatest English Tory—the Duke of Wellington. Then Mackenzie King sat down.

When the nominations for the leadership were entered, Mackenzie King began to look like a winner. He was nominated by Sir Allen Aylesworth and seconded by the Hon. Sydney

[1] *The National Liberal Convention; the Story of the Convention and the Report of the Proceedings* (Ottawa, 1919), p. 134.

Fisher. Martin had decided not to stand. This eliminated two possible English-speaking colleagues of Laurier who had remained loyal in 1917. When the first ballot was counted he had obviously won. He had 344 against Fielding's 297 votes, while Graham and McKenzie each had 153. The candidates loyal to Laurier thus had 497 votes against 450 for the deserters. Quebec had voted for Mackenzie King by a large majority. 222 Quebec votes out of 297 had gone to King. Lemieux and Lapointe were for Mackenzie King. The only Quebec politician who might have forced a change in the voting on the second ballot, Sir Lomer Gouin, was immobilized on the platform as one of the Joint Chairmen of the Convention.

The Quebec vote was Mackenzie King's real victory.[1] Laurier had not pronounced for him, but he had found a new means of victory in Lapointe. The Quebec delegation at the Convention was, in fact, divided and unstable, when it arrived in Ottawa. Lemieux had lost his head. He was reported to be first for Fielding and then for Mackenzie King and then for someone from Western Canada. If Lemieux had lost his head, Gouin had lost control of the body of delegates. He had enjoyed absolute control of the provincial machine for so long and he had been so free to indulge his social prejudices favourable to great wealth that he seems to have lost the capacity to come to terms with reality. He entertained the notion that the best candidate for the Leadership was W. S. Fielding. Fielding was socially reactionary like himself. In fact Fielding was so reactionary that he proposed to stand for the leadership only if it was understood that he would be free to repudiate the mildly progressive platform of the Party adopted by the Convention. This sort of stupidity seems to have suited Sir Lomer Gouin. But not so the majority of the Quebec delegation. One group of compromisers wished the Quebec delegation to abstain from voting, thus leaving the selection of a leader to the other eight provincial delegations. In the midst of this confusion Sir Allen Aylesworth intruded to declare that he would quit the Party if a traitor to Laurier were elected leader. If French-Canadians had to learn loyalty to Laurier from an Ontario man, where was their self-respect?

Lady Laurier attempted to undo the emotional damage to

[1] *Lemieux Papers*, King to Lemieux, 12 February, 1932.

Mr. Fielding by sending a message to the Convention to the effect that her late husband had considered Mr. Fielding a suitable successor capable of re-uniting the party. By this time the feeling was so intense in the Quebec delegation that the messenger from Lady Laurier, a man of wisdom and great loyalty to his party, decided not to deliver his missive lest the Party split publicly with all the consequences which would inevitably ensue.

At this stage Lapointe took charge. He declared emphatically against any course of withdrawal, and this rallied the whole delegation. Then, A. R. McMaster and Sydney Fisher declared that Mr. Fielding was a tool of St. James's Street. This sentiment Lapointe supported. Who was not a tool of St. James's Street? The answer? Mackenzie King. Sir Lomer Gouin was incapable of playing in a game like this. The feeling against St. James's Street was too much for him. Thus did St. James's Street's policy of backing all the candidates in the field prove itself once more. If one is rich enough to back both the black and the red, one is bound to win, and in real life roulette on these terms is worth playing.

On the second ballot Graham lost 29 votes and McKenzie lost 93. Of these 122 votes Mackenzie King gained 67 and Fielding 47. Eight delegates refrained from voting on the second ballot. On the third ballot twenty-five delegates, who originally cast ballots, did not vote. Graham and McKenzie withdrew leaving 184 votes to be collected of which 60 were votes for a Laurier loyalist and 124 for a deserter. Of these 184 votes Mackenzie King gained 65—McKenzie's vote plus a few others. Fielding gained 94. Had every delegate who voted for Graham, voted for Fielding, and only those who voted for McKenzie had gone over to Mackenzie King, Mackenzie King would have had only 3 votes to spare. Had those delegates who dropped out in the second ballot also voted, the third ballot might have produced a stalemate. As it was Mackenzie King won by 38 votes.[1]

Any mathematical calculation shows that Mackenzie King did not get all of the 47 votes which represented the superiority of the Laurier Loyalists in the first ballot. But mathematics cannot explain politics. Obviously his victory turned mainly

[1] *The Story of the Convention*, etc., pp. 181, 185, 196.

on his loyalty to Laurier but finally upon other factors at which we can only guess. As between him and Fielding there was the choice between youth and age. Mackenzie King was not yet 45 years old. Fielding was 71. Mackenzie King was supposed to have rebel blood in his veins, and the times were rebellious. Did this influence the odd vote? His enemies said he was a deserter during the war. Did this influence the odd vote among those who hated war?

These are small factors which constitute the Mackenzie King luck. But luck cannot explain the solid fact of his victory. Those who wanted him planted in the Liberal leadership had won. They had secured the Quebec *bloc*. That was the real object of the pressure applied to Laurier before his death, for, as long as Laurier lived Mackenzie King could not win without the Old Chief's blessing. Laurier's death paved the way for the swing of Quebec to Mackenzie King. In the interval between Laurier's death in February and the Convention in August the backroom boys working for Mackenzie King had fixed things in Quebec.

Given solid Quebec support, Mackenzie King was able to win left support elsewhere on the strength of his loyalty to Laurier. Aylesworth and Murphy among the big men and hosts of little people were influenced by his outward loyalty to Laurier in 1917. His statement in 1917 that the Union Government was "a fraud designed to win the election and not the war" evoked great sympathy, and concealed his approval of conscription and the support for the Wilsonian drive for victory at all cost. His supposedly progressive and sympathetic attitude towards labour, his promise of jobs in the bureaucracy for labour leaders and his verbal radicalism attracted others to his cause.

There was much happiness and satisfaction at the outcome of the Convention. Everyone's illusions were intact. As they left the Convention Hall, Lemieux was observed to slip his arm through Murphy's and was heard to say: "Well, Charlie, unto us a child is born."

CHAPTER XI

Conclusion

Mackenzie King first appeared upon the political stage, in 1895, playing a leading role in a minor but interesting political drama. At that time his country occupied an obscure place in the political affairs of the world. As a factor in the economy of the nations Canada was then of no great importance. But in 1895 Canada was on the eve of a great transformation, which, in the course of the next twenty-five years, changed profoundly the character of the Dominion and its weight in world affairs and in the universe of its own experience. When Mackenzie King was a very young man Canada was still thought and spoken of as a colony lacking in many things the character of a mature state. By the time he reached middle life and a position of eminence as leader of the Canadian Liberal Party, Canada had been caught up completely in the turbulent courses of industrial society. By 1919, her people had also died upon the battlefields of the Great War in greater numbers than any other people in the Americas.

It is difficult to appreciate or explain Mackenzie King unless we keep firmly in mind the nature of the transformation of Canada and the world, which was contemporaneous with his rise from obscurity to eminence. When Mackenzie King left his native town for the provincial metropolis in 1891 Canada was primarily a commercial and raw material-producing country of less than 5,000,000 people. By the time he entered the House of Commons as Leader of the Opposition, Canada was an industrial nation of more than 8,000,000 people. Some of the

Canadians of the early '90's lived in cities like Montreal or Toronto, but a high percentage lived in small towns, on scattered homesteads and in isolated lumbering and mining camps, where the main business of production was carried on. In 1871, only 14 per cent of Canadians lived in cities of more than 10,000 inhabitants, and there were only 9 cities of such size in the country. In 1881 the percentage of town dwellers was still the same. By 1911 this percentage had mounted to 45.5 per cent.[1]

In the old Canada before its industrial revolution there were many wage earners, but a substantial percentage of Canadians in those days were owner-workers of farms, fisheries, shops, contracting enterprises for building, cutting lumber and pulp wood and moving commodities to market. By the end of World War I more than half of all Canadians lived in cities, and considerably more than half were wage earners. From a nation composed primarily of people of Anglo-Saxon, French and Celtic descent Canada had been transformed into a white cosmopolis. During the course of this economic revolution the farmers and small business men, so important and so weighty in the community of old Canada, were afforded new opportunities; while they were, at the same time, faced by the competition and financial pressure of large scale financial, industrial and transport interests.

The increasing importance of domestic financial capital and the increased invasion of Canada by British and foreign financial interests presented the community with a number of serious economic and finally political problems. The total investment in the Canadian economy in the form of stocks, shares, debentures, bonds, loans and mortgages—some at fixed interest, some depending for their value to their owners upon the profitability of enterprises—mounted very rapidly. It has been estimated that between 1900 and 1911 the fixed interest capital and the share capital in Canada increased by $3,000 millions.[2] By 1913 the equity of British investors in Canada was $1,753,118,000 and that of American investors $629,794,000.[3] But the physical factors of production did not increase as rapidly as the claims

---

[1] R. H. Coats, *The Rise in Prices and the Cost of Living in Canada, 1900–1914* (Department of Labour, Ottawa, 1915), p. 40.

[2] Coats, *Prices and Cost of Living*, p. 31.

[3] J. Viner, *Canada's Balance of International Indebtedness* (Cambridge, U.S.A., 1924), p. 126 and p. 134.

and expectations of the investors. Agricultural capital increased, for example, by 136·4 per cent between 1900 and 1910, but the acreage of improved lands by only 60·8 per cent and the total number of livestock by only 55·7 per cent. The total labour force increased by only 35 per cent between 1900 and 1910 and 45 per cent by 1913.[1]

A study of physical productivity during the years 1910–11 further reveals the precarious nature of the prosperity of the Laurier epoch. In the face of the huge increases in investment, the productivity of agriculture increased only 36·8 per cent during the decade 1900–10. The production of fish scarcely increased at all, the 55 per cent increase in net value of fish being accounted for very largely by an increase in price of 50 per cent. The output from mines increased only 64 per cent and lumber only 54 per cent. The manufacturing sector of the economy showed much better results; manufactured miscellaneous articles increased 126·5 per cent and food and household articles 87·9 per cent. The only remarkable increase was in bar and sheet metal (1,384 per cent), pig iron (312 per cent) and castings and machinery (544 per cent).[2]

The prosperity of the Laurier epoch was not bringing corresponding prosperity for the wage-earners. Wealth accumulated and men decayed in accordance with the law of the poet. The consumption of liquor and tobacco increased by 60 and 66 per cent respectively, but the consumption of staples like cheese and apples declined. Apples became so costly that they began to be replaced by oranges. Imports of jewellery, perfume and precious stones increased by hundreds per cent. In the old Canada the one-family house had been the general rule, but between 1900 and 1910 this condition began to change. The number of families living in one room increased by 74 per cent from a percentage of the whole of 4·3 per cent to 5·7 per cent. On the other hand the number of houses having 11 rooms or more increased by 6 per cent from 7 per cent of the whole to 8·3 per cent of the whole. The increase in house rents in Canada was among the highest in the world[3] amounting to 60–70 per cent.

[1] Coats, *Prices and Cost of Living*, p. 37.
[2] Coats, *Prices and Cost of Living*, pp. 41–3.
[3] Coats, *Prices and Cost of Living*, pp. 46–8.

According to the official study by Canada's ablest statistician and social scientist of that time, R. H. Coats,

". . . an examination of the course of 'real' wages . . . over a wider range . . . leaves it open to question whether in spite of the great rise in money wages the standard for workers as a whole is appreciably higher,—this not withstanding the abundance of employment which has prevailed and the many evidences of greater comfort in the modern family. Wages, speaking generally, have risen 43 per cent. . . . But there has been considerable inequality as between classes like agricultural labour and the printing trades on the one hand and less skilled industrial workers on the other. Wages of the former have risen faster than the rise in retail prices, wages of the latter not so fast. This, however, leaves out the important item of rent . . . it may be noted that although the earnings of the average employee in manufacturing establishments increased 40 per cent, according to the census, between 1900 and 1910, proportionately to the value of the product the total wages bill declined from 23·5 per cent to 20·6 per cent."[1]

Given facts of this kind, we are not surprised by the unrest, the zeal for organization, the desire to influence the labour market and the increasing consideration among Canadian labour of alternative forms of society.

In her colonial epoch Canada had been isolated from the great world and largely independent of it. By the time Mackenzie King achieved Cabinet rank she had become a nation with an economy characteristic of the great states. The economic isolation and independence of Canada tended to diminish. Commercially and financially Canada became more and more tied to the markets and financial centres of the United States and Europe. $2,500,000,000 of capital bound her with golden chains to the owners of their investments in Europe and the United States. A bricklaying contractor in Calgary could be ruined by a war in the Balkans. The Balkan War of 1913, in fact, impaired the credit of promoters of Canadian enterprise in the capital markets, and this blow precipitated the crisis and unemployment which afflicted Canada in 1913–14.[2]

Politically, too, Canada's isolation came to an end. Canadians were debating whether and in what form they should become involved in the growing rivalries of the Great Powers. Abroad the Canadian Government was confronted by the

[1] Coats, *Prices and Cost of Living*, p. 48.
[2] Coats, *Prices and Cost of Living*, p. 53.

effects of the growing restlessness of the Asiatic and African peoples in the presence of the increasing pressure of European and American interests. In India, China, Japan and the Philippine Islands the masses of people, poorer, more insecure and more cruelly treated by man and by circumstance than any in the world, were beginning to bestir themselves. The Canadian Government, pushed on by forces which it could not control and which it was unwilling or unable to educate, placed itself in blank opposition to the claims of would-be Asiatic immigrants to a share in the unused resources and abundant opportunities of the Americas.

Living in a world of growth, transformation and rapidly shifting social tides, Mackenzie King proved himself a skilful navigator. He was supposed to be lucky. We do not believe that Mackenzie King was especially blessed by the fates. He made his own fate. Taught by men of profound insight, such as Sir William Ashley, Archdeacon Cunningham and Professor F. W. Taussig, he had a much clearer view of society than a superficial examination of his sentimental rhetoric would lead one to expect. His analysis revealed to him that there was developing everywhere, including Canada, a sharp antithesis which was increasingly becoming the subject matter of politics. Rule-of-thumb politicians like Sir Wilfrid Laurier recognized the existence of this antithesis, but their theories, in so far as they had any, could not explain it. Mackenzie King not only recognized it, but understood it.

The social antagonism which Mackenzie King so clearly appreciated was a product of the economic growth which his country had experienced during the years of his manhood. On the one hand there were what Laurier and the Liberals called the Big Interests—the financial and industrial magnates of Montreal, Toronto, Winnipeg and Vancouver. No one knew their political influence better than Laurier. They were the inheritors of the past and possessors of the present. But as their power increased so did their perils. In the youth of Sir Wilfrid Laurier a merchant or a plough manufacturer had few enemies and a secure place in the community. Free traders might object to his advocacy of tariffs, but he lived at peace with the dozen men whom he employed and called by their Christian names. But in the old age of Sir Wilfrid Laurier the sometime plough manufacturer did not know the men on the assembly lines of his farm implement empire. The ratio of employers to employees had changed radically. As capital accumulated, moreover, the economy fluctuated more wildly, and the soft tolerance of prosperous times disappeared. Then came the impact of the First World War. Until the age of industrialization, Canada had had no wars capable of shaking the social fabric and of provoking the question, why must such things be?

On the other hand there were what Laurier and the Liberals called the Common People. Because of the youth of Canadian industry, these, the wage-earners, were a young and inexperienced social group: inexperienced in both thought and action. Many of them could not even speak the English language, many could do little more than read and write, and some not even that. But the common people were developing as a social force with every stride made by industry. The problems of individuals—low wages, bad houses, meagre educational opportunities and periodic unemployment—were beginning to be recognized as social problems. Nor were there wanting Canadians who saw the problems of the common people in the round, and who sought political solutions for their difficulties. The potential of the common people was very great.

Mackenzie King understood this fundamental element in Canadian politics. He appreciated both the actual power of the rich and the potential power of the poor. The power of the rich he believed to be an agency of beneficence; the potential power of the poor to be an agency of chaos. He believed, however, that an equilibrium between the two might be maintained; and he worked to create faith in the powers of "conciliation".

Although Mackenzie King possessed an understanding of the anatomy of industrial society, superior in its realism to that of Laurier and the representatives of traditional Canadian Liberalism, he was not on that account a better politician. He himself had a very considerable measure of the responsibility for the disaster suffered by the Liberal Party in 1911. After the election of 1911 Mackenzie King could think of nothing to help the Liberals repair their fortunes. He jumped around from position to position like a bull in the presence of the banderilleros. Laurier, the rule of thumb politician, laid the political foundation of the resurrection of the Liberal Party when he abandoned first reciprocity and the American connection, then imperialism and an armament policy, and finally stood against conscription. On these subjects Mackenzie King never had any clear line, and more often than not he can be discovered in an attitude of opposition to Laurier, particularly on that most fundamental of all issues—conscription.

It is important to notice how profoundly he differed intellectually from the traditional Liberals of his party. The problems to which he addressed himself had nothing in common with those posed by the classical Liberals of Europe and America. The classical liberal thinkers, Adam Smith, Hume, Condorcet, Bentham and the older Mill, and the great Canadian Liberals, politicians like William Lyon Mackenzie, Alexander Mackenzie, Mowat and Laurier, had held the belief that a society organized as a free, competitive market would be stable, just and vital. Their problem was to destroy the control exercised over the mind and spirit by established churches, to end the economic control exercised by guilds of employers and/or workers, and to uproot the control over land and people exercised by feudal landlords, laws and customs. Once these things were done, they believed, man would be free, rational, happy, just, productive and good.

Mackenzie King had nothing in common with the classical Liberals except the name of his grandfather. He faced different problems and offered different solutions. Laurier, like Bentham, believed in going to the people. Mackenzie King talked about the merits of publicity, but repudiated the idea that abuses can be corrected by telling the people about them. The people must be filled with Faith not information. They themselves can devise neither ends nor means. Only capitalists and managers are endowed with such capacities. Welfare must depend upon the consciences of such men as John D. Rockefeller.

To the "natural" Liberals of Canada, the small farmers and small merchants, Mackenzie King paid comparatively little attention. They were not big enough or important enough. He concentrated upon the forces of labour and capital, and strove to capture their support for his political machine. He also strove to cultivate the great mass of uncommitted people who are not rich but who do not like to think themselves poor; who are wage-earners even though they do not carry a lunch pail. These people are in the grip of the social conflict, and often more cruelly affected by it than the man in overalls, but are reluctant to face the reality of their situation. They comfort themselves in their suburban bungalows with the hope that there will be peace and prosperity unto eternity. These people Mackenzie King strove to make his supporters.

About Mackenzie King's alignment with the opposing forces in Canadian political life, there can be no doubt. The ghost of his grandfather never walked to any effect among the artificial ruins with which Mackenzie King adorned his country estate. Philosophically and practically his grandfather was opposed to the big interests of his day; Mackenzie King was on the side of the big interests of his. As early as 1919, an unmistakable pattern emerges from the final positions he had adopted in all the major situations in which he had found himself.

When he examined social conditions in Toronto, in 1897, his analysis was favourable to large scale enterprise, and his handling of his material was such as to save the Government from embarrassment. When he went to Valleyfield, in 1900, we find him acquiescing in a conclusion favourable to the employers. As the secretary of a Royal Commission on Industrial Disputes in British Columbia we find him associated with recommendations to strengthen the Government's control of the labour movement and to divide it. On the question of Oriental immigration the pattern appears to break. He was on the popular side and opposed to the big employers who favoured the importation of Oriental labour. But here we find him on the side of racial discrimination—one of the most debilitating serums which can be injected into society. He fathered the Industrial Disputes Investigation Act, which had the effect of weakening and dividing the labour movement. His Combines Investigation Act did little more than strengthen the hands of the lawyers and public relations experts of large firms. In the Grand Trunk strike of 1910 he made effort after effort to smooth the path for the employers, to transfer to the Government and the people the cost of a settlement, to help President Hays to discipline the men who went out on strike and to bring matters to a conclusion before a united front of all the Grand Trunk workers brought the management to its knees. In the election of

1911, he took an extreme pro-American position, suggesting that association with Great Britain meant an attack on Germany and endeavouring to persuade the electors of the advantages of being part of the "protected" American market. During 1912–14, we find him cultivating the big interests in Toronto, and in intimate association with their representatives such as N. W. Rowell, P. C. Larkin and Sir Edmund Walker. The Rockefeller phase of Mackenzie King's career reveals his dependence on and belief in the very wealthiest of industrial and financial magnates. In the election of 1917, we discern the same pattern. While Laurier manoeuvred in a popular direction, Mackenzie King was pleading for a policy acceptable to the plough manufacturers and biscuit kings of North York. In *Industry and Humanity* he talked much of representative institutions in industry, but for the managers of big enterprises he recommended unrestricted authority. In 1919 we find him being sponsored for political leadership by tea magnates, senators and members of the St. James's Club in Montreal. There can be no mistake about the forces with which he aligned himself. He died a wealthy man, and his wealth came largely from gifts from wealthy Canadians and Americans. After he became leader, the Liberal Party never wanted for money, and the longer he remained leader the more money was available.

If Mackenzie King could command the affections of the big interests how did he garner the votes of the common people? A general strategy emerges from an examination of his activities. In 1897, he was the partisan in print of the sweated clothing worker, but in the library of Sir William Mulock he was ready to befriend the Government whose contractors were responsible. In Valleyfield he penned the message of hope which brought the workers back to their machines, but made no effort to fulfil it. The Industrial Disputes Investigation Act was promised to striking miners as a guarantee of Union recognition. Its actual effect was to reduce the pressure of labour on employers. For the Grand Trunk workers he had fine words which won him a free hand to fight for them. As a result many of them lost their jobs and their pensions. Employing slogans of free trade and free food in the election of 1911 he busied himself betraying Canadian business and Canadian labour to American interests. During the years 1914–15, he explored new levels of deliberate inconsistency. He advised the Canadian people to help save the British Empire, while explaining to Rockefeller how he might "reap the full measure of the harvest" for *his* Empire. To the terrorized and beaten workers of Colorado he came not with more terror but with a plan which actually granted the right to join a union. Then they discovered that the plan concealed a company union, and that the real unions, which they were free to join, had no place as bargaining agencies. In the election of 1917, he ran as a Laurier Liberal, but advocated a policy so like the "Unionists" that only his "passion for accuracy" enables us to discern the difference. In 1919 he appeared before the Liberal convention as a sudden arrival from Great Britain bearing an innocent message of Industry and Humanity, but behind the scenes organized a pressure group of the big interests to secure his election. Some people may denominate all this as "smart politics"; we prefer to think of it as the kind of conduct which in the long run discredits Parliamentary democracy.

Mackenzie King had a tender heart and a hard head; a tender heart for labour and a hard head for the employers. This combination suited the times. The use of violence, police repression and espionage in dealing with labour movements had obvious disadvantages; "hard" policies are uneconomic, once labour begins to gain in maturity and experience. Constant repression and indignity reduce productivity and increase discontent. They have the added disadvantage of alienating the uncommitted elements of the community. As a normal policy, force is not only expensive but impossible. Mackenzie King believed that talk was a more appropriate weapon. He would use phrases as forceful as the temper of the people, and then betray them.

Great artists have a capacity for grand conceptions. Their success, however, depends more often than not upon attention to detail. In matters of detail Mackenzie King was ever a man of genius: shrewd, amoral and a nice judge of human passions and weaknesses. He realized that in a business society one must have something to sell. He made his way into political life by trading an embarrassing piece of information for an appointment as a commissioner to inquire into abuses. Once he was on the inside of politics, he proceeded to build his own machine.

He was loyal to the Liberal Party, but he knew that loyalty is not enough. One must command a platoon of followers, or a company or a regiment.

While other politicians built their followings like medieval soldiers in their home districts, Mackenzie King like a Renaissance monarch constructed his following on the most ample scale at the centres of power. In this process he transformed substantially the character of the Canadian Government.

Today the Canadian bureaucracy is no longer simply an instrument of government, but a part of the government itself. It makes the policies of the Canadian state, and, through its connections with the Liberal Party, gives leaders to Parliament and the Cabinet. The growth in size and power of the Canadian bureaucracy has been a noticeable phenomenon only during the period since the outbreak of World War II in 1939, but we can see that one of the formative incidents in its growth occurred when Mackenzie King accepted the Deputy Ministership of Labour in 1900.

Mackenzie King was a classical example of the modern Canadian bureaucrat. He entered the Civil Service, not as a clerk, but as an executive officer under the authority of a Minister. He was, moreover, in possession of expertness in a new field; university trained and possessed of refinements of knowledge which Sir William Mulock, his formal superior, could never master. From the first moment of his entry into the Civil Service, Mackenzie King proceeded to build his own organization—a centre of power and propaganda—operating parallel to the traditional organs of authority. He brought in personal friends and acquaintances from the University and the newspaper offices to assist him in his work, while he built up his connections in the community at large. He soon learned to control men through his ability to give offices. He may not have been widely liked by his superiors and inferiors but he discovered—perhaps he had always known—that for certain purposes power is more important than affection.

With the advent of Mackenzie King upon the Ottawa scene, as we can now see, a blow was struck at the hopes entertained by some thoughtful citizens that Canada might develop in its civil service a body neither of rulers nor of party retainers, but of educated, enlightened and disinterested advisers, who could bring to bear upon the consideration of public questions the thought and energy of cultivated men and women free of partisan zeal and undisturbed by personal ambition. Mackenzie King was so fiercely partisan, he once declared he would never serve as a deputy to a Tory minister. As a politician he demanded unbelievable "accommodation" from civil servants. Furthermore, he set the example of seeking a political career from a place in the Civil Service. He taught the ambitious and the interested to build political machines within the service and to establish through their control over information a retinue among journalists and through their capacity to find jobs an elaborate connection in the Universities, the Churches, business and the trade unions. A man with a profound respect for Parliament, such as Laurier entertained, can hardly have guessed the consequences which were to flow from appointing to the Civil Service a partisan so able and so ambitious.

If the Civil Service was the first and remained the principal engine in his political powerhouse, Mackenzie King did not neglect other agencies. He cultivated governors-general, British Cabinet Ministers, American university personalities and Church dignitaries. He told Rockefeller he was indispensable to Laurier and he told Laurier he was indispensable to Rockefeller. If he was careful to make the right friends, he was also judicious in making the right enemies. The Canadian Manufacturers' Association and the American Labour Unions had common ground in their dislike of Mackenzie King. His enemies were by his own lights either mean reactionaries, or impractical anarchists; but they were always some person or institution disliked by the business interests or by a section of the Canadian labour hierarchy, or by both. He contrived always to keep clear, or seem to keep clear, of compromising associations and out of the way in compromising situations. He posed as the student in politics; the earnest would-be-professor torn reluctantly from scholarship. He wore the mantle of disinterested independence.

Once Mackenzie King was within sight of the highest office he displayed the greatest skill. He was a delicate strategist and a nimble tactician. Surveying the broad panorama of Canadian politics he committed his forces at the critical points. In an area like the province of Quebec, his task was comparatively simple.

He was a Laurier Liberal, or so it seemed. He had stuck to Laurier when Laurier stood before the Canadian people as their champion against conscription. That and Lapointe were sufficient.

It was to the uncommitted elements that Mackenzie King addressed himself. His advocacy of conciliation had originally been directed exclusively to organized labour and to employers, but later he gave it an extended meaning. Conciliation became a slogan suited to the temper of the times. The bloodshed in Quebec and in Winnipeg during 1918 and 1919 was frightening to everyone, and most of all to those who were neither rich nor poor. Conciliation became a species of magic. It was laden with hope and promise, for the people, who came in large numbers to the Liberal Convention in 1919 and applauded the kind words and generous phrases of the new Leader.

It embraced things beloved by the uncommitted: generosity, respectability, fairness. Class strife is repulsive to the majority of both rich and poor alike, no matter how exclusive the rich may be and how bitter the poor may feel. To people as naturally tolerant and pragmatic as most Canadians are, conciliation was an excellent slogan.

Mackenzie King realized, too, that the mass of mankind hate war, greed, arrogance and bloodshed. By 1919, the hatred of war was intense in Canada as well as throughout the world. Unlike others, who had benefited from the war, Mackenzie King did not appear before the people as a mouthpiece of the professional officers and war profiteers. Instead, he uttered a cry against war and waste on behalf of Industry and Humanity. He appealed to man's better self, and he won first the leadership of the Liberal Party and finally power.

On August 7th, 1919, the age of Mackenzie King dawned amid the shouts of the multitude of Liberals over whom he had won power.

A Note Concerning Sources

THE information in this book has been derived from seven main sources:

(1) Letters and papers available for public inspection in the Public Archives of Canada, in Ottawa. The main collections of papers, upon which we have relied, have been the newly completed collection of the Laurier Papers, the Lemieux Papers, the Willison Papers, the Graham Papers and the Murphy Papers. Although they contain relatively little information of value on Mackenzie King himself for the period 1874–1919, we have also examined the Dafoe, Cameron, Jacobs, Rowell, Hudson, Woodsworth, Dixon and Ewart[1] Papers for the picture they give of the age.

(2) Letters and papers in the possession of private institutions or individuals, such as the Eliot Papers in the possession of the President and Fellows of Harvard University, the correspondence and papers of Edward L. Doyle, sometime Secretary of District 15, United Mine Workers of America, the Lloyd George Papers in the possession of the Rt. Hon. Lord Beaverbrook, and the personal papers of Mrs. F. N. Pratt, Rev. Canon Harding A. Priest, Dr. R. H. Coats, the Hon. T. A. Crerar, the Hon. C. A. Dunning and the Hon. Charles G. Power.

(3) Official publications of the Governments of Canada and the United States, such as the *Debates of the House of Commons* and *Senate of Canada*, the *Congressional Record*, the *Labour Gazette*, *The Report of the United States Commission on Industrial Relations*, and

---

[1] The *J. S. Ewart and Fred J. Dixon Papers* are to be found in the Manitoba Provincial Archives.

reports of various Royal Commissions and Boards of Inquiry, such as those on Industrial Disturbances in British Columbia, 1903, on Anti-Oriental Riots, 1908, and on the Cost of Living, 1915, etc., etc.

(4) Contemporary newspapers and periodicals, such as the *Globe*, Toronto, *Mail and Empire*, Toronto, *The Star* and *Star Weekly*, Toronto, the *Gazette*, Montreal, the *Citizen*, Ottawa, the *Western Labor News*, Winnipeg, the *Free Press*, the *New York Times*, and above all the *Canadian Annual Review*.

(5) The recollections and memories of living persons who were concerned in the events depicted in this book or who were acquainted with the leading personalities. In making use of the recollections of people, we have recorded only the recollections which can be checked or are rendered inherently correct by reference to evidence more reliable than the human memory.

(6) Contemporary books and pamphlets of which there are a multitude, many of a high order of value both as information and criticism.

(7) The information contained in the work of other scholars.

Acknowledgments for Quotations

THE authors and publishers gratefully acknowledge the permission of the following to use extracts from copyright books: The Macmillan Company of Canada Ltd, for *Robert Laird Borden: His Memoirs*, edited by H. Borden, and for W. L. Mackenzie King's *Industry and Humanity, A Study in the Principles underlying Industrial Reconstruction*: The Oxford University Press, Canadian Branch, for O. D. Skelton's *Life and Letters of Sir Wilfrid Laurier*: Miss A. Ashley for her *William James Ashley, A Life*: and The Viking Press for J. Dorfman's *The Economic Mind in American Civilization*.

Biographical Notes

Frederick Albert Acland (1861–1950). Born Bridgewater, England. Migrated to Canada 1883 where he engaged in journalism. News Editor of *The Globe*, Toronto, 1890–1902. Western Editor of *The Globe*, 1906–07. Entered Department of Labour 1907 with right of reversion to Deputy Ministership. Entered upon his reward, 1908. Deputy Minister of Labour until 1923. King's Printer, 1921–33.

Jane Addams (1860–1935). Born Cedarville, Illinois. Educated at Rockford College. Spent two years in Europe, 1883–85. Founder and resident head of settlement house in Chicago, 1889. An inspector of streets and alleys, Chicago. Wrote extensively on social reform and welfare. Advocate of American neutrality during World War I. A pacifist. Shared Nobel Peace Prize with Nicholas Murray Butler in 1931.

Sir William J. Ashley (1860–1927). Born in London. Educated St. Olave's Grammar School and Balliol College, Oxford. Fellow of Lincoln College, Oxford. Professor of Political Economy and Constitutional History, University of Toronto, 1888–92. Professor of Economic History, Harvard, 1892–1901. Professor of Commerce and Finance, University of Birmingham, 1901–25; Vice-Principal of University of Birmingham, 1918–25. Author of numerous works on English economic history and economic problems.

Sir Hugh Graham, 1st Baron Atholstan (1848–1938). Born Huntingdon County, P.Q., into a family of newspaper proprietors. Educated Huntingdon Academy. President *Daily Star* and *Weekly Star*, Montreal. Developed the Montreal *Star* as a mass circulation English-language newspaper.

Joseph Atkinson (1865–1948). Born in Newcastle, Ontario. Educated at Newcastle High School. The most successful popular journalist and newspaper proprietor in Canadian history. A Liberal. President of the Toronto Star Publishing Company, 1899–1948.

Hon. Sir Allen Bristol Aylesworth (1854–1951). Born Camden Township, Ontario. Educated Newburgh Academy and University of Toronto. Practised law in Toronto for half a century. Counsel in many legal cases before the Judicial Committee of the Privy Council, and Hague Tribunal. One of the Canadian representatives in the Alaska Boundary Commission and refused to sign the award agreed to by the American and United Kingdom representatives. Member of Canadian House of Commons, 1905–11. Briefly Postmaster-General and Minister of Labour, 1905. Appointed to the Senate, 1923. Supported Sir Wilfrid Laurier during conscription crisis. Played an active role in securing Leadership of Liberal Party for Mackenzie King after his own candidate dropped out of race.

Most Rev. Louis Nazaire Bégin (1840–1925). Born Levis, P.Q. Son of a peasant. Educated Levis Model School, St. Michel Commercial College, Quebec Seminary and Rome. Professor of Theology, Laval University, 1868–84. Bishop of Chicoutimi, 1888. Coadjutor of Cardinal Taschereau, 1891; Administrator of the Archdiocese of Quebec, 1894; Cardinal, 1914.

Hon. Henri S. Béland (1869–1935). Born Louisville, P.Q. Educated Trois Rivières College and Laval University. A physician. M.L.A. Quebec, 1897–1901. Member of House of Commons for Beauce, 1902–25, except for an interval in a German prison camp, 1915–18. Appointed to Senate, 1925. Postmaster General, 1911; Minister of Soldiers' Civil Re-establishment and Public Health, 1921–26. A member of one of the orders of chivalry of the Crown of Belgium.

William H. Biggar (1852–1922). Born Carrying Place, Ontario. Educated at Trenton Grammar School and Upper Canada College, where he was head-boy. Assistant and then General Counsel of the Grand Trunk Railway from 1903. Director of numerous enterprises connected with the Grand Trunk.

Hon. Edward Blake (1833–1912). Born Cairngorm, Ontario. Successful lawyer and reluctant office holder and politician. The list of his appointments refused is impressive in range and number. Member of House of Commons and Ontario Legislature. Leader of Liberal Party, 1878–87. Member of British House of Commons, 1892–1907.

Hon. Sir Frederick William Borden (1847–1917). Born Cornwallis, Nova Scotia. Educated at Universities of King's College, Windsor, N.S., and Harvard Medical School. Member of Canadian House of Commons, 1874–82 and 1887–1911. Minister of Militia and Defence, 1896–1911. Appointed an Honorary Surgeon-General in the British Army, 1911.

Rt. Hon. Sir Robert Laird Borden (1854–1937). Born Grand Pré, Nova Scotia. Educated Acacia Villa Seminary, Horton. Called to bar, 1878. Member of Canadian House of Commons, 1896–1904, 1905–21. Leader of Conservative Party, 1901–21. Prime Minister, 1911–20. Member of Imperial War Cabinet. Chief Canadian delegate to the Paris Peace Conference, 1919. A man of moderate views, he more closely resembled in temperament Sir Wilfrid Laurier than the more outspoken enthusiasts of his own party. He resisted economic colonialism and tended to regard the variety, volume and skill of the nation's work as the foundation of its well-being rather than the accumulation of large profits by commercial interests supplying the United States and other industrial nations with raw materials.

Henri Bourassa (1868–1952). Born in Montreal. Educated privately. Fascinated by the name of his revolutionary forebear Louis Joseph Papineau. His mother was a Papineau; so was his wife who was born in Papineauville, a town of which Bourassa subsequently became mayor. Liberal member of Canadian House of Commons, 1896. Resigned in 1899 in protest against Canadian participation in the South African War. Re-elected by acclamation 1900, and again in General Election of that year and again in 1904. Entered provincial politics in 1907. Founded Le Devoir in 1910. Supported Canadian participation in War World I. Subsequently an Independent member of the House of Commons.

Hon. Louis Philippe Brodeur (1862–1924). Born Beloeil, P.Q. Son of Toussaint Brodeur, a rebel patriot of 1837. Educated at St. Hyacinth College and Laval University. A lawyer. Member of the Canadian House of Commons, 1891–1911. Deputy Speaker, 1896–1900. Speaker, 1901–04. Minister of Marine and Fisheries, 1906–11. Considered his great achievement to consist in the fact that under his guidance the St. Lawrence River was "made navigable under all conditions whether during night or day or in foggy weather".

Hon. George Brown (1818–1880). Father of Confederation. Born Alloa, Scotland. Migrated with his father to the United States following the failure of the family business during the panic of 1837. Migrated from U.S. to Canada, 1843. Proprietor and editor of Toronto Globe newspaper. Member Canadian Legislative Assembly, 1851–67. Defeated in first Dominion election. Appointed Senator, 1873. Bitter opponent of Tories and Roman Catholics. Advocated Confederation of provinces of British North America and westward expansion. Leading Liberal Reformer in the Executive Council during Confederation negotiations.

z

William Jennings Bryan (1860–1925). Born Salem, Illinois. Educated Illinois College and Union Law College. Elected to the House of Representatives of the U.S. Congress for Nebraska, 1890 and 1892. Democratic candidate for the Presidency of the United States, 1896, 1900 and 1908. Threw his support to Woodrow Wilson in 1912, who appointed him Secretary of State. Resigned from this office because he advocated U.S. neutrality in World War I.

Hon. William A. Buchanan (1876–1954). Born Fraserville, Ontario. Educated in Trenton, Ontario. Journalist and newspaper proprietor. Migrated to western prairies where he established a newspaper in Lethbridge, Alberta. Active in provincial politics. Member of the House of Commons, 1911–21. Senator, 1925–54.

Hon. Jacques Bureau (1860–1933). Born Trois Rivières, P.Q., educated at Nicolet College and Laval University. Practised law briefly in Manitoba and Wisconsin. Liberal member of Canadian House of Commons, 1900–25. Solicitor-General, 1907–11; Minister of Customs and Excise, 1921–25. For many years one of the most powerful and energetic figures in Quebec politics. Later elevated to the Senate.

Rt. Hon. Sir Richard John Cartwright (1835–1912). Born Kingston, Ontario. Educated Trinity College, Dublin. First elected to Legislative Assembly in 1863. Henceforward in and out of Parliament as a Liberal. Minister of Finance, 1873–78. Minister of Trade and Commerce and Government leader of the House, 1896–1911.

Hon. Frank Broadstreet Carvell (1862–1924). Born Bloomfield, New Brunswick. Educated public schools of N.B. and Boston University. Liberal member of the New Brunswick Legislature 1899–1900, and member Canadian House of Commons, 1904–19. Joined the Union Government in 1917 and withdrew to the Board of Railway Commissioners of Canada in 1919, of which he became Chairman.

Hon. Thomas William Crothers (1850–1921). Born Northport, Ontario. Educated in public schools, Albert College, Belleville, and Victoria University, Cobourg. Successively a headmaster, lawyer, and politician. Conservative member of Canadian House of Commons, 1908–21. Minister of Labour, 1911–18.

Archdeacon William Cunningham (1849–1919). Born Edinburgh. Educated at Edinburgh Academy and University and Trinity College, Cambridge. Lecturer in History, Cambridge University, 1884–91. Professor of Economics, King's College, London, 1891–97. Archdeacon of Ely. Author of the monumental *Growth of English Industry and Commerce*.

John Wesley Dafoe (1866–1944). Born Combermere, Ontario. Educated Arnprior High School. At the age of 20 became editor of the *Ottawa Journal*. Editor *Montreal Herald*, 1892–95. Editor in Chief of *Manitoba Free Press*, 1901–44. Chancellor of University of Manitoba, 1934–44.

Eugene Victor Debs (1855–1926). Born Terre Haute, Indiana. Educated in the common schools. Secretary of the Brotherhood of Locomotive Firemen, 1880–93. Member of the Indiana Legislature, 1885. President of the American Railway Union, 1893–97. Strong believer in large, militant, industrial unions. Chairman of the National Committee of the Social Democratic Party, 1897–98. Socialist candidate for Presidency of the United States, 1900–04. In 1918 he was sentenced to ten years' imprisonment under the Espionage Act. Was released from gaol after widespread popular agitation.

Lt. Col. the Hon. James Domville (1842–1921). Born Belize, British Honduras. Educated Royal Military Academy, Woolwich. Settled in Canada in 1866. Engineer, financier, politician, soldier and traveller. Built and operated the first British vessel in the Yukon trade, 1897. Originally a Conservative but became a Liberal before 1896. Member of House of Commons, 1872–82 and 1896–1900. Appointed Senator, 1903. Chairman of important Select Standing Committees of Senate and House.

Rt. Hon. Victor Alexander Bruce, 9th Earl of Elgin and Kincardine, (1849–1917). Born near Montreal shortly after a mob in that city had expressed their opinion of his father by burning down the Legislative Buildings. Educated at Eton and Balliol College, Oxford. Viceroy of India, 1894–99; Secretary of State for the Colonies, 1905–08. A Liberal.

Dr. Charles William Eliot (1834–1926). Born in Boston, Mass. Educated at Boston Public Latin School, Harvard University and variously in Europe. Assistant Professor and Professor of Chemistry and Mathematics at Harvard, 1858–1865. Professor of Chemistry at Massachusetts Institute of Technology, 1865–69. President of Harvard, 1869–1909. Played an important role in adapting American higher education to the needs of a complex industrial society. Advocated freedom of choice of subjects for undergraduates from a wide variety of studies. Helped develop highly specialized post-graduate studies. Closely associated with leading American industrialists and financiers whom he advised on a variety of subjects. Energetic and optimistic critic of many features of American life including culture, labour relations, income distribution and foreign policy.

John S. Ewart (1849–1933). Born Toronto. Educated Upper Canada College. Called to Bar, 1891. Practised law in Ontario and Manitoba. Counsel for Roman Catholics during Manitoba School controversy. Established a legal practice in Ottawa where he specialized in Supreme Court and Privy Council work. Vice-President of Canadian Bar Association. Author of several technical works on law. Retired in 1914, and devoted remainder of his life to advocacy of Canadian independence.

Rt. Hon. William Stevens Fielding (1848–1929). Born Halifax, Nova Scotia. Educated in Halifax. A journalist and politician. Member of the Legislature of Nova Scotia, 1882–96. Premier of Nova Scotia, 1884–96. Member of Canadian House of Commons, 1896–1911; 1917–25. Minister of Finance, 1896–1911, 1921–25. Following the election of 1908 Sir Wilfrid Laurier offered to resign the Leadership in his favour, but he persuaded Sir Wilfrid to remain. Advocate of Imperial Preference in tariff policy and later of economic reciprocity with the United States. Generally a moderate on all issues affecting race and religion, but separated from Laurier on the issue of conscription. Refused to join the Union Government.

Hon. Sydney Arthur Fisher (1850–1921). Born Montreal. Educated Montreal High School, McGill University and Trinity College, Cambridge. A gentleman farmer and cultivated man of leisure. Member of Canadian House of Commons for Brome, P.Q., 1882–1891 and 1896–1911. Minister of Agriculture, 1896–1911. Intimate friend of Sir Wilfrid Laurier. Gave Mackenzie King invaluable help during his campaign for Leadership of the Liberal Party.

The Hon. Mr. Justice Joseph Napoleon Francoeur. Born 1881 at Cap St. Ignace, P.Q. Educated Normal School, Quebec; Seminary of Quebec; Laval University, Quebec. Called to the Bar of Quebec, 1905; created K.C., 1913. Elected to Quebec Legislature for Lotbinière, 1908; re-elected, 1912; re-elected by acclamation, 1916, 1919, 1923 and 1927; re-elected 1931 and 1935; Speaker of the Legislative Assembly, 1919–28; appointed Minister of Public Works, June 5, 1930; Minister of Game and Fisheries, July 24, 1934, and Minister of Mines, March 13, 1936; resigned August, 1936; elected to House of Commons, December 27, 1937. Appointed Judge, Court of King's Bench, Quebec, P.Q., 1940.

Austin Bruce Garretson (1856–1931). Born Winterset, Iowa. Educated at Osceola (Iowa) High School. A Quaker, Republican, railway conductor and labour union executive. Worked as a conductor on railways in United States and Mexico. Vice-president Order of Railway Conductors, 1889–1906; president, 1906–19. Member of Commission on Industrial Relations, 1912–15, before which Mackenzie King appeared as a witness in 1914 and 1915.

Samuel Gompers (1850–1924). Born in England. A cigar maker. Helped found the Cigar-makers' Union in New York. One of the founders of the American Federation of Labour and its first president from its foundation until his death, except for a break of one year, 1895, when he lost control. A skilful bargainer on behalf of established union organizations.

Hon. Sir Jean Lomer Gouin (1861–1929). Born Grondines, P.Q. Educated at Sorel College, Levis College and Laval University. Admitted to P.Q. bar, 1884. Married the daughter of the Prime Minister of Quebec, Hon. Honoré Mercier. Law partner of Hon. Rodolphe Lemieux. Liberal member of Quebec Legislature, 1897–1920. Minister of Colonization and Public Works, 1900–04. Prime Minister and Attorney-General of Quebec, 1905–20. Member of Canadian House of Commons, 1921–25. Minister of Justice, 1921–24. Appointed Lieut.-Governor of Quebec shortly before his death. A director of the Bank of Montreal, Royal Trust Co., City and District Savings Bank, Shawinigan Water and Power Co., Canada Power and Paper Co., Montreal Light Heat and Power Co., Royal Exchange Assurance Co., Lake of the Woods Milling Co., Crédit Foncier Franco-Canadian, President of the Title Guarantee and Trust Co. Ltd., and President of the University of Montreal.

Rt. Hon. George Perry Graham (1859–1943). Born Eganville, Ontario. Educated in Iroquois and Morrisburg. A journalist, business man and lodge brother. A Grandmaster of the Ancient Order of United Woodmen of Ontario. Among the variety of his offices he numbered the presidency of the Victorian Order of Nurses. A director of numerous small industrial and financial enterprises in eastern Ontario. Sat in the Ontario Legislature from 1898 to 1907. Leader of the Liberal Opposition there, 1907. Entered Canadian House of Commons, 1907. Minister of Railways and Canals, 1907–11. Defeated in 1911, but re-entered the House in 1912. Supported conscription in 1917, but refused to enter the Union Government. A candidate for the Leadership of the Liberal Party in 1919. Minister of Militia and National Defence, 1921–23; Minister of Railways and Canals, 1923–26. Senator, 1926.

Jerome Davis Greene. Born in Yokohama, Japan, 1874. Educated at Harvard and the University of Geneva. Assistant to the general manager of the Harvard University Press, 1899–1901. Secretary to the president of Harvard, 1901–05. Progressed through a succession of secretaryships, including that of the Rockefeller Foundation to directorship of numerous American educational, philanthropic, cultural and political organizations.

Rt. Hon. Thomas Hamar, 1st Viscount Greenwood of Holbourne (1870–1948). Born Whitby, Ontario. Educated Whitby Collegiate Institute and University of Toronto. A United Empire Loyalist. Employed in Ontario Department of Agriculture. Migrated to England. Bencher, Gray's Inn. Liberal member of British House of Commons, 1906–22. Conservative M.P., 1924–29. Under-Secretary to Rt. Hon. W. S. Churchill, 1910. Served in British Army, 1914–16. Minor government offices, 1916–20. Chief Secretary for Ireland, 1920–22. Treasurer of Conservative Party, 1933–38. President of British Iron and Steel Federation, 1938–39.

Rt. Hon. Albert Henry George, 4th Earl Grey (1851–1917). Educated at Harrow and Trinity College, Cambridge. Liberal member of the British House of Commons, 1880–86. Administrator of Rhodesia, Director of the British South Africa Company. Governor-General of Canada, 1904–11.

Rt. Hon. Edward, 1st Viscount Grey of Fallodon (1862–1933). Educated at Winchester and Balliol College, Oxford. Liberal member of the British House of Commons, 1885–1916. Secretary of State for Foreign Affairs, 1905–16. Agreed to continue policy of supporting France against Germany, but failed to inform Cabinet colleagues, Parliament, the British people and the Governments of the Dominions of the undertakings he made and their meaning.

Hon. Hugh Guthrie (1866–1939). Born Guelph, Ontario. Educated Guelph Collegiate Institute and Osgoode Hall, Toronto. Called to Bar, 1888; K.C., 1902. Member of the House of Commons, 1900–35. Before 1917 was regarded as one of the ablest Liberals in the House; after that date one of the ablest Conservatives. Solicitor-General, 1917–20; Minister of Militia and Defence, 1920–22, and July–September, 1926; Leader of Conservative Party in House of Commons, 1926–28.

Minister of Justice and Attorney-General, 1930–35; Chairman, Board of Railway Commissioners from 1935.

Marcus Alonzo Hanna (1837–1904). Born New Lisbon, Ohio. Educated in the common schools and Western Reserve University. Started business in the wholesale grocery trade, and ended a director of coal, shipping, mining and banking enterprises. U.S. Senator for Ohio, 1897–1904. A skilful political manager.

James Keir Hardie (1856–1915). Born Lanarkshire, Scotland. Commenced his career as a miner at the age of seven. Self-educated. Secretary of Lanarkshire Miners' Union. Labour candidate for Mid-Lanark, 1888. Elected to British House of Commons, 1892. One of the founders of the British Labour Party.

Hon. Arthur Charles Hardy, Born Brantford, Ontario, 1872. Educated Brantford Collegiate Institute, Upper Canada College, University of Toronto. Son of a sometime Prime Minister of Ontario. President of the Ontario Liberal Association, 1919–32. Appointed to the Senate in 1922. Briefly Speaker of the Senate in 1930. Appointed to the Privy Council that year.

John Hay (1838–1905). Born Salem, Indiana. Educated in Warsaw, Illinois; Springfield, Illinois and Brown University. Private secretary of President Lincoln. Author of standard work on Abraham Lincoln. Secretary of State of the United States, 1898–1905.

Charles Melville Hays (1856–1912). Born Rock Island, Illinois. Educated St. Joseph, Missouri and Philadelphia. Became a railway clerk at the age of seventeen. By the age of 21 was secretary to the General Manager of the Missouri Pacific Railway. Managed various railway enterprises in United States and consolidated the Wabash Railway system. President of Southern Pacific Railway Company, 1901. Came to Canada as general manager of Grand Trunk; appointed President of G.T.R. in 1910. Also officer of numerous enterprises connected with Grand Trunk system. Drowned during sinking of S.S. *Titanic*.

William Randolph Hearst (1863–1951). Born San Francisco. Son of a wealthy mining magnate. Expelled from Harvard. He revealed an astonishing talent for popular journalism. Owned newspapers in many American cities. Opposed United States entry into World Wars I and II. Wished to annex Canada and other American neighbours to the United States. Aspired to be President of the United States, but failed even to become a State Governor.

John Castell Hopkins (1864–1923). Born Dyersville, Iowa, of Canadian parents of British descent. Educated Bowmanville and Toronto, Ontario. Journalist and bank clerk. Founded the first branch of the Imperial Federation League in Ontario. Founded Empire Club in Toronto. President of the Ontario Conservative Association, 1891–92. Founder, editor and author of the *Canadian Annual Review*, a formidable and valuable source of information.

Lt. General Hon. Sir Sam Hughes (1853–1921). Born Darlington, Ontario. Educated at Toronto Model School, Toronto Normal School and University of Toronto. School teacher and editor and proprietor of a weekly newspaper in Lindsay, Ontario. Served in Boer War. Member of Canadian House of Commons, 1911–16. Minister of Militia, 1911–16. An Orangeman, Freemason and Forester.

Robert Jaffray (1832–1914). Born Bannockburn, Scotland. Educated at Stirling Academy. Migrated to Canada in 1852. Founded a retail and wholesale grocery business with the profits of which he gained control of numerous enterprises among them the Toronto *Globe Printing Co*. Director of companies operating in nearly every province of Canada. Appointed to the Senate, 1906.

Alfred P. Jury. Born Kent, England. A tailor. Migrated to Canada, 1873. Wrote and spoke widely on the condition and problems of the working class. Unsuccessfully contested East Toronto as a Liberal-Labour candidate, 1887. Employed by the Liberals as Government Immigration Agent in Liverpool, 1897–1912.

John King (1843–1916). Born Toronto. Educated Upper Canada Grammar School and Toronto University. Briefly a journalist. Called to Bar, 1868. Author of *The Law of Defamation*; *Slander and Libel in Canada* and of numerous articles, personal reminiscences, pamphlets and books on aspects of the law in relation to contempt, libel, slander and the editing of newspapers.

Rt. Hon. Ernest Lapointe (1876–1941). Born St. Eloi, P.Q. Educated at Rimouski College and Laval University. Practised law at Rivière du Loup and Quebec City. Member of Canadian House of Commons, 1904–41, first for Kamouraska, but succeeded Sir Wilfrid Laurier as member for Quebec East. Minister of Marine and Fisheries, 1921–24. Minister of Justice, 1924–30, 1935–41. Also Attorney-General, 1935–41. First Canadian to sign a treaty with a foreign state on behalf of his country. Gained control of the Liberal Party machine in Quebec during Mackenzie King's struggle for the Leadership in 1919. Unquestioned master of Quebec Liberals from 1919 until his death.

Hon. Peter Charles Larkin (1856–1930). Born Montreal. Educated Montreal and Toronto. Became a tea merchant. Originated sealed lead tea packet for selling tea. Creator of Salada Tea Company of Canada and United States. Known as "the Tea King of America". For ten years a director of the Toronto *Globe*. One of the founders of the Ontario Liberal Club. For many years treasurer of the Ontario Liberal Association. Intimate friend of Sir Wilfrid Laurier and Mackenzie King. 1911 appointed Canadian representative on Royal Commission to investigate resources of the Empire. 1922 appointed to the Privy Council and became High Commissioner for Canada in England, which post he retained until his death in London. Financial patron of Arts, Letters, Toronto General Hospital and Liberal Party.

Rt. Hon. Sir Wilfrid Laurier (1841–1919). Born St. Lin, P.Q. Educated L'Assomption College and McGill University. Member of the Canadian House of Commons, 1874–1919. Minister of Inland Revenue, 1877–78. Elected Leader of the Liberal Party, 1887. Prime Minister, 1896–1911. Leader of the Opposition until his death. The true architect of the modern Liberal Party. By rigidly adhering to principle of provincial autonomy won extensive support of powerful minorities everywhere in Canada. Presided over an epoch of rapid expansion.

Armand Rénaud Lavergne (1880–1935). Born Arthabaska, P.Q. Educated Quebec Seminary and Laval University. A lawyer and journalist. Liberal member of Canadian House of Commons 1904–08, 1930–35. Member of Quebec Legislature, 1908–12 where he supported Henri Bourassa. An assistant editor of *Le Devoir*. Deputy Speaker of the House of Commons during the Prime Ministership of the Rt. Hon. Viscount Bennett. An intransigent nationalist who specialized in attacking British imperialism.

Ivy Ledbetter Lee (1877–1934). Born Cedartown, Georgia. Educated at Princeton University. A Doctor of Laws of Oglethorpe University, Atlanta, Georgia. Commenced his career as a journalist, but transferred his talents to the profession of public relations. Public relations adviser to anthracite coal operators and Pennsylvania railroad and various stockbrokers and bankers. Member of the personal advisory staff of John D. Rockefeller, 1915–16. Assistant to the Chairman of the Red Cross War Council, 1917–19.

William Granville Lee (1859–1929). Born at La Prairie, Illinois. Educated at the public schools of Illinois; brakeman and conductor on the Atchison, Topeka and Santa Fé Railway and the Union Pacific. Vice-president Brotherhood of Railway Trainmen, 1895–1909. President, 1909–29. A Republican.

Hon. Rodolphe Lemieux (1866–1937). Born Montreal. Educated Nicolet Seminary and Laval University. Barrister, politician and *bon viveur*. Member of House of Commons, 1896–1930; of the Senate, 1930–37. Postmaster-General, 1906–11; simultaneously Minister of Labour, 1906–08. Minister of Marine, 1911. Speaker of House of Commons, 1922–30. Chevalier of the Legion of Honour. Knight Commander of the Order of St. Gregory the Great. President of the Royal Society of

Canada, 1918. Went to great lengths to launch Mackenzie King on his public political career in 1908.

Hon. Sir James A. Lougheed (1854–1925). Born Brampton, Ontario. Educated in Toronto. Called to the Bar, 1877. Migrated to North West Territories, 1882. Lawyer, stock broker and insurance executive. Appointed to the Senate in 1889, where he supported the Conservative Party. Strenuously fought Reciprocity with the United States. A minister without portfolio in the Borden Government.

Seth Low (1850–1916). Educated at Columbia University. Clerk and later a partner in his father's importing firm. A mayor of Brooklyn, 1882–85. President of Columbia University, 1890–1901. Mayor of New York, 1902–03.

Rt. Hon. Sir Claude Maxwell Macdonald (1852–1915). Received a military education. Soldier and diplomat with much experience of fighting and negotiation. In command of the Legation Quarter of Peking during the Boxer Rebellion, 1900.

Edward Mortimer Macdonald (1865–1940). Born Pictou, Nova Scotia. Educated Pictou Academy and Dalhousie University. Lawyer and minor politician. Member of Canadian House of Commons, 1904–26. Esteemed himself a man of consequence on the strength of an invitation to tour Canada with Sir Wilfrid Laurier in 1910. Minister of Defence, 1923–26.

Dr. James A. Macdonald (1862–1923). Born Middlesex County, Ontario. Educated Toronto and Hamilton Collegiate Institutes, Edinburgh University and Knox Theological College, Toronto. Pastor of Knox Presbyterian Church, St. Thomas, Ontario, 1891–96. Progressed from religious to political journalism. Editor of *The Globe*, Toronto, 1902–17. Pacifist, extreme prohibitionist and advocate of Canadian integration with the United States.

Alexander Grant Mackay (1860–1920). Educated at University of Toronto. A barrister. A Liberal member of the Ontario Legislature, 1903–12, Commissioner of Crown Lands, 1904–05. Leader of Liberal Opposition in Ontario, 1907–11. As a result of the character assassination to which he was exposed, Mackay migrated to Alberta where he rebuilt his political career. Minister of Municipal Affairs and Minister of Health in the Government of Alberta, 1918–20.

Daniel Duncan McKenzie (1859–1927). Born in Cape Breton, Nova Scotia. Educated Sydney Academy. Articled law clerk. Liberal member of Canadian House of Commons, 1904–06, and 1908–23. Appointed temporary Leader by the Liberal caucus following death of Laurier. Appointed Justice of the Supreme Court of Nova Scotia, 1923.

James William Maddin. Born Westville, Nova Scotia, 1874. Educated Pictou Academy and Dalhousie University. A lawyer. Conservative Member of House of Commons, 1908–11.

Hon. William Melville Martin. Born Norwich, Ontario, 1876. Educated Clinton Collegiate Institute, University of Toronto and Ontario Normal School. Successively a classics master in secondary schools, lawyer, politician and judge. Liberal member of Canadian House of Commons for Regina, Saskatchewan, 1908–16. Resigned to become Premier of Saskatchewan, 1917–22. Appointed Justice and later Chief Justice of the Saskatchewan Court of Appeal.

Gilbert John Murray Kynynmond Elliot, 4th Earl of Minto (1845–1914). Educated Eton and Trinity College, Cambridge. Ensign in Scots Guards, 1867–70. Fought in various minor wars for fifteen years. Chief of Staff during second Riel Rebellion, 1885. Contested Hexham in the interests of the Liberals, 1886. Governor-General of Canada, 1898–1904. Viceroy of India, 1905–10. Married into the family of Earl Grey, who succeeded him as Governor-General of Canada. Knight of the Garter and member of the Guards Club.

Hon. Walter G. Mitchell (1877–1935). Born Danby, Mass. Educated Montreal High School, Bishop's College School and McGill University. Member of legal firm of Greenshields, Greenshields, Heneker and Mitchell which represented some of the biggest industrial and financial enterprises in Canada. In 1903 formed his own legal firm of Laflamme, Mitchell and Callaghan. Although never a member of any political body was invited to become Provincial Treasurer of Quebec in 1914 and was elected to the Legislature by acclamation. Appointed Minister of Municipal Affairs in 1918. Resigned 1921.

Hon. Frederick Debartsch Monk (1856–1914). Born Montreal. Educated at Montreal College, McGill and Laval Universities. A lawyer. Professor of Constitutional and International Law, Laval University. Leader of Conservative Party in Quebec, 1900. Supported Federal interference in Manitoba School question. Advocated the development of a dual language civilization in Western Canada. Opposed reciprocity with or annexation by the United States. Minister of Public Works in Borden Government, 1911–12.

Rt. Hon. John, 1st Viscount Morley of Blackburn (1838–1923). Born in Blackburn, England. Educated Cheltenham and Lincoln College, Oxford. Member of British House of Commons, 1883–95 and 1896–1908. Twice Chief Secretary for Ireland. Secretary of State for India. Liberal biographer and philosopher. Resigned his Cabinet office upon outbreak of World War I.

Hon. William Richard Motherwell (1860–1943). Born at Perth, Ontario. Educated at Perth Collegiate Institute and Guelph Agricultural College. Commenced farming at Abernethy, North-West Territories later Saskatchewan in 1882. Liberal member of the Saskatchewan Legislature from its establishment in 1905 until 1921. Minister of Agriculture in Saskatchewan Government, 1905–18. Member of the Canadian House of Commons, 1921–40. Minister of Agriculture, 1921–26 and 1926–30.

Sir Oliver Mowat (1820–1903). Born Kingston, Ontario. Father of Confederation. Member of Canadian Legislative Assembly, 1857–64. At various times a member of the Executive Council before and during Confederation negotiations. Liberal Prime Minister and Attorney-General of Ontario, 1872–96. Laurier's Minister of Justice and Leader in the Senate, 1896–97. Lieutenant-Governor of Ontario, 1897–1903.

Hon. Sir William Mulock (1844–1944). Born in Bond Head, Ontario. Educated Newmarket, Ontario, Grammar School and University of Toronto. Lawyer and expert in the management of mortgage companies. Liberal member of the House of Commons, 1882–1905. Postmaster-General, 1896–1905. Also first Minister of Labour, 1900–05. Chief Justice of Exchequer Division of Supreme Court of Canada, 1905–23. Chief Justice of Ontario, 1923–36. Chancellor of the University of Toronto, 1924–44.

Hon. James Murdock (1871–1951). Born Brighton, England. Trainman on C.P.R., 1900–05. Vice-President Brotherhood of Railroad Trainmen, 1905–21. Unsuccessfully contested South Toronto in Liberal interest, 1921. Appointed Minister of Labour and had a seat found for him. Defeated again 1925 and 1926. Remained out of office until appointed to the Senate shortly before the defeat of Mackenzie King's Government in 1930.

Hon. Charles Murphy (1863–1935). Born Ottawa. Educated in Christian Brothers' School, Ottawa Collegiate Institute and Ottawa University. Member of Canadian House of Commons, 1908–25. Appointed to the Senate, 1925. Secretary of State, 1908–11; Postmaster General, 1922–25. A skilful political organizer. Believed in Irish Home Rule. Organized Liberal Convention of 1919 where he supported election of Mackenzie King. One of the first to fall in the purge of the Liberal Party in 1926.

William Barton Northrup (1856–1925). Born Belleville, Ontario. Educated at Belleville Grammar School, Upper Canada College and Toronto University. A lawyer. Conservative Member of House of Commons, 1892–96, 1900–17; Clerk of the House of Commons, 1917–24. Belonged to a small minority of Canadian cricket enthusiasts.

Hon. Frank Oliver (1853–1933). Born Peel County, Ontario. Educated there. A printer. Migrated to western prairies and founded the Edmonton *Bulletin*, 1880.

Manager and Editor of *Bulletin* until 1923. Elected to North-West Council, 1883; elected to Legislative Assembly which succeeded Council, 1888–96. Elected to the House of Commons, 1896, as Independent Liberal, and re-elected 1900–08 and 1911 as Liberal; defeated 1917 and 1921. Minister of Interior, 1905–11. Commissioner, Board of Railway Commission, 1923–28.

Hon. Frederick Forsythe Pardee (1867–1927). Born Sarnia, Ontario. Educated at Upper Canada College. Called to the bar, 1891. Liberal member of the Ontario Legislature, 1898–1905. Member of Canadian House of Commons, 1905–21. Liberal Chief Whip, 1909–11. Deserted Laurier in 1917 but did not enter the Union Government.

Sir Joseph Pope (1854–1926). Born Charlottetown, Prince Edward Island. Educated in his native province. Entered Civil Service of Canada, 1878. Private Secretary to Rt. Hon. Sir John A. Macdonald, 1882–91. Wrote a biography of the same. Assistant Clerk of the Privy Council. First Under-Secretary of State for External Affairs, 1909–25.

William Thomas Rochester Preston (1851–1942). Born Ottawa. Educated in public schools and Victoria University, Cobourg. Successively shopkeeper and commercial agent, journalist, political organizer, civil servant and acid commentator on political affairs. Secretary of Ontario Liberal Association, 1883–93. Several times unsuccessful parliamentary candidate. Alderman in Toronto, 1896–98. Librarian of the Ontario Legislature. Inspector of Emigration Agencies of the Canadian Government in Europe, 1899–1911. Acted as a Canadian Government agent in negotiations in Japan, Netherlands, China, Korea. Collected vast body of information on election frauds in 1917.

Hon. William Pugsley (1850–1925). Born Sussex, New Brunswick. Educated in public schools and University of New Brunswick. A lawyer and Liberal provincial politician who held various ministerial offices in the provincial government. Federal Minister of Public Works, 1907–11. A supporter of conscription. Appointed Lieutenant-Governor of New Brunswick, 1918. Resigned, 1923.

Hon. John Dawsley Reid (1859–1929). Born Prescott, Ontario. Educated in public schools and Queen's University. Intended to practise medicine, but was lured into politics by Sir John A. Macdonald. Conservative member of the Canadian House of Commons, 1891–1921. Minister of Customs, 1911–17; Minister of Railways and Canals, 1917–21. Appointed to the Senate, 1921.

Hon. William R. Riddell (1852–1945). Born Hamilton Township, Ontario. Educated Cobourg Grammar School, Victoria University and Osgoode Hall. Called to the Bar, 1883. Appointed Justice of the Supreme Court of Ontario, 1906. Author of numerous books, pamphlets and articles on historical and legal topics.

John Davison Rockefeller (1839–1937). Born Richford, New York. A Republican and a Baptist. Reputed in his time to be the richest man in the world.

John Davison Rockefeller, Jr. Born Cleveland, Ohio, 1874. Educated at Brown University. Closely associated with his father in numerous business enterprises. Known for many years principally as an industrialist, financier and philanthropist. A Republican and a Baptist.

Hon. Sir George William Ross (1841–1914). Born in Middlesex County, Ontario. Educated in public schools and Normal School, Toronto. A successful lawyer. Liberal member of the Canadian House of Commons, 1872–83. Entered provincial politics. Minister of Education, 1883–99. Prime Minister and Provincial Treasurer of Ontario, 1899–1905. Appointed to the Senate, 1907. Was chairman of the Committee which raised $120,000 as a present for the Rt. Hon. W. S. Fielding. Director of several financial and journalistic enterprises.

James Hamilton Ross (1856–1932). Born London, Ontario and educated there. Went to the North-West Territories at an early age and established a ranch near Moose Jaw. Sat in the Assembly of the N.-W.T. Held various offices in the Territorial executive council. Commissioner of the Yukon Territory. Appointed to the Senate in 1904. A genuine Western pioneer and political patriarch.

Hon. Newton Wesley Rowell (1867–1941). Born Middlesex County, Ontario. Educated in the public schools and at Osgoode Hall, Toronto. A very successful barrister in Toronto. Entered parliamentary politics at the top as Leader of the Opposition in the Ontario Legislature, 1911–17. The most important of Liberal Unionists in 1917. President of the Council, 1917–20. Vice-Chairman of the War Committee of the Cabinet, 1917–19. Member of the Imperial War Cabinet. A Canadian delegate to various bodies such as the League of Nations. Appointed Chief Justice of Ontario in 1936. Conducted an abortive inquiry into the working and non-working of the British North America Act. Lifelong friend of Mackenzie King.

Hon. Sir Clifford Sifton (1861–1929). Born Middlesex, Ontario. Educated London (Ont.) High School, Boys College, Dundas, Victoria University, Cobourg. Established a legal practice in Manitoba in 1882. Liberal member of Manitoba Legislature, 1888–96. Member of the Canadian House of Commons, 1896–1911. Attorney-General and Minister of Education in Manitoba Government, 1891–96; Federal Minister of Interior, 1896–1905. Successfully led a movement in Manitoba to separate church and state in matters of education. Resigned from Laurier's Cabinet in 1905 because of refusal of Laurier to extend this principle to new provinces of Saskatchewan and Alberta. Proprietor of *Manitoba Free Press*. Opposed economic reciprocity with United States in 1911 and supported conscription in 1917.

Dr. Oscar Douglas Skelton (1878–1941). Born Orangeville, Ontario. Educated Cornwall High School, Queen's University and University of Chicago. Professor of Political Science, Queen's University, 1908–25. Under-Secretary of State for External Affairs, 1925–41. A strong Liberal partisan. Author of several important works on political subjects including an interpretation of the life of Sir Wilfrid Laurier.

Alexander Smith (1866–1928). Born Saugeen, Ontario. Educated at Collingwood Collegiate Institute and the University of Toronto. Successively a school teacher, journalist and lawyer, but always a Liberal political organizer. The "Available Jones" of his day and country. Claimed to have won the General Elections of 1896, 1900 and 1904 for his Party by a technique known as "Ontario management". After the election of 1904 established a "law" office in Ottawa.

Frank W. Taussig (1859–1940). Born St. Louis, Missouri. Educated in St. Louis and Harvard University. Professor of Political Economy at Harvard, 1892. Author of several textbooks and articles on economics, including *Tariff History of the United States, The Silver Situation in the United States, Wages and Capital*. Appointed to several Government Boards examining economic problems following World War I.

George Taylor (1840–1919). Born Lansdowne, Ontario. Educated in local schools. Member of House of Commons, 1887–1911, when appointed to the Senate. Conservative Whip for many years. Described as liberal-minded, but claimed to be "an Orangeman and proud of it".

Thomas Phillips Thompson (1843–1933). Born Newcastle-on-Tyne of Quaker parents. Migrated to Canada, 1857. A journalist, humorist and socialist. Correspondent of various newspapers in which he often wrote under the *nom-de-plume* "Jimuel Briggs, D.B. of Coboconk University". Author of *The Politics of Labour* and *The Future Government of Canada*, etc.

John Gillanders Turriff (1855–1930). Born Little Métis, P.Q. Educated in Montreal. Early migrated to Western provinces. Represented Moose Mountain in the N.-W. T. legislature, 1884–1891. Part of the Sifton political machine. Commissioner of Dominion Lands, 1898–1904. Federal M.P., 1904–18. Elevated to Senate, 1918.

Alphonse Verville. Born Côte St. Paul, P.Q., 1864. Educated Sault au Recollet. A plumber and steamfitter. Learned about labour organization in

Chicago, 1882–93. Business agent and President of the Plumbers' Union, Montreal, 1900. President of the Trades and Labour Congress of Canada on several occasions. Standing in the Labour interest he defeated the Government (Liberal) candidate in Maisonneuve in 1906. Refused to accept the whip of any party. Re-elected, 1908–11. Returned unopposed in St. Denis, 1917. In 1918 appointed by the Quebec Provincial Government one of the Commissioners to administer the municipal government of the city of Montreal.

William Wainwright (1840–1914). Born Manchester, England. Educated in Manchester. Secretary to the General Manager of Manchester, Sheffield and Lincolnshire Railway. Entered service of the Grand Trunk Railway, 1862. Held many leading offices in Grand Trunk. Senior Vice-President, 1911.

Frank Patrick Walsh (1864–1939). Born St. Louis, Missouri. Educated at St. Patrick's Academy in St. Louis. Early interested himself in social welfare and labour problems. Represented organized labour in numerous arbitration proceedings. Chairman of the U.S. Congress Commission on Industrial Relations, 1912–15. Member of the National War Labour Board from which he resigned in 1918. Lawyer and director of transit enterprises in New York after World War I. Appointed a member of the New York Public Utilities Commission by Governor Franklin D. Roosevelt in 1929. Chairman of New York Power Authority, 1931. Trustee of St. Patrick's Cathedral, New York.

Rt. Hon. Sir William Thomas White (1866–1955). Born Bronte, Ontario. Educated Brampton High School and University of Toronto. Called to the bar but became a journalist, municipal civil servant in Toronto and manager of a Trust company, 1900–11. Conservative member of the House of Commons, 1911–1921. Minister of Finance until his retirement from House.

Sir John Stephen Willison (1856–1927). Born Hills Green, Ontario. Educated in a country school. Shop assistant who became a journalist. Parliamentary correspondent Toronto *Globe*, 1882–90. Editor of Toronto *Globe*, 1890–1902. Editor of Toronto *Daily News*, 1902–10. London *Times* correspondent, 1910. Chairman Ontario Commission on Unemployment, 1914–16. Chairman Ontario Housing Committee, 1918–19. For fifteen years a Governor of Upper Canada College. President Canadian Reconstruction Association, 1918–21. President Mortgage, Discount and Finance Ltd. Director Western Canadian Colonization Association. Strong imperialist and opponent of economic reciprocity with United States.

Woodrow Wilson (1856–1924). Born Staunton, Virginia. Educated Princeton, University of Virginia and Johns Hopkins. Professor of History, Political Economy and Jurisprudence at Bryn Mawr and Wesleyan University. President of Princeton, 1902–10. Governor of New Jersey, 1910–12. President of the United States, 1912–20.

Rev. James Shaver Woodsworth (1874–1942). Born Islington, Ontario. Educated Wesley College, Winnipeg, University of Toronto and Oxford. A Methodist minister who was early troubled by the contradictions between formal religious orthodoxy and the social consequences of the economic system. Turned from conventional pastoral to social welfare work. Secretary of Canadian Welfare League, 1913–16. Director of Bureau of Social Research financed by Western provincial governments until dismissed in 1917 on account of his pacifism and refusal to co-operate in recruiting soldiers. Following Winnipeg General Strike spent a period in a federal penitentiary and was later elected to the Federal Parliament as Member for Winnipeg North Centre, 1921–42. Leader of Cooperative Commonwealth Federation from its formation until his death. Always strongly moved by social distress and economic injustice.

Professor George Mackinnon Wrong (1860–1948). Born Grovesend, Ontario. Historian. Educated at University of Toronto, Oxford and Berlin. Teacher of theology and subsequently of history, University of Toronto. Professor of History, 1894–1927. Wrote extensively and well on Canadian history. Played an important part in organizing historical scholarship in Canada.

Index

About the authors

Henry Ferns was born in Calgary and educated at the University of Manitoba and at Cambridge. He now lectures in social science at the University of Birmingham.

Bernard Ostry was born in Wadena, Saskatchewan and studied at the University of Manitoba and the London School of Economics. He has held several senior posts in federal government agencies and is now Secretary General of the National Museums of Canada.